Religious Intolerance, America, and the World

Religious Intolerance, America, and the World

A History of Forgetting and Remembering

JOHN CORRIGAN

University of Chicago Press
Chicago and London

The University of Chicago Press, Chicago 60637
The University of Chicago Press, Ltd., London
© 2020 by The University of Chicago
All rights reserved. No part of this book may be used or reproduced in any manner
whatsoever without written permission, except in the case of brief quotations in
critical articles and reviews. For more information, contact the University of Chicago
Press, 1427 E. 60th St., Chicago, IL 60637.
Published 2020
Printed in the United States of America

29 28 27 26 25 24 23 22 21 20   1 2 3 4 5

ISBN-13: 978-0-226-31393-1 (cloth)
ISBN-13: 978-0-226-31409-9 (e-book)
DOI: https://doi.org/10.7208/chicago/9780226314099.001.0001

Library of Congress Cataloging-in-Publication Data

Names: Corrigan, John, 1952– author.
Title: Religious intolerance, America, and the world : a history of forgetting and
    remembering / John Corrigan.
Description: Chicago : London : University of Chicago Press, 2020. |
    Includes bibliographical references and index.
Identifiers: LCCN 2019031492 | ISBN 9780226313931 (cloth) |
    ISBN 9780226314099 (ebook)
Subjects: LCSH: Toleration—United States—Religious aspects—History. |
    Toleration—United States—History. | Persecution—Public opinion. |
    Religion and international relations—United States—Public opinion. |
    Protestants—United States—Attitudes. | Christians—United States—
    Attitudes. | United States—Religion.
Classification: LCC BR517 .C68 2020 | DDC 277.3/058—dc23
LC record available at https://lccn.loc.gov/2019031492

♾ This paper meets the requirements of ANSI/NISO Z39.48-1992
(Permanence of Paper).

For Ben Ray

Contents

Introduction: Religious Intolerance, Trauma, and the International	1
Concord and Contention	1
Trauma	2
Identity and International Relations	6
International Relations and American Religious History	11
1 Proscribing Amalekites: Violence, Remembering, and Forgetting in Early America	18
Colonists, Indians, and War	18
Memory and Intolerance	26
Trauma and Identity	29
The Amalekites of the Old Testament	31
Amalek in America	34
Amalek and the War against Native Americans	36
Blotting Out, Remembering, and Forgetting	42
Catholics and Mormons as Amalekites	45
The Instability of Identity	53
2 Projections: Antebellum Americans and the Overseas Crisis	56
Triumph of Religious Liberty	56
Sectarian Secrecy	58
Conspiracies in Boston and Philadelphia	63
Intolerance in Foreign Lands	71
The Problem Overseas	71
Fear of Global Catholicism	75
The Aftermaths of Boston and Philadelphia	78
Making Foreign Policy	88
Toward a New Era	88
Intervention	96
3 Protections: The Nineteenth Century Turns—to the South	102
The Foreign Spaces of Americans	102
Foreign Time and the Puritan Specter	111

viii   CONTENTS

Forays into Internationalism   121
Rescuing the Twin   126
Civil and Religious Liberty in South America   135
U.S. Policy in South America   138
Wilsonianism   144
The New Danger   151

4   **Pursuits: The Cold War and the Hunt for Intolerance**   154
A World of Protestants   154
Anti-Communism   160
Intolerance   165
   Communists and Cults   165
   Anti-Catholicism   174
   African American Churches   177
Human Rights and Religious Persecution   180
Religious Freedom Legislation   186

5   **Persecutions: The Importation of Intolerance in the
Twenty-First Century**   192
White American Christians   192
Identifying with the Persecuted   198
Stages of Persecution   203
Religious Intolerance and Post-Christian America   210

Acknowledgments 213

Notes 215

Index 273

Introduction

Religious Intolerance, Trauma, and the International

Concord and Contention

James Madison in 1785 characterized religious freedom as "the lustre to our country."[1] Americans since have celebrated it continuously. The collective voice of a mammoth catalogue of speeches, sermons, articles, and textbooks for over two hundred years has extolled the national history of religious concord. That voice tells a story of a brilliant realized ideal at the core of American identity.

The history of religious intolerance in America has proven less fascinating to Americans. Except for the protests of those who have suffered it, or the occasional critical observer, fewer have recognized it. It has not been the topic of speeches or the stuff of textbooks. Americans have labored, instead, to forget the national history of religious intolerance. It interferes with faith in a past characterized by religious harmony. It is a painful and messy history which, if taken seriously, opens a Pandora's box of trauma.

The unforeseen election of Donald Trump in 2016 on a wave of support from evangelical Christians brought the issue of religious intolerance into the foreground of national discussion. Trump's core campaign proposal to end Muslim immigration figured prominently in the ensuing national debate. But equally as important was the decade-long rising tide of Christians' complaints that they were in fact the most persecuted group in America. Driven partly by bitterness over their own political losses (involving same-sex marriage, among other issues), they prevailed upon the new administration to rescue them. Trump's attorney general Jeff Sessions certified their complaints as legitimate when he created the Religious Liberty Task Force in 2018.

During a political season full of surprises, white Christians' sudden willingness to define America as an intolerant nation stood out for its irony. Evangelical Protestants and their allies had dominated the culture. They

2   INTRODUCTION

had practiced intolerance toward many religious groups over two centuries. In the new Trump era, Christian conservatives who complained that they were persecuted evinced a sense that their cultural standing was in decline. Though they historically had been reluctant over two hundred years to see their religious competitors as victims, now, imagining themselves fallen from power, they pictured their own victimhood with luminous clarity.[2]

Americans forgot about intolerance and then remembered it. Or so it appeared. That drama of forgetting and remembering in fact emerged out of complex historical circumstances that involved much more than mere expediency in national politics. It was grounded in early American history and took on its characteristic features over many decades. Most importantly, American thinking about intolerance developed in tandem with emerging American thinking about the rest of the world.

While this book is not an international history, international relations play a key role in its narration of the American history of religious intolerance. Here is a discussion of how American thinking about religion in other parts of the world has reflected the realities of religious intolerance at home. Those realities were trauma, the bid to repress memory of it, and the complex vibration between remembering it and forgetting it.

These introductory pages and their accompanying endnotes address in a preliminary way the historical and theoretical issues that frame the discussions of evidence in the respective chapters. They are at the same time meant to diagram analytical superstructures that interrelate identity, memory, trauma, international relations, and religious intolerance. It is thus conjointly an afterword of sorts, equally meant to be read after the chapters—after the presentation of the historical data—as a way of placing the arguments of the chapters in a broader field of debate about history and theory.

Trauma

Since the nation's founding, Americans have been congratulating themselves for fashioning a politics that regulates relations between religious groups. Americans from colonial times were keenly aware of the religious violence of dreadful scale waged in early modern Europe. American editors published Friedrich Schiller's frightening *History of the Thirty Years' War* (1790) no fewer than thirteen times in the second half of the nineteenth century alone. Americans read reports of and wrote often about ongoing wars of religion in Europe and elsewhere. They remained wary, but they believed that through their forethought they had managed to dodge the horrors of mass religious warfare. In America there never was religious violence on the order of the campaigns that razed thousands of European towns and villages in the early seventeenth century. Americans nonetheless knew what was possible. They understood something of the suddenness and unpredictability of religious violence—on any scale—as well as its catastrophic results. The European wars of religion haunted them.

Americans likewise knew about religious violence because, in spite of their professed determination to forbear it, they could not. Religious violence came early and often, as colonial New Englanders executed a series of devastating military campaigns against Native Americans. They conceptualized Native Americans as savage enemies and planned their slaughter by drawing explicitly upon Christian scripture and theology. They believed that God approved their violence, even commanded it. They celebrated their victories as proof of both God's favor toward them and God's judgment upon the Indians, the heathens whose beliefs were an offense to Christianity. They wrote at length about their victories over the Indians, painting the battle scenes as figurations of Old Testament heroes vanquishing their foes. They spared no ink chronicling the specifics of their destruction of entire communities, detailing the screams, terror, and agony of the Indians, and the laughter of the victorious Christians.

Even as Puritans and their descendants in New England rejoiced in their triumphs over the Indians, however, they worried about their similarity to them. New Englanders saw something of themselves in the Indians. Sometimes they reckoned out loud that through increased encounters they were becoming more like them. That possibility was disconcerting, and early New Englanders struggled to deny it even as evidence for it seemed to compound. Telling themselves they were not savages, the white Christians pushed back against a sense of the darkness in their own souls, a darkness manifested in Indian genocide. The fact of their religious violence and all that it implied was trauma too painful to face. And although they sought to repress memory of it, it inhabited them.

In antebellum America the ghosts of colonial religious violence troubled Protestants' relations with other religious groups. Those ghosts animated the rhetoric that followed fresh encounters with Indians, and spread to confrontations with Mormons, Catholics, and new religions that were emerging from Protestantism itself. It was a rhetoric starkly visible in Protestant responses to anti-Catholic violence in Charlestown, Massachusetts, and in Philadelphia. In the former case, a Protestant mob in 1834 burned down a Catholic convent situated on a hill across the river from Boston. While attacks on Catholic buildings in the area previously had occurred, the destruction of the convent proved a galvanizing event for commentary for and against Catholics in

America. In Philadelphia, the violence was more widespread and of longer duration, taking place at several times during the summer of 1844. It included pitched battles between Catholics and Protestants and ended with the deaths of many persons and the destruction of Catholic churches and homes.

The spectacle of hostility and loss in Boston and Philadelphia prompted Protestants to address the problem of religious intolerance. Troubled by their past but unable to come to terms with it, they took action by discovering and condemning religious violence not in America but in other nations.

Unable to face the fact of their own historical culpability in the religiously inspired genocide of Indians, but aware of the religious intolerance that was taking place in American cities, Protestants spatially displaced that intolerance. Unwilling to admit that America was not the model of a realized ideal of religious harmony, they projected overseas America's religious frictions. As instances of intolerance against Catholics, Mormons, Indians, and others multiplied, Protestants more energetically scanned the globe for places where intolerance was a problem. They raised their voices to condemn that intolerance and urged the U.S. government to take action against it.

The initiatives of American Protestants, bedeviled by the memory of a traumatic past that resisted efforts to fully repress it, produced an agenda of foreign policy reforms regarding intolerance. Protestants made gradual headway in effecting those reforms. In the immediate aftermath of the Boston and Philadelphia riots, Protestants wrote excitedly about the problem overseas. They targeted Catholic Spain, Portugal, Austria, Italy, and their respective possessions around the world as strongholds of religious intolerance. To those they added China, Burma, and assorted places in Asia, Africa, and Europe. With stiffening Protestant resistance to seeing America as a place where religious intolerance occurred—even as victims complained publicly of it—came more ambitious and detailed reports of religious intolerance elsewhere. Protestants undertook to project the problem of religious intolerance to spaces beyond the United States, and the means by which they pursued implementation of that was through U.S. foreign policy.

The Protestant effort to shape foreign policy regarding religious intolerance developed in stages. In the late nineteenth and early twentieth centuries, as American imperial aspirations grew, Protestants achieved some success in pressuring the U.S. State Department to take a strong stance with the emerging Latin American states. Commanding a small army of overseas missionaries, Protestants reported with increasing frequency the impediments to their efforts to bring their brand of Christianity to inhospitable countries. The Catholic nations of South America were the worst offenders, according to Protestant lobbyists and agitators, but there were other places as well where

RELIGIOUS INTOLERANCE, TRAUMA, AND THE INTERNATIONAL   5

agents had discovered intolerance. At a time when the resurgent Ku Klux Klan was engaged in constant violence against Catholics, Jews, and others, Protestants looked ever more determinedly for those places overseas that were guilty of religious intolerance.

The unprecedented organization of Protestant evangelical power during the Cold War era resulted in further efforts to influence foreign policy. Evangelicals, together with some Catholic and Protestant allies, depicted the U.S.S.R., China, North Korea, Vietnam, and Eastern European nations as godless communist states that were at the same time religious opponents. For many religious Americans, communism was itself a religion and its oppression of Christians therefore all the worse an instance of religious intolerance. Muslim nations eventually also earned the scorn of American Christians, who ever more vigorously worked to discover religious intolerance overseas and pressure the U.S. government to address it. The International Religious Freedom Act of 1998 (IRFA), much-heralded by evangelicals as a victory in the war against religious intolerance in other countries, was first and foremost a program to identify overseas sites of religious intolerance. Additionally, the plan was to punish them, not systematically to install some version of religious liberty in the client countries. At a time when arsons of African American churches dominated the national news, the supporters of IRFA chose to demonstrate forcefully against religious intolerance—as long as it was overseas.

Having expended so much energy on discovering religious intolerance overseas—a project that demanded a significant psychological investment alongside a financial one—American Christians who long had complained about the persecution of Christians in other countries began to characterize themselves as equivalent victims. Having identified so thoroughly with those who suffered persecution in other countries—having learned to feel so deeply about them—some American Christians effectively imported back into America the problem that they had so determinedly been tracking overseas.[3] American Christians became the persecuted Christians for whom they had long voiced sympathy. They accomplished that feat, moreover, without having to confront the American history of religious intolerance. They did not admit that there had always been a problem, that the ideal was never fully implemented, and that religious groups in power had always acted in their own self-interests. Initially, they made themselves out to be religious persons who suffered as part of a global, not specifically American, persecution of Christians.

Finally, American Christians who had seen themselves as victims of a global persecution of Christianity reframed their suffering as a fully *American*

6   INTRODUCTION

persecution. For some conservative Christians, America in 2018 was no longer the Christian nation that they had believed it to be. Blaming secularists, gays, women, and other groups for having broken the foundation of national identity, disenchanted Christians found an additional way to admit that there was in fact religious intolerance in the United States. That was because America as they knew it was gone, and a different America had taken its place. For them, the identity of the nation had changed.

Identity and International Relations

Identity, in spite of the seeming ease with which scholars deploy it in historical analyses, is a slippery term. There has never been consensus about what is meant by the term "identity," exactly whom it applies to, how racial and ethnic groups are involved, the roles of religious organizations, or the relevance of class, among other variables. The *Encyclopedia of the Social Sciences* published by Macmillan in 1930 had no entry for "identity." Even over fifty years later, the historian Philip Gleason ventured that "identity is a new term," adding, significantly, "as well as being an elusive and ubiquitous one."[4]

American historians and literary scholars nevertheless have not flinched in building interpretation around the concept of a specifically American identity. Among the latter, Sacvan Bercovitch was effusive about the roots of American identity. In attempting to locate *The Puritan Origins of the American Self* (1975), he offered a bold thesis about "the rhetoric of American identity." He looked to New England beginnings and claimed that theological crisis in mid-seventeenth-century New England "marks a high-point in the formulation of American identity."[5] That interpretation, even as it has been criticized and amended over decades, has been broadly influential among Americanists, alongside several others. But questions about American identity remain.

The very notion of national identity poses challenges to the historian, who must navigate around a number of conceptual potholes and recognize an assortment of contingencies in order to arrive at plausible, deployable definitions of it. National identity rarely represents the experience of subaltern groups, and it is constantly in motion as demography changes, subcultures emerge, power shifts, and national priorities are recalibrated. In referring to it as a component of international relations, particular care is required.

The ascent of identity as a central component of international relations took place rapidly after it emerged as a topic of interest in the 1980s.[6] In the early twenty-first century, it was advanced in a widening circle of theoretical and historical studies, becoming an important stream of scholarship as researchers increasingly tied national identity to international relations. A "cultural turn" began as scholars with an interest in diplomacy incorporated ideas about national identity into their research, and historians and political scientists examined more closely the collective psychologies, emotional communities, and national mythologies that affect the policy agendas and international diplomatic performances of nations.[7] Attention to power and policy has not been diminished by the cultural turn. Rather, both are becoming clearer as analyses of culture are made a part of the investigation of familiar subjects, namely the state, national security, and international contention.

National identity presumes nationality, and academic debate about how to define the state has been as lively as debates about identity. One starting point is to view a nation as the product of imagination. Members of a state envisage their connections with each other in a way that elides the fact that they have no personal contact with each other excepting their own tiny circles of acquaintances. There may be significant differences among the population, including in key areas such as race, religion, class, and language, yet all imagine that they are joined in a common venture, a shared idea. The attachments between persons in a state, moreover, are profoundly emotional. Individuals feel themselves to be engaged in a collective project of the utmost importance. The affectual attachments that comprise collective life are deep and constant, and they fortify the state against social disintegration while powering its domestic and international initiatives. As persons recall the history of the state, as they remember the ideals, struggles, setbacks, and victories that have advanced the state, they rededicate themselves to it and strengthen the attachments they feel to it.[8] National identity intertwines memory and feeling.

States build collective memory and depend upon memory for their survival. Forgetting, understood as the screening from memory of events that do not square with national ideals and perceptions, likewise is crucial to the viability of the state—even though trauma can never be entirely screened. Ernest Renan's oft-cited observation that "the essence of a nation is that all individuals have many things in common, and also that they have forgotten many things," expresses how social solidarity, paradoxically, is grounded partly in amnesia.[9] That amnesia is not purely accidental. It is a product of ongoing historiographical invention that endeavors to massage out of national memory events and ideas that do not conform with familiar, comfortable, and inspiring narratives of national achievement.[10] Remembering is a process that regulates emotional attachment to the state by reinvigorating positive affect regarding the state. Forgetting, a related process, serves the state by endeavoring to sweep negative feelings under the rug, even though those feelings periodically can reemerge, prompted by events and by shifting narratives of national identity.[11]

As individuals will repress traumatic memories but not entirely vanquish them, nations labor to forget events in their past but are haunted by them.[12] Nations are not persons, but the processes of memory and forgetting that are observable in the lives of individuals are qualifiedly present in the behavior of collectives.[13] We glimpse national identity when we understand how people act as one psychological group. As in the case of individuals, moreover, the development and maintenance of national identity is never an entirely self-contained process. That is, the struggle to secure national identity, like the psychic turmoil of the individual, is unpredictable in its course. It can cross its territorial boundaries and extend to a global arena.[14]

Patterns of national forgetting and remembering are sometimes enmeshed in habits of encounter with other nations or regions. A nation after all is one community among others. A nation both compares itself to other nations and contrasts itself to them. The dialectics that structure relationships with other nations enhance the definition of national identity through a back-and-forth movement between affinity and antipathy. National narratives objectify other states in ways that serve, through that back-and-forth movement, domestic identity-building.[15]

The dialectics of international relations are hard to read because national identities are never so fully elaborated and so well secured as to exist as ontologically secure entities. They are unstable in some measure because ambiguities, contradictions, and uncertainties are always present in them. Those complications are especially perceptible in the state's positioning itself vis-à-vis other states. Encounters between states bring to the surface the ambiguities and contradictions of national identity because the process of encounter is itself fraught with contradiction: the state identifies with another state even as it senses its difference from it. Encounter of another state prompts a toggling between different versions of national identity, sometimes between versions that seem contradictory. In spatial terms, the state perceives the other as exterior at the same time that it senses that state as an extension of its own national interests. That gymnastic draws upon the coexistence in national identity of different, even discordant, versions of what the nation is. National identity accordingly is fashioned "not simply in the difference between the self and other but in those moments of ambiguity where one is other to oneself, and in the recognition of the other as like."[16] In other words, narratives of national identity are to some degree in flux. They take shape and are recast as nations perceive that their interests are in accord with those of other nations and, alternatively, at odds with them.

When a state even partly identifies with an external entity, it projects itself outward, bestowing upon the client state certain attributes symbolic of national identity. Americans, for example, might find democracy, a commitment to personal freedom, and respect for property ownership in the portfolios of other nations. At the same time, a state so engaged with another might paradoxically leverage that sense of likeness to picture that other state as an example of its own worst traits. That is, a state projects onto the other various negative national traits as well as positive ones. So, a nation with which the United States senses the common cause of freedom and democracy can be cast—in a continuous back-and-forth fashion—as an example of those traits that Americans would prefer not to see in themselves, such as the corruption of politics by money, the denial of freedoms to minorities, or arrogance rooted in a trust in national exceptionalism. The projection of a nation's worst traits, the assignment of those traits to other nations in lieu of recognizing them domestically, sometimes is a part of the process of international relations. And such projection of ugly national traits can itself be an act of remembering what some national narratives have struggled to forget.

Edward Said famously argued that the West had constructed an "Orient" as an inferior Other against which the West defined itself as an exceptional civilization. Among the many strands of interpretation of such "Orientalism" is one within postcolonial theorizing and international relations scholarship that has critically pursued Said's claim that Orientalism was "a kind of Western projection onto" the Orient.[17] While rejecting parts of Said's argument,[18] scholars have built on some of his claims to suggest how "in *Orientalism*, the 'Oriental' exists only as a useful creation of the West, a projection of Western desire and fear, a subject without its own identity."[19] Furthermore, "the Orient as constructed by the West can be interpreted as a projection of repressed desires and fears," and in that process it "signifies the West's own dislocation from itself, something inside that is presented, narrativized, as being outside."[20] While the reliability of parts of Said's account of Western academic construction of the Orient is debatable, the notion of Western projection of its own unseemliness onto other nations is a serviceable observation, and especially relevant to understanding American history.[21]

Trauma, the powerful residue of terrible events that have occurred in a community's past, is embedded in national identity. It is a scar that does not fade and is constantly at work shaping identity, sometimes below the surface of awareness.[22] Nations typically demonstrate an effort to forget trauma, and typically fail in accomplishing that. But the effort nevertheless is significant, and the practice of forgetting is a crucial component of the maintenance of national identity. Amnesic response to trauma is as much a part of the construction of national identity as memory, and it is the complicated movement back-and-forth between the two that characterizes the efflorescence of that identity.[23]

Trauma is ambiguous, profound, and often willfully hidden. National identity, understood as constituted in part by historical trauma, is fluid and at times paradoxical. National trauma "is felt but not understood; it is memorized and recalled, but not necessarily experienced; it defies language but insists on being communicated; it refuses to be incorporated into normality, but goes on perpetuating itself in memory; it is triggered at a specific moment in time but alters its linearity; it must be forgotten but is always being recalled and relived."[24] It has an existential component, a sense of dread or intense anxiety. It sometimes underlies the perception of what has been termed the "ontological insecurity" of the state, a discernment of essential impermanence or the dangerous volatility of the state.[25]

National identity that is haunted by painful memories of trauma but yet requires remembrance of the past takes shape through myths that emerge out of that negotiation. Those myths, drenched in feeling, are themselves dressed in images and symbols that represent the ambiguities and polyvalencies of national identity. Myths are supple, allowing for creative reinterpretations of the past as befits the requirements of the present, and they are plastic, allowing for expansive incorporation of new cultural material, or its deletion. National myths, while thus adaptable, nevertheless can linger where they are no longer useful, exerting influence in ways that complicate, rather than ease, the struggle of the present. Myths keep anxieties alive even as they serve to soothe them. A national mythscape is ever-shifting, deeply emotional, and conducive to sudden outbursts of remembering, all alongside its legitimating and stabilizing role for state business.[26]

National identity is given narrative form in a national myth, or set of myths. In America the myth of the exceptional nation, the providentially authorized beacon to the world, lingers. It is powerful, its capability to direct national resources and policy visible both in domestic affairs and in international relations. Its clout is detectable not only in the assignment of priorities in foreign policy but in the ways in which the myth, once it is forcefully projected outside the nation, returns on rebound to reinforce and sometimes edit familiar national narratives regarding domestic affairs.[27] Domestic and foreign affairs in such a way can collaborate in making national identity. That is, national identity is subject at times to a looping process in which that which is projected returns recursively in some form to affect the ongoing formulation of national identity.[28]

To return by way of example to the problem of religious intolerance in

America: Attorney General Sessions's Religious Liberty Task Force of 2018 emerged in the context of late twentieth-century American foreign policy invented to discover and alleviate religious persecution abroad. The U.S. State Department indeed found that persecution abroad. And then, in a process of recursion that seemed a feat of cross-national identification, Americans who promoted that foreign policy came to believe that they in fact were the persecuted. The recursive effect of that particular American foreign policy was to influence its American supporters to identify as victims of the persecution they discovered overseas.[29] And it contributed to them changing their thinking about what America was, who it was for, and how its future might unfold.

International Relations and American Religious History

Thinking about American identity in ways that join the insights of humanities scholars to those of international relations researchers offers advantages to the study of nation and religion. When American historians, literary scholars, or other humanities researchers write about national identity, they typically do so with a view to understanding culture as it emerged among a distinct people who call themselves Americans and who imagine their collective life in conjunction with certain specific ideas and practices. Scholars invoke such a framing of national identity as a means to understanding how certain literatures emerged and became influential, how political traditions were created and maintained, how economic power developed, how race was defined, or how men and women lived their daily lives.

The idea of national identity has proven useful across a wide range of scholarship, serving as an effective organizing concept for the integration of disparate kinds of data, the analysis of various social forces, and the charting of historical cause and effect, of change over time. American religious historiography makes especially good use of the concept of identity, however, when it considers it in the context of Americans' thinking about the rest of the world.

Religious intolerance has been central to the religious history of North America since the European settlement of the continent. American Christian groups since the colonial era defined themselves in terms of what they were not, identifying other groups as their opponents and accentuating the differences between themselves and those other groups as a means to constructing identity.[30] Most of the time that process of aggressive differentiating took the form of debates about doctrine and rituals, arguments over polity, and rhetoric aimed at undermining the authority of competing groups. In a nation without tax support for religion, such competition became particularly pointed as groups sought to build the memberships needed to ensure the financial viability of religious community.

In many instances, however, the tactics of differentiating one community from another led to active discrimination by a powerful religious group—typically (but not exclusively) Protestants, who were dominant for most of the nation's history—against minority groups. Sometimes that discrimination culminated in physical violence. The campaigns against Native Americans, legitimated by religion, were the most vicious of those instances. Violence against Native Americans, and against other groups as well, was animated by a rhetoric claiming that opponents were so corrupt as to deserve extermination.

The legal historian David Sehat asked at the beginning of his recent book: "But what if U.S. religious history was not a history of progressive and unfolding freedom? What if, instead, it was a history of religious conflict? And what if that conflict involved extended periods of religious coercion and the continual attempt to maintain power and control?"[31] It is a question that others[32] likewise have asked, and it begs a corollary question about why we find ourselves wondering how we missed the story in the first place: How did Americans forget their history of religious conflict? How did they *practice* that forgetting?

It is clear that an exceptionally robust veneration of the ideal of religious freedom, including the trust that it was successfully implemented in America, served well as a distraction from the painful chore of confronting a frightful past. The constitutional commitment to an ideal of religious liberty was an impressive historical achievement, and Americans have enthusiastically saluted it since the earliest days of the Republic. But scholars increasingly are skeptical that even the ongoing fervent celebration of the First Amendment was so successful a coup of misdirection that it fully screened from collective memory the religious violence that occurred both before and after the amendment's adoption in 1791. Americans did not completely forget the trauma of their past. It came back repeatedly to haunt them, appearing at times dressed in complaints registered by members of minority religions and sometimes, but rarely, in the public laments of conscience-stricken white Protestants.[33]

When haunted by memories of religious violence, Americans fought back against them by projecting that violence elsewhere. Americans denied the religious violence in their past—and their present—by picturing it as a problem for other countries, not for the United States. Repeatedly, Americans exported their record of religious violence overseas. They outsourced the ugliness of their own culture. America, drunk on self-congratulations for enacting a protection of religious freedom, was unable to come to terms with the trauma of religiously inspired genocide and recurring instances of religious violence. America projected those events out and away, to nations where there were no American-style protections for religious practice.

Paradoxically remembering trauma and at the same time forgetting it, Americans imagined their own history of religious intolerance as the predicaments of other nations. The dominant Protestant majority of the United States at various times led campaigns to call out the intolerance of other nations and to create legislation that would in some way address that intolerance—initially by protecting Americans who wished to practice their Protestant Christianity while living overseas. Such campaigns were especially visible during periods when domestic religious intolerance flared up in the nineteenth and twentieth centuries. Americans consciously identified as members of a nation that was a divinely ordained "city on a hill" and not a place of religious violence. As such, they believed it their right and duty as an exceptional people to press upon other nations a code of protections for the practice of religion.

Writing a book about American religious history by placing America's international relations among its core themes has required that I draw upon two differing scholarly literatures. Those literatures do not always have the same starting points in their quests to make sense of the American past and present. And in some instances, the goals of research are discrepant. In endeavoring to join insights drawn from the field of international relations to the investigation of American religious history, I have tried to tread carefully. It has required that I find grounds upon which I can remain faithful to what I sense are the intentions of research in both areas by adapting the insights drawn from each to inform a history that might look at first glance like neither. The potential advantages of enhanced analytical breadth and precision are worthy of an experiment, however, and with apologies to practitioners in both fields—and with thanks to them—I have endeavored to find ways to integrate two distinctive areas of research.

With regard to approach, then, this project first of all is a decentering of American religious history in a fully spatial sense. It presents a view of American identity and religious history that looks outside the borders of the United States in order to understand what has happened within those borders. More precisely, it historically tracks how Americans themselves looked beyond those borders and were changed by what they saw. It is not a project consonant with older expectations for "decentering" as a movement away from the history of white Protestant males, colonial New England, and religious doctrines. All of those are here in abundance. White Protestant males occupied the seats of power, and religious intolerance is a matter of the vindictive exercise of power. The "crises" of colonial New England had an enormous bearing on the course of American religious history. Doctrines having to do with time, space, suffering, justice, evil, and divine vengeance are the bones upon which much else rests in an American religious history that takes seriously questions about why force is applied and how it is justified.

Additionally, this history, while drawing on scholarship in international relations, is less focused than some research in that field on the state activities of other nations in their relations with the United States. There is some limited discussion of regimes in South America and elsewhere, but the goal here has been to investigate how national identity has been entangled with Americans' views of issues abroad. In terms of approach, this book hopefully betrays the salutary influence of work by other scholars who have written similarly about religion and American internationalism.[34]

The topic of religious freedom arises at many points throughout this history. In most cases it is because historical actors put it there. The arguments set out in this book are not articulated in direct engagement with the current surge of studies about religious freedom. Americans throughout the nation's history often have taken religious freedom to be a transcendent ideal, a principle so true by common sense, by Enlightenment science, by resonance with great scriptures and literatures, or by simple tests of trial and error that it is considered as an essential thing, as a quiddity, all-but-insuperable in its truth and power. There is a quasi-theological tone to much discussion about religious freedom among historical figures, and still among a few contemporary authors, that sets up the discussion of religious conflict as an unnatural condition, as a disease that can be cured by an application of religious freedom, in the same way that transcendent grace might effect the cure of a sick soul. Some recent scholarship has been especially concerned with the challenges redolent in its legal enforcement, a concern informed by considerations of how both religion and religious freedom are defined. But that is not the approach here. Religious freedom is not the starting point. Instead, it is the fact of religious violence.[35]

This introduction began with references to religious violence. Chapter one continues the discussion of religious intolerance in America by describing Americans' justification of it through the citing of Old Testament stories about the annihilation of one's enemies. The story of the Amalekites was especially important in the conceptualization of and justification of religious intolerance. The Amalekites were kin to the Jews. The Jews accordingly, by Old Testament standards, were attached to them, albeit dysfunctionally. The Amalekites were duplicitous, and conspired to attack the Jews. For their secret plottings as much as for their actual raids, the Old Testament God sentenced them to extermination, commanding the Jews to "blot out" the Amalekites as well as all remembrance of them. The Jews obeyed.

The example of the Amalekites served in America as the imagistic basis for campaigns against Indians, Catholics, Mormons, and others. The destruction of the Amalekites and the ventured erasure of their name from history was an act of vengeance that pressed upon the Jews an ongoing responsibility: to forget the Amalekites. God said, kill and forget.[36] Americans, a Bible-believing people, tried to learn that lesson. But they never completely forgot.

Chapter two continues the discussion of religious intolerance and notably of antebellum violence in Boston and Philadelphia. In the immediate aftermaths of the anti-Catholic mobbery in those two cities, Protestants wrote excitedly about the persecution of Christians overseas and especially about offenses against American Protestants in Catholic countries. That enthusiasm for locating foreign incidences of religious intolerance translated into a campaign in Congress to enact legal protections for Americans who wished to practice their religion in other countries. The campaign was described by nineteenth-century observers as the dawn of a "new era" in American international relations and by twentieth-century scholars as the beginnings of a U.S. policy of human rights in foreign relations. It also provided a sturdy platform upon which Americans could build out their project of looking for intolerance outside the United States during times when it was especially problematic within the United States. It was an effort at spatial projection that became a model for subsequent outsourcing ventures.

After the Civil War, during a period of expansion and immigration, Protestants grew more wary of Catholics and Mormons, among other groups that they believed were conspiring to overthrow American democracy. Chapter three begins by outlining how Protestants imagined such religious groups as un-American, fantasizing them spatially as foreign communities, as groups that did not exist in the American state but instead were geographically located elsewhere. Puritans, who increasingly were diagnosed as intolerant, likewise were conceptually relocated to a different place, Protestants explaining that the time period during which Puritans lived was also a different space. Spatial othering of domestic opponents was partnered with the spatial projection of American trauma into international territories.

As Protestant intolerance of Catholics and Mormons reached critical levels, Protestants discovered that South America was suffering badly from oppression by its Catholic regimes. Decrying offenses against Protestant missionaries and their followers in South America, Protestants rededicated themselves to shaping a foreign policy that would protect the rights of Protestants in other countries. South America, called the "twin" of North America, was both like and unlike the United States. It was ruled by Catholics whose ultramontanist agendas issued in alleged conspiracies to ruin Protestantism there, before moving northward as part of a plot to take over the United States. South America at the same time was deemed like the United States in that its peoples either were Christian or, in the views of Protestant missionaries, yearning to become Christian. Protestants organized against the perceived threat of Catholic conspiracy and succeeded in influencing the State Department to press South American nations to guarantee religious freedom to Protestants, both to those visiting from the United States as well as to the mission communities that Protestants had founded.

In the wake of the South American endeavor, President Woodrow Wilson made an effort to extend the cultural reach of Anglo-Saxon Protestantism worldwide. He undertook that mission at a time during which organized violence against Catholics and Jews was cresting in America. His foreign affairs agenda, which included some achievements and some failures, boosted an American propensity to discover religious intolerance worldwide during times of severe intolerance at home.

With the Cold War came a more pointed and politically engaged effort to locate religious intolerance overseas. Chapter four begins by attending to the coalescence of the American crusade for "world Protestantism," an invention (with European cognates) that encouraged American Christians to conceive of themselves as part of a great "worldwide family" of brothers and sisters mystically united in Christian love.[37] Christian leaders encouraged their followers to identify with the suffering of Christians who were persecuted overseas, to feel their pain, to emotionally know their persecution. At the same time, Americans were building higher walls between themselves and a large part of the global population, "the communists." Communist governments in the Soviet Union, China, and various other places behind the Iron Curtain were not hospitable to Christianity, and Americans made much of that fact in arguing the necessity of defending and promoting Christianity overseas. Americans were certain that communists, and especially Asian communists, were not like them. But at the same time, American Christians who were committed to the vision of a worldwide Christianity felt obliged to embrace those others as family members yearning for the truth. Americans identified with them, often in a decidedly affectual manner, even as they rejected them.

During the Cold War there was domestic intolerance of Asian religions, New Religious Movements, and Catholics, among other groups. Race and religion were strikingly joined not only in the animus toward Asian religions[38] but with regard to African American congregations. Many black churches were destroyed by arson in the latter part of the twentieth century, but it was in the immediate post–Cold War decade that a string of black church arsons drew the attention of the nation. During that period of time, while political leaders focused closely on the arsons as a national disgrace, a growing contingent of Christians became ever more determined to find religious intolerance overseas. That focus eventuated in federal legislation creating a commission to hunt down religious intolerance overseas and to report it to Congress with an eye to sanctioning nations that allowed it.

The Religious Right, and prominently its evangelical component, celebrated their success in influencing legislation to make religious intolerance a standing item on the agenda of the State Department. As discussed in chapter five, they simultaneously lamented what they believed was a failure to win the battle to retain their moral standing in American life. Following a series of defeats on issues of same-sex marriage, school prayer, reproduction, and other matters, they came to the conclusion that they, as Americans, were a persecuted people. Having learned over generations to identify with persons abroad who suffered persecution because of Christian belief, they looked at America, recognized it as a foreign country, and identified themselves as the persecuted subjects of that country.

Moreover, evangelicals and their allies, having imported their problem from overseas, imported as well their persecutors, the Muslims—who were in fact responsible for much persecution of Christians overseas. That is, American Christians claiming victimhood identified Muslims—ranging from President Barack Obama (who actually was Christian) to various groups allegedly plotting to make Shari'a the law of the land—as culprits in their oppression. Christians on the Religious Right, while taking control of the White House, Congress, the Supreme Court, and a majority of statehouses, depicted themselves as a group persecuted by agents of a Muslim/secularist/Marxist conspiracy to destroy America.

The project, developed over two centuries, of looking away from religious intolerance in America to intolerance overseas was an exercise in projection that came full circle. A robust group of Protestants, together with some persons drawn from other religious groups, in the early twenty-first century remained consistent in their views about historical America: religious intolerance did not take place in the American past. But America was no longer the country that they believed it to be. It had been lost to the enemies of Christian religion. Having projected American intolerance overseas, a powerful religious cohort of Americans received it back by recursion, welcoming it as political capital while publicly bemoaning it as oppression.

1

Proscribing Amalekites: Violence, Remembering, and Forgetting in Early America

Colonists, Indians, and War

The British who arrived in North America in the early seventeenth century fantasized the land as empty, a *vacuum domicilium*. They construed their settlement of its northern coast, a place they called New England, as a refiguration of the delivery of the Jews into the Land of Canaan. New England, the Promised Land given them by God, was in their imagining theirs before they arrived. They claimed land inhabited by the natives, offering no compensation for it except the promises of Christian theology. They brought confidence in their superiority to Native Americans alongside an uneasy sense of their similarity to them. Even as they took Indian land, they sought to understand their acts of oppression as gestures of collaboration.

Roger Williams, who settled in Plymouth Colony in 1631, thought harder than most about relations between the British and Indians. He addressed a complaint to King Charles, probably in 1632, challenging the British claim to land occupied without compensation. While he subsequently answered for it in court, the treatise itself did not survive. In a written summary, John Cotton, the religious overseer of the community at Massachusetts Bay, made plain the gist of it. Indians hunted over great expanses of land, and tended to the environment, such as by periodically burning out undergrowth, in order to maximize its bounty. "As noble men in England possessed great parks, and the King great forests in England only for their game, and no man might lawfully invade their property," related Cotton, "so might the natives challenge the like propriety" of English settlement.[1]

Expelled from Massachusetts for his theological opinions as much as for his views on social order and relations with Indians, Williams established himself farther south on land he purchased from the Narragansett. He remained critical of New Englanders who displayed a "depraved appetite" for "great portions of land." Writing from Rhode Island to Major John Mason in 1670, he warned that land was "one of the gods of New England, which the living and most high Eternal will destroy and famish." Castigating the British for their mistreatment of the Indians, Williams characterized his countrymen as gluttons who chased land as if it were "like platters and tables full of dainties." In so doing, the British "but pull or snatch away their poor neighbors' bit or crust" of bread, worsening the Indians' "continual troubles, trials, and vexations."[2]

Major Mason himself was well acquainted with the Indians, having served as captain in the British force that, with its Indian allies, fought the Pequot War. Decades after that war, and seven years after receiving Williams's plaintive letter on behalf of the Indians, Mason published his own *Brief History of the Pequot War*. It amounted to a cataloguing of some of the more spectacular "trials and vexations" about which Williams previously had written Mason. In tone and perspective, it in fact was a proud memoir of the British massacre of Pequots at Mystic in 1637.

Mason's, and New England's, Pequot War began in 1636 against the background of contestations involving land and the fur trade among the Pequot, Wampanoag, Narragansett, Algonquians, and Mohegans. The English and Dutch colonies sought stable relationships with the Indians of the Connecticut River Valley for the purpose of trade and growth. They calculated that often it was worthwhile to pursue those relationships through force. A series of confrontations between the English and Indians, resulting in deaths on both sides and the destruction of several Niantic and Pequot villages, prompted an English military campaign. The central event in that campaign was the surprise attack by the English, together with their Narragansett and Mohegan allies, on the Pequot fortified village of Mystic. Overwhelmed by the dawn attack, the Pequot were wiped out. After initially entering the village to fight, the English chose to burn it, and stationed their forces around it to kill any who sought to escape. The resulting inferno took the lives of 500–700 Pequot men, women, and children. Several survived to be taken prisoner or disappear into the woods.

Captain Mason led the attack and began the burning that some historians refer to as a genocide.[3] His account, published in 1677, was conspicuously republished in 1736 by Thomas Prince and then again in 1897 with three other seventeenth-century accounts of the war, in a collection edited by the Ohioan Charles Orr. Mason wrote that once the fire was kindled, "the Indians ran as men most dreadfully amazed." Seeking to escape the English who had entered the village, "such a dreadful terror did the Almighty let fall upon their spirits, that they would fly from us into the very Flames where many of them perished."[4] The English with "great Rejoycing" recognized that "God was above them, who Laughed his Enemies and the Enemies of his People to Scorn, making them as a fiery Oven." Such was "the just Judgment of God" upon the "heathen" and a show of the mercy of God toward the English.[5] Mason exulted: "Our Mouths were filled with Laughter and our Tongues with Singing." The delivery of the faithful to victory was plain: "Was not the Finger of God in all of this?"[6] Mystic was, as historian Bernard Bailyn wrote, "holy war."[7] It was battle, recalled Rev. Thomas Shepard of Cambridge, in which the English triumphed because of their Christian faith: "the Providence of God guided them to . . . the divine slaughter."[8]

Other accounts of the battle at Mystic add human detail and echo the Christian certainties of God's intervention and the justice enacted upon the heathen Pequot. The slaughter was too much for the younger English soldiers, wrote Captain John Underhill, one of the leaders of the attack on Mystic. They blanched at how "great and doleful was the bloody sight . . . to see so many souls lie gasping on the ground, so thick, in some places, that you could hardly pass along."[9] The Indian allies of the English, said Underhill, cried out that the burning of the Pequot was no good, because "it is too furious and slays too many men."[10] Wondering if Christians should not show more compassion and mercy, he affirmed that "Sometimes the Scripture declareth women and children must perish with their parents." And there was "sufficient light from the word of God for our proceedings."[11] For Mason, similarly, God was "burning them up in the fire of his wrath, and dunging the ground with their Flesh."[12] In the end, Mason summarized it in a telling turn of phrase: "the Face of God is set against them that do Evil, to cut off the remembrance of them from the earth."[13] The clergyman Philip Vincent, present in New England during the war, concurred: "the Pequetans are now nothing but a name."[14] The General Assembly of Connecticut endeavored to make sure of the erasure by outlawing even the name, including for the few survivors, and rendering the Pequot River the Thames and the site of the village New London.

Charles Orr, in his introduction to the collected accounts of the conflict, believed that the Pequot War was a defining event for those who lived through it, and for their descendants. "No event in the early history of New England," he asserted, "had a greater influence on its destiny than that known as the Pequot War."[15] The war indeed occupied the memories of early New Englanders and served subsequently as an important point of reference for their understanding of their relationship with the Indians. It is important as well for its instancing of the habitual mingling of violence and religion in early America. And it illustrates the complexity of encounters between English and

Indians. The English, casting Indians as heathen, were deeply suspicious of them, suspecting them of collaboration with the Devil and countless corruptions, from their filthy sexuality to their duplicity, cruelty, and physical and mental inferiority. Roger Williams, who studied their languages assiduously, who insisted on paying them for land, and who served them as broker and negotiator in their encounters with other English, confessed at various times that he was terrified of them for the evil in their hearts.[16]

But as much as the English registered their hatred of Indians, they also expressed their admiration for them. In the accounts of the Pequot War are references to the mettle of the Pequot and their display of virtue, and praise specifically for their courage in battle. Captain Underhill observed on the one hand that Indians typically played at war, behaving as if the "fight is more for the pastime than to conquer and subdue enemies." But at the same time he declared that in the midst of the conflagration at Mystic that exterminated them, "most courageously these Pequeats behaved themselves." There were, he said, "many courageous fellows unwilling to come out . . . and so perished valiantly."[17] Roger Williams became convinced, in the aftermath of the Pequot War, that there was more in common between the Christian English and Native Americans than he had thought. He saw virtue in the Indians, and he saw violence in the English. The war "convinced Williams that religion never justified violence and that Native Americans and Christians shared a moral code."[18]

The Pequot War of 1637 illustrates the manner in which religion supplied an intellectual and emotional framework for violence against Indians in New England. It was a furnace, indeed, in which was forged a crude self-understanding of New England among the British who colonized it. King Philip's War, fought forty years later, was an equivalent disaster for the Indians and as profound a lesson for the English as the Pequot campaign. That lesson was again about the differences between Indians and English, the instabilities of their relationship, and the mixed sorrow and jubilation of a war. Less visible to the English at the time but apparent to later generations, it was a lesson about the role of religion in justifying and prosecuting war, and about resemblances alongside disparities.

King Philip's War was led on the Indian side by Metacom, son of a Wampanoag chief known to the Pilgrims at Plymouth as Massasoit. In 1675, amid increasingly frictive relations between the Wampanoag and the English colonists, he directed a year-long offensive against English towns, aided by Indian allies from other tribes who remained aligned with him for various lengths of time. Destroying a dozen towns, killing many English, and severely disrupting the social and commercial structures of southeast New England, the war eventually spread northerly as far as Maine, where it festered and erupted in periodic violence until the middle of the next century. In the south, English losses were about ten percent of the population. Indian losses by mid-1676 were as much as half their population. As Metacom's allies left him, and the Mohawks, entering the conflict, inflected severe losses on the Wampanoag, the acute phase of the war wound down.

Metacom, known as King Philip, was killed in Rhode Island during the summer of 1676. The English cut his body into pieces, which they hung in trees. They placed his head on a pike and brought it to Plymouth, where Cotton Mather, a rhetorician of religious war, reputedly made off with the jaw as a trophy. The bone of the Indian was a remembrance—of war, of providence, and of unpredictability. In the end, "for Cotton Mather, as for his father, King Philip's War was a holy war, a war against barbarism, and a war that never really ended."[19] Mather, for all his cheerleading of Christian retributive justice, at the same time lamented that the battles with Indians had taken a long-term toll: "But our *Indian* Wars are not over. We have too far degenerated into *Indian* Vices. . . . We have shamefully Indianized in all these abominable things."[20]

New Englanders, prolix in their depictions of tragedy since earliest settlement, wrote at length about King Philip's War. Mather's *Brief History of the Warr with the Indians* (1676), William Hubbard's *Narrative of the Wars in New England* (1677) and, eventually, Mary Rowlandson's popular narrative of her captivity among the Indians, like many other writings, celebrated the god on the side of the English. Rowlandson's narrative, however, also depicted the complexity of relations between Indians and English. Her eleven weeks of captivity blurred for her the categories of savage and civilized, heathen and Christian.[21] Eating Indian food and liking it, observing Indians in English dress, recognizing that some prayed to the Christian God as she did, and perceiving even how her own behavior drifted into Indian ways complicated for her the conceptualization of Indians as the polar opposite of the Christian colonists. That sense of the fluidity of roles played by English and Indians was present elsewhere among New Englanders who left literary traces of their experiences of the crises of the seventeenth century. As a collective memory it endured.

The Indian Wars were crises that bore deep and lasting consequences.[22] Benjamin Tompson's long poem *New England's Crisis* (1676) typified the expression of popular understanding of King Philip's War as an epic confrontation of Protestants with "Pagan spirits." who, possibly urged on by "some Romish agent," indulged their "lust to make a Christian bleed." For Tompson, the "crisis" was war in the usual sense of bloodshed and loss, of "unheard of crueltyes." But the poem additionally was apocalyptic in tone, a bloody witness to the deficiencies of New England Christians.[23] The tragedies of killing and loss were interwoven with religious ideas about just punishment, about God's displeasure with Christians straying from their commitments to their faith. It was a warning, and a reminder of the precariousness, the instability, of the world. It was a call to New Englanders to remember who they were, but a call in the form of a question: "Who are we?"

New Englanders were, first of all, an anxious people. They worried about their piety. They wondered if it was enough and if their choices were moral choices, acceptable to God as well as to the community. They fretfully examined their lives for failings, intent on reviewing every aspect of their behavior and feeling, rarely expressing satisfaction that they had mapped their sins adequately. For such a meticulous religiosity, little that happened was free of religious meaning. Shoeing horses, gazing into glowing embers on the hearth, or picking apples could be occasions for profound spiritual realizations. Traumas likewise were religious business. War with the Indians, layered with fear, joy, guilt, hope, and anguish, and with ideas about the destiny of a chosen people in a Promised Land, was a fraught experience. Narrated into the larger, apocalyptic religious worldview of New Englanders, it acquired over time a powerful historical gravity. It survived within the collective as a memory not only of battle, but of who New Englanders were, how violence was involved in their religious calling to North America, and how the line between good and evil, savage and civilized, English land and Indian land, could be vague.

Scholarly discussion of crisis in early New England has taken as points of departure a number of events, including the Antinomian crisis, commercial transformations, the Indian Wars, and turbulent politics in England. Scholars have been particularly interested, however, in how the Indian Wars brought to the surface the complex dynamics of race, colonization, and religion. They have been observant of the shiftiness of relations between Indians and English colonists. Among many useful discussions of these themes, Richard Slotkin's careful delineation of how Indians and English recognized themselves in each other has remained a central organizing idea for much scholarship about the period. For Slotkin and like-minded scholars, the New England Indian Wars eventuated in a foundational literature: "It was within this genre of colonial writing that the first American mythology took place."[24]

The core American mythology was not solely engendered by John Winthrop's oft-cited speech about the Massachusetts Bay colony as a beacon to the world but rather arose as a cultural formation from the troubled relationships between colonists and Indians. Colonial literature communicated how in relations with the Indians, "the Puritans saw a darkened and inverted mirror image of their own culture, their own mind." Drawn, fascinated, to the Indian, Puritans simultaneously feared descending into "savagery." They glimpsed in Indians' lives the failures and violence of Indian societies, but sensed kinship as well. If "the Indian cultures were the devil's city on a hill," there was more to the story than that grim circumstance because "the Indian was not totally alien to the world of the saints."[25] Through meetings as both friends and foes, English and Indians sought to steady themselves, as they advanced their encounter, by drawing from each other's cultures just enough to conceptually abet a shared project of mutual definition. It was a kind of "double vision." English writers who spent time in the North American colonies "held the Indians up as a mirror in which English readers could examine their own society." The encounter took the form of a "face off."[26]

From such a colonial world of mirrors came important components of an emerging American identity. In *The Name of War: King Philip's War and the Origins of American Identity*, Jill Lepore refined and extended some of Slotkin's arguments, and provided additional perspective. The war, she said, eventuated in "new, firmer boundaries between English and Indian people, between English and Indian land, and between what it meant to be 'English' and what it meant to be 'Indian.'"[27] Those boundaries, while more clearly drawn than before the wars, remained oddly tenuous, however, and relationships between Indians and English remained unstable as frontiers moved farther inland.

While King Philip's War should not be taken as an "archetypal Indian war," it nevertheless served as an enduring American "allegory" about competition for land and the paradoxes of cultural encounter in North America. And one of the components of that encounter was the mutual dread of English and Indians that each was being acculturated to the other. The English feared that they were gradually being drawn into savagery, while the Indians feared being absorbed into English traditions that would compromise their own. In this context of ongoing distress over their identity, "New England colonists waged war to gain Indian lands, to erase Indians from the landscape, and to free themselves of doubts about their own Englishness."[28] But the "English" identity of New Englanders remained profoundly haunted by a feeling of kinship with the Indians, and as much as the wars were an attempt to bury that feeling through annihilation of the other, they only served to preserve it.

New Englanders kept thinking about the Indians. Their ongoing and intense reflection on their relationship to the Indians was fostered by their predilection to understand themselves "by demonstrating, in word or in deed, who we are not." New Englanders were constantly drawn back to pondering the Indians because they wished to push off from them. Their literature expressed the trust that "New England could best be defined by contrast to those whom New Englanders had sequentially opposed." The feeling of kinship with Indians then was at the same time a central aspect of New Englanders' attempts to understand themselves by remaining aware of how they differed from Indians.[29]

As New Englanders pushed off from Indians they imagined as kin, they abetted that enterprise by framing their relationship with Indians in racial terms. New England identity accordingly was a racial identity as well as a religious one. That racial identity, while of deep local importance, moreover was expansively geographic in terms of its many constituent parts. It was so thoroughly shaped with reference to a broad Atlantic world that it would not have served as an effective marker of identity and difference apart from its immersion in that setting. It was framed by overlapping contexts of vast and differentiated space, including national territories, metropoles and peripheries, and mainland and oceanic frontiers. Race in Benjamin Tompson's corpus, for example, was more than an expression of just Tompson's New England experiences. It took shape as part of a "global flow of cultural goods," a circulation of ideas, genres, and language, among other aspects of culture, that emerged in the Atlantic basin in a number of distinct but related contexts.[30] New Englanders looked to both far-off overseas and close-by Atlantic world territories for their leads about race, importing them and adapting them to meet the requirements of their local process of identity construction. Space and race were reciprocally defined. To think about a faraway place often meant to think of a faraway people, a different race. Thinking about race invoked imaginings of space.

Racialization in the New England colonies was a process that drew upon an awareness of a great geography—not only the western edges of the New England colonial territory but also Africa, the Caribbean, New Spain, and New France, in addition to Europe.[31] The racial categories that informed the treatment of Indians after the seventeenth-century wars in New England evidenced that expansive spatial context of race. Following the Pequot War and King Philip's War, defeated Indians were shipped to slavery in Barbados, Bermuda, Jamaica, the Azores, Spain, and North Africa.[32] At the same time, Governor Winthrop drew a more complicated plan, negotiating proposals to trade Indian slaves for Africans. The construction of identity in New England always was in process within an Atlantic world of emerging and shifting racial conceptualizations and related religious arguments.[33] Race and space were conceptually coupled under an umbrella of impressions about linkages between the many different territories of the Atlantic world. Religion, war, race, and world all were joined in the continuous effort of New Englanders to understand themselves, the land, and their destiny.[34]

MEMORY AND INTOLERANCE

The complex connections among race, religion, war, space, and identity in early New England are intimated in the changing ways, over time, that New Englanders remembered Indians. It is a truism that New Englanders thought and wrote about their regional history at great length. That includes their literary representations of the Indian Wars. But it was, as well, the reappraisals of those wars in the eighteenth and nineteenth centuries that are particularly revealing.[35] Sometimes those reappraisals were made by persons whose own histories connected them closely to the wars. The well-known example of William Apess, a Pequot minister, who addressed a gallery of affluent Bostonians at the Odeon theater in 1836, suggests how the white identity of those Bostonians that had partially coalesced in the seventeenth century remained open-ended and at times enigmatic in the nineteenth. Apess's "Eulogy on King Philip" upheld the honor of the Indian leader who had sought to destroy the ancestors of those in attendance at the Odeon. A direct descendant of Metacom, Apess called out the British colonists who sought to destroy the Indians, condemned their "black and hypocritical heart," compared Metacom to George Washington, and pictured his cause "as glorious as the American revolution."[36] Apess's speech was enthusiastically applauded.

Apess's viewpoint, moreover, was likely no surprise to his audience. There were similar views of Indians in circulation in the early nineteenth century. For years the actor Edwin Forrest had been playing to sold-out houses, starring in a play that cast Metacom as a hero. *Metamora; or, the Last of the Wampanoags*, a romantic tragedy written by John Augustus Stone and launched during the Christmas season of 1829, concluded with a mortally wounded Metacom pronouncing, "Curses on you, white men!" Audiences cheered it wildly, and it had a sixty-year run in playhouses across the nation.[37] Lydia Maria Child's *The First Settlers of New England*, which was published in the same year that Forrest's play was launched, painted Philip as a hero and early New Englanders as heartless persecutors of the Indians, "whom they had barbarously destroyed."[38] Publishing her book just as the Indian Removal crisis involving the Cherokee was cresting, Child noted that "it appeared to me that but little attention had been given" to the treatment of Indians by New Englanders. Her task was "to prove, from the most authentic records, that the treatment they have met with from the usurpers of their soil has been, and continues to be, in direct violation of the religious and civil institutions which we have heretofore so nobly defended."[39]

Other writers of the time, such as Congressman Salma Hale of New Hampshire, compared Indians to English colonists and likewise found them similar in terms of character. In his *History of the United States* (1820), which featured many stories of "brave" soldiers, especially during the Revolutionary War, Hale offered the by-then-common positive descriptors of the Pequot at Mystic, such as deeming them "brave and obstinate" in their defense of their village.[40] Timothy Dwight, president of Yale and leader of the evangelical revival there in 1802, wrote that Sassacus, the leader of the Pequots, was courageous, sagacious, and bold, "unquestionably a great man," and one who, "had he been born in an enlightened age and country, might perhaps have been a Charles, or an Alexander."[41] Catharine Sedgwick, a colleague of Child's and author of the romance *Hope Leslie, or, Early Times in the Massachusetts* (1827), depicted like Child how "the courage of the Pequods was distorted into ferocity" by the cruelties of the English.[42] And in that story the English, in their relations with Indians, similarly showed their savagery even while aiming to behave as civilized Christians. The Pequot and the Puritan mirrored each other.[43]

In Sedgwick's rendering and in other early nineteenth-century writings, Puritans and Indians became more like each other, both manifesting valor and honor, but both also savage for their violence against those who stood in their way. Each feared the other, but they were drawn to each other. The potential for unwitting transformation, for merging with the other, remained a constant concern, as was clear in Benjamin Franklin's *Narrative of the Late Massacres* (1764), a commentary on the murder of a number of Six Nations Indians by a large posse in Lancaster County, Pennsylvania. Franklin exclaimed: "Do we come to America to learn and practice the manner of Barbarians?" Pennsylvania had become, he said, a "Neighbourhood of the Christian White Savages."[44] Americans, poised between a sense of kinship with Indians and equally opposed to them, continued in their efforts to construct an identity that could make sense of the issues that were embedded in that relationship, including race, religion, space, and providence. As they did so, they invested themselves more and more deeply in a paradigm of self-defining that, in a United States that was to continue to expand westward and eventually outward from the continent, built in a measure of uncertainty.

The constant migration of Americans to the frontier guaranteed continued clashes with Indians. In the South, the machinery of Indian Removal established a direction for national policy, and set an official example for the mass application of violent means. A religious idea of manifest destiny, the future of Protestants in a Promised Land, kept religion at the forefront of American thinking about those clashes. But religiously inspired violence was not limited to encounters between EuroAmericans and Native Americans.

In addition to the conflicts with Indians, the British fought among themselves. Often those fights were about religion. New England Puritans executed Quakers, imprisoned or exiled religious opponents of various sorts, hanged accused witches, and generally threatened any religious group not in accord with local principles. From Georgia, where the colonial charter withheld religious freedom from Roman Catholics, to the colonial Piedmont, where armed militias of Presbyterians, Baptists, Catholics, Puritans, Anglicans (and Episcopalians), and others fought pitched battles, to statutes limiting Catholics in New York, early America was a place of constant religious conflict.[45] Religious intolerance, which sometimes led to violence, was everywhere, including in Pennsylvania and Rhode Island, which had been founded as refuges for the persecuted. What Bernard Bailyn called the "holy wars" between early New Englanders and Indians were aspects of a broader pattern of religiously justified violence in the United States.

Religious intolerance did not go unrecognized by colonial-era Americans, nor by historians who subsequently wrote about the beginnings of the nation. Colonial-era Catholics and Quakers understandably were quick to condemn it, as were some Baptists and Presbyterians. Congregationalists eventually spoke more of it, especially in the mid-eighteenth century as relations with England frayed.[46] Observers sometimes took circuitous routes in naming it, but religious violence weighed on the minds of many. One of those was the loyalist Charles Inglis, who published a treatise in 1779 that argued, somewhat extravagantly, and belatedly, for avoidance of conflict with England. One claim that he made had to do with his vision of ingrained religious intolerance run wild in a land without British authority to control it. For Inglis, holy war was contagious. The consequences of the Revolution would be ongoing religious wars in North America, as eventual extensions of the rebellion against England currently in progress: "Religious prejudices would certainly operate, and struggles for superiority would ensue; for whatever may be the opinion of some to the *contrary*, it is absolutely certain, that on the part of many, the present is a *Religious War*."[47]

Early Americans such as Hannah Adams recognized the everydayness of intolerance. Attempting to polish the reputation of Governor John Winthrop, she reached hard in her efforts to address his standing as a man who was known for "maintaining the necessity of using coercive measure in religion." She affirmed that Winthrop, who kept Pequot slaves, "finally rose superior to the prejudices of the age in which he lived, and, in his dying moments, feelingly regretted that his conduct had been tinged by the spirit of religious intolerance."[48] Whereas Adams wrote about the history of "bigotry and intolerance"[49] in early Massachusetts, the influential English historian Edmund Burke, a proponent of toleration, pointedly identified the "religious violence, which was the chief characteristic of the first settlers in New England."[50]

TRAUMA AND IDENTITY

Many Americans, however, did not see religious violence, including the religiously legitimated slaughter of Indians. Or, seeing it enacted, they did not wish to remember it. If EuroAmericans, as Benjamin Franklin suggested, might forget who they were and become like Indians, another kind of forgetting was equally important. There were those who simply did not wish to remember any of the history of massacres, the religious wars, the intolerance that fostered those wars, or the racial problem. Forgetting could be easier than remembering. Defending forgetting, some nineteenth-century writers believed that the forgetting of conflict amounted to a recognition of the superiority of the present to a past that was best left to fade from memory. Thomas Loraine McKenney could write straightforwardly of the founders of New England in his *History of the Indian Tribes of North America* (1855), "Their great fault was their religious intolerance. Theirs was an intolerant age, and they were a bigoted race."[51] But there were Americans who, like B. B. Cahoon writing in the *American Journal of Politics*, believed that it was good to forget: "If in the past the Catholic Church persecuted, as did the Puritans in New England, because of religious differences, that can well be forgotten in the broader and better era in which we live, which represents a purer Christianity and a better civilization. We shall never return to the religious intolerance of the past in all denominations but leave it behind us."[52]

Cahoon's pitch followed the many British journal writers who were read in America and who made the same proposal about history more broadly. The *North British Review* published a book excerpt in 1850 that opined, regarding Scottish history: "We would not burden our remembrances with a heaviness that's gone. A new civilization had called into being new habits of thought; and had buried the persecutions of the Stuarts as completely as those of Caligula and Nero."[53] The *Quarterly Review* was more forthright in 1880, describing England emphatically as "a country which has forgotten religious intolerance."[54] The American *Catholic World* agreed, framing the religious violence of English history as "a forgotten and happily buried age of persecution."[55] The *United States Magazine and Democratic Review*, returning to the North American context, made the point in 1850 in commenting approvingly on the "almost, or we might well suppose, quite forgotten persecution" of Quakers in colonial Massachusetts.

Quakers might have disagreed with those renderings of history. So might have many other religious groups who found themselves on the wrong end of power. Certainly Robert Ingersoll, the outspoken champion of unbelief in America, was not willing to forget. He saw religious intolerance everywhere in the United States, and he thought it no less dangerous than the excesses of the French Revolution. He complained loudly that Americans were content to forget about it. Writing in the *North American Review* in 1881, he recited a litany of reasons Americans should review their own past just as the French do the religious crimes of the French Revolution, where church and state colluded in intolerance. The French, he said, "will remember the sufferings of the Huguenots. They will remember the Massacre of St. Bartholomew. They will not forget the countless cruelties of priest and king. . . . Behind the revolution they will see altar and throne—sword and fagot—palace and cathedral—king and priest—master and slave—tyrant and hypocrite. They will see that the excesses, the cruelties, and crimes were but the natural fruit of seeds the church had sown."[56] Ingersoll hoped that Americans likewise would remember their history of intolerance.

Instead, Americans shied from memory of trauma. For many, the trauma of the colonial-era Indian Wars was best forgotten. Religious violence that was fundamental to those wars was abundantly in evidence elsewhere in early America as well, in persecutions of various orders. While a few pressed for remembrance of religious intolerance, others were content to forget Indians, the wars, and all intolerance, from the distant past as well as recent. But remembering and forgetting, seemingly two very different ways of processing trauma, were never available as two distinct options. Forgetting included a kind of remembering, and remembering was joined to forgetting. If, for example, twentieth-century African Americans forged "collective identity through a dialectic of remembering and forgetting within the process of cultural trauma begun earlier,"[57] white Americans as a whole did similarly with their own religious and racial history of traumatic, Old Testament–legitimated violence (experienced as oppressors rather than the oppressed) that took place in early British North America. It was a back-and-forth process.

The traumas of early America, in which are located "the origins of American identity,"[58] are crucial to understanding the history of religious intolerance in America. More precisely, what matters is the way in which American identity remained haunted by religious intolerance, by the Indian massacres, the Quaker hangings, Salem, the pitched battles between religious militias, and many other tragic instances of religious violence that followed over time. There was a tendency for Americans to forget that trauma, and there was a tendency, though a much more subtle one, to remember. Americans blended remembering and forgetting in paradoxical fashion. There are differences with regard to both of those behaviors, depending on factors of race, region, social class, and religious affiliation. But the American history of religious violence, of various "holy wars," and the process of engaging trauma were central to the ongoing, zigzag construction of a national identity.

In as much as American international relations eventually were conducted with reference to an American identity as a nation, they were troubled by factors that were ingrained early on in the nation's history. International relations, especially with regard to religious issues, were steeped in the history of intolerance, violence, trauma, and the urge to forget. When American leaders promoted "religious freedom" abroad, they did so standing on a platform made of fear, suspicion, and forgetfulness as much as confidence and hope.

The Amalekites of the Old Testament

Americans learned to justify religious violence and equally to forget it with the help of the Old Testament. The Old Testament provided a series of stories that modeled religious violence as the product of a dysfunctional attachment between competing groups. It likewise taught that erasing the memory of vanquished enemies went hand in hand with remembering the ruthlessness of the violence. Americans, a people largely in agreement with President Andrew Jackson's deathbed utterance "The Bible is true," saw themselves in the Bible, and imagined that they were reenacting the providentially guided campaigns of the Jews against their enemies. They found inspiration in the Bible, but just as importantly they embraced the biblical vocabulary of violence, not only with regard to the enactment of violence but to the memory of it.[59]

Dysfunctional attachment is a concept that appears in psychological research, and it offers some advantages for analysis when applied to the study of social groups.[60] Social groups can be said to be dysfunctionally attached when they are relationally situated to each other in a way that discloses both the connections between them—the shared norms, ideas, and goals—and the differences that cause friction between them. In some cases, there are feelings of connectedness alongside feelings of fear and distrust, a sense of kinship alongside a sense of oppositeness. Religious groups in America, when they have clashed, presume themselves to be attached to each other in certain ways at the same time that they view themselves as diametrically opposed to their others.

In America, religious groups that are dysfunctionally attached have a religious way of explaining their predicament. It involves deploying a vocabulary different from psychological or sociological science. It nevertheless articulates, in heavily freighted linguistic images, both the attachment and the problem of the attachment. Those images are drawn from the Bible, which furnishes a rich set of narratives illustrating dysfunctional attachment without naming it in that way. Specifically, the Old Testament stories about relations between the Jews and the Amalekites serve as the point of reference for understanding religious others. The message of those stories is that a group can be kin and enemy at the same time.

The twentieth-century literary historian Perry Miller observed that the "Old Testament is truly so omnipresent in the American culture of 1800 or 1820 that historians have as much difficulty taking cognizance of it as of the air people breathed."[61] Arguably it was even more present to colonial New Englanders, who habitually imagined themselves into the stories about the Israelites, seeing their own causes joined with those of Moses, Abraham, Saul, Ruth, Isaiah, Jeremiah, and others: they named their children after such figures. The colonial setting encouraged such identifications with ancient heroes. Contact with the Indians, especially, prompted recourse to the Old Testament as a source of instruction about those emergent relations. New Englanders settled on depictions of the Amalekites, and their defeat by the Jews, as the touchstone for their encounters with Native Americans.[62]

The Amalekites, descended from Esau, appear in several places in the Old Testament. Or, more properly, they disappear, for their fate at the hands of God is to serve as fodder for a massacre that, when recalled by the Israelites over time, will instruct the faithful in the importance of obeying God's commands. The Amalekites were a wandering tribe that trailed the Hebrews during their flight from Egypt, falling upon the sick and weak in the rear, killing them and claiming their possessions.[63] Moses presided over a miracle in the desert in which the Jews defeated the Amalekites, but did not entirely destroy them. Many generations later the prophet Samuel informed Saul, Israel's first king, that God wished the Amalekites annihilated: "Thus says the Lord of hosts: 'I will punish Amalek for what he did to Israel, how he ambushed him on the way, when he came up from Egypt. Now go and attack Amalek, and utterly destroy all that they have, and do not spare them. But kill both man and woman, infant and nursing child, ox and sheep, camel and donkey.'"[64] Saul, however, spared the life of Agag, the Amalekite king, as well as the livestock, which he intended to sacrifice formally to God. Consequently Samuel reprimanded Saul that "to obey is better than sacrifice," put Agag to the sword, and abandoned the king to his regrets for his disobedience.

Old Testament references to the Amalekites are important less for their lesson in obedience to God, however, than for their illustration of the theme of genocide.[65] Even before the successful campaign of Saul, God had promised to "blot out" the Amalekites and, more specifically, to "blot out the remembrance" of them, as he spoke to Moses: "I will utterly blot out the remembrance of Amalek from under heaven."[66] In Deuteronomy, the extermination of the Amalekites is specifically linked to God's awarding possession of the land to the Hebrews, and to the underhandedness of the Amalekites: "Remember what Amalek did to you on the way as you were coming out of Egypt, how he met you on the way and attacked your rear ranks, all the stragglers at your rear, when you were tired and weary; and he did not fear God. Therefore it shall be, when the Lord your God has given you rest from your enemies all around, in the land which the Lord your God is giving you to possess as an inheritance, that you will blot out the remembrance of Amalek from under heaven. You shall not forget."[67]

Crucial to the meaning of the story told in these lines is the closing command. It stressed to the Israelites, prior to Saul's victory, the necessity of remembering the evil done by the Amalekites, at the same time that God vows to erase all memory of them. This association of remembering with forgetting is essential to appreciating the complex logic informing subsequent religiously driven campaigns to exterminate one's opponents. Such campaigns are undertaken not only to blot out the existence of an enemy, but to bury the memory of that enemy as well, the act of violence itself an enactment of a simultaneous urge to forget. At the same time, however, crusades to exterminate the other are contrived to remember that the other has been erased from memory. So, the scriptural recounting of the act of annihilation of the Amalekites and God's promise to purge from collective memory all traces of them is itself a testimony, a remembering.

Noted in a related way by Benedict Anderson in his discussion of imagined community, it is that ambivalence, the choppy movement between hatred and forgetting, that historically has been central to relations between religious opponents. That ambivalence, moreover, reaches more broadly into confrontations between religions, framing the self-understandings of groups in conflict. In many encounters we find the oppressors constructing the oppressed as the mirror of certain negative characteristics of themselves, that is, as a *doppelgänger* of the Amalek within the oppressor. American Protestant groups that perceived Mormonism as a threat, for example, met secretly in order to condemn the "secrecy" and "predilection to violence" of Mormons and to lay plans for their extermination.

There is an English and even a Continental background to the Christian

34   CHAPTER ONE

embrace of the Amalek stories. New Englanders and other Americans did not invent the application of the story to their religious, ethnic, or political others. That background is detailed elsewhere,[68] and here the focus is directly on how the Amalek stories served as inspiration and justification for violence between the British and Native Americans, American Protestants and Roman Catholics, and Mormons and various other American religious groups. It is possible to see in such instances the manner in which forgetting, remembering, violence, attraction, and repulsion were intertwined in the invocation of an authoritative biblical image, a reference for all of those things.

Amalek in America

American religious leaders in New England and elsewhere, through the nineteenth century, were familiar with the story of Amalek, as would be any Christian minister, and especially a Protestant one, whose sermonizing required knowledge of the Bible. Protestant leaders, from the beginning of the settlement of New England, invoked Amalek in making points about Christianity in the New World. John Winthrop, in his well-known "covenant" speech aboard the *Arbella* just prior to the Puritans' arrival in Massachusetts Bay in 1630, drew his auditors into a consideration of the core meaning of covenant by raising the specter of the Amalekites. He compared the importance of obedience to God in the work of building a Christian community in New England to God's commission to Saul "to destroy Amalek."[69]

The imagery deployed by Winthrop informed generations of Anglophone literature about North America. The colonial theologian Jonathan Edwards, in *A History of the Work of Redemption*, a series of sermons preached in 1739 that he intended to be his great work of divinity, made more precise application of Amalek to the unfolding of history. "The dangers that the saints must meet with in their course through the world," he wrote, "were represented by the fiery flying serpents which the children of Israel met with in the wilderness. The conflicts the church has with her enemies, were represented by the battle with the Amalekites, and others they met with there."[70]

The trope passed from Edwards to a succession of writers in the following century. The early nineteenth-century revivalist and abolitionist Charles Grandison Finney invoked it in reflecting on the enemies of the church in his *Systematic Theology*. Finney argued that the terrible Old Testament justice administered the Amalekites was in fact an aspect of love. But it was tough love, to be sure. The "prayers for the punishment of the wicked" that "abounded" in the Old Testament were, Finney warned, "no vindication of the spirit of fanaticism and denunciation that so often have taken shelter under them. As well might fanatics burn cities and lay waste countries, and seek to justify themselves by an appeal to the destruction of the old world by flood, and the destruction of the cities of the plain by fire and brimstone." But Samuel's hewing the Amalekite leader Agag in pieces, and King David's "strongly developed" inclination toward annihilation of the wicked, were models of right action because "those sinners deserved to die."[71]

Alexander Campbell, founder of the Disciples of Christ, asked in the title of one lecture, "Is capital punishment sanctified by divine authority?" Answering in the affirmative, he observed, "And what shall we say of the father of the faithful [Moses], returning from the slaughter of the confederate kings? . . . of Samuel, the pure and pious Samuel, hewing to pieces with his own hand the king of Amalek?" Such were cardinal instances in which "God has made the purest, the holiest and the best of men, as well as angels, the executioners of his justice."[72] The Adventist prophetess Ellen Gould White similarly referenced Amalek. In more than one instance, she demonstrated her familiarity with a line of interpretation that had emerged in the late seventeenth century and that made gradual gains in popularity into the nineteenth century. White, in referring to the Amalekites in 1870, made a point about reversal. Noting that Amalek had overstepped his bounds in claiming the superiority of the Amalekites over the Israelites, "God marked their boastful words against him, and appointed them to be utterly destroyed by the very people they had despised."[73]

Such thinking was in fact continuous over several centuries, as evidenced in the message of Mary White Rowlandson, who, in narrating her captivity in 1682, had remarked on her predicament: "Another thing that I would observe is the strange providence of God in turning things about when the Indians at the highest and the English at the lowest." The Indians, "thinking surely, Agag-like, 'the bitterness of death is past,'" the Lord opened the gates of hell and "hurled themselves into it" just at the time that the Christians that they persecuted had nearly abandoned hope.[74] For American interpreters, the affiliation of the Amalekites and Jews—the kinship between them—was framed by religious enmity. Rowlandson's and White's and many other writers' imagining of inversions, and their declaring of social changes to be reversals, were manifestations of the mirroring of two parties dysfunctionally attached.

The applicability of the lesson of the Amalekites to groups beyond Native Americans was evidenced early in the colonial era. The practice of marking out-groups as Amalekites in England had been refined with particular at-

36 CHAPTER ONE

tention to Catholics, and that tendency was transmitted to America, where Catholics initially were associated with Indians and soon afterward attacked as a separate North American group.

Colonial New England minister Cotton Mather, never one to miss a chance to publicly bless the New England Puritan cause or to foretell its destiny, called up Amalek to rally colonial forces to the "just war" against the Indians in 1689. "Turn not back till they are consumed," urged Mather. "Tho' they Cry; Let there be none to Save them; But beat them small as the Dust before the Wind." We pray, he said, for "vengeance upon our murderers. . . . against the Amalek that is now annoying this Israel in the Wilderness." In this sermon is a glimpse as well of a stage in the developing intersection of seventeenth-century Puritan rhetoric about papal plots and the call for extermination of the Indian. Mather made note of Catholic association with the Indians in tones meant to indicate its meaningfulness. "The Papists," he declared, "contribute what help they can" to the Indians, "and say Mass with them (as of Late) after their Little Victories." Which, in the broader scheme of things, should not dispirit or confuse the soldiers, "but the rather from thence prognosticate their Approaching Ruine."[75] The joining of anti-Catholic polemics to the condemnation of Native Americans was an important stage in the American rendering of the Amalek story, vesting it in richer detail and interlocking themes that suited it eventually to wholesale reapplication to American Catholics, Mormons, Jews, Jehovah's Witnesses, Asian immigrant religious groups, and others.

Amalek and the War against Native Americans

Violence between New Englanders and Indians was most deadly when colonists imagined Indians as kindred who had turned against them, that is, as Amalekites. Again, while English colonists believed that Indians were contrary and inferior in many ways, they also recognized them as kindred. Crucial to the English construction of the Native American was a belief that Indians, whatever their differences with Europeans, shared a bond with the English. There were various understandings of what that bond was, but one strand of it was that kinship between Christians and Indians lay buried deep in the religious history of both groups. Many of the settlers of British North America, and New Englanders especially, arranged the image of the Indian in their minds in keeping with theologically grounded historical categorizing of people and place that were familiar to them through preaching and religious literature. Participants in the Virginia Company's colonization of North America imagined Indians as examples of how the English themselves had lived at an earlier point in time. That is, they shaped a vision of Native Americans as "Britons," England's Saxon ancestors, heathens all until the Romans forced Christianity upon them. English reports about Native Americans in this vein were "mirrors in which English readers could see their own virtues and vices reflected."[76]

More importantly, some English quickly came to regard Native Americans as the descendants of the Ten Lost Tribes of Israel. Western writing about the fate of the twelve Jewish tribes of the Old Testament previously had concluded that in the aftermath of social and political pressures upon the Jews, two tribes had remained in Judah, and the other ten had been "lost," meaning dispersed. Beginning with the Spanish and French, European explorers and missionaries in the Americas had developed detailed arguments for taking Indians as lapsed Jews, and in some cases as lapsed converts to Christianity. The renowned Dominican missionary Bartolomé de Las Casas, for example, considered the possibility of the Indians being descended from the Jews.

Spanish writers such as Garcilaso de la Vega, Pedro Cieza de León, and José de Acosta, in their histories of the Incas and other writings, found linkages between Indian mythologies and material cultures and the religions of Jews and Christians. Indians, said those writers, had over time "forgotten" the monotheistic revelation. Moreover, as the Spanish considered Indian culture alongside the stories in their New Testaments, they began to argue that in fact traces of Christian preaching—moreover, by one of the original apostles of Jesus—were visible in the background of Indian life. Some Spanish accordingly concluded that Indians had fallen away from Christianity over time, and that Amerindian religion was *praeparatio evangelica*, that is, preparation for the gospel.[77] French missionaries came to some of the same conclusions as the Spanish. The writing of missionaries such as the Capuchin Pacifique de Provins expressed the view that the role of the missionary was to recover the faith, to reawaken it, in Amerindians. In his words, the missionary labored to "bring these savage people *back* to the knowledge of the true God we adore." The abbé Bobé in 1719 likewise explained how "Israelites under the dispersion by Salmanasar passed into North America," and he linked them specifically with the Sioux.[78]

Among New Englanders, the paradigm of the Lost Tribes was "optimistic in that, like the Old Britons model, it assumed the Indians to be ripe for conversion."[79] The Puritan missionary John Eliot embraced the theory and helped popularize it in the mid-seventeenth century. His cause was joined in Amsterdam by the rabbi Menasseh ben Israel, whose *Hope of Israel* (1650) proclaimed "*that the first inhabitants of* America *were the ten tribes of the* Israelites." In Norfolk, England, the Presbyterian clergyman Thomas

Thorowgood, author of *Iews in America; or Probabilities that the Americans are of that Race* (1650), lent his voice to the claim.[80] Other writers, in England and the Americas, expressed support for the theory throughout the colonial period, from earliest settlement. They learned from each other's writings.

Cotton Mather, in *The Mystery of Israel's Salvation Opened*, declared that the time was coming "when all Israel will be saved, and then will converting work go on gloriously . . . even among the Indian." Planting his analysis firmly in the soil of Puritan theology, Mather argued that "they are broken off from that covenant and church relation which once they stood in. This is true concerning the Israelites or ten tribes. . . . But there is a day coming, when God will receive them into favour again. . . ." Other well-known advocates of the theory were Roger Williams, William Penn, Samuel Sewall, and Jonathan Edwards. Edwards, in *History of the Work of Redemption*, argued that the Indians were led from Canaan by the Devil, who by degrees was able to persuade them from their worship of God to worship of himself.[81] Charles Crawford's essay *Upon the Propagation of the Gospel*, published in Philadelphia in 1799, carried the theory into the eighteenth century, as did James Adair's *History of the American Indians* (1775), which was largely about "observations, and arguments, in proof of the American Indians' being descended from the Jews." Adair offered detailed explanation for residual Jewish culture in everything from the Indian manner of counting time, to healing, burial, religious rituals, language, theocratic ideas, naming, and numerous other topics. In representation of the swirling alteration of identities that marked the fluid, volatile relationship between English and Indian, the Pequot William Apess published in 1831 *The Indians: The Ten Lost Tribes*.[82]

Not all Americans rushed to embrace the theory that the American Indians were of the Ten Lost Tribes. Anne Bradstreet had questions about it, and so, too, did the Cotton Mather of the *Magnalia*.[83] Those who found it appealing, however, were drawn to it not only because of some interest in the human history of the American continents, but because of a view of history that included the belief that the Jews were to be converted before the return of Christ to the world.

In New England, the notion of Indians as descendants of the Jews offered an exhilarating challenge to Christians who looked forward expectantly to the glorious end of time. Ministry to Indians was not merely an undertaking to convert heathen. It was activity that fell squarely in the center of a theologically driven agenda of history, and of human participation, through initiative, in the events that would lead to the culmination of history in Christ. Puritans knew from their Bibles that the Jews were to be converted before the dawn of the millennium. The Indians were considered ripe for conversion because ministering to them was a way to bring them back to the revelation of God originally given to them as Jews. It is unlikely that any New Englander who had encountered Indians believed that they would suddenly convert in droves to the Christian faith. In fact, their conversions were not impressive in terms of either numbers or staying power. But missionaries approached the Indians with a sense of their own participation in a key episode in the unfolding of a divine plan. They fully expected Indians to become Christian, to remember that they were children of God who had lapsed from the revelation given them centuries earlier. Christians who believed that Indians were the remnant of the Lost Tribes approached them as kindred, expecting Indians to respond by professing belief in Christian monotheism. Accordingly, "missionaries loved the notion, for Christianizing pagans who were also descendants of Jews fitted the Bible's prediction for the millennium and would fulfill, in fact, one of its preparatory demands."[84]

Relations between Indians and New Englanders—and with other Euro-Americans—did not go well, however. Contestation of land and resources, the clashing of cultures, and the frictions between personalities, among other factors, led to violent engagement. EuroAmerican depiction of Indians, who were kindred to Christians because they were descended from Jews and ripe for conversion, relied in such circumstances on the religious imagery of the Amalekites. Looking backward, a report of a U.S. commissioner of Indian affairs in 1863 observed that "there is a deeply rooted antipathy between the habits, religion, and customs of a savage race, and the pursuits and teachings of civilization."[85] In the seventeenth century, trust in that antipathy already grounded colonial New England thinking about removing Indians from the land. Typically, when this aspiration was expressed with reference to the Amalekites, it was in circumstances that had delivered relations between Indians and colonists to the precipice of military engagement. So, for example, the New England Confederation in declaring war on the Narragansett tribe in 1675 asserted that the "Narrohigansetts and their confederates" had been stirred up by Satan in the same way that "Amalek and the Philistines did confederate against Israel."[86]

The English opponents of Indian deviltry were cast as heroes on the order of Old Testament figures, including those involved in the war with the Amalekites. At key moments in the English conquest of the northeastern tribes, Christian sermons and speeches focused on the battlefield leadership of specific persons, much in the same way that English rhetoricians had placed figures like the Duke of Marlborough at the center of their narratives. During the eighteenth century, as filiopietistic New England chroniclers were canonizing the heroes of the first generation and bestowing laurels upon the heads of contemporary defenders of the New England way, they also commended Indian fighters in eulogies and remembrances. Their memories of such persons were of Moses-like or Joshua-like heroes who prevailed over evil Amalekites. And in cases where colonial soldiers died in battle against Native Americans, they were celebrated as martyrs, including in cases where their sacrifice did not immediately suggest heroism, or even competence, in the face of the enemy.

Heroes were praised as the hammers of Amalek. In relating details of the "fight at Piggwacket" in 1725, Thomas Symmes sermonized that Captain John Lovewell, who lost his life, the battle, and a majority of his force while bounty-hunting Indian scalps, resembled Joshua, Moses's "Renowned general, in his wars with the Aborigines of Canaan," the Amalekites.[87] Just how far the colonial imagination had come in picturing the collective future of Native Americans as empty of promise, as already on course to be blotted out, is redolent in Symmes's preaching. Offered by Symmes as "a very Celebratory Elegy," the sermon is grounded in a trust that extermination of the Indian was only a matter of time.[88] That was the faith likewise of Captain Samuel Appleton, who wrote to a friend regarding his role as commander of the colonial forces arrayed against the Narragansett in 1675: "By the prayers of God's people, our Israel in his time may prevail over this cursed Amalek; against whom I believe the Lord will have war forever until he have destroyed him."[89]

Some nineteenth-century American writers, looking back on the colonial period, wrote forthrightly about New Englanders' belief that Native Americans were Amalekites deserving of annihilation. In some cases, the polemical goals of those writers were complicated, as in the case of Confederate Army veteran Robert Lewis Dabney, who, in the course of defending the honor of the South post–Civil War, raised the issue of slavery in the North, that is, "the enslaving of the Indians. The pious 'Puritan fathers' found it convenient to assume that they were God's chosen Israel, and the pagans about them were Amalek and Amorites. They hence deduced their righteous title to exterminate or enslave the Indians. . . ."[90] Dabney, in his eulogy for General Thomas "Stonewall" Jackson in 1863, on the other hand, apparently had no difficulty in identifying Jackson himself as the hammer of the Amalekites, that is, the Union.[91] *Putnam's Magazine* observed in 1857 that Christians in colonial North America treated Indians "as the Amalekites and Canaanites had been treated by the Hebrews." George Bancroft, in his monumental *History of the United States*, discerned that New Englanders assumed that they had "a right to treat the Indians on the footing of Canaanites or Amalekites." The *North American Review*, remarking on seventeenth-century English encounters with Indians in the northeast, concluded: "Heathen they were in the eyes of the good people of Plymouth Colony, but nations of heathen, without question, as truly were the Amalekites. . . ."[92]

Edward Eggleston looked back in 1883 on the "scenes of savage cruelty" at Mystic in 1637, a Pequot genocide, Eggleston said, that ministers rhetorically justified through "citation of Joshua's destruction of the Canaanites." As *The Living Age* likewise observed of the event, "As the Israelites slew the Amalekites, so did the Pilgrims slay the Pequot." Bostonian Frederick D. Huntington, who eventually became a bishop of the Protestant Episcopal Church, commented in 1859 that the military exercises against Native Americans in New England were led by men who were "evidently of an energetic spirit and quite an Old Testament cast of mind."[93]

Some nineteenth-century writers recognized the problem. Looking backward, they had seen the genocidal results of campaigns grounded in Old Testament militarism and proposed ground-level solutions. They challenged reckless teaching of Old Testament texts in Bible study groups, pulpits, and Sunday schools. Even at the end of the nineteenth century, however, such efforts were still sporadic, desperate, and ideologically compromised. The Rev. James M. Whiton, for example, published in the *New Englander and Yale Review* in 1884 an impassioned plea that Sunday school teachers tone down their presentation of the story of Amalek. Arguing that "it is one of the most unfortunate mistakes of ordinary Bible readers, which Sunday school teaching has done nothing to correct," that the story of the Amalekites is presented in a "literally objective sense," Whiton explained that in Samuel's time, "this robber tribe of Amalek were hanging about the southern frontier of Judah very much as Indian tribes about our own western settlements." The Israelites were forced to come to terms with the necessity of waging a war of annihilation against the Amalekites just as "in the case of white farmers against red savages—a clean sweep of the pests, men, women, and children, like so many wolves. It had to be done." Whiton's objection to this version of the story was not directed to the genocide itself. Rather, it had to do with God's role in it. "Not that God *actually* ordered it," he argued. "To Samuel, however, it was *as if* God had ordered it." And so it was done, and without remorse.[94]

While some easterners were looking back with remorse, or at least mixed feelings, on the Puritan campaigns against the Indians, settlers out west were extending it. Exploration of the western frontier brought with it bloody contestations and a reinvigorated language advocating the extermination of the Indian. Speechmakers and writers who commented on those clashes still wrapped their remarks in Old Testament language, and especially images of Amalek. In the stripped-down ferocity of the battle for land and power in the West, however, the reference to biblical heroes that provided a shorthand for an ideology of genocide was often put to the side, well-enough known already to make unnecessary its ongoing rehearsal for an audience of migrants arriving from back east.

What the West retained were specific wordings that were grounded in those ingrained Old Testament stories, linguistic codings that carried forward the frameworks for thought provided by biblical accounts. The *Western Monthly Magazine* reflected in 1833 on "the cause and operation of these feelings," that "the dweller upon the frontier continues to regard the Indian with a degree of terror and hatred . . . which can neither be removed by argument nor appeased by anything other than the destruction of its object."[95] In 1856, Commissioner George W. Manypenny already had imagined in biblical terms the tragic ending of the Native American collision with westward expansion, and was "so sure will these poor denizens of the forest be blotted out of existence, and their dust be trampled under the foot."[96] In the Pacific Northwest, James Y. McDuffie, superintendent of Indian affairs for California, wrote to his boss A. B. Greenwood in 1860 about settlers' antipathy toward Indians, remarking on "the determination of a portion of the settlers to exterminate them from the face of the land."[97] The *Humboldt Times* abetted the genocidal impulses of settlers in the area by declaring in 1863 that "the Indian must be exterminated or removed. . . ."[98] A few years later the *Chico Courant* reinforced the religious framework for hatred of the Indian by arguing that "it is a mercy to the red devils to exterminate them."[99]

Such pronouncements were built upon the assumption, thickly woven out of various bits of cultural fabric over three centuries, that as non-Christians Native Americans were religious opponents, that by their sneaky and duplicitous behavior they had earned a sentence of extermination, and that the land belonged to the EuroAmerican population. The American trust in manifest destiny, which, in its decidedly Christian dress, meant that God had awarded Europeans possession of the land, continued to inform relations with Indians throughout the nineteenth and twentieth centuries.

Blotting Out, Remembering, and Forgetting

We understand more of the extremist manner of speaking and thinking about Native Americans when we consider the widespread but specific use of the term "blot out." The expression, adopted from key passages in the King James Bible about annihilating the Amalekites, of destroying them and "blotting out" the memory of them, was widespread. It occurred as well in biblical and theological writings suggesting that God had the power to "blot out" the sins of a person.[100] The expression was in use in colonial America and appeared more frequently in religious and, later, social writings, especially alongside the word "exterminate," in the decades leading up to its frequent usage in the mid-nineteenth century. Its deployment in religious rhetoric was varied.

The Westminster Confession, the seminal Presbyterian statement of faith that had informed colonial religious life from the middle of the seventeenth century, warned that Satan labored "to blot out the Glory" of the Sabbath "and even the memory of it" as a day set aside from business for the worship of God.[101] John Hale, in his 1702 retrospective on the events at Salem a decade earlier, worried over innocent blood that might have been shed and who was culpable, and prayed to God to be of a forgiving mind, so that "when he shall visit, he will not visit this sin upon our land, but blot it out and wash it away."[102] By 1845, writers could refer shorthandedly to "the sentence of extermination issued against Amalek," a phrase that was repeated regularly, including nearly twenty years later, prominently, in the massive *A History of All Nations*.[103] Princeton theologian William Henry Green, in reminding his readers in 1877 of the "perpetual authority of the Old Testament," wrote that the Israelites "were commanded to treat the Canaanites with the utmost barbarity and cruelty, utterly destroying all that breathed, men, women, and children; they were likewise commanded to exterminate the Amalekites." Green defended the directive as part of God's plan.[104] Susan B. Anthony employed the term, as had others before her, in the interest of a cause other than American Israelism: she lamented during the Civil War that "to forever blot out slavery is the only possible compensation for this merciless war."[105]

Anthony's Old Testament–flavored depiction of the war against slavery suggests the problem of whites' relations with African Americans more generally. In fact, although many Americans came to conceive of Native Americans as Amalekites, they did not extend that conception to African American slaves. Slaves were valuable as property, and aside from scattered campaigns of retaliation against participants in slave revolts, the Old Testament imagery of Amalek, the enterprise of "blotting out," had little relevance to a plantation system founded on a scheme of human chattel. Ironically, white uninterest in pursuing a characterization of African Americans as Amalekites took place alongside African American Christians' embrace of another Old Testament image, Ham, whose genealogy (the Amalekites were his descendants) in fact furnished them with a platform for self-understanding.[106]

The struggle against slavery itself, however, was figured a crusade against Amalek by numerous writers and ministers during the Civil War. C. A. Bartol rallied his congregation at Boston's West Church in 1861 by telling them that the North's struggle resembled the Israelites' battle against "the wild tribes of Amalek, the freebooters and enslavers of their day." Presbyterian minister J. P. Cleaveland laid out in full detail the evil attributes of Amalek in angrily condemning the South for their "butcheries" during the war. Speaking in Newark in 1865, several days after the execution of the notorious Andersonville commandant Captain Henry Wirz, he reminded his audience that the Amalekites had "turned traitor to Heaven and humanity," and "killed in cold blood every defenceless woman and babe." Citing Exodus 17:14, "I will utterly put out the remembrance of Amalek from under heaven," and identifying the Union as "Canaan," he declared: "Let all loyal America ponder upon this decree now. Let them remember too that Amalek was due *South* from the 'Holy land.'" The lesson of Amalek, he concluded, "solves the perplexing problem, what to do with your enemies when you have them in your power." Such likely were the sentiments of Eben Conant when he wrote to Abraham Lincoln earlier that year about South Carolina: "I propose to blot out that state forever."[107]

"Hatred" of one's enemies, said a western writer, led to "extermination" of them.[108] But hatred was about blotting out not only one's enemies but ostensibly the memory of them as well—and, paradoxically, of somehow remembering at the same time that such a cleansing had occurred. It takes little imagination to see how American writing about religious and social conflict during the nineteenth and early twentieth centuries (alongside American consumption of English literature) joined the fantasy of utter destruction of opponents with the dream of eliminating memory of them. The linkage between annihilation and forgetting was well formed in an assortment of literary genres.[109]

New England Puritans, building on the foundation provided them by English writers, condemned Indians as Amalekites, wrote and preached excitedly about blotting them out, and rhetorically presented the Indian-fighter in the figure of a biblical hero. Before the middle of the nineteenth century, a crucial linkage had formed among several component ideas, namely, the Indian as both distant other and religious kindred, the desirability of exterminating one's enemies, and of destroying their traces in collective memory—forgetting them. Those linkages were enabled and justified through appeal to a well-known, even ingrained, biblical narrative.

From the seventeenth century forward, colonialist conceptualization of the other was grounded in the distinction that early English colonists made, like French and Spanish before them, between Christian and heathen. That distinction was complicated, however, because some who embraced it also theorized that Indians were of the Ten Lost Tribes. Indians were the religious other at the same time that they were religious collaborators—distant brethren, but brethren nevertheless. The religious interpretation of difference that relied on the Amalek story promoted the ideas of extermination and of forgetting the exterminated other. Paradoxically, Americans, following the bold phrasing of Old Testament passages, at the same time were expected to remember that they had forgotten. Forgetting and remembering thus were thought to be intertwined in the biblically informed organization of thinking about difference, encounter, violence, and resolution.

Catholics and Mormons as Amalekites

Early New Englanders brought to the fore of thinking about religious opponents the ideas of extermination and of blotting out memory. They also began to develop the rudimentary notion of conspiratorial secrecy as a trait of the other. Those who commented on relations with Indians in those terms fully expected that their readers and auditors grasped the Old Testament framework for those ideas. That rhetoric developed over the course of the nineteenth century, and in so doing, it gradually shifted its primary reference from the story of Amalek per se to a more precise focus on the modus operandi of the other, to the secrecy, duplicity, and cowardice of the other. Americans continued to make explicit reference to Amalek in their discussion of Indians, and, increasingly, in complaints about Catholics and Mormons. But the emphasis was moving to certain characteristics of the religious other, to the other as a traitor and a coward and a conspirator in secret schemes against "real" Americans. All of those character traits were rooted in American renderings of Amalek and the Amalekites.

Like EuroAmerican mistreatment of Native Americans, the history of anti-Catholicism in America has been well documented.[110] From its manifestation as Protestant harassment of Catholics in colonial Maryland, to arson that destroyed Catholic buildings in Boston, Philadelphia, and other cities in antebellum America, through the hate-driven campaigns of the late nineteenth and early twentieth centuries, violence against Catholics has attracted the attention of many historians who research religious intolerance. The story begins with the intolerance of English writers who cast Catholics as Amalekites from the sixteenth century onward. The trope of the Amalekites was more important to depictions of Indians in colonial America, but it did not disappear from discussions of Catholics. Enriched over time through application to Indians, the language of intolerance, with its Old Testament emphases on extermination, trickery, and cowardice, remained linked to campaigns against Catholics throughout the history of the United States.

The French and Indian War (1755–1763), which pitted Protestant New

Englanders against "papist" French and their Indian allies, featured lively denunciations of Catholic Amalekites. As James West Davidson has shown, the logic of the millennial thought of New Englanders included an English willingness to see French Catholics as hopelessly corrupt and therefore fit to be annihilated during the approach of the eschaton.[111] In was in this frame of mind that Nathan Stone preached a sermon following English victories in Canada in 1760 that cast the defeated French adversaries as "Amalektish enemies," and reminded his auditors that the Bible taught that "Thou shalt blot out the remembrance of the Amalekites from under heaven."[112] Such language was progressively reinforced through the incorporation of other texts into the Old Testament core of stories about the Amalekites.

For example, the application of texts drawn from the Revelation to John, an apocalyptic book of the New Testament, had been standard in Protestant writing about Catholics since the Reformation, and it continued in America. It was in this tradition of intertestamental patterns of interpretation that the *Christian Monitor* reminded its readers in 1809 that "the ten-horned beast therefore represents the Romish church," a conclusion drawn throughout the century by many other Protestant exegetes of the text, as they engaged the Revelation to John alongside Old Testament condemnations of the enemies of God. Such interpretation added muscle to the other biblically framed calls to arms against Amalekites, and built momentum for intolerance of Catholics. In more general terms, combinations of Old and New Testament justifications for annihilation of the other were interwoven so thoroughly by the nineteenth century that a writer for the *Boston Investigator* had no trouble in 1844 making sense of the meaning of a Jonesboro, Tennessee, *Whig* editorial that declared, "Our opinion is, that there is to be no peace in this country, till the Mormons and Catholics are exterminated." The editorial, said the *Boston Investigator*, was about "blotting out Amalek," that is, Mormons and Catholics, and doing so in anticipation of the coming "millennium."[113] By bringing an end to the existence of the other, some Christians expected to bring an end to time itself, the final resolution of the struggle against Amalek being the end of history, a forgetting on a mass and absolute scale.

American Protestants increasingly voiced their anxieties about Catholics with interlocking references to both testaments. Dr. Joseph F. Berg, who wrote animatedly about the perils of popery in antebellum America, asserted that "Rome is the Amalek with which God will never make peace. . . . Rome is that wicked one whom the Lord will destroy," linking that vision to Catholicism as "the system of popery . . . the Master-piece of Satan . . . the impudence of AntiChrist."[114] The heart of the message remained a call to action, to blot out the other. Accordingly, the picturing of Catholics as Amalekites throughout the nineteenth century fueled calls for their extermination, or pronouncements that they be "blotted out," memory and all.

In early twentieth-century retrospect, an observer of anti-Catholic violence wrote that a previous generation of German Protestant immigrants "thought nothing of shooting at a window behind which they suspected a cardinal in Cincinnati, or of shying bricks in the direction of a priest in Milwaukee. . . . There could be no peace with Amalek." The anti-Catholic American Protective Association and the League for the Protection of American Institutions endeavored, as the *North American Review* observed, to "blot out from memory" Catholic figures from the American past. Toward the end of the nineteenth century, it was still the case, wrote the Reverend William Barry, that "Old Protestant hatred still breeds men, neither few nor feeble," who wanted to "abolish" Catholicism in America. The oath sworn by members of the American Protective Association, which was founded in Clinton, Iowa, in 1887, included the telltale promise to "erase the name on the ticket" in the voting booth if it identified a Catholic. And, as was often the case, such claims were reinforced with reports that Catholics, in fact, were the ones who wished to destroy Protestants, not only in the United States but elsewhere in the Americas as well. This conceptual reversal of position, so important in the cultivation of intolerance, was reported continuously by the Protestant press. Looking southward, the *Methodist Review*, for example, claimed that Catholic clergy in Mexico had inspired mobs with a "hatred of Protestantism" and had set out to "exterminate Protestant congregations in all that region."[115] Many other accusations of Catholic plots at home were likewise aired in print. Many of those stressed the secret, heretical, and anti-democratic spirit of Catholicism.

The influence of English anti-Catholicism[116] was felt in other ways besides the survival in New England and elsewhere of English anti-Catholic rhetoric. Protestant military actions against Catholics in Maryland overturned the vaunted Catholic order of that colony in the seventeenth century, and other colonies discouraged Catholic settlement by denying Catholics the right to worship and by banishing priests. In Boston in 1647, priests were threatened with execution. At street level, the regular enactment of anti-Catholic dramas in New England built anti-Catholic momentum in the eighteenth century. Puritans changed Guy Fawkes Day to Pope Day, and the occasion was celebrated in America with burnings-in-effigy and, eventually, rioting. In Boston, Pope Day riots resulted in anti-Catholic violence on November 5 in 1745, 1747, 1755, 1762, and 1764. Persons were killed and maimed in such rioting, and in some cases, such as the anti-impressment Knowles riot of November 1747, mob action spilled over in Boston into other causes. These incidences set the

48   CHAPTER ONE

pattern for other lethal incidences of mob hatred directed against Catholics in the nineteenth century.[117]

Before turning to a consideration of those specific attributes of secrecy and heresy that Protestants accentuated in exciting themselves about the Catholic threat, it is important to consider how Mormons were likewise cast as Amalekites and how the characteristic features of Amalek—conspiracy, plotting, cunning—were given definition as well through Protestant complaints about Mormons.

As in the case of anti-Catholic campaigns, the history of violence against Mormons has been described in detail by historians.[118] Mobs attacked Mormon communities intermittently throughout the nineteenth century. It occurred often enough that some Mormons came to believe that the government had sanctioned mob violence against them. In the decade after the founding of the Church of Jesus Christ of Latter-Day Saints religion by Joseph Smith in New York State, and on the heels of a series of run-ins with non-Mormon populations in several communities, a cycle of escalating threats traded between Mormons and non-Mormons in Missouri led to armed conflict with the Missouri militia. Mormon elder Sidney Rigdon, protesting the persecution of Mormons, delivered a Fourth of July speech in 1838 in which he declared that the "mob that comes on to disturb us, it shall be between us and them a war of extermination; for we will follow them until the last drop of their blood is spilled; or else they will have to exterminate us. . . ."[119] Joseph Smith shortly thereafter characterized the situation in Missouri: "The Governor is mob, the militia are mob, and the whole state is mob."[120]

In the midst of an increasingly threatening war of words, and in the wake of skirmishes between Mormons and non-Mormons, Governor Lilburn Boggs eventually responded in kind, in late October, in a letter to General John B. Clark of the militia: "The Mormons must be treated as enemies and must be exterminated or driven from the state. . . . Their outrages are beyond all description."[121] The "mobbers," as Mormons called the militia, attacked and killed twenty Mormons, including children, at Haun's Mill, Missouri, on October 30, precipitating the mass exodus of Mormons across the Mississippi River to Nauvoo, Illinois.

The rhetoric of "extermination" traded in confrontations such as that in Missouri illustrated the manner in which religious minorities in some cases adopted the language of those who sought to destroy them. As part of an ongoing, reflexive, mimetic process of religious groups in conflict accusing each other of extermination schemes, the battles between Mormons and their enemies in Missouri and elsewhere, like the battles between Catholics and Protestants, evidenced the fluidity of violent rhetoric. Each side, by the nineteenth century, could adopt the position of victim, and each side criticized the other for similar offenses, including secrecy, conspiracy, and a plan to exterminate the other.

As the imagery associated with Amalek was enriched and focused in a Bible-conscious American society, it proved useful not only for dominant groups in picturing their religious enemies, but for minority religions to do so as well. Protestants, for example, could imagine Catholics seeking to blot out Protestantism, and therefore called upon Protestants to blot out Catholics, at the same time that Catholics claimed that Protestants wished to blot out Catholicism. Moreover, in the dysfunctional attachment that is religious intolerance, the sharing of rhetoric underscored the "kindredness" of the groups in conflict. It elaborated their attachment in certain ways, alongside their enmity, and facilitated their mirroring of each other, as far as their fears were concerned. Mormons and their largely Protestant opponents, for example, could see each other as Amalekites who must be destroyed. They likewise pictured each other as cowardly, crafty, and covert.

Anti-Mormon perception of the kindredness of Mormonism to the Christianity of well-established denominations was crucial to the organization of resistance to Mormonism. Mormons called themselves Christians, but anti-Mormons considered the followers of Joseph Smith to have misinterpreted scripture and to have abandoned many of the fundamental precepts of Christianity as practiced by Protestants and Catholics. The opponents of Mormonism, from the 1830s onward, made elaborate theological and historical arguments aimed at proving that Mormonism was not Christianity.[122] But underneath those polemics was a profound sense of Mormonism as a wolf in sheep's clothing, a cancer that had somehow entered the body of Christianity and was corrupting it from the inside. Mormons accordingly were imagined as deceived and misled followers of a compromised Christianity at the same time that they were constructed as non-Christian, as fully other. Like the Amalekites, they were related to God's people, but acted in such a way as to indicate their clear difference from the truly faithful. "The doctrines of Mormonism," wrote one critic, "profess to be derived chiefly from the Old and New Testament Scriptures, and constitute a corrupt form of Christianity." Another, in discussing the need to "inoculate" persons against the "viruses of superstition," protested that Mormonism was sickening the souls of God's children like "deadly poison," and was even more detrimental to spiritual life than "those forms of Christianity which are exceedingly corrupt."[123]

Who portrayed Mormons as Amalekites who must be exterminated? A resolution by civic leaders in Warsaw, Illinois, following the death of Joseph Smith in 1844 reportedly announced that "we hold ourselves at all times

50   CHAPTER ONE

in readiness to cooperate with our fellow-citizens of this state, Missouri, and Iowa, to exterminate, utterly exterminate, the wicked and abominable Mormon leaders."[124] Thoroughly Old Testament in its vision of "abominations" and "wickedness," the language of the resolution recurred frequently throughout the nineteenth century as frictions between Mormons and other religious groups cycled through periods of varying intensity.

The evacuation of Mormons to Utah did little to slow the war of words — or the war of swords. The Mormon *Messenger and Advocate*, in Kirtland, Ohio, published in 1836 the prophecy of Elder Orson Hyde, who drew precisely on his Old Testament lexicon in lamenting the persecution of Mormons "in a republican government holding out the delusive, fallacious profession of equal rights. The arch fiend seems to have marshaled all his forces; every art is tried, every stratagem invented, every weapon put in requisition to destroy the influence of the saints [Mormons], and if it were possible to blot out their name from under heaven."[125] A few years later, as one of the many seeming confirmations of Hyde's prophecy that appeared in the form of hateful articles, *Atkinson's Saturday Evening Post* observed the troubles in Missouri and remarked that "there is no doubt that very strong measures must and will be adopted" there, "to extirpate the whole fraternity of Mormons."[126]

As the nation began its recovery from the Civil War and turned its attention westward, the polemics heated up. A Protestant clergyman in San Francisco could warm his audience with reports of his visit to Utah, where he saw "the most dreadful blasphemy in the face of heaven, and the most horrible insult to the Christian civilization that ever came out of hell."[127] The *New York Times* reported in 1882 a meeting of the Presbyterian Ministerial Association in Cincinnati, at which attendees planned another session at which "resolutions will be offered providing for the preparing of petitions asking Congress to take immediate and energetic means to blot out Mormonism. . . . It is thought that the Methodists will follow much the same plan that the Presbyterians are planning to adopt."[128]

Mormons resisted such rhetoric by turning it back upon their critics. As the Nauvoo *Times and Seasons* declared shortly after Joseph Smith's death in 1844, "prophets . . . die for the sake of the truth . . . and no man, no mob, no king, no potentate has been able to blot it out."[129] Such resistance included, said one turn-of-the-century writer, raising ten million dollars to arm a militia for the purpose of "resisting troops sent (as they supposed) to exterminate the Mormons."[130] More importantly, that resistance featured an escalating cycle of threats and rejoinders, leading to a state of affairs described by an anti-Mormon convert to Roman Catholicism, Orestes Brownson, in 1857: "'You must exterminate us,' said a Mormon elder to the writer, 'or we, as we become strong enough, shall exterminate you.'"[131] Each side saw Amalek in the other. When President Buchanan sent an army to Utah to enforce federal rule there, Brigham Young immediately surmised its purpose and announced it in a broadside issued in Salt Lake City in 1857: "We are evidently invaded by a hostile force who are assailing us to accomplish our overthrow and destruction." Said Mormon leader Mormon leader Isaac C. Haight: "they are sending an army to exterminate us."[132]

The federal force arrived in Salt Lake City on June 26, 1858. The Mormons had gathered a 2,000-soldier militia, but there was no spilling of blood because Brigham Young and other Mormon leaders voiced to the federal commander Albert Johnston their love of the Constitution and their agreement to live according to it (although the polygamy issue would not be settled for many years). But that confrontation came on the heels of another encounter between Mormons and non-Mormons that had not ended so well. In 1857, near Enterprise, Utah, Mormon militia and Indian confederates massacred 120 unarmed men, women, and children, nearly an entire caravan of persons on their way overland from Arkansas to California.

Investigators such as Judge John Cradlebaugh, who vigorously pursued responsibility for the case into the Mormon hierarchy, believed that the massacre had taken place in accord with an oath added to the temple ceremony (initiation liturgy) after the murder of Joseph Smith. Mormons vowed revenge upon Smith's murderers in these words spoken to the initiates: "You and each of you do covenant and promise that you will pray and never cease to pray to Almighty God to avenge the blood of the prophets upon this nation, and that you will teach the same to your children and to your children's children unto the third and fourth generation." The language remained a part of the temple oath until 1927.[133]

Thorough coverage of the massacre and its aftermath by the press condemned Mormons for treason and human slaughter. Essayists, travel writers, and autoethnologists such as Mark Twain made certain over the years that it remained fresh in memory, with Twain sympathetically recalling after his own trip out west in the 1860s the words of Cradlebaugh that "it was one of the most cruel, cowardly, and bloody murders known in our history."[134] Although many contemporaries as well as historians believe that the orders to murder the caravan came from the top of the Mormon organization, a Mormon bishop, John D. Lee, eventually was executed for the crime. Lee employed the familiar language of Amalek in describing how he came to be involved in carrying out the commands of church superiors: "The substance of the orders were that the emigrants should be *decoyed* from their stronghold, and all exterminated."[135]

If Mormons were to be blotted out, the massive Protestant domestic missionary enterprise that was close to full stride by the mid-1870s needed some rethinking as far as Utah was concerned. Even Protestant missionaries whose call to ministry led them into contact with groups whose beliefs and customs often seemed to them corrupt or immoral balked at the prospect of evangelizing Mormons. Thus the American Home Missionary Society, as it aimed itself westward in the mid-nineteenth century, planned evangelical forays to "the cities of Romanism, 'great and fenced up to heaven,' in New Mexico, Arizona and elsewhere," but seemed less confident of its goal of reaching "the Amalekites of Mormonism in Utah."[136] Mormons for their part continued to turn the tables on their critics, characterizing "Gentile" Americans as the Amalekites. A writer back east noted that Mormons expressed their religious views in a "long train of Hebraic similes: the Church was in bondage in Egypt,—it was in the wilderness of Zin,—it was to overthrow the Amalekites (Missourians) and repeat all the wonderful achievements in the fruitful annals of Israel."[137]

Mormons likewise characterized defectors from their own faith with reference to a "Hebraic simile." A visitor from New York reported on a Mormon sermon preached in Salt Lake City that was "of a denunciatory rather than a benevolent nature, and turned upon the wrath of God toward apostates, and the propriety of rooting out those who had gone astray after Amalek."[138] Some non-Mormon observers got the message, and noted in various ways that Mormons considered other religions to be idolatry, and that they were as unlikely to embrace "Gentile" Christianity "as it would have been for the children of Israel to have surrendered Moses or Joshua or the Decalogue for the idolatrous rule of Pharaoh or of Amalek."[139] Mormons themselves knew about the Amalekites not only through their familiarity with the Old Testament, but because their distinctive scripture, the *Book of Mormon*, made reference to the Amalekites as a wicked and murderous people who inhabited pre-Columbian North America.[140] Those "Amalekites," also portrayed as "evil Nephites" in Mormon scripture, made war on the righteous Lamanites, another group that inhabited North America according to Mormon accounts.

Keeping in mind that "Amalek, the Arab" enjoyed a run in the Boston theater in the 1840s,[141] and that Arabs were identified in nineteenth-century magazines, such as *Littel's*, as "the modern representatives of the ancient house of Amalek,"[142] it is not difficult to understand how Mormonism came to be characterized by non-Mormons as a species of Islam. Viewed as Amalekites by their critics, Mormons were easily cast as participants in a North American performance of Islam, that is, the religion of Arabs. Almost from the beginning of the denomination's history, it attracted comparison to Islam that eventually ran so deep, and was so detailed, that a book such as Bruce Kinney's *Mormonism: The Islam of America*, published in 1912, could draw a large popular readership well after Utah had entered the Union and the pitched battles between Mormons and their enemies had subsided.[143] In the nineteenth century, Mormon polygamy invited comparison to Arab harems, and Mormon prophets such as Joseph Smith were understood as perverted charismatic leaders on the order of Mohammed.[144] Almost from the beginning of Mormonism, its detractors pictured its membership as Amalekites, as bad Arabs, and it was on that perceptual foundation that writers elaborated the comparison with Islam.

The Instability of Identity

In the Old Testament framework for thinking about religious opponents, to exterminate was to blot out. To erase the name of a group, as early New Englanders did in the case of the Pequot, was to destroy that group. Blotting out the Pequot, for example, occurred both through war and through the renaming of places that carried a Pequot name. The opponents of Catholics and Mormons asserted in their most intense moments of anxiety their intentions to blot out those groups, to ensure that their names would be buried. The biblical command grounding American thinking about extermination of others, the necessity of blotting them out, also inveighed "not to forget." The specific message of the text, "you will blot out the remembrance of Amalek from under heaven. You shall not forget,"[145] was a mixed message, a call to destroy memory wrapped in a command to remember.

To practice genocide, to attempt genocide, is traumatic. For the victim, it is a horror. For the agents of genocide, however successful they might be in achieving their goals, it also is a horror, but of a different type, and in the end still a trauma. That trauma typically is buried in memory. As such, it exists in groups as well as in individuals. To destroy a people is to erase but equally an effort to forget, two entwined aspects of extermination that characterize paradoxically both the finality of extermination and its ongoing open-endedness for the perpetrators, who continue to remember what they have erased.

Acts of religious intolerance in America, their promotion, theorization, connectedness to various aspects of culture and power, in as much as they have been grounded in Old Testament views of just vengeance, have shaped an American identification with regard to religion. There is an ingrained American memory of religiously inspired campaigns to exterminate religious others. That memory is generally a vague one, not fleshed out in detail, but still imbued with affect, and while fleeting, it is substantial enough to burst occasionally into public discourse (and increasingly so since the late twentieth and early twenty-first centuries). It is a narrative that has been kept alive alongside the powerful urge to forget it. It has been present in the complaints of minority religions such as Catholics and Mormons, among many others, and, occasionally, in the observations of certain Protestants whose sense of justice and whose interpretation of the First Amendment has led them to challenge American amnesia about religious conflict in the nation's past.[146] Those narratives of remembering have always been in tension with narratives that forget.

National identity is shaped by the remembering of trauma alongside the unwillingness to remember. The trauma within national identity "is felt but not understood . . . it must be forgotten but is always being recalled and relived."[147] That complex character of trauma is present in the story of the Amalekites, which in its own abbreviated way expressed the same paradox.

It is possible to underestimate the importance of trauma in the construction of national identity because the unwillingness to remember trauma is a part of the power of trauma. For a long period of time, Americans did not wish to remember the trauma of the Indian crises in New England. Twenty-first-century discussion of Native Americans still has difficulty coming to terms with that trauma, which lies at the heart of American identity. The trauma involved in battles between EuroAmerican religious groups, from the hanging of Quakers to the Bible Wars, Mormon Wars, and other bloody events, extended and deepened the trauma of early colonial encounters with Indians. It is woven into the cloth that makes up American national identity. Indians, Catholics, Mormons, and many other groups together comprise a college of the oppressed, a collective target of rhetoric that calls for their extermination. Just as America attempted to bury memories of Indian genocide, so also did it refuse to come to terms with the broader national history of intolerance involving various religious groups. That resistance was never fully realized, however, as trauma remained a powerful force in the maintenance and development of American identity. It left its traces.

One of those traces is a deep sensitivity to secrecy, to hidden agendas and conspiracies.[148] Americans, invested for centuries in their forgetting of trauma involving Indians, Catholics, Mormons, and others, remain aware that they are keeping a secret. American culture keeps secret the repressed memories of things that happened in colonial New England, in nineteenth-century Missouri and Illinois, in religiously divided cities such as Boston and Philadelphia, and in numerous other places where religious intolerance issued in violence. In one sense, a secret is a dialogue between remembering and forgetting. To suspect others of having a secret is to imagine that they know something that they are not telling. Americans everywhere, by virtue of the fact that they are Americans, have secrets they are not telling.

American national identity is made up of many components. Many kinds of memories are involved. Some are repressed memories, and some are not. Some have to do with religion, and some do not. But the religious history of the nation is crucial to making sense of American identity and, consequently, to how that identity is involved in American views of the world. Rhetoric about Amalek enabled the refusal to remember trauma having to do with religious violence, and in so doing helped frame the enterprise of projecting that violence overseas.

2

Projections:
Antebellum Americans and the Overseas Crisis

Triumph of Religious Liberty

The projection of American intolerance overseas began with enthusiasm for religious liberty at home. It began with the cultivated remembrance of the rebellion against England and a broad satisfaction with the political outcomes of the Revolutionary era. Americans celebrated the founding of the Republic, with its visionary Constitution and Bill of Rights, well into the nineteenth century. The village liberty trees that had signaled resistance to England and served as markers for gatherings of rebellious colonists remained the focal points of celebrations for generations. Americans sang songs of liberty, enacted plays celebrating liberty, penned poems and stories about glorious liberty, and organized jubilant parades. Nineteenth-century Americans moreover revered liberty in a multitude of ways in everyday life, from flag-waving to patriotic historical dress, painting their homes and barns in red, white, and blue, and teaching their children its American history.

Antebellum Americans were especially proud of religious liberty. They spoke often and passionately about how religious liberty was a singular and momentous achievement in America, and how it distinguished the United States from Europe—and everywhere else. In books and newspapers, correspondences and works of art, speeches and sermons, Americans expressed their pride in what they believed was an elusive ideal that had at last been realized in America.

Hezekiah Niles, the founder and editor of *Niles' Weekly Register*, one of the most widely circulated periodicals in America, published in 1830 a speech that had been delivered during a public celebration of rights and liberties that July. Its reference to religious liberty in America was typical in its exaltation of its global significance, rejoicing in "the triumph of religious freedom . . . which has flashed upon the world, after a long night of darkness and bigotry."[1] Some writers traced the roots of that freedom into pre-Revolutionary history. The *Baptist Memorial and Monthly Record*, in "The Final Triumph of Religious Freedom," unsurprisingly made Roger Williams the foundational figure, and likewise asserted that since his pioneering efforts, "the spirit of freedom has been extending its salutary influence in various parts of the world." The American example was so complete, and so powerful, "that its final triumph [worldwide] will be universal and glorious."[2]

The South was as proud as New England. Robert Reid Howison's influential[3] *A History of Virginia* (1848) proudly lauded that state's role in "the triumph of religious liberty" in America—a phrase that became common in both the United States and afterward in England. Some writers used other language to celebrate it.[4] A Fourth of July speech in North Carolina in 1830 celebrated the founders who "on this memorable day established religious freedom," another familiar phrasing of the achievement of religious liberty.[5] Early New Englanders who were not Roger Williams were sometimes accused of intolerance. But antebellum writers generally were forgiving, and often cast them as laudable for their determination to finally get it right, for the fact "that they made great progress toward it, and ultimately secured it." That viewpoint was strongly promoted by the New England religious press, which rejoiced in "the continuous triumph of religious liberty in New England," linking it to early Revolutionary-era figures such as Boston's Rev. Jonathan Mayhew.[6]

The point of American celebration of religious liberty, regardless of the language used or the figures referenced, was that religious freedom was a fact of American life. The broadly adopted textbook *Introduction to the Science of Government* (1836) by Andrew W. Young informed students that religious liberty was "effectively secured, both by the national and state constitutions," and thus "enjoyed in the United States" to its "full extent."[7] *McGuffey's New Fifth Eclectic Reader* (1857) spelled it out more specifically in case there was any doubt about whether religious freedom remained an aspirational ideal or was a reality in America. The nation's founders understood that religious rights "were not merely things to be talked of, and woven into theories, but to be adopted with the whole strength and ardor of the mind, and felt in the profoundest recesses of the heart, and carried out into the general life, and made the foundation of practical usefulness." Because of the founders' effective practical-mindedness, God since "has raised their descendants to such hights [*sic*] of civil and religious liberty."[8] Religious liberty was a profound good that had won out over an equally profound evil. According to one orator, "the triumph of religious liberty—for this great principle now covers almost the entire union with its aegis"—was not only a legal reality but a

58   CHAPTER TWO

spiritual one. "Once downtrodden, it has Antaeus-like arisen with renewed vigour and has ultimately driven the dark spirit of religious intolerance from the Statute-book and the high places of the land."[9]

Americans rejoiced in the victory of religious liberty over intolerance. But at the same time, some nevertheless fretted that the "dark spirit" of intolerance remained invisibly alive. Protestant Americans, and members of other denominations as well, clung to the idea that religious intolerance was a thing of the past in America. But they often expressed a vague anxiety about it, a paradoxical worry that it yet lurked as an unwelcome animating spirit of the social order. Like the repressed memory of genocide against Indians, the ostensibly unseen but somehow perceptible evil of intolerance haunted their world. They made attempts to identify it—but not among themselves—and most often did so by pointing their fingers at Catholics and Mormons.

Sectarian Secrecy

A crucial part of Protestant nervousness about non-Protestants, and a foundational key to Protestant mappings of religious intolerance around the world, was the belief that Catholics and Mormons were sectarians bent on domination, and that they schemed to accomplish that through secrets and conspiracies. The narrative of conspiracy—nourished by repressed trauma—was highly developed in antebellum America, rooted in the violent colonial past, and enlivened by emotional language. Anyone and any group could be a conspirator. But the majority of Protestant discussion of conspiracies in antebellum America was about Catholics. Mormons also were on the minds of most Americans. However, at the time they more often were treated as a related but secondary case, an important example of secrecy, but one referenced to make points when describing the corrupt plans of the Catholic Church.

American opponents of Catholics and Mormons knew them to be secretive and cowardly, because those two character flaws were central to the Old Testament depiction of Amalek. As betrayers of their kindred relationship with the ancient Jews, Amalekites also were seen as traitors of a particularly vile and dangerous sort, as conspirators and heretics. English writers' previous characterization of Catholics as secretly planning the overthrow of both Protestantism and liberty in England developed in America into a more complex profiling of Catholics and Mormons. Americans took from their colonial depredations of Indians some measure of a sense of righteousness in exterminating their opponents, added to it specific concerns about covert scheming on the part of American Catholics, and expressed it in angry rhetoric about heresy, and, especially, sectarianism that came to the fore in denunciations of Mormonism. A letter to the *New York Observer* just before the Fourth of July 1857 reflected the tendency of anti-Mormon and anti-Catholic writers to conflate the two religious groups in cataloguing their offenses against Protestantism:

> The fact is, Mormonism, (it is not denied,) is a modern form of Islamism, the former seeking to engraft itself upon Christianity. . . . Besides this, there is a large mixture of popery in the councils of the "Saints" and no little Freemasonry. On the one hand there is the adaptation of teaching and on the other the secrecy of carrying it out. The end sanctifying the means, is as much a principle in Mormonism as it is in Romanism, and the secrecy of the confessional is the safety valve of both. . . . The popish priesthood screen the assassin who murders for the good of the church, and the Mormon priest will do the very same thing. . . . In point of fact, there is no feature in the worst characteristics of Irish or Italian Popery, but that its type may be found in anti-Christian Mormonism.[10]

"What stratagems have been invented? What deep and artful plots have been laid?" asked the Rev. William Adams, referencing the plottings of the Catholic "Amalek" in a thanksgiving sermon in 1760. Later, in an elaborately gendered nineteenth-century American culture where secrecy often was judged the equivalent of cowardice, the two flaws came to be intertwined in speechifying about Amalek. Presbyterian pastor John M. Lowrie, of Fort Wayne, Indiana, in his essay "War with Amalek" (1865), could boil it all down to the bone in typically economical Scotch prose: "But theirs was not the bold and open defiance of a manly foe."[11] Secrecy and conspiracy had for centuries been associated with heresy, and especially with sectarianism, a social development identified with religious violence since the Reformation. Americans who believed themselves native defenders of a Protestant culture of Bible and democracy made certain to emphasize those associations in their warnings about Catholics, Mormons, and other religious groups with whom they clashed.

Protestant anxieties about Catholics, Mormons, and some other religious groups and fraternal organizations were grounded in a tradition of anti-sectarianism that had crossed the Atlantic with the earliest European settlers. American movements that arose in opposition to minority religious groups embraced ideas that had a long transatlantic history, manifesting what the historian David Brion Davis called "a cultural continuity" with early modern Europe. That continuity included fidelity to the practice of denouncing minority groups as "sects," and as representative examples of a broader "proliferation of sects" that, in the view of members of dominant groups, were a plague upon society.[12] The accusation that a group had come into being as part of a "spirit of sectarianism" implied a portfolio of negatives: secrecy, conspiracy, duplicity, and treason. The term "sect" as an epithet accordingly was applied to a range of religious groups.

Some Americans believed that sects lurked everywhere, under an assortment of denominational covers. The Presbyterian minister Lewis Cheeseman wrote in 1849 that Protestant revival religion, including that encouraged by Lyman Beecher and Charles G. Finney, was as corrupt as Mormonism, "popery," and "Christianism," and lethally dangerous. Writing about the same time, the *New Englander* lumped together "Papists," Jews, Shakers, Swedenborgians, Mormons, Universalists, and "Socialists," as "sectarian" and "heretical" groups. It nevertheless surprisingly noted that while the first of these promoted a "deadly heresy," in the larger scheme of things Rome posed no distinct threat vis-à-vis any of the others because "the papist here is nothing but a sectarian among sectarians." A leading nineteenth-century exponent of rational religion, Thomas J. Vaiden, spoke for most of those who by midcentury had weighed in on the matter when he stressed that "secret societies" were "sectarian societies" opposed to the ideal of "universal brotherhood" and therefore dangerous. In the wake of the anti-Catholic riots in Philadelphia in 1844, a widely circulated effort at conciliation, *The Olive Branch*, defined intolerance as sectarian strife and proposed that the pathway to civility was through an overcoming of the sectarian spirit that pitted religious groups against each other.[13]

If religion is the primary locus for the practice of cultural secrecy,[14] the history of religion in America is an instructive case of how religion and secrecy thus were imaginatively braided. When Americans thought about secret organizations, they thought about secretive religious groups, and especially during the nineteenth century. They read about ancient, seemingly exotic religions that appeared to be highly secretive, and they found parallels to them in contemporary religious groups in North America and beyond. Immersing themselves in narratives about secret religion, Americans reinforced a biblically grounded view of their religious opponents as potential traitors, as practitioners of dark arts scheming to overthrow the social and political order.

Americans read about Gnostics, discovering that "the highest source of knowledge, with these heretics, was a secret tradition."[15] They learned that "the worst corruptions of Paganism, and particularly the secret mysteries, introduced from Asia into Italy at about the time of the Antonines, long survived the establishment of Christianity, and were secretly propagated by men who may best be described as credulous deceivers." Those ancient mystics "were banded together in secret societies, or rather in secret sects."[16]

Americans were well informed about the "secret sect of Tao," with its magic elixirs that bestowed immortality upon those who drank them, and about other "secret societies" in China, which continued up to the present day, including in the nineteenth century the "appearance of a secret sect in the rites of which . . . there are to be traced the remnants of a debased Christianity." The "Druses" were a secret society who, some believed, survived as the remnant of Christian communities established by the Crusaders in the Holy Land.[17] The Nusaris of northern Syria, said the *North American Review* in its notice of a book on the subject, were "like the other secret sects of the East" in that "they are as unwilling as the Druses or the Yesidees to give any clew to their religious opinions" through analysis of their genealogy.[18] The community of Freemasonry, like other secret sects, was thought to practice a form of priestcraft, and did so early on in its European beginnings. Such "secret societies were established in Germany . . . and encouraged by princes against their French despots," and their "dark and mysterious rites" horrified the clerics of Iberia. Masonry was even said to be "Judaism in a mask."[19] Americans read as well that "the secret sect of the Rosicrucians" was linked to Jewish Cabalistic mysticism.[20]

Rumors of secret sects fed the fears of Americans as they listened to readings of Old Testament texts during sermons. Sermons helped clarify that fear, so when Reverend E. H. Sears prefaced his sermon on the need for military efficiency during the Civil War with a reading of Psalm 83, his auditors likely knew where his sermon would be headed: "For lo! Thine enemies begin to rage: and they that hate thee lift up their heads. They form secret plots against thy people, and consult together against thy chosen ones. 'Come,' they say 'let us blot them out from the number of the nations. . . .'"[21]

Anti-Catholic and anti-Mormon voices cast members of those out-groups as Amalekites who conspired to overthrow Protestant authority and American democracy. They claimed that Catholics met secretly to lay plans for that revolution, and, remembering Guy Fawkes and the Gunpowder Plot, they often sounded the alarm of nefarious Catholic designs. The controversial Illinois clergyman Edward Beecher, commenting on Catholicism and democracy, explained in *The Papal Conspiracy Exposed and Protestantism Defended* (1855) that "the systems are diametrically opposed: one must and will exterminate the other." His father, the busy and influential Presbyterian revivalist and reformer Lyman Beecher, already had warned Protestants that Catholics intended to subvert Protestant efforts to win the West. In 1835, in *A Plea for the West*, the elder Beecher was exasperated that "the religious and political destiny of our nation is to be decided in the West," and he lamented that immigrant Americans, emptied out of European poorhouses and the barely civilized backcountry, were plotting, under the spell of Catholic priestcraft, to vote as a bloc against American traditions of democracy and to put an end to Protestant control of society and government. Samuel Morse, the inventor of the telegraph and Nativist Party candidate for mayor of New York in 1836, began serialized publication of *The Foreign Conspiracy Against the Liberties of the United States* in 1834. He explicitly linked the influx of Catholic immigrants to Rome's secret agenda of defeating democracy and Protestantism in America.[22]

The prose in such publications was paranoid in tone and often rich with references to secrecy and conspiracy, even in asides about the lives of Catholics or the leadership of the church in Rome. The corrupted Christianity of Rome was said to have "flourished within the secret recesses" of monasteries and in the "secret passageways," the catacomb-like tunnels, that linked nunneries with the homes of male clergy. Washington Gladden, a leading Protestant theologian of late-century Social Gospel, reported Protestant whispering "that the Catholics are meeting by stealth, from night to night, in the basements of their churches, to drill for the impending insurrection." Remarking specifically on the paranoia of the anti-Catholic American Protective Association, he reported similarly that "The members of the order in Toledo . . . only a few months ago, were buying rifles, and alleging that they were arming themselves against the very uprising commanded by the Pope."[23]

The fear of an uprising was rooted in a deep literature about Catholic plans to overwhelm the nation. *The Cloven Foot*, published in Boston in 1857, warned of the "numerous evidences of a vast conspiracy to crush our liberties and destroy the sacred influence we have on other nations. One vast and powerful agent for the accomplishment of this purpose is the church of Rome." Popery "has a grave design of subverting our liberties," and "she has conspired with the tyrants of the world to effect this object."[24] Other writers warned of "the great Roman conspiracy," the "designing Jesuit Papists," and "the *Roman Confederacy*," which, under cover of "the Roman conspiracy from New Orleans to Quebec," was by degrees strengthening its hold on the nation.[25] All such alarms emphasized the international nature of the Romanist threat. The conspiracy was global.

Fear of a Catholic conspiracy grew steadily throughout the first half of the nineteenth century into a Protestant political organization opposing it, the Know-Nothing Party.[26] That fear found expression in numerous acts of violence against Catholics, some fomented by Know-Nothingism and others occurring in less organized fashion through mobbery—although mobs sometimes formed as a consequence of inflammatory ministerial rhetoric. The claim of one magazine writer in 1835 that "for several years the religious protestant papers of our country, with but few exceptions, have teemed with

PROJECTIONS

virulent attacks against the Catholics" was, while boldly stated, successful in capturing something of the mood.[27] The strong resurgence of anti-Catholic intolerance was evidenced in the 1830s and 1840s by attacks on convents in New Orleans, Galveston, and Charleston and arson that destroyed or damaged Catholic churches in New Jersey, Connecticut, Maine, and upstate New York. By mid-century the intolerance was so common that by one account minor riots, fomented by street preachers, took place in New York on almost every Sunday in 1854.[28]

The attacks on Catholics—and Mormons—were, however, showing signs of being more than just a nervousness about the secret plottings of religious opponents. The alleged secrets of Catholics were joined to the actual secrets of Protestants. When Protestants manifested their worries about Catholics, they sometimes glimpsed their responsibility for their history of intolerance toward Catholics and others.[29] They tried to forget that, in a way similar to how white slaveowners attempted, through various kinds of rationalizations, to forget their violence toward slaves.[30]

Conspiracies in Boston and Philadelphia

Protestants expressed their fears of a Catholic conspiracy through violence against Catholics. That antebellum violence occurred in many places, but most dramatically in Boston and Philadelphia, two cities where immigration had changed the religious demographics. In both cities violence was the result of mob action, but in neither case was it a surprise. The Protestant press—both religious publications and Protestant-controlled public newspapers—had a role in provoking the rioters.

Anti-Catholicism in antebellum Boston was a complicated problem involving not only religious difference but social change that came with the rapid growth of the Irish immigrant population, frictions arising from debate about parochial education, gender and race issues, and the role of the media in fomenting intolerance. In 1829 Bostonians attacked Irish Catholics in their homes over the course of several days, and during the next few years mobs periodically sacked and then set fire to houses in Irish neighborhoods. By the late 1830s, Catholics had established armed security patrols of their churches, while property and insurance companies balked at providing coverage for Catholic buildings. Anti-Catholic literature such as Mary Martha Sherwood's *The Nun* (1834)—which was quickly followed by similarly incendiary literature such as *Awful Disclosures of Maria Monk* (1835), William Nevins's *Thoughts on Popery* (1836), and Richard Baxter's *Jesuit Juggling: Forty Popish Frauds Detected and Disclosed* (1835)—helped the opponents of Catholics imagine criminality within convents and picture other secret and treasonous proceedings of Catholic clergy and laypersons. What is clear is that the burning of the Catholic convent in Charlestown, Massachusetts, on August 12, 1834, followed directly on the heels of Lyman Beecher's preaching his sermon *A Plea for the West* in three separate locations on the previous day: at the Bowdoin Street Church, the Old South Church, and the Park Street Church.[31]

Located just across the Charles River from Boston, the convent founded by the Ursuline Sisters about 1820 had grown to include a boarding school for upper-class Boston girls, all told about forty Protestant girls and about ten Catholic girls in 1834. The Sisters had located themselves on a hill that had been fortified during the Revolutionary War. Two of the women who lived inside the fence, a nun, Sister St. John, and a novice, Rebecca Reed, had complained outside the convent of abuse within, and those complaints were taken seriously by the town selectmen as well as by the alcohol-fueled mob that looted and burned the convent.

The Protestant emphasis on secrecy and conspiracy among Catholics remained strong following the destruction of the Charlestown convent. The apocalyptic imagery in books such as Morse's *Foreign Conspiracy*, which appeared as a series of essays by "Brutus" beginning a few weeks after the convent burning, offered an imagery that was built upon a foundation of anti-Catholic polemics that had taken shape over centuries. It featured—borrowing here the phrasing of a later writer—presumption of a "'vast' or 'gigantic' conspiracy" as "the motive force in historical events."[32] Writings such as Morse's, republished, interpreted, and enhanced continuously in newspapers and magazines, imbued the matter with a deep sense of urgency. Even posters in the street brought the news of papal plots to pedestrians, as in the case of one in Charlestown in 1831, which in its insistence on the duplicity and cowardice of Catholics might have reminded persons of the wicked Amalekites:

> Be it known unto you far and near, that all
> Catholics and all persons in favor of the Catholic
> Church, are a set of vile impostors, liars,
> villains and cowardly cut-throats. (Beware of
> False Doctrines) I bid defiance to that
> villain,—the Pope.
>
> A TRUE AMERICAN[33]

Protestant fears of Catholic secrecy and conspiracy similarly framed the religious scene in Philadelphia. There had been violence between Protestants and Catholics in Philadelphia prior to the summer of 1844, and there had been much public airing of frictions between other groups as well. In the end, the much-commented-upon Bible Wars,[34] fought over which Bible to use in public schools (the Catholic Douai translation or the Protestant King James version), climaxed in violence.

Rioting in Philadelphia began in a neighborhood in the Kensington area of town on May 3, 1844, when persons associated with the Native American Party speechified against Catholicism to the neighborhood's residents, who were almost entirely Irish Catholic. Chased off, the nativists returned a few days later several thousand strong and fighting broke out, leading to injury and loss of life. The following day the rioting continued, with nativists burning down blocks of Catholic houses, St. Michael's Church, the rectory, and the adjoining Female Seminary, the convent of the Sisters of Charity, and St. Augustine Church. Following an anti-Catholic Fourth of July parade some weeks later, anti-Catholic nativists destroyed St. Philip Neri Church in the suburb of Southwark. Troops sent to guard the Catholic buildings during most of the rioting proved ineffective, and by the time the rioting had subsided, the death toll had reached a dozen civilians and two militiamen, and blocks of houses and religious buildings had been destroyed.

In a part of the country, the "middle colonies," that had seen religious diversity in colonial times on a scale that significantly exceeded diversity anywhere else on the eastern seaboard,[35] it might seem puzzling that there should have been so much criticism of Philadelphia as a stronghold of sectarianism. But even Thomas Jefferson, whose own visits to Philadelphia had proven important to his reflection on the nature of democracy, thought the city plagued by sectarianism by the 1820s. Writing to Dr. Thomas Cooper in 1822, Jefferson lamented that "The atmosphere of our country is unquestionably charged with a threatening cloud of fanaticism, lighter in some parts, denser in others, but too heavy in all. I had no idea, however, that in Pennsylvania, the cradle of toleration and freedom of religion, it could have arisen to the height you describe. This must be owing to the growth of Presbyterianism." Jefferson clarified his blame of Presbyterianism by noting its sectarian spirit: "Their ambition and tyranny would tolerate no rival if they had power. Systematical in grasping at an ascendancy over all other sects, they aim, like the Jesuits, at engrossing the education of the country, are hostile to every institution which they do not direct, and jealous at seeing others begin to attend at all to that object."[36]

Subsequent writers reiterated Jefferson's opinion. The *Princeton Review*, not far away on the other side of the Delaware River from Philadelphia, remarking on Dr. Andrew Wylie's *Sectarianism Is Heresy* (1840), cast its own Presbyterian eyes on the world and found itself having to agree that religious

66   CHAPTER TWO

sectarianism was rife (but not because of Presbyterians). "When the convert looks away from the Bible to the world around him, what does he see?" asked the *Review*. He sees "endless division, subdivision, separation, alienation, animosity. Instead of a church, he sees conflicting sects; the seamless robe of Christ rent and parceled out among armed men."[37] Quaker publications for decades in Philadelphia had complained about the sectarian spirit that had taken hold of the city, so that, as one writer in 1845 reported: "Many persons cry out against SECTARIANISM." The author added for emphasis: "If by *sectarianism* be meant such a bigoted and exclusive attachment to a particular religious association as excludes all feelings of brotherly regard and tenderness,—all sentiments of Christian charity towards others, we can fully concur in the views just mentioned."[38] Such opinion, deeply ingrained, conveniently framed the "Catholic problem" as a matter of sectarian ambition to dominate all other groups.

Thomas Jefferson, who as creator of the reputed "Jefferson Bible" remained to some extent an outsider as far as nineteenth-century American Christianity was concerned, and certainly the Quakers, whose experience in America had been one of persecution from the earliest years of English settlement, both were able to see what not all were able to acknowledge, namely, that "almost every . . . religious organization is in commotion."[39] That commotion in Philadelphia in the 1840s, moreover, was not in essence reducible to political or social issues that merely were expressed in religious terms. The religious disagreements were primary and motivated persons to face each other in the streets as enemies.

In Philadelphia, religion often was at the forefront of public conversation over social differences. Social worlds, political worlds, and religious worlds were interwoven, and at different times one or the other became the lead theme of debate even as it remained joined to the other two. An analysis of the anti-Catholic riots of 1844, *The Truth Unveiled*, published by a self-identified Protestant writer shortly after the hostilities, addressed in one of its sections on the cause of the riots the role of the Native American Party, a precursor to the Know-Nothings, which was founded in Louisiana in 1841. Under the heading "NATIVE AMERICAN PARTY; ITS SECTARIAN CHARACTER; POLITICAL OBJECT ONLY SECONDARY," the book claimed that the organization was first and foremost "sectarian," meaning religious in its orientation and agenda. "The Native American party is sectarian; decidedly sectarian. It is not political; and its leaders, they who are behind the curtain, dare not" declare it so. Though the party publicly claimed to serve as a means of resistance to "foreigners," that claim was false. Its "standing theme" was "nothing but 'Roman Catholics,' 'Irish Papists,' 'degraded slaves of the

Pope,'" and other such religious subjects. "In a word," said the author, "if 'Native Americanism' be not sectarian, how comes it, THAT TWO CATHO-LIC CHURCHES, ONE CATHOLIC SEMINARY, TWO CATHOLIC PAR-SONAGES, AND A CATHOLIC THEOLOGICAL LIBRARY, WHICH CAN-NOT BE REPLACED IN THE WIDE WORLD, HAVE BEEN BURNT?"[40]

Similarly, Sister Mary Gonzaga wrote from Philadelphia to her superior during the riots with the same message as that offered (a short time afterward) by the Protestant author of *The Truth Unveiled*: "The truth is, it is nothing but a party of Protestants leagued against the Catholics under the name of Native Americans. . . . It is believed to be more religion than politics which is the cause of the riot."[41] Sydney George Fisher likewise saw religion leading the way alongside political motives: "Religious is mixed with political feeling & the ancient hatred of Protestant against Catholic is combined with the jealousy of natives toward foreigners."[42] Serious consideration of such views—which taken together evidence a historical sense of such conflicts as religious problems—informs understanding of why in the aftermath of crises such as Charlestown and Philadelphia Protestants were so active in attempting to frame specifically *religious* policy for American international relations.

There was a strong emotional component to events such as the Philadelphia riots. Sydney George Fisher's sense that "feelings" lay behind the riots, and that the emotion of "hatred," especially, was involved, was shared by other Philadelphians, and by onlookers from other parts of the country. In a sermon preached in the Universalist Church in Charlestown, Massachusetts, ten years after the arson of the convent there, Edwin Chapin pointed a finger at Philadelphia and made an obvious play on the city's nickname: "The city named 'Brotherly Love,' has become an arena of unbrotherly hate, of savage slaughter, of mad intolerance, of lawless violence, of armed force." For Chapin, it was the lack of "religion which controls the affections, subdues the passions," and "directs the consciences of men" that lay behind the problems in Philadelphia. The problem, simply put, was "sectarian hatred," observed *Zion's Herald*.[43]

Other nineteenth-century writers who had no immediate stake in the Philadelphia troubles likewise took unregulated feeling to be a central part of undesirable sectarian religion. Andrew Jackson Davis knew about "exclusive, sectarian, prejudicial feeling," the influential psychologist Laurens P. Hickok believed that "sectarian feeling" had a way "of attaching good or bad men together," and William Ellery Channing thought "sectarian feeling" easily translated into "an epidemic passion." Washington Irving knew about its destructive consequences for Islam, and Frederick Jackson Turner observed that religious sects had an unusually strong "emotional responsiveness."

Religious magazines lamented how "religion became much a matter of feeling, and sectarian strifes took the place of Christian zeal," while remarking that years after the events of 1844 there was even "more sectarian hatred and bitterness." The religious writer Thomas J. Vaiden stated the matter this way: "How unwise is the sectarian feeling of a peculiar faith towards all sects not its own . . . !" Accordingly, "sectarian hatreds," wrote the predictable *Christian Union* magazine, "are the bane of religion."[44]

The rioting in Philadelphia and Boston illustrated how affect breathed life into the suspicion that the long game for any sect was to dominate and destroy all others. In keeping with the "paranoid style" of Americans, that affect was given expression in the sounding of alarms about secrecy and conspiracy. Such alarms were a part of many Protestant discussions of Catholic ecclesiology and the various Catholic practices that were both fascinating and frightful for Protestants.

Some aspects of religious practice, such as auricular confession and the use of Latin in Catholic services, were especially vexing for Protestants. Both of those issues in their own way aggravated Protestant fears that Catholics were plotting to overthrow the government and establish a papal territory in North America. Protestant awareness of a secret language that could be used for plotting treason was taken for granted in much anti-Catholic writing. Auricular confession was an even more thrilling and intuitively appealing focus for Protestant dread and became a popular topic for published opinion and speeches during periods of mass violence between Protestants and Catholics.

In 1845, *Spiritual Direction, and Auricular Confession: Their History, Theory and Consequences*, a translation of lectures by French historian Jules Michelet, was published in Philadelphia. It intensified interest in the Catholic ritual of the confession of sins to a priest, and focused previous suspicions that the secrecy of the ritual was a cover for Catholic machinations in America.[45] On the heels of publication of the book, a former Catholic, identified in the press as a Dr. Giustiniani, campaigned courtesy of the American Protestant Society against auricular confession, delivering scathing lectures in various eastern states in which he warned that the ritual was designed to enable manipulation of Catholics by their priests. At the same time, anti-Catholic writers inflamed the claims of Michelet's already highly critical analysis of confession, concluding that secret confession led women to commit adultery with their confessors. From early in the nineteenth century, there had been legal proceedings involving the claim of Catholic clergy to exempt themselves from giving legal testimony that involved revealing the contents of a confession made to them as part of the sacrament. That exemption was withheld in a case in New York City in 1813, but debate about the practice was constant throughout the nine-

PROJECTIONS

teenth century, particularly during times when Catholics were immigrating in large numbers.[46] Complicating the debate was the fact that the Protestant Episcopal Church was experimenting at the time with auricular confession and members of the Anglican Church in America were defending auricular confession as sacramental means.[47] There were inconvenient commonalities, a measure of connectedness, to high church Protestantism.

The specific threats posed by auricular confession were clustered around its capability to serve as a means of covert administration of programs subversive of Protestantism and democracy. "There is no institution in the Catholic Church to which the average Protestant, whether he be an American or an Englishman, has a more deeply rooted antipathy than to the practice of auricular confession," lamented the Jesuit Rev. R. F. Clarke during the high point of Catholic immigration late in the century. For some Protestants, auricular confession was dangerous because it was theologically phony, a ritual purported to bring divine forgiveness to the sinner, but, as the *New Englander and Yale Review* observed, what "about that 'godly sorrow' for sin, 'without which forgiveness cannot be obtained?'" More to the point was lawyer and essayist Ezra C. Seaman's rehearsal in 1853 of claims previously made against Catholic auricular confession, with Seaman claiming that it allowed the clergy "to plan and promote political intrigue, to the ruin of many an individual and family; to the injury of the state; and to the dishonor of religion." Richard W. Thompson, in *The Papacy and the Civil Power*, similarly complained about "its threatening aspects toward the political and social foundations of the state," that it was "so at war with the whole genius and spirit of our institutions. Protestants have not duly considered what a tremendous engine of power this is." Other writers called it a "humbug," an elaborate machinery for concealment of papist scheming, and a pathway to violence, one writer punctuating his warnings with the remonstrance that auricular confession would be the "farewell to national liberty."[48]

In short, auricular confession represented for Protestants a secret Catholic campaign to overthrow the Protestant order in America. The fact that Catholic ritual unfolded through "the use of an unknown tongue," Latin, made matters worse. The Indians—always on the periphery of memory when Protestants worried about Catholic conspiracies—likewise had spoken in mysterious tongues when they undertook campaigns against early New Englanders. That flashing memory of the colonial past amounted also to the recall of fears that Indians intended nothing short of annihilation of European settlers. When American anti-Catholic writers referred to Catholic plans to exterminate all other religions in a monumental and conclusive Inquisition, they were at the same time engaging their own colonial-era trauma. That experience was deeply troubling, and nativists often operated at the edge of panic. The unspoken question of whether it was advisable to exterminate Catholics first could occasionally surface through that panic. *Romanism and the Pope* (1846), published in Philadelphia following the riots and in defense of the mob action, reminded readers that "seventeen bishops and six hundred and thirty-four priests" of the Roman Catholic Church in America were "*sworn enemies* and persecutors of a very large majority of the people of this country." Accordingly, some of them seemed to have gotten what was due them.[49]

Rhetoric about secrecy and conspiracy, about profound feelings of religious hatred among one's enemies, and about plans to usurp Protestant America was not limited to anti-Catholic writing. Opponents of Mormonism, including some Catholics, condemned it for secrecy, heresy, conspiracy, its ruthless opposition to non-Mormons, and its sectarianism. Attacked in the nineteenth-century press early in its emergence as a religious community, Mormonism fared little better at the end of the century, when, as one Bostonian observed, "the newspapers teem with articles attacking Mormonism in the most hostile and prejudiced way." *Scientific American* in 1845 advised that "it is well-known that Mormonism is a groundless heresy," while another publication associated Mormonism with Catholic "heresy and fanaticism." *The Liberator*, which published a wide range of opinion—in part because of its inability to resist republishing rhetorically juicy morsels from other periodicals—ran a short piece in which the author, "disgusted with Mormonism," insisted somewhat nervously that "the established religion of the United States is the evangelical system," which, being rooted "in the strongest emotions of the population . . . *can never be destroyed.*"[50]

But Protestant enemies of Mormonism, and Mormon foes from other religious backgrounds as well, did in fact fret constantly about the destructive power of Mormonism.[51] That power was evidenced, as many writers pointed out, specifically in the body count from Mormon killings of non-Mormons, and more generally in the treachery and treason of Mormons, who "are as careless of their oaths as a Chinaman, and bear as little allegiance to the United States government as do the Chinese."[52] Mormons, while not typically identified as immigrants in the way that Irish Catholics were, were sometimes imagined as foreigners, as a novel, perverse species of Chinese, Native Americans, or other ethnic group. Only foreigners, it seemed, could be so regularly involved in "neighborhood wars, local raids, and extraordinary mobs" as well as grander events such as the Mountain Meadows massacre in Utah, where, a magazine reminded its readers, "a hundred and thirty-one Gentiles were murdered!"[53] Many Americans likewise viewed Mormon polygamy as an assault on the nation's women, Christian virtue, and the American way of life.

Sectarianism, secrecy, conspiracy, treason, and murder all were joined in Protestant anxieties about religious difference. The religious battles of the antebellum period were more than matters of immediate denominational difference, however. They served as stages upon which deep misgivings and unease about colonial events emerged in rhetoric that foisted responsibility for religious intolerance onto the minority groups that suffered it. Protestant denial of the past and Protestant denial of responsibility for violent antebellum acts of intolerance were two sides of the same coin.

Intolerance in Foreign Lands

THE PROBLEM OVERSEAS

Many Americans were intolerant, but many also wanted to make religious intolerance go away. Americans were disturbed by their perception of the powerful and complex emotion of hate between religious groups, and they feared for democracy, the Republic, and the American Protestant order. There was much public bragging about the American achievement of the First Amendment and much pledging of fidelity to the cause of religious freedom. But under the surface of that, there could be doubts. One who had doubts was Thomas Jefferson, whose *Virginia Statue for Religious Freedom* (1786) had set the bar for free exercise of religion. Jefferson, writing to Mordecai Manuel Noah, a American playwright and diplomat descended from Portuguese Sephardim, confessed a national failing that lay just below the surface of much American discussion of religion. Referring to the "religious intolerance inherent in every sect," Jefferson observed that "our laws have applied the only antidote to this vice, protecting our religious as they do our civil rights." But, said Jefferson, "more remains to be done, for although we are free by the law, we are not so in practice; public opinion erects itself into an inquisition, and exercises its office with as much fanaticism as fans the flames of an *auto-da-fe*."[54]

The public to which Jefferson referred was the same public that found it difficult to come to terms with the American history of religious intolerance and the violence and trauma that it had caused. He referred to what the public believed about the difference between America and Europe: religious violence had been left overseas, and the rule of law in America had ensured that. When James Madison in his *Memorial and Remonstrance Against Religious Assessments* in 1785 reminded his audience that "Torrents of blood have been spilt in the old world" because of the state's attempts to proscribe "all difference in religious opinion," he was inviting them to engage with a cultural geography of a North America that existed essentially apart from Europe. He offered a vision of "the lustre to our country" juxtaposed specifically to the intolerance and religious violence of the Old World.[55]

The great ramping-up of the Protestant Christian missionary industry in the early nineteenth century—a byproduct of growing evangelical zeal and the diminished momentum of a public Deism and "infidelism"—played a key role in directing Americans' attention overseas. While missions to Native Americans remained important and regularly were reported in the religious press and in the notes of religious association meetings, stories of the challenges and successes of overseas missions captured the imaginations of readers who were drawn to the exoticized and romanticized portraits of life in the Orient and elsewhere. The overseas missions field was, as historian Christine Heyrman wrote in conveying the feelings of missionaries, "a perfect romance."[56]

The depiction of missionaries as heroes made for good reading, and the diaries and journals of overseas missionaries delivered particularly poignant stories about risk of life, the overcoming of bad odds, and success through patience and reliance upon divine guidance. When the newly created American Board of Commissioners of Foreign Missions sent eight missionaries to Asia in 1812, the goal was no less than a beachhead for the Protestant conversion of the world. The ABCFM eventually sent over a thousand missionaries to all corners of the earth, fostered the cultivation of a missionary spirit in students at the lively Andover Theological Seminary and at other Protestant institutions, and popularized the notion that the ABCFM-coordinated march of the gospel to every nation would result in a world fully Protestantized.[57]

As intolerance of Catholics and Mormons increased in antebellum America, and as infighting among Protestant sectarian movements intensified, Americans increasingly looked away. Turning their gaze to the world, they searched abroad for instances of intolerance. Americans retreated from recognizing the distressing predicament of religious intolerance in their traumatic past and confusing present, and instead projected their awareness of it into overseas scenarios that they detailed and condemned in letters, newspapers, journals, and other kinds of writing. Like Edward Said's Europeans who projected the worst parts of their cultures—the corruptions, failures, violence, and trauma with which they could not come to terms—onto the Orient, Americans projected their failures, in this case their religious intolerance, onto places across the sea, to every continent where missions might venture.

American thinking about intolerance overseas was shaped by the emergence of a missionary literature. Their lives dramatically portrayed in the religious press, missionaries to overseas lands became celebrities among Protestants in antebellum America. Two of the best known were the Baptist couple Adoniram Judson (1788–1850) and Ann Hasseltine Judson (1789–1826). Adoniram was a founding member of the ABCFM, and the Judsons were among the first to embark on a missionary career under its flag. Ann died in the course of her activity overseas, and her memoirs furnished the basis for a biography by James D. Knowles, the *Life of Mrs. Ann Judson, Late Missionary to Burmah*. First published in 1829, it was republished almost every year thereafter until 1856. It was so popular that Lydia Maria Child remarked that it was "a book so universally known that it scarce need be mentioned."[58] By 1833, the book had become "constitutive of American Protestant culture."[59]

Ann and Adoniram Judson's activities in Burma (where they began their work of conversion after having found no welcome for it in India) became the "Mission to Burmah," as it was reported regularly in Baptist newsletters—and copied in other publications. What stands out in the Judsons' own memoirs and correspondences was the uninterrupted flow of their reports about their struggle with the intolerance of the Burmese civil authorities, whose religious intolerance they constantly decried.[60] The religious intolerance of the Burmese in fact became a central motif of the Judsons' missionary accounts and framed almost every phase of their reports of their efforts to engage potential Burmese recruits to Protestant Christianity.

What the Judsons reported was repeated in the American press. Soon, Protestantism in America had cast the "Mission to Burmah" and cognate overseas missions as dangerous forays into intolerant territories, where brutal persecution involving torture, imprisonment, and execution was an everyday reality. It was, as the *Religious Intelligencer* wrote in republishing an account from the *Baptist Magazine*, "The War in Burmah," a rhetorical entwining of the fact of political struggle there with the historic Christian battle against intolerance.

Reporting on overseas missions was rich in affect, cultivated by prose suggesting that catastrophe was imminent. Among Protestants who read denominational periodicals and audited sermons and lectures, religious life in the world outside the United States took shape as activity in a war zone in which intolerance commanded a powerful and intimidating army of enforcers. Death was a possibility. In the course of courting Ann in 1811, and prior to going overseas, Adoniram wrote to her father, asking him "whether you can consent to her departure for a heathen land, and her subjection to the hardships and sufferings of a missionary life; whether you can consent to her exposure to the dangers of the ocean; to the fatal influence of the southern climate of India; to every kind of want and distress; to degradation, insult, persecution, and perhaps a violent death."[61]

74   CHAPTER TWO

The War in Burmah in fact was a war over political control involving the Burmese and the Bengali government, but for an American Protestant readership, it was equally or more so a battle against religious intolerance. "Now we well know," said the *Intelligencer*, "that the great obstacle in the way of the progress of Christianity in this empire has been the intolerance of the government. The natives are intelligent, thoughtful, and candid, willing to examine any other religion, and only withheld from doing so by the fear of persecution." In the hands of Protestant promoters of missions, the story of a willing potential clientele and a repressive, persecuting government became a central trope of mission literature. The story was repeated relentlessly in every kind of writing about religion overseas.[62] It was, moreover, told with a sense of urgency, as if something was about to break forth that could be terrible or wonderful. There was hopefulness for success in conversions, and there was a deep, ingrained anxiety about the real possibilities of cataclysm, about the world-changing dangers posed by religious intolerance. At various points during their Burmese residency, both of the Judsons expressed that intuition. In Adoniram's words, a "storm was gathering," and it was "something worse, and more to be dreaded, than our own personal inconvenience and persecution."[63]

The storm was gathering not only in Burma.[64] Beginning early in the nineteenth century, Protestants filled their religious publications with stories of intolerance throughout the world. In 1833, the *Proceedings* of the ABCFM reported on "The Religious Intolerance of the Chinese Government," an account of the Chinese campaign against "heterodox sects" and their punishment: "The Emperor has been rather severe in punishing these people, and many of them have been thrown into prison, scourged, and transported."[65] The persecution of Sikhs in India often was condemned, one observer of it there extrapolating that "religious persecution is always revolting, and exercises a baneful influence in every age and country."[66] Muslims were of an "aggressive and intolerant spirit," and their treatment of Hindus amounted to "bigotry and intolerance," contemptuous, violent, and sacrilegious.[67] The *New York Observer*, advancing the theme of terrible religious intolerance in India, reported a spate of "19 deaths from violence recorded during the month of November in the mortality tables, amongst which poisoning, stifling, strangling, and hacking to pieces from religious intolerance stand in awful and bold relief."[68] The Presbyterian missionary Daniel McGilvary in Siam reported back over the course of much of the nineteenth century about the ups and downs of missionary work there. He voiced his alarm at the fact of people "executed for no crime whatever, except for being Christians," an intolerance that amounted to "atrocity that seemed beyond belief," while noting as well how so many others were regularly accused of witchcraft, in a process that amounted to "the most dreaded means of oppression and persecution."[69]

The regular ABCFM reports, while often describing mission fields abroad in guardedly upbeat terms, also detailed the challenges posed by intolerance in literally every geographic area of the world. Religious outlets such as the *New York Evangelist* and the *Christian Observer*, among many others, circulated the reports, and in so doing progressively dramatized the problems of religion in foreign lands. From "a new spirit of intolerance in the Persian government" to "outbreaks of fanatical violence" in a "persecution that raged" in Turkey—in spite of Turkish efforts to promote toleration—the problem was vividly portrayed for an American Protestant readership. There were Muslim traditions of intolerance at work in Africa, where Copts had gone to "escape the ferocity and intolerance" of Arabian conquerors but where local religious groups also continued to fight with each other and with Christians.[70] Everywhere, governments as well as popular movements crushed minority religions and communities that showed signs of heterodoxy.[71]

For American readers of accounts of worldwide intolerance, "heathens" often were to blame for it. But there were others. Sometimes the Buddhist or Muslim or Hindu governments were the root cause of intolerance. And neither England nor Europe more broadly was exempt from criticism. Antebellum periodicals continuously criticized European governments for their intolerant acts, especially if they were against Methodists and Baptists. "Religious Intolerance in England" (1822), like numerous other articles of the time, called out officials for intolerance of "the Primitive Methodist sect" there. The more expansive *History of American Baptist Missions in Asia, Africa, Europe, and North America* (1849), while noting difficulties everywhere, paid full attention to Europe, such as in German areas where "acts of persecution were not confined to" Hamburg. "They were repeated, with greater or lesser aggravation, at Oldenburg, at Berlin and other cities in Prussia; at Stuttgart, and in several of the towns of Hessia, Bavaria, Pomerania,—and even in the kingdom of Hanover, where . . . we might hope to find the exercise of religious freedom unrestricted." Affronts to Baptists in those places "all were acts of intolerance, called for by no crime but that of dissenting from the established faith of the country."[72]

FEAR OF GLOBAL CATHOLICISM

For all of the intolerance that Protestants were able to locate and condemn overseas, the most vocal complaints they registered were about the influence of the Roman Catholic Church. The American Protestant stage was ready for the literary enactment of fears about the power of Catholics overseas because beginning early in the nineteenth century numerous local stories about Catholic designs on subverting American democracy had been gathering authority among the growing Protestant evangelical readership. In the 1830s and 1840s, the decades of the mob attacks on Catholic property and persons in cities such as Boston and Philadelphia, the emotional tenor of Protestant dissatisfaction had deepened, so that articles about Catholic intolerance overseas increased not only in number but in the aggressiveness of their polemics.

Protestants read about how "outrage on the principle of religious liberty was committed in Italy, where the facts . . . of religious intolerance are uncontested." Persecution of Protestants was said to be widespread in Italy—in Rome, Tuscany, Genoa, and "all parts of Italy."[73] But for American Protestants who had their own global mission agendas, the real crime of Catholic intolerance was Catholic enforcement of it in foreign places where Catholic missions had gained a toehold. Portugal, itself often scolded for Catholic intolerance, was overseer of the much-reported colony of Macao. In spite of British progress in Hong Kong, Protestants fretted about Catholic growth in China, and the Catholic policies that followed, as harbingers of a China turned away from Protestants because of Catholic power advanced through intolerance. Protestants feared that the "bigoted jealousy of a Popish priesthood" would limit their possibilities in China.[74] That priesthood, warned George Smith, was "intimately connected with the local government . . . and ready to crush, at the earliest stage, any attempts to make converts in Protestantism."[75] *Sketches of China* (1830) viewed the colonial religious terrain similarly, emphasizing how "bigotry and intolerance, are assiduously cultivated and cherished by the inhabitants, who are, with a few exceptions, priest-ridden, and ignorant to the last degree."[76] In Portuguese Goa, the case was the same, where the Portuguese brought their "prohibitory laws, their system of violence, and their religious intolerance."[77] Portuguese intolerance ironically presented another, potentially worse problem in Brazil. One publication explained that in the decades after independence, the sharp Brazilian reaction against Portuguese religious intolerance ironically was a problem for all Christian religion. The *Christian Statesman* published an opinion that "the Brazilian Empire in repudiating its connection with Popery will repudiate the Christian religion."[78] The severity of Catholic intolerance could lead circuitously to a whole new order of threat to Protestant aspiration.

Catholic mission initiative in Africa allegedly had accomplished the same trick of misleading the local populations. The *Independent* explained, in language that was common in Protestant discussions of Catholic missions, that in a certain exemplary instance the arrival of Jesuits in Africa led to "a

PROJECTIONS   77

deplorable act of intolerance." The *Independent* asserted that "soon the report spread that Protestantism would be put down by force, and it proved only too true." The Catholics ensured that "the public professions of no other religious belief" would be permitted. Because "soldiers had orders to fire on everyone who might dare" to defy Catholic power, Protestant missionaries fled.[79]

Spain was the most feared of the Catholic nations for its tendency to excess—Americans frequently cited the Inquisition as well as the Black Legend of the Americas—and was constantly criticized by American Protestants for its gross religious intolerance. The Spanish empire in the Americas and elsewhere, while not as extensive or powerful as it once had been, nevertheless still loomed in Protestant imagination as a threat to Protestant progress worldwide. A Protestant report in 1828 began with the principle: "The truth is, that the Portuguese and the Spaniards are so generally and completely under the influence of the popish priesthood, that all appearances of their being favorable to free government, when put to the test prove to be delusive." While Protestantism made small inroads here and there around the world, deadly Catholic conspiracy loomed everywhere. Moreover, the longer that Catholics were engaged in Africa, Asia, and South America, the graver damage they wrought not only to religion but to liberty and democracy. After the triumph of Bolivar in South America in the 1820s, the Protestant report bemoaned the religious scenario there: "It appears now, and we have always feared it would so turn out, that the present generation of South Americans are too ignorant, and have been too long under the influence of bad habits to become at once good republicans." The thinking of South Americans had been poisoned by Catholic leaders who imposed a rigid and oppressive system on them, and at the core of that system was the rotten truth of Catholic lust for power. Accordingly, "there can never be real freedom in any state in which religious intolerance exists, in all of the new South American States."[80]

Mexico, the Catholic nation neighboring the southwest borderlands, was the subject of much discussion and especially during the years of Texas independence (1836–1845) and the subsequent Mexican War (1846–1848). Published during the Mexican War, George Wilkins Kendall's *Narrative of the Texan Santa Fé Expedition* explained that the clergy in Mexico "retain their supremacy and their fat benefices . . . and continue to gull their simple flocks—to hold the downtrodden mass in the same ignorance in which they have so long been kept—and hence their open intolerance towards all other sects . . ."[81] The Rev. Fitch W. Taylor, a U.S. naval chaplain, extended the criticism about religious intolerance in Mexico to include the broad condemnation of the repression of liberty, a common theme among other Protestant writers who discussed the effect of Catholic rule in the declining Spanish and Portuguese empires. "Liberty of thought is a sin, according to their creed. Liberty of action is denied to those who adopt their creed. Liberty of person is even precarious, where the creed of the Papal church" is enforced by a "politico-religious Hierarchy."[82]

THE AFTERMATHS OF BOSTON AND PHILADELPHIA

Protestants were particularly keen in noticing Catholic intolerance overseas in the immediate aftermaths of the mob violence against Catholics in Boston and Philadelphia. In the several months following the attack on the convent in Charlestown—just across the river from Boston—and continuing for several years, Protestants saw with particular clarity the problem of intolerance abroad, and they wrote extensively about it. Mexico was a popular topic for many writers late in 1834, partly because of the mounting political tensions with Texas but especially for partisan Protestants who could infuse political observation with complaints about religious intolerance. Even ostensibly neutral (but actually partisan) publications such as the *American Annals of Education*, which was located in Boston, participated. The *Annals* published an article that appeared several weeks after the destruction of the convent that took direct aim at Catholic Mexico. In Mexico, there was "gross superstition, which is generally diffused, the despotic influence of the clergy over the greater part of the inhabitants, and intolerance, which is even sanctioned by the constitutions of the Union and the States." The article, summarizing a lyceum speech by a visitor from Mexico, pled for someone to free "the imprisoned minds of Mexico."[83]

By the same token, the Holy Land, which in antebellum America was becoming an increasingly fascinating place for Protestants, was also lamented for the intolerance there. In the immediate aftermath of Charlestown, numerous Protestant publications reported their concerns. The "mission church at Beyroot" had discovered there the extent of the "bigotry, intolerance, unreasonableness, and worldly-mindedness of the priests," among other problems.[84] Religious intolerance in Palestine generally, entwined with civil despotism, had "done much to lay waste the land."[85] The Holy Land was suffering as Catholics, even though declining in influence in some parts of it, tortured Protestant efforts to preach their gospel. It was a scene of Protestant struggle at the hands of "Papal Christians."[86]

In thinking about the Holy Land, Protestants took the further step of trying to get a bead on the nefarious interplay of Roman Catholicism with Islam. The "Mission to Persia," a lecture read in the Amherst chapel the night before

PROJECTIONS 79

the final riot in Charlestown—that is, during the period when growing Protestant intolerance already was highly visible in the streets of Boston—was an exhortation to young men to commit to missionary labor. It informed them that in the Holy Land, "you, as a Christian missionary, can expect only an inhospitable reception" underwritten by "the strength of prejudice and intolerance."[87] That intolerance was the product of years of connivance by a congeries of religious groups, including Muslims and degenerate Latin and Byzantine Christians whose crimes included "idolatrous worship of departed men." But Protestants were not entirely sure of the relationship of Muslims to Catholics there and elsewhere, and the point in any event was that Catholics were terrible at allowing freedom of conscience. Henry Stuart Foote, a historian of Mexico, likely bearing in mind his readers' prejudice against Muslims, attempted to make a more pointed criticism of Catholic intolerance through an atypical but instructive comparison. He maintained that Muslims in Spain in fact historically had been tolerant of Catholics, and by contrast it was the Spanish Catholics who instilled "a barbarous bigotry," an "intolerance in religious matters," that they spread throughout Iberia and their empire overseas.[88] Catholics, because of their intolerance, were worse than Muslims.

Even hope for the future in Spain, following the official dismantling of the Inquisition there in mid-July 1834, was tentative. "One Curse Removed!!!" proclaimed the *Religious Intelligencer* from New Haven the following November. Then, in terms that would have comported with the Amalekite story, it continued, "The Inquisition of Spain is annihilated!!!" But the *Intelligencer* eventually added discussion of the event that indicated its own mixed feelings about whether the Inquisition truly had been annihilated. It still existed outside Spain, and the event was more about "the example of Spain," which, "we earnestly hope," would translate globally.[89] The *New-England Magazine* similarly was a bit more confident during that November in a future for world Protestantism, but still, there was a degree of reticence. The magazine treated the event as the victory of truth over "pride, ignorance, and bigotry." But much remained to be done: "All these evils are now seen—they are felt—they are known to be remediable—they will be remedied; priest-craft will be shaken."[90] But it was still, as the *Intelligencer* phrased it, just "one curse removed."

In October 1834, the Hartford *Christian Secretary* published a chapter of Samuel Morse's "Foreign Conspiracy Against the Liberty of the United States," in which Morse offered a short summary of Protestant thinking about the global conspiracy. "Let me not be charged with accusing the Catholics of the United States of intolerance," the author pled. "They are too small a body as yet to fully act out their principles," and beyond that, "they are not genuine and consistent Catholics," but rather "a small insulated body under the restraints of the society around it." Catholics in America for the most part were friends, not enemies, who demonstrated an "ardent love for the republican, tolerant institutions of our government." Real Catholic power, including the core players in the Catholic plot to dominate, were in Spain, Portugal, and Austria. Morse eventually admitted that a number of Catholic subversives were at work in America, but the crux of his argument was that Catholic designs were, as the title of his eventual book claimed, a "foreign conspiracy." The heart of that conspiracy was in Austria, a Catholic country, where "the great master-slave Metternich . . . obeys his illustrious master the Emperor." Austria was the model nation for intolerance, and the expert practitioner in secrecy, conspiracy, and vicious use of power, all exercised in the interest of undermining democracy and replacing it with a religious hierarchy.[91]

When the *Christian Advocate and Journal* published for its Protestant readers another installment in Morse's serialized treatise in December 1834, the message was again the role of Austrian Catholicism in leading a global conspiracy. The language was more emotional, however, and the sense of urgency more palpable. America, he warned, was on guard against "the *Austrian conspirators*," a plot that "sends its serpents to lurk within his [America's] cradle," by means of "its secret agents in this country."[92] Morse's alarm was an extension of a broader American anxiety about its place among other nations. Americans had been on alert for conspiracies to subvert liberty and democracy since the founding of the nation. During the early nineteenth century when Deism and "infidelism" claimed newspaper space, observers such as Yale president Timothy Dwight and the geographer Jedidiah Morse (1761–1826), a preacher who had been Jonathan Edwards's student and was Samuel's father, warned of republicanism endangered by the vast Illuminati network. The Austrian conspiracy, as the point of the spear of Catholic intolerance, was a decidedly anti-Catholic version of ongoing American worries about foreign plots that predated by decades the Charlestown and Philadelphia mobs. Nevertheless, it was in the several years following Charlestown, and later Philadelphia, that the Protestant concern about Catholic conspiracy abroad and the threat to American democracy became a full-blown preoccupation.[93]

The discussion of religious intolerance in newspapers and other periodicals after Charlestown was robust. It was so robust that it prompted investigations into what the term "religious intolerance" actually meant. It also engendered debate about how culture and history served as contexts for understanding intolerance. There was agreement among most who wrote about religious intolerance that at its worst, it was an emotional event along the lines of what Diderot wrote in his *Encyclopédie* (1751–1772). The *Boston Recorder*, shortly after the burning of the convent, published that definition: "INTOLERANCE—A ferocious passion, which leads those who feel it to hate and persecute those who entertain erroneous opinions." The *Recorder* also excerpted the definition of intolerance in the *Encyclopédie Méthodique* (1782–1832), which added the following to Diderot's definition: ". . . erroneous opinions, and to practice all sorts of violence against those who think differently from us concerning God and his worship."[94] The latter definition, which qualified the previous one by referring to "different" rather than "erroneous" opinions, was a more Protestant take on religious intolerance in its implied claim that people can have different opinions about God. Both definitions, however, allowed for the generally accepted understanding of religious intolerance that can "exist in the heart" even if it does not show "itself in open acts of violence."[95]

The quasi-philosophical discussion of intolerance—was it a feeling, a thought, a motive, an action?—that took place in Protestant publications signaled a broad concern among the readership about the appearance of intolerance in places such as Charlestown. Protestants, as well as Catholics, asked how it could happen, and why. Harrison Gray Otis, a Boston Protestant and wealthy Federalist politician, condemned the arson in strong language, framing it as a "horrible outrage" and persuading his audience at Faneuil Hall—which included local government leaders who were Protestant—to resolve that "the attack on the Ursuline convent in Charlestown, occupied only by defenceless females, was a base and cowardly act, for which the perpetrators deserve the contempt and detestation of the community."[96] Protestant publications such as the *Christian Watchman, Western Christian Advocate,* and *Christian Examiner* all regretted that such an offense took place in America, where religious freedom was a constitutional principle. The *Examiner,* expressing its "indignation and abhorrence," wondered just how the perpetrators "and the wretches like them, exist in the bosom of our community."[97] Lyman Beecher himself, who had just inflamed his audiences against perceived Catholic schemes to take over the nation, repented of his rhetoric by castigating the mob from his pulpit.[98]

Beecher's turnabout represented the complicated, sometimes confused or contradictory thinking about America when it came to identifying intolerance and those who practiced it. Samuel Morse professed to be satisfied that Catholics in America, except for any who might be acting as foreign agents, were for the most part tolerant. That opinion, stated in the context of his larger, profoundly anti-Catholic screed on foreign conspiracies, represented another kind of complexity in American thinking about intolerance. It raised the question of whether cultural context and spatial location changed the character of a group, rendering it more or less intolerant. For Morse, it did. A religious group on the whole could embody a passion for persecuting opponents, but discrete communities within that group might by virtue of their spatial situatedness practice toleration. At least that was the case for America, which for Morse, like most other Americans, was an exceptional nation.

The arson in Charlestown prompted discussion about the earliest immigrant New Englanders, the Puritans. During the 1830s–1840s, some of the most illustrative discussion of the historical and cultural contexts of intolerance in America in fact was undertaken in considerations of the behavior of Puritans in early New England. In those discussions can be glimpsed the complexity of American thinking about the Puritans, and about the meaning of intolerance in antebellum America. At times, Puritans were praised as heroes of Christian history, liberty, and democracy. At other times, they were condemned — as is well evidenced in early nineteenth-century literature — as hate-filled persecutors of any who dared to differ from them.

Catholics, understandably, tended to be sharply critical of Puritans, and especially in Boston after the arson. In the months following the burning of the convent in August, Catholic publications raged against it, offering up a litany of criticisms of anti-Catholic prejudice that had festered for decades. "Wonder is expressed at the outrageous proceedings at Charlestown," observed a Catholic magazine in "On Religious Intolerance and Persecution." But "this is absurd. . . . When probably a dozen of the so-styled religious papers have been for years sedulously employed in exciting the hellish passions of our nature against the Roman Catholics."[99] In late August, the *United States Catholic Miscellany* published "The Dawn of Religious Persecution in America," in which the author emphasized that "the reign of liberty both civil and religious, is now on the wane." It was obvious that "no person can any longer hesitate in believing" that Catholics "are now marked out in the land of their adoption as objects and victims of that outrage which they could not brook in the land of their nativity."[100] Continuing the theme for weeks, the magazine in October, after loudly condemning American anti-Catholicism, turned to an especially salient issue, the Puritans. "But I will now take a totally different ground," wrote the author (probably the Catholic writer Mathew Carey), "and admit for the sake of argument" that Catholics in the past had persecuted their religious opponents and that "all the atrocious accusations brought against our ancestors are perfectly just." Protestants, said the author, must then acknowledge their own culpability, and accept the judgment of those who aim "to charge the existing Protestants with the follies, errors, aberrations of their ancestors."[101] Those ancestors, the Puritans,

PROJECTIONS

haunted Protestant memories, and Catholic reference to them aggravated a difficult process of Protestants' coming to terms with Puritan persecutions of Amalekitish foes.

Protestant writers in the months after Charlestown addressed the issue of the culpability of the Puritans, and the transmissibility of Puritans' sins to nineteenth-century Protestants. One way in which they did that was to play with definitions of intolerance and to frame Puritan intolerance as an error committed within a historical past in which that error was less egregious than it might appear to later generations. Conveniently, the first volume of George Bancroft's *A History of the United States, from the Discovery of the American Continent to the Present Time* was published in 1834, and reviews of it began to appear late that summer. Bancroft was a Unitarian descended from the earliest settlers of Massachusetts Bay. His belief in progress and divine providence informed his view of American history. He praised New England Puritans for their idealism and especially for their "undying principles of democratic liberty," but he criticized their religious intolerance, and in no uncertain terms.[102]

Bancroft wrote a lengthy section on Puritan intolerance and illustrated it with references to the many cases of persecution of those who disagreed with Puritans. Early Massachusetts, even as a transitional society, was a society where "bigotry exhibited its worst aspect." That was in spite of the fact that the Puritan venture overall was "a war against tyranny and superstition."[103] Bancroft left a lot of wiggle room for interpreters of Puritan intolerance, opening the door especially for Protestant characterizations of Puritans as a group that behaved in ways that were not unusual or particularly offensive for the time in which they lived.

The *American Quarterly Review*[104] issue published in early September 1834 included a long review of Bancroft's history. It urged readers to follow Bancroft's revisionist lead, to accept "the necessity of looking beyond the mere narrative of the original adventurers and old historians." It informed readers that "the most interesting and attractive portions of Mr. Bancroft's volume, are those which relate to the Puritans." The Puritans, indeed, were intolerant. But, said the review, "turn not in disgust away from the bigotry of doctrine and intolerance of deed, which too frequently meet your eye" in reading about the Puritans. Rather, see them as pious, idealistic, defenders of liberty, and visionaries of a better world. And, in the meantime, remember that they were not as intolerant as the Spanish. "An ardent, enthusiastic, religious feeling was more characteristic of the Spaniards of that day than, if possible, it was of the Puritans." The Spanish were more vicious and far-reaching in their oppression of heathen peoples, their intolerance more intense and corrupt.[105]

84

CHAPTER TWO

The *New York Evangelist* chimed in (somewhat exaggeratedly) about the same time that Bancroft lauded Calvin as a valuable influence on Puritanism and asserted that "the intolerance of Roman superstition was rebuked by the keen dialectics of Calvin."[106]

The Puritans, for all their acts of bigotry and their oppression of dissenters, were made to look better than Catholics. In 1834, in the aftermath of Protestant violence against Catholics in Boston, those Protestants who sought to understand the problem of intolerance in America were better off studying Catholic conspirators in Europe and their global schemes than to search the New England past.

As was the case in Boston, the deadly riots in Philadelphia during the late spring and summer of 1844—a decade after Charlestown—were followed immediately by Protestant discussion about Catholic conspiracies abroad. Much of the discussion was identical in tone and theme to what had been in the papers after Charlestown. However, there was more of a sense of intolerance as an ongoing, entrenched problem, and an increasingly exhausting one for everyone, regardless of their religious affiliation. The prominent Jewish reformer Rebecca Gratz, a Philadelphian, wrote to her younger brother Benjamin in the week after the worst rioting, "Intolerance has been too prevalent of late, and many of the clergy of different denominations are chargeable with its growth." She relayed that "the present outbreak is an attack on the Catholic Church, and there is so much violent animosity between that sect and the Protestants that unless the strong arm of power is raised to sustain the provisions of the Constitution," there would be in America "no secure dwelling place for religion."[107]

Some publications devoted months to explaining, typically in partisan terms, the causes of the violence in Philadelphia. The debate about what version of the Bible should be used in public schools was often a part of those discussions. But, as had been the case in Boston, many writers turned their readers' attention away from America toward Europe, where Catholic plots far worse than what was happening in Philadelphia were said to be ruining the lives of Protestants. In the several months after the riots, the Protestant press publicized Catholic intolerance in Brazil,[108] and in Spain, a nation that because of "superstition, bigotry and intolerance seems to have been rendered incapable of self-government."[109] In Mexico, the Spanish had taught the natives about religious violence, turning them immoral, cunning, and artificial in their relations with others. "The New Mexicans appear to have inherited much of the cruelty and intolerance of their ancestors [the Spanish], and no small portion of their bigotry and fanaticism."[110] Austria, as previously, was the focus of Catholic plotting against Protestants in Europe. The Unitarian *Christian Register,* in its article on "Romish Intolerance" just after the riots, stressed how "an Austrian law punished with banishment a convert to Protestantism."[111]

Protestant criticism of Rome followed much of the same lines as it had in the months after the violence in Boston. There were some fresh developments, however. There was more discussion of the dangers of civil government merged with ecclesiastical institutions. "The term *to legislate,*" said the *Christian Observer,* "is ordinarily used in a well-defined sense, and implies the exercise of power which is not vested in any of our ecclesiastical judicatories."[112] Rome legislated religion, and "whenever men make laws for the church, they persecute their fellows who reject the authority of their enactments." The *Register* added that when "the Pope is a sovereign as well as a Pope," intolerance and persecution follow. In Philadelphia in 1844, Protestants illustrated the problem with reference to Rome's legislating the use of a Catholic Bible in Italy, and disallowing the Protestant Bible wherever it could.

The Bible issue remained salient. *Rome's Policy Toward the Bible; or, Papal Efforts to Suppress the Scriptures,* published by James Campbell in Philadelphia in 1844, tracked that problem from the Waldenses and Lollards, through Wycliffe and Tyndale, and the Inquisition, up to its American climax in the summer of 1844. The book concluded that "Rome hates the Bible always and everywhere the same," and that because of its collaboration with civil authorities, Rome had been able to suppress the Bible throughout history.[113] A story thought to exemplify the problem was often stated, in various forms, during the period of the riots: "Armed sentinels and officers of the customs are stationed at every entrance into the Pope's dominions to search the trunks of travelers and to seize upon every Bible which they find, that the forbidden book may be destroyed."[114]

What also distinguished the public debate about religion in Philadelphia from that in Boston a decade earlier was the greatly increased attention to religious intolerance as a problem affecting commerce and the material improvement of life. The "market revolution" that had gathered momentum by the end of the eighteenth century advanced rapidly in the 1830s and 1840s. There was much writing about everyday commerce, productivity, free enterprise, trade, and the improvement of the common good.[115] The problem with the Roman Catholic Church, as it exercised its power globally, was not just its suppression of the Bible, exercise of priestcraft, and fostering of superstition. The Catholic mentality was bad for business. At a time when conversations about religious tolerance were deepening to regularly include its relation to other kinds of liberties, writers developed the argument that freedom to conduct commerce was part of a larger package of rights that included freedom to practice religion.

In October 1844, the *Christian Advocate and Journal* published "The Progress of Christianity-Hindrances-Prospects." The article was more about hindrances, and chief among those were the roadblocks to Protestant progress set up by Rome. In Italy, "where Popery is absolute," the hierarchy are "the most uncompromising opposers of all attempts to educate the common people." The result was that Italy contained "more ignorance and beggary than any other country in Europe." Italy was even worse than Ireland, where the Catholic Church "is the source of the poverty, ignorance, and wretchedness of the people."[116] Wherever the Catholic Church had established itself, poverty followed. Writers noted how Catholic mission enterprises over time drained the ambition from people, destroying their interest in bettering themselves and turning them into lazy, indolent enactors of a Roman script to dominate the world. The Philadelphian Samuel Augustus Mitchell made the point precisely in explaining the damage done by the Portuguese in Brazil:

> Considering the time that has elapsed since Brazil was colonized, its extent, fertility and favourable situation for commerce, its progress in population and wealth has been very slow. Its tardy growth, like that of the late Spanish colonies, was owing entirely to the vicious principles on which it was governed by the mother country; to the restriction laid on its trade and industry . . . Portugal could bequeath nothing to her colonies but pride, superstition, and intolerance.[117]

The topic of commerce came to the forefront of writing about the religious situation in Philadelphia in 1844 in part through the efforts of one of the most important figures involved in provoking the riots, Lewis C. Levin.[118] A Know-Nothing, an outspoken anti-Catholic, and the first Jew to serve as a Representative in the U.S. Congress, Levin was an editor for the *Daily Sun*, which, with the *Native American*, drove a vigorous anti-Catholic campaign after 1843. In September, two months after the riots had ended, Levin explained that "nature has made us a manufacturing people, by providing every facility to enable us to attain perfection" in industry, mining, agriculture, mechanics, and commerce. All of the raw materials had been provided by nature "so as to make us, in all of the elements of National wealth and greatness an *American people*." The "national character" was "based on the substantial virtues of industry, genius, invention, and patriotism, and a religion . . . which, at the *reformation*, struck out the sparks of liberty." "That religion," wrote Levin, "which ever was, and ever will be the concomitant

PROJECTIONS

of manufacturing," was a world apart from the despotism of the Roman Catholic Church. "The Catholic nations of the earth are restricted to *pastoral* occupations and supplied with manufactures from Protestant kingdoms. Everywhere Popery and manufactures are antagonist powers." Portugal, Spain, Italy, and Ireland, among other places, countries where there is not a "religion, corresponding with the laws and liberties which protect them," were doomed to economic failure.[119]

During the 1840s, both before and after the Philadelphia riots, business and industry magazines, as well as the religious press and the urban dailies, published articles about the importance of commerce in America. In many cases, those articles remarked on its relation to religion, and especially on what they termed religious freedom or religious liberty.[120] In 1840, the *Merchants' Magazine and Commercial Review* published a lecture by Charles King, a descendant of Captain John Underhill (of Pequot War fame) and soon-to-be anti-slavery president of Columbia College. King's talk, "Commerce as a Liberal Pursuit," aimed to defend commercial pursuits as decent and productive and to recognize those members of the "commercial class" as among the top ranks of society. A section of the talk was given over to explication of the relation of commerce to religion. King asserted that "this nation had its foundation in the love of liberty, and the spirit of commercial adventure. Impatience of political oppression and religious intolerance, founded the colonies."

Reason had concluded and history had shown that religious intolerance was to be avoided because it was a hindrance to the development of commerce. The liberty to engage in commerce and to practice religion were tightly braided. Moreover, it was through the free spread of religion—the efforts of missionaries in places such as the Sandwich Islands—that commerce was developed in places around the world where previously "superstition" together with "barbarism, licentiousness, and the bloody arts of paganism held undisputed sway." Religion was "instrumental in advancing commerce," and it did so when it was left free to do its work. Accordingly, where religion— that is, Protestantism—was left to do its work, without interference or intolerance, commerce flourished.[121]

The *Merchants' Magazine* reiterated the argument a year later, in 1841. Putting a finer point on the previous discussion of the topic, the magazine gave the example of Catholic Spain as a commercial failure. "Spain presents a striking instance," the magazine said, "of the deleterious effects of religious intolerance upon the enterprise and ingenuity of mankind." Spain's intolerance prevented her from properly developing in commercial enterprise the resources that she had claimed in the Americas. The "blighting effects of

88   CHAPTER TWO

superstition," alongside that intolerance, ruined Spain's chances. So also with Portugal in the Americas.[122]

In the immediate aftermath of the Charlestown and Philadelphia riots, Protestant writers energetically attacked Catholic intolerance around the world. They did so not only by repeating standard phrases about Romish priestcraft and popish superstition, but by pinning on Catholic territories additional charges of economic ineptness, destructive character flaws, and the caustic mingling of church and state, among other faults. Critics of Catholic territories took strong initiative in lengthening the list of charges against Catholicism and coloring it as even more dangerous than previously imagined. It was a leap ahead in anti-Catholic rhetoric and a new, determined effort to discover and catalogue all the various evils of Catholic rule overseas.

This occurred simultaneously with a Protestant bid to protect its flanks by redefining the behavior of New England Puritans as excusable given the time and place of the colonial setting. Later in the century Protestants would build on that depiction of Puritans, but first they would raise their voices more forcefully against overseas intolerance. And they would define themselves as righteous saviors of the persecuted as they campaigned to influence American foreign policy.

Making Foreign Policy

TOWARD A NEW ERA

Prompted by Protestant outcry, American politicians began in the 1840s–1850s to observe more closely the ways in which the United States conducted its relations with the various countries whose religious regimes they considered corrupt. At mid-century, political, military, commercial, and cultural interests all were central to discussions about what was happening in Russia, England, China, Austria, and other countries. But religion increasingly emerged as a salient topic in the process of American theorizing about how to construct foreign relations. Following the razing of the convent in Charlestown, and increasingly so after the Philadelphia riots, as Americans looked overseas for examples of the religious intolerance they had trouble acknowledging at home, they began to think about ways in which to address intolerance in other nations. The promoters of missionary enterprises overseas had been in conversation for several decades with U.S. government officials whom they thought might help them establish safe bases for their overseas conversion ministries. After Philadelphia, and in the midst of the sporadic but dramatic Mormon Wars, some concluded that the United States should take more initiative in its foreign relations with regard to religion. The idea that the United States should involve itself more directly and forcefully in campaigning against religious intolerance in other countries gained traction. That development is seen most clearly in the activities of a small but influential cluster of politicians in Washington at mid-century.

Momentum for the idea of American involvement in influencing the religious policies of other countries grew slowly, and in some cases required that government officials evolve in their thinking. Joseph R. Underwood (1791–1876), a U.S. Representative from Kentucky, was one of those persons who over the course of several years in the 1840s and early 1850s altered his view about the importance of religion in U.S. foreign relations. An agitator for emancipation who financed his own slaves' relocation to Liberia, Underwood, a lawyer, was an independent thinker when it came to conceptualizing America's place in the world. His speech in Congress in early 1848, a week after the signing of the Treaty of Guadalupe Hidalgo to end the Mexican War, strongly discouraged American annexation of Mexico while challenging the very idea of American manifest destiny.

Pleading with an audience that he read as desiring "not only the annexation of the whole of Mexico, but the whole of North and South America," Underwood argued that "it is alleged to be our 'manifest destiny' to overrun all this continent with the Anglo-Saxon race, and to extend the 'area of freedom,' and the liberty of conscience" to the world. But that project, of bringing freedom of religion to the world as part of an imperialist mission grounded in a manifest destiny, was, he said, unrealistic and improper. "I am unwilling," he asserted, "to enter upon military crusades with a view to teach our politics or religion to the other nations of the earth." It was not possible for "man to be taught true religion or the true principles of civil liberty and republican government at the point of a bayonet." American campaigns to forcefully Protestantize the world, as part of a program grounded in eradication of religious intolerance and promotion of freedom, would fail. Addressing those Americans who believed in manifest destiny, he concluded: "If these Christian people desire the extension of civil and religious liberty," they "must persuade and not attempt to drive."[123]

Five years after his speech on Mexican annexation, influenced by the burgeoning collective missionary initiative of the Protestant denominations and the increased post-Philadelphia Protestant finger-pointing at other nations for their intolerance, Underwood viewed things differently. He did not convert to an ideology of manifest destiny, or to the idea of militarily forcing religious freedom upon another country, but he began to articulate a new understanding of foreign relations that foregrounded religion. He submitted to the Senate a report on the importance of arbitration in international relations that catalogued the damage done by war and proposed measures that would, through diplomacy, reduce that risk. It recommended that treaties include language regarding the arbitration of differences. Underwood's report emphasized how "civilization and Christianity are making vigorous efforts to penetrate and enlighten the dark lands of barbarism and idolatry," and it implied that commerce and religious freedom should be conjoined. He observed, "It is difficult, where peace and commercial intercourse exist between a Christian and anti-Christian nation, for the missionary of the former to penetrate into the territories, and conciliate the favor and esteem of the heathen." Because war would make that even harder, arbitration was preferable. Underwood reported that his committee, in fact, had been keenly attentive to the voiced concerns of the American public in the preceding years, and that his thinking had been influenced by advocates for missionary work and for their safety overseas. "The political strength of the Christians of our country is such as to command attention and respect on all occasions," he confessed. "The members of this committee heartily concur with what they believe to be the Christian sentiment of the country."[124]

That same week in February 1853, Underwood filed another report. Its full title is self-explanatory: "Report of the committee on foreign relations to whom were referred numerous petitions praying for the adoption of measures as may secure our citizens residing in foreign countries the right freely and openly to worship God according to the dictates of their own consciences."[125] That report quickly garnered support from members of Congress and from the press. The measure had been the subject of correspondence among Representatives for two months, including a flurry of letters from mid-December 1852 that included Representatives John Allen Wilcox (Mississippi), Charles E. Stuart (Michigan), John L. Taylor (Ohio), Alexander H. Stephens (Georgia), John P. Hale (New Hampshire), Samuel W. Morris (Pennsylvania) and, especially, Senator Lewis Cass of Michigan.[126] It emerged from committee with strong backing.

Underwood's report found an especially sympathetic supporter in Lewis Cass (1782–1866), a pivotal figure in nineteenth-century American foreign policy. He considered the freedom to practice religion of one's choosing a human right, and has been identified as the groundbreaking petitioner for a U.S. policy of human rights in foreign relations.[127] His leadership was crucial to the launching of a long arc of foreign policy that reached a milestone in 2012 when Secretary of State Hillary Rodham Clinton tweeted that religious freedom was "a bedrock priority of our foreign policy."[128]

Cass, a brigadier general in the War of 1812, served as secretary of war under Andrew Jackson, as a U.S. Senator from Michigan for over a decade, and ended his career as secretary of state under President James Buchanan. He was the Democratic nominee for president in 1848. He did not identify as religious, but he brought his wife, Elizabeth, and their children to Presbyterian services on Sundays when he was in Detroit with them, dropping them off at the door and picking them up afterward.[129] His hallmark was his political pragmatism, which was construed as opportunism by his critics. His views of foreign policy were, according to his most recent biographer, constituted by his "politics of moderation." His view of religion was that it was useful in keeping order. One of his nineteenth-century biographers believed that "no man in his official character could be more tolerant or friendly to the religious rights of others." Another quoted him before the Senate professing that the United States had "grown powerful and prosperous by toleration," but "intolerance, religious and political, finds zealous [*sic*: zealots], and it may be that they will prove successful advocates, in this middle of the nineteenth century." Pragmatic, moderate, and professing a commitment to religious tolerance, Cass increasingly paid attention to religion in his thinking about foreign relations.[130]

Cass, like many Americans, was nervous about Austria. After Charlestown and Philadelphia, Americans blaming overseas countries for religious intolerance were especially perturbed by the Catholic leadership of Austria, which they believed was set on advancing the corrupt conspiratorial agenda of Rome. Cass does not seem to have been invested in the anti-Catholic aspect of the animus toward Austria. His son, Lewis Cass Jr., in fact was the U.S. minister to Rome at the time (1852–1860). But Cass was pragmatic, and he believed that religious intolerance was in the end bad for religion, and that meant that it was bad for order, commerce, and international collaboration. He believed that Austria was intolerant in its treatment of non-Catholics and that its intolerance was intertwined with its ruthlessly violent engagement of its political enemies.

In December 1849, Cass had become concerned about the brutal manner in which Austria had crushed the Hungarian Revolution in 1848, and he wished to explore the possibility of breaking diplomatic relations with Austria in protest. In January, he entered a resolution to the Foreign Relations Committee complaining that Austria, "a Power thus setting at defiance the opinion of the world, and violating the best feelings of our nature, in the very wantonness of successful cruelty, has no bond of union with the American people." After debate, legislators rejected the resolution. But it "nagged the national conscience," and it clearly nagged at Cass.[131] And there was public support. Senator Robert M. T. Hunter of Virginia, in a speech opposing the resolution, admitted that "a large portion of the press has sustained it."[132] Over the next several years, Cass kept himself informed about the situation in Austria and looked for an opening.[133]

Five years after his failed resolution, and in the wake of Underwood's proposal to diplomatically construct protections for Americans wishing to practice their religions overseas, Cass found his opening. He made the most of it. On May 15, 1854, he gave a speech in the Senate on the topic "The Protection Due to American Citizens When Abroad, in Their Rights of Conscience and Public Worship." A strongly worded proposal, but one that oddly claimed as well not to give offense to Austria, it commended Underwood's report but greatly extended and detailed it. More tellingly, Cass made clear that his proposal was a response to certain events that had recently taken place. It cited at the outset the "destruction of a convent in Charlestown" and the violence "in Philadelphia when churches and convents were burned to ashes by the intolerance of the mob," and it returned to discussion of those events later in its argument. At the same time, it criticized Catholic intolerance throughout.

In making his case through his speech for the need for protections of Americans overseas, Cass provided a thumbnail popular geography of religious intolerance in Europe. He condemned Spain, which "stands prominently forward in this unholy warfare" against religious conscience, and branded "Spanish Intolerance" a "byword and reproach among the nations of the earth." He reviled Spain's decree of November 1852 forbidding travelers in Spain from religious worship outside the Roman Catholic Church. Portugal was the "land of iron religious despotism," where innocent American Christians were shut up in prisons for attempting to practice their religion. Chile presented similar problems. Even Protestant kingdoms—Sweden, Norway, and various parts of Germany—oppressed Christian groups that did not comport with state views of legitimate religion, under a despicable system of "legal intolerance." In Russia, "imprisonment and Siberia await the missionaries. It is the most cruel intolerance formed into a system." The speech, overall, was a vivid overview of religious intolerance that began with sober recognition of the problems in America, but moved immediately to extensive and vigorous discussion of the intolerance of other nations. It largely focused on Roman Catholic countries, but briefly referenced a few that were not officially Catholic. Cass reminded his audience of their history as "the American people, founded, as they are, upon those principles of religious freedom which make part of our very political existence." He closed with a plea that Americans "see the persecutions and oppressions abroad," and firmly address them with a "new national policy."[134]

The response to the speech was immediate and overwhelmingly positive.

The *Christian World* advised that "the country owes much to the veteran general for this great speech. We trust that it will be extensively circulated and read." The magazine predicted that "great good will be done by this noble speech. It puts the question on its proper foundation." It raised consciousness across the nation, so that "indeed the whole subject of religious liberty, is exciting great attention."[135] It was by looking abroad that the Americans known by the *Christian World* were turning their attention to the problem of intolerance and its antidote, religious freedom. One of those who was hopeful for progress on that front was New Yorker Elizabeth Emma Stuart. She wrote to her son-in-law William Baker two weeks after Cass's speech: "Have you read Cass on Religious Freedom in a Foreign Country? It is good, & I believe will work good."[136] Stuart, a Roman Catholic, seemed to be able to read a sharp rebuke of Catholic intolerance overseas without connecting the dots to the predicament of her own American denominational membership.

Americans appreciated Cass's speech because they were primed to do so. There had been much public discussion of several specific cases of intolerance in Europe just previous to Cass's speech, and that discussion tended to be emotional, often outraged. Two events were of particular importance in setting the stage for Cass's speech in 1854. The first of those was the Jonas King case in Greece, and the other was the Madiai Affair in Italy. Both raised the issue of the practice of religion by Americans overseas and the question of U.S. responsibility in protecting Americans against foreign religious intolerance.

Jonas King was a single-minded and driven student at Andover Theological Seminary who began missionary work overseas in the early 1820s. He served in Palestine and Turkey, learned modern Greek, and assumed leadership of the mission to Greece in 1830. The schools he founded flourished, but he soon ran afoul of Greek law. His proselytism was aggressive and hypermasculine.[137] It included denigrations of Greek Orthodoxy and active discouragement of membership in the local Orthodox churches, and was not protected under Greek law. In fact, religious preaching outside the auspices of the Orthodox Church was prohibited. The independence movement that freed Greece from Ottoman rule in 1832 had set an agenda that subsequently included the severe limiting of any religious influence in the country outside of Orthodoxy. Missionaries were required to teach the Orthodox catechism if they wished to teach at all about Christianity. King did not comply with those laws, and in 1845 the government charged him. The Greek press described his crime as blaspheming and mocking Orthodoxy. King refused to stand down, however. He was tried and convicted for teaching "false doctrines," briefly imprisoned, and then exiled in 1852. Greek conservatives applauded the action, while Greek liberals criticized it.[138]

The ABCFM energetically publicized the case in America, characterizing the limitations placed on King's missionary work as an insult to the U.S. government. During 1852 the press stoked American indignation about the case, protesting repeatedly that Greek intolerance was unacceptable and that Americans must be free to practice their religion abroad. The issue of religious intolerance was an especially salient one given the events that had been occurring in the United States, and because the nation had begun to alter its views about its role in world affairs.

After mid-century, a group known as the "Young Americans" had formed as a small but ambitious reforming wing of the Democratic Party. Among their recommendations was that the United States reconsider the American policy of nonintervention that had coalesced during the presidency of George Washington.[139] Their efforts dovetailed with the related initiatives of groups and individuals with specifically religious interests. It found expression in publications such as the *National Era*, a reformist and abolitionist newspaper in Washington, DC, that had glimpsed in Catholic countries the vision of "a hell of religious intolerance."[140] Noting that "questions affecting our Foreign Relations have generally held a subordinate position, owing to our long established policy of Non-Intervention," the paper broached instead that the United States pursue a "policy of intervention in the affairs of the civilized world . . . where encouragement and aid could be rendered to the cause of Popular Rights."[141] The paper urged an "effort to place our Government actively on the side of Human Liberty, at home and abroad."[142] The paper seemed to have its finger on the public pulse. In considering the King case and the issue of religious rights of Americans abroad, some began to shift in their thinking about U.S. foreign policy.[143]

The similar case of the Madiai Affair unfolded over the course of several years in the early 1850s. It involved religious policy with respect to Italy. In the early nineteenth century, the Grand Duchy of Tuscany permitted Protestant chapels for British and Prussian diplomatic envoys, their staffs and visitors, and even the occasional local convert to Protestant religion. In those Protestant chapels were Protestant Bibles. After the Italian Revolutions of 1848 were put down by the French and Austrians, Pope Pius IX, who had become more reactionary during the revolution, together with Leopold II of Tuscany implemented conservative reforms. They forbade Protestant proselytism and prohibited Tuscans from attending Protestant meetings.

Tuscans Francesco and Rosa Madiai were middle-aged converts who provided lodging for visiting British families in the Piazza Santa Maria Novella in Florence. In August 1851, they were charged with breaking the laws regarding religion, and after court proceedings were imprisoned. They appealed to their Protestant clients and friends, and soon their cause was broadcasted throughout Europe in the religious press. Protestant groups in England were furious. They were strident in their protests, and they were heard. Protestants elsewhere, including in America, took up the call, and soon heads of state had become involved in the matter. Formal diplomatic protests, public demonstrations, and fraught negotiations with the Catholic Church and the Tuscan government eventually led to the release and exiling of the Madiai on March 15, 1853. But the affair so offended Protestant sensibilities and caused such an avalanche of critical discussion of religious rights that it remained a popular topic of discussion, engendering a nineteenth-century English-language neologism used to describe one's being persecuted for religious belief: to be "Madiai'd." A more important shorthand for the case that circulated widely was the Protestant summary of its root cause: they were punished for reading the Bible.[144]

Americans paid close attention to the Madiai. The affair prompted much debate between Protestants and Catholics, most of which involved the airing of opinions about the relationship of civil government to religious institutions. Some Catholics, aware of their difficult circumstances in America, sought to play it down. Father Patrick Moran, writing in the *Newark Daily Advertiser* in 1853, expressed doubt that the Madiai were incarcerated for reading their Bible.[145] Others among the clergy set out to defend Rome. One of those was John Hughes, "Dagger John," the newly elevated Archbishop of New York. At a time when the virulently anti-Catholic Know-Nothing political party was forming, Hughes, who previously had proven himself a formidable debater in public confrontations with Protestants, decided to stake out a strong Catholic position. He addressed the Madiai Affair in a long letter in the *New York Freeman's Journal,* an ultramontanist organ that he published for a time. "I claim to be a friend of civil and religious liberty," he wrote. He then proceeded to explain that in countries "already divided and broken up into sects, mutual toleration" is required. But in states where there was no diversity, no such responsibility existed. "Neither am I of the opinion that the Sovereign Pontiff, whose subjects are entirely Catholic and united in belief, is bound to throw his state open for the preaching of every form of Protestantism."[146] When Cass gave his influential speech in May 1854, he framed it as a response to Hughes's open letter, responding point by point to Hughes's claims while addressing the broader issue of intolerance overseas and the need for protection of Americans there.[147]

The international fuss over the Madiai Affair, Hughes's open letter, the King case, several related incidents involving British and American missionaries, and Representative Underwood's proposal of early 1853 all formed the immediate background for Cass's well-received speech. The recent violent conflicts between Protestants and Catholics—and increasingly Mormons—provided a deeper background. A crucial part of American memory, the forgettings and rememberings of trauma, was a third component. It constituted a powerful, ingrained identity that prompted an impulse to project American failures overseas—casting them as the failures of foreign nations—at the same time that it allowed grudging, but fleeting, recognition of those failures as national history. All of those components worked together to frame an idea about the rights of conscience of Americans abroad as an issue worthy of international intervention. Cass, as historians later observed, was advocating a new kind of foreign policy.

Archbishop Hughes, who was both an insider and outsider in American religious politics, saw clearly what was happening. Cass, said Hughes, was endeavoring to launch "a new national policy."[148] Foreign policy in fact was inching closer to an interventionist approach. The protection of American citizens abroad, and especially their liberty of conscience, was its focus. The *National Era*, in an article on "Our Foreign Relations" in 1853, remarked favorably on the signs of the emergence of that nascent interventionist foreign policy, and prospected something big: "We seem to be on the threshold of a new era."[149]

INTERVENTION

Cass's speech, for all the attention that it received and all the discussion it sparked, was not actually as dramatic an innovation as some editors believed it was. Interpreters of his proposal took it as a vision of foreign policy that would protect the consciences of Americans overseas.[150] And it was important in that regard. The rise at mid-century of the concerns that Cass articulated was centrally important in setting the course for coming decades. But in perspective those specific concerns were part of a broader network of issues having to do with foreign policy and religious intolerance. Cass's petition at the very least was indebted to a history of American treaty-making that long had prioritized freedom of conscience in American relations with other states. It is unlikely that the American public knew much about that history, as few Americans outside of State Department corridors were likely to be aware of the provisions of treaties with countries whose names they might not even have recognized. So, even though there already was an American track record, treaty-wise, the increasingly noisy public discussion that was assiduously fostered by the American Board of Commissioners of Foreign Missions and other evangelical organizations (together with the strident

Evangelical Alliance founded in London in 1846) evinced newness, a sense of American power freshly put to use in the service of Christianity. For the Protestant religious press and its allies, it was a rising up, the next step in the march of Protestant progress. But there was no great innovation in policy, only in rhetoric and vision. It was the spectacle of religious intolerance at home, and particularly anti-Catholicism, that made the effort to put religious protections in treaties appear more innovative than was actually the case.

Had Americans looked over the accumulating body of treaties with other nations, from the beginnings of the Republic up through the time of Cass's proposal for protection of American travelers, they would have learned that those treaties typically had included a clause making clear the expectation that foreign countries would allow freedom of worship for American visitors. The various treaties of "amity, commerce, and navigation," which established frameworks for relations between the United States and other nations, listed a treaty article—usually after a dozen others had addressed boundaries, trade, and maritime issues—that concisely stated that expectation.

Two early nineteenth-century treaties set the tone. The treaty with Algiers in 1816 included Article 15, where "it is declared by the contracting parties, that no pretext arising from Religious Opinions shall ever produce a disruption of Harmony between the two Nations; and the Consuls and Agents of both nations shall have liberty to celebrate the rites of their respective religions in their Own houses."[151] The treaty with Brazil in 1828 similarly included Article XIII, which addressed the issue in language that served as a template for subsequent treaties:

> It is likewise agreed that the most perfect and entire security of conscience shall be enjoyed by the citizens or subjects of both the contracting parties, in the countries subject to the jurisdiction of the one and the other, without their being liable to be disturbed or molested on account of their religious belief, so long as they respect the laws and established usages of the country. Moreover, the bodies of the citizens and subjects of one of the contracting parties who may die in the territories of the other shall be buried in the usual burying grounds, or in other decent or suitable places, and shall be protected from violation or disturbance.[152]

Together, the two early treaties expressed in language that was to become common the idea that Americans should be able to practice their religion in foreign countries "unmolested."

Subsequent treaties with Chile (1831), Venezuela (1836), Siam (1838), Mexico (1831), China (1858), and Japan (1858), among others, included the wording in some form. The treaty with Venezuela specifically asserted that: "Nei-

98   CHAPTER TWO

ther shall they be annoyed, molested, or disturbed in the proper exercise of their religion in private houses, chapels, or places of worship." At least seventeen treaties ratified between 1828 and 1860 provided for such protections.[153]

The extent to which Congress had awakened to the issue of religious intolerance overseas—how they began to take it seriously as a component of treaties rather than a boilerplate add-on—is visible in the case of a treaty of amity with Switzerland. In a convention at Bern in 1850, diplomats signed a treaty of "Friendship, Reciprocal Establishments, Commerce, and Extradition." Arriving at the U.S. Senate for ratification, it was rejected because it did not guarantee the protection of Jewish Americans in their practice of religion in Switzerland. Swiss discrimination against Jews was a simmering issue between Switzerland and several other European countries, and France in particular. Some Swiss cantons were especially rigid in their intolerance of Jews. The United States, aware of that problem, wished in foresight to secure its Jewish citizens in Switzerland as part of a treaty involving commerce and international legal collaborations.

Negotiations with Swiss diplomats were undertaken, but the relevant language remained: "The citizens of the United States and the citizens of Switzerland shall be admitted and treated upon a footing of reciprocal equality in the two countries, where such admission and treatment shall not conflict with the constitutional or legal prerogatives as well as Federal or State and Cantonal ones of the contracting powers."[154] Americans opposed the language because it would leave cantons free to treat Jews intolerantly. But the outcry against the treaty was driven by fears that it "could establish a precedent for discriminatory policies against American Protestants in Catholic countries."[155] For that reason, the Senate strenuously resisted, as did the White House, but the Swiss would not budge.[156] The treaty, when finally proclaimed in 1855 after several years of negotiation, included some altered language, but it did not protect the religious rights of American Jews in Switzerland.

The failure of the Swiss treaty in the early 1850s, just as the clamor for the protection of American citizens abroad was rising in Washington and in the press, reminded Americans that there was work to be done. It was a thorn in the side. The treaties of amity that had long seemed to guarantee religious liberty to Americans in various foreign countries appeared to mean little if the United States, in negotiations with a relatively weak European country, could not deliver assurances of protection to its citizens. A "new foreign policy," as Archbishop Hughes had critically characterized it, would be needed. Some Protestants believed that the turn to a new foreign policy was taking place. And it was true that Washington was viewing the business of religion overseas

PROJECTIONS   99

from a new perspective. But what was more certain was that the Protestant search for intolerance overseas now had a formal state machinery with which it could collaborate in projecting intolerance out of the United States into the affairs of other nations.

A further lesson derived from a look at antebellum treaties has more directly to do with American national identity. Foreign policy can be recursive in terms of its relation to the state that constructed it. That is, once projected, policy can rebound in various ways to influence domestic affairs. The processes by which that happens can be complex. But important changes in foreign policy, the new directions taken during transitional periods, sometimes leave traces of their unfolding. Those traces in some instances are visible in the process by which American ideals projected abroad came back to inform American life. As we shall see, the dynamics of such recursion with regard to religion have been especially important for understanding early twenty-first-century developments, but they already are in evidence in the mid-nineteenth century.[157]

An important consequence of antebellum U.S. insistence on religious protections for Americans abroad, expressed in a string of treaties over several decades and intensified at mid-century in public outcry, was the rebounding of that concern to the domestic setting. Treaties providing for religious protections, among other state documents, are official expressions not only of rules governing relations with other nations, but idealizations of America, of American aspirations to be a place where religious freedom is everywhere implemented and respected. What is conceptualized as good for an overseas setting can acquire a seeming objectivity and power that make it in turn adoptable domestically. What is advanced as a plan for religious liberty overseas can project aspiration on the part of a nation that has yet to fully implement the ideals that it preaches.

In certain circumstances, treaties serve as ways in which a state can define itself with regard to religion, by taking the opportunity of what would seem to be a document broached as essentially about another nation to express desiderata for its own political-religious order. Such circumstances, and outcomes, are represented by the Treaty of Guadalupe Hidalgo (1848), which ended the Mexican War. It was not a casual treaty of amity but a surrender document that addressed the rights of foreigners who were about to live as Americans in territories ceded to the United States. The treaty accordingly attended to the lives of people crossing the cultural and political threshold from Mexico to the United States. They could be addressed, in the treaty, to a certain degree as Others, as foreign objects, but at the same time had to be considered U.S. citizens. They occupied, during the brief period of the treaty negotiations, a liminal position in terms of citizenship. The treaty as a result was an unusual document, in that it offered a view of how a foreign population should be protected from religious intolerance at the same time that it directly defined how that also should be the case in America.

A bare-bones but clear vision for religious tolerance in America was embedded in the Treaty of Guadalupe Hidalgo. It is visible in an article added to the treaty that provided an explanation for the rights of Roman Catholics in annexed territories. Mexican Roman Catholics who suddenly found themselves citizens of the United States in 1848 were promised political and religious "rights" that would be, as the treaty stated it, "at least equally as good as that of the inhabitants of Louisiana and the Floridas."[158] In a statement longer than those in other antebellum treaties, the treaty guaranteed protection specifically to churches, schools, hospitals, "and other foundations for charitable or beneficent purposes." Furthermore, the treaty specifically explained that "ecclesiastics, corporations, and communities" received "the same most ample guaranty." Catholics were entitled to "the enjoyment of all civil rights," and none of their property, "whether individual or corporate," could be diverted to other uses. They were to be "free and exempt from all hindrance whatsoever." Moreover, the new Catholic citizens of America would be free to answer to their religious authorities, "even although such authorities shall reside within the limits of the Mexican Republic."[159]

The treaty of Guadalupe Hidalgo, in short, said what America was supposed to be, namely, a nation where there was no intolerance and where the free practice of religion was the everyday norm. Signed four years after the destruction of Catholic churches and neighborhoods in Philadelphia, it was in reality a strongly aspirational statement about religion in America. As such, it was part innocence, part benevolence, part condescension, and part memory of how bad things could get. It was a conceptualization of religious tolerance grounded in a recognition of the roles of houses, bank accounts, bureaucracies, political boundaries, hospitals, and human bodies. It articulated a reality more materially rich and complex and, simply, *lived*, than did the religion clause of the First Amendment or the language of previous treaties.

America was not yet ready to begin the process of looking inward, however. During the remainder of the nineteenth century and into the twentieth century, there were occasional attempts by persons from across the denominational spectrum to draw attention to the problem of religious intolerance in the nation. The direction, literally, had been set, however, and it pointed outside the United States and North America to the "twin" continent to the south. As intolerance spiked domestically, Protestant efforts to locate it internationally increased. There was not going to be a reckoning to reverse the pattern of denial and outsourcing that had coalesced at mid-century. South America became the object of concern, and the stories of intolerance there increased in number and were enriched with detail.

3

Protections:
The Nineteenth Century Turns—to the South

The Foreign Spaces of Americans

Some Americans condemned violent incidences of religious intolerance. There was pleading, among some Protestants as well as minority communities, for a more determined and effective implementation of state guarantees for religious freedom. Nevertheless, the national pulse beat Protestant and nativist for much of the period 1860–1940. The period opened with continued acts of violence against Catholics, Mormons, and other groups, and ended during the 1930s with an assortment of nationally influential religious demagogues who promoted religious intolerance through print media and the new communications technology of radio. Jews, Jehovah's Witnesses, and others emerged as additional popular targets for such intolerance, and Protestantism's certainty of its glorious destiny in North America and in annexed territories offshore remained strong.

Consideration of how a process of spatial othering took place internally in the United States during this period can help clarify how that process unfolded in an international context. From the era of the Civil War to the end of the Great Depression, a process of "internal orientalism"[1] consigned Catholics, Mormons, Jews, and several other groups to a status that was akin to how Edward Said defined the predicament of colonized populations. Internal orientalism in America, an exercise in spatial othering, shared much of the characteristics of the internationally projected orientalism that Said described. There were binaries that enabled the articulation of dominant group identity, distinguishing it from caricatures of subjected communities. Internal orientalism sustained an exalted national identity—in the case of America, it was an Anglo-Protestant identity—by setting and resetting cultural boundaries so as to maintain power. Because "a spatial dimension is usually inherent in the definitions of the Other,"[2] any process of making an other against which a nation can define itself will express that spatiality.

In recent years, "scholars have moved from applying an international scale of analysis to examining the operation of orientalist discourses *within* states." That process of orientalizing consists "of a deeply imbedded tradition and practice of representing the subordinate region as afflicted with various and sundry vices and defects." American writers, for example, have portrayed the South in that way.[3] In such a characterization it is a world apart, and one into which white non-Southerners through imagination have emptied the ugly parts of their own regional cultures. The result is not quite the same as if the Other was another nation, an overseas territory. But there are close similarities. Because the othered region is part of the national state, persons have a keener "dual attachment," a "sense of belonging to both the othered region and the national state."[4] There is, to invoke a term broached previously, a "dysfunctional attachment" between the othered region and the state (which is to say, in this instance, a dysfunctional attachment of non-Southerners to Southerners). But on those grounds there is also a likeness of internal othering to external othering. To conceive a group as an internal other enables a definitional drift into imagining that group as external. The elements of the relationship in each case are similar: for the dominant group there is a strong perception of spatial apartness, a feeling of threat, an effort to construct identity in opposition to the negative features of the Other, a complex and troubled attachment, and asymmetry of power.

In the case of religious groups, Protestant identification of internal others and conceptualization of them as spatially located apart from the territory associated with the exalted national identity is evidenced in nineteenth-century religious frictions. In such cases politics is imaginatively interwoven with space, and that politics is drawn in terms of dangerous relations between opponents. For example, the "popular geopolitics" that informed the internal othering of Mormons in the twentieth century exemplified how "geopoliticized space is also often represented as a fundamental threat to the nation-state."[5] Mormons, consistently defined spatially as a people apart, as members of a distal kingdom or political body outside the boundaries of a dominant Protestant culture, were considered a threat to the nation. Their threat was written into the spatialization of their otherness. It underwrote depictions of their community as a strange land, a foreign land, a far-off state.

Protestants' spatial othering of their religious opponents is evident in their relations with multiple religious groups, beginning with Catholics. Catholic immigration to the United States over the century commencing about 1820 took place in several waves. The steady immigrant trickle of Irish Catholics greatly increased during the potato famine of the 1840s. There were more immigrants from Germany and England as well. Although Catholic immigration during the antebellum era cannot be precisely calculated, one estimate puts the Roman Catholic denomination as the largest in America by mid-century.[6] In the late nineteenth and early twentieth centuries, another surge took place. In addition to Irish and German Catholics, there were Italians, Poles, and others, including an influx of French Canadians. By the 1920s, Catholics made up seventeen percent of the population. And as their numbers grew, so did the forces opposing them. Anti-Catholic publications, social movements, political initiatives—and everyday discrimination that was exemplified by the "No Irish Need Apply" signs that began turning up in employment advertisements in the 1850s—became more widespread and entrenched as the backlash against Catholic immigration grew.[7]

The messages coming from Rome in some cases frustrated Catholic efforts to find common ground with other Americans. Pope Pius IX, having experienced a strong rightward conversion after the revolutions of 1848, expostulated an increasingly conservative view of Catholicism. His *Syllabus of Errors* (1864) rejected the principle of separation of church and state and decreed as erroneous any claim against the Roman tenet that "the Catholic religion should be held as the only religion of the State, to the exclusion of all other forms of worship."[8] The doctrine of papal infallibility (1870) and later encyclicals that scolded some reform-minded Catholics for their "Americanism" contributed to Protestant fears that Catholics would not accept American democracy and would resist acculturation more generally.

The history of anti-Catholicism in America is well documented.[9] However, the full workings of Protestant imagination that made Catholics, as historian John Higham wrote, "strangers in the land" are less clear. Protestants, as Higham observed, took Catholics to be persons who did not belong in America. But Protestants did not object merely to the fact of a Catholic presence in American cities. Their objections were more complicated than that. Protestants were aware that Catholic religious loyalties were with Rome. And Protestants were troubled by the Catholic reverence for authoritarian hierarchy and the implications of that for Catholic capability to embrace democratic traditions. In many other ways, as well, Protestants thought Catholics simply did not fit into the picture. So, they took Catholics out of the picture. For Protestants, Catholics were not just politically un-American. Protestants imagined Catholics as geographically out of place. They were strangers in a profound sense: their hearts and minds were not in North America, but rather in Italy. For the most fervid Protestant nativists, Catholic bodies, and the communities they formed, paradoxically were there, too.

Protestant nativists conceptually banished American Catholics to Rome. They imagined Catholics to occupy a different territory, a different space, than did American Protestants. Of course Catholics were neighbors of Protestants in urban environments such as Boston, New York, and Philadelphia. But Protestants pictured Catholics as foreigners, and that meant abstracting them as inhabitants of foreign places. The imaginative process by which they did that was, to borrow a term from religious studies scholar Thomas A. Tweed, a kind of "translocation." Tweed has pointed out how Cuban Americans in the late twentieth century "translocated" themselves back and forth between Havana and Miami. Members of the immigrant congregation of a church in Miami, through rituals and symbols, and their devotion to "Our Lady of the Exile," inhabited, said Tweed, two religious spaces. In the context of Catholic devotional exercises, "the translocative diasporic rituals move participants spatially. They ritually remap Miami and reclaim Havana. To sing songs to the patroness is to travel to the land she protects."[10]

Protestants as observers and opponents of Catholics—and also as members of a community that was dysfunctionally attached to Catholics—"thought" them back across the ocean in the same way that the Miami Catholics ritually re-emplaced themselves in Havana. Protestants who consumed the enormous body of anti-Catholic writing over the century from 1860 to 1940 built stories out of what they read, and one of those stories was that the Catholic strangers truly were foreigners who somehow maintained a primary spatial relationship with Rome. In a way similar to how Tweed, as an outsider, believed that he recognized a community that was translocating to another country, Protestants believed they could recognize the Catholic community translocated overseas. There were crucial political differences and interpretive strategies that distinguished one case from the other, but the work of imagination in each was comparable.

The process of Protestant thinking about American Catholics as paradoxically citizens of Rome began with the belief that the first loyalty of Catholics was to Rome, not to the United States. That belief was repeated in myriad ways over decades and served as a foundation for other components of Protestant anti-Catholic reasoning. According to John L. Brandt's widely publicized *America or Rome, Christ or the Pope* (1895), bishops, first of all, swore an oath to the Pope. Brandt cited an oath given in the consecration of Bishop Burke in Albany in 1894, which included promises "to preserve, to defend, increase, and promote the rights, honors, privileges and authority of the holy

Roman Church," among other strong statements of loyalty to Rome. Brandt then remarked: "If that is not swearing allegiance to a foreign potentate, what is?" Remarking that no man can serve two masters, Brandt concluded: "The loyalty of the true papist is pledged to Rome. He is Romanist first."[11]

Priests also swore the oath, as *Popery: An Enemy to Civil and Religious Liberty, and Dangerous to Our Republic* stated in 1835. That oath made priests "the subjects of a foreign despot." And the rank and file, led by priests and bishops sworn to Rome, all gave themselves up to the service of Rome, whatever it might be. Joseph van Dyke explained in 1872 that they "lick the dust and swear eternal loyalty to a distant spiritual despot; who openly proclaim that their first allegiance is due to Rome's Sovereign Pontiff."[12] Catholics, according to the popular *Anti-Papal Manual: A Book of Ready Reference for American Protestants* (1876), "hold that their first and highest allegiance is due to the Pope of Rome. . . . They belong to him body and soul, and know no law save that which issues from the Vatican."[13] Not just the soul but the body was committed to Rome, a point that the most widely read anti-Catholic publication,[14] *The Menace*, repeatedly stressed. For the editors of *The Menace*, all Catholics were imprisoned, body and soul, within the walls of Rome, like nuns in a convent, whose bodies Protestants imagined as if they were in Rome: "Those within Rome's prison walls belong to Rome, body and soul."[15]

Their minds and bodies tied to Rome, Catholics, in Protestant imagination, lived apart from the United States of America. "These people belong to the Holy Father," said *The Menace*. Catholics lived on the other side of a boundary that separated them from the United States. "Yet no law can be thought of which will penetrate the inner places, the dungeons and passages where no light but that of a Catholic candle can pierce the gloom. THIS IS INDEPENDENT TERRITORY BELONGING TO ROME."[16] And just as the soul and body were located in Roman territory, so also were Catholic communities places unto themselves, foreign to the space of America. Germantown, Illinois, where German Catholics were the "sole inhabitants," was the subject of "a personal investigation by a *Menace* man" in 1914. His conclusion, trumpeted in the newspaper's headline, was that Germantown was a place "where Rome Rules Supreme!," a "Real 'Little Rome.'" And it was a place, ironically, where the school emphatically did not teach "geography."[17] Other Catholic towns and neighborhoods earned the same title from *The Menace*. "Buffalo, N.Y., the little Rome of the new world" was typical. It was a place where "Roman Catholic priests and their bamboozled lawyers and henchmen are conducting an Inquisition."[18]

When the Catholic Eucharistic Congress convened in Chicago in 1926, it was no wonder that the journalist Stanley B. Frost, author a few years earlier of a widely read book on the Ku Klux Klan, found the entire public proceedings "something foreign, something alien." The gathering was the "strongest proof of the actual alien character of Catholic instinct, thought, and the particular kinds of conduct derived from them." The displays of priestcraft, and particularly the spectacle of the subjection of the Catholic multitudes to ecclesiastical royalty, was "utterly at variance with our American tradition." Nothing about the event was American, and those who participated behaved as if they were visitors to America from overseas. Frost concluded that "one fact stands out: it was alien and foreign to America of the past, and even to America today."[19]

The enormous anti-Catholic print campaign, which remained strong through the Great Depression, provided Protestant readers with a vast amount of information and opinion about Catholics. Protestants, as they read, arranged that information, given in so many different kinds of stories, into patterns that allowed them to make sense of it. Readers of *The Menace* and other anti-Catholic publications were "cued" by those stories to think about the larger problem of Catholicism. Protestant readers, moreover, were "active readers" in that they sought to connect the dots in ways that reinforced narrative lines about the corruptions of Catholicism and its dangers to the nation. In general, "the genre of journalism begs for linking, for it is almost by definition incoherent. It is a daily sampling of a rushing flow of occurrences and observations, which has no beginning and no end. Readers must find (create actually) coherence through connection, interpretation, and inference. In a word, they link." That process normally led to certain kinds of inferences, and in the case of anti-Catholicism, one strategy in particular was important. That strategy was to uncover secrets, because "the most vivid form of linking is the detection of conspiracies."[20] In a cultural setting where secrecy and conspiracy already were of paramount importance, Protestants who created conspiracies out of news stories placed Catholics outside of an America committed to democratic ideals. The conspirators came from somewhere else. They were immigrants, strangers, foreigners. They lived in "independent territory." That territory might as well have been overseas.

Mormons, like Catholics, were an "alien people." The fact that they made the Rocky Mountains their "Deseret" after the departure from Nauvoo in the 1840s abetted Protestant understanding of them as inhabitants of a foreign land. The sense of them as spatially apart preceded their settlement of what later became the state of Utah and remained in full effect throughout the twentieth century.[21] But the combination of their residency in Utah and the strangeness of their religious beliefs and practices, in Protestant eyes, made the spatial othering of Mormons particularly strong.

Protestant thinking about Mormons became more entwined over the course of the nineteenth century with Protestant hopes to convert Mormons. Mormons, who were themselves the most determined of missionaries and the most ambitious, were always on the minds of Protestant mission leaders who dreamed of bringing Mormons into the fold of official American Protestantism, and in the process making them true Americans. But Protestants admitted that success in the mission field of Utah and other places where Mormons made their lives would not come easily. Trying to convert the Mormons was like trying to convert the inhabitants of an overseas country.

On their good days, Protestants such as Methodist minister C. P. Lyford could spin the problem so as to make it sound appealing: "Utah is a foreign mission field come to our own shores." Mormons deserved the same effort that Protestants might expend in going to Asia or Africa. But Protestants recognized the oddness of the circumstances, and frequently stated it in terms that captured the perception of similar/different that characterized their relations with all of their religious opponents: "Shall there be less effort to Christianize the very heart of our own country than we would give to the same people were they located in a foreign land?"[22] Hugh Latimer Burleson, the Episcopal Bishop of South Dakota, in the triumphalist missions narrative *The Conquest of the Continent* (1911), saw little difference a half century later: "The strongholds of Mormonism, then as now, represented essentially the problems to be found in a foreign land."[23] The author of *The Mormon Usurpation* (1886), addressing the U.S. House of Representatives, filled in the picture with human detail: "I am fully persuaded that it requires as much courage, patience, perseverance, and consecration to work in Utah as in a foreign country."[24]

Protestant missionaries and their supporters spoke for many Americans when they portrayed Mormonism as a foreign country. The machinery of Protestant missionizing influenced the foreign policy of the United States, and the language that missions writers used sometimes became watchwords for government officials who were charged with making foreign policy. So too did that language influence domestic policy. In addition to the writings and lobbying of missionaries, moreover, were everyday Protestants whose knowledge of Mormonism often came from missionaries—just as did their knowledge of Native Americans. Those Protestants, too, had a role in shaping policy by virtue of their influence conducted through other channels. Their sense of the spatial otherness of Mormonism was integral to their discussions of it. Even in the first decade of Mormon settlement in the Rockies, rank-and-file Protestants had spatially othered Mormons. According to the nineteenth-century constitutional historian George Ticknor Curtis, a non-Mormon defender of Mormonism, during the late 1840s "public opinion throughout the United States was at that time of one unanimous tenor. . . . They are well beyond the mountains, they are in a foreign land. . . ."[25]

The spatial othering of Jews, like the cases of Catholics and Mormons, had its own distinct circumstances. The spatial geopolitics of American Catholicism linked Catholics to Rome. The spatial othering of Mormonism was reinforced by the Mormon migration westward. The mapping of the Jews was influenced by beliefs that Jews formed an internationally coordinated network of corrupt financiers and other powerful figures who sought to direct world events from their secret headquarters. The rise of Zionism at the end of the nineteenth century reinforced the view of many Americans that Judaism was foreign, as did likewise the partially imposed and partially chosen consolidation of Jewish populations in urban ghettos. The Jewish self-understanding as a people in diaspora, a theological idea articulated by Jews and appropriated by antisemitic writers for their own purposes, likewise played a part in the forming of an American notion of Jews as spatially other.

American antisemitic propaganda grew more strident and was more widely circulated as the nineteenth century wore on. In the early twentieth century it reached a climax in the publication of *The International Jew*, a selection of columns from Henry Ford's *Dearborn Independent* that was published in the 1920s. Its influence on American thinking about Jews was significant. It is likely that "more than any other literary source, these articles spread the notion that Jews menaced the United States."[26] The book was partly fashioned out of a translation of the fabricated *Protocols of the Elders of Zion*, which had evolved over several decades before its publication in a fully developed screed in Russia in the early twentieth century. The book's depiction of the displacement of the Jews from any particular national territory through appeal to the imposed identity of the "International Jew" was a profound spatial othering of Jews. Its appeal among antisemites in America played, first of all, on the fact of Jews as an immigrant group, and thus to some extent displaced, but also upon Jewish self-understanding of diaspora, as a scattered community in exile. Overlaid on that initial conceptualization were an assortment of specific claims about the greed of the Jews, their deceptiveness and treason, their unethical business practices, lust for power, efforts to control the press, and intractable corruptness in relations with other groups. Having plotted against the world from the time of the Sanhedrin in antiquity, the aggregation of those features "is the ancient machinery that the Jew used" to acquire and maintain power.[27]

The Jew as the International Jew met secretly in locations all over the world to plan the undermining of governments and institutions. The international conspiracy that bound all Jews together was itself a surrogate nation, a space unto itself, with its own spatial perspective on the nations where Jews lived. The international cabal that lived in the interstices between states had its own ambitions to control world affairs through secret maneuvering: "There can be little doubt, however, as to the existence of what may be called a 'foreign policy,' that is, a definite point of view and plan of action with reference to the gentile world." Jews lived in their own territory, even as they were dispersed around the world as International Jews. "The Jew feels that he is in the midst of enemies, but he also feels that he is a member of a people—'one people.'" That spatial identity means that "he must have some policy with regard to the outer world." As Protestants thought about Jews in a territory set apart from the nations of the world, they recognized themselves as a community on the receiving end of a "foreign policy." Spatial othering of Jews was so thorough (and not just in America) that it resulted in a belief that there was actually a Jewish foreign policy—further proof that Jews were foreign. For American Protestants drawn to the notion of the International Jew, Jews populated a foreign place.[28]

Besides Catholics, Mormons, and Jews, other religious groups up to 1945 experienced intolerance. But in most cases they were not spatially othered. If there was a strongly perceptible connection to Protestantism, such groups were scolded, or attacked, or their members were jailed, but they were not imagined as inhabitants of another land. Even in the case of Jehovah's Witnesses, who began calling themselves by that name in 1931 and suffered badly through mob attacks on their houses of worship and mass arrests for refusing to salute the flag, there was no expression of a sense of their spatial apartness in the religious press. Having grown out of a Bible study group, the Watch Tower Bible and Tract Society, the denomination gave the appearance of an enterprise on the edges of Protestantism but still within the fold. For Protestant supervisors of national order, it was a community to be brought from the margins more solidly into fellowship with the large well-established churches rather than labeled foreign. That hopeful impulse likely was reinforced by the unrelieved tirades of anti-Catholicism that poured from the mouths of Jehovah's Witnesses leaders. It nevertheless remained common for critics to characterize Jehovah's Witnesses as deviants of some sort, and particularly so when their refusal to salute the flag during wartime earned them coast-to-coast disapprobation.

Foreign Time and the Puritan Specter

The early history of New England was a potential problem for Americans who proclaimed religious liberty and who believed in its deep roots in an American imaginary of divinely directed exceptionalism. Catholics, Mormons, and Jews could be spatially othered easily enough. But the case of the Puritans was more complicated. Puritans were the founders, the claimers of North American space, the makers of place, and indispensable actors in a foundational American myth. The cost of outrightly geographically othering them was too high a price to pay for whatever might be gained in narrative consistency. So the Puritans remained, but the time they lived in took on new significance, and because space and time are mutually constitutive, a way was found to relocate them as well: they were consigned to the space of a past so distant as to be a foreign space. It was a bold move for the guardians of the story of religious liberty, and a desperate one. And it was an indication of just how intensely Americans labored at repressing what they knew was true.

In antebellum America there was much public celebration of the "triumph of religious liberty." In later decades, as fear of religious others intensified and led to spatial othering, there was continued celebration of religious liberty. The United States, a place in North America, was not the land of Catholics, Mormons, Jews, and others. For Protestants who were busy imagining themselves more deeply into a religio-national identity as a collective shining city on a hill, those groups inhabited a different space. Thus in America, according to the most mature version of the Protestant fantasy of the Promised Land, there could be no religious intolerance. And throughout the post–Civil War period of intensifying Protestant rhetoric about the unsuitability of Catholics, Jews, and others as American citizens, the discourse of adoration of the principle of religious freedom coalesced more firmly. It also incorporated thinking about time alongside space, arguing that any intolerance that might have occurred in America was in the past—itself a foreign country.

As was the case in antebellum America, Baptists, somewhat self-congratulatorily, were among the most vocal in their praise of religious liberty. Samuel Howard Ford, addressing the United Baptist Congregations in 1889, offered anecdotes ending with the lesson of "the triumph of the principle of religious freedom" in America.[29] In Cincinnati, the *Baptist Quarterly Review*, in an article on the beauties of "Liberty and Toleration," used the same language in proposing that "much credit be given us for the triumph of the principle of religious freedom."[30] In Boston, as a campaign to honor Roger Williams by erecting a monument to him gathered momentum, the Baptist minister who served as a leader in that effort made a case for

Williams by linking him to the "triumph of religious liberty over irreligious bigotry and intolerance."[31] In nearby Connecticut, also in the late nineteenth century, the centennial celebration of the Baptist church in Meriden was animated by the claim that the congregation there "saw the full triumph of religious liberty in Connecticut, ten years before that desirable result was attained in Massachusetts."[32] The *Baptist Quarterly Review* in 1882 identified a special aspect of the triumph of religious liberty in America: "Religious liberty is not the offspring of mere greatness of mind or political sagacity. It was the child of *principle.*"[33]

Baptists were not the only ones who were happy about religious liberty. Spokespersons for other denominations used the same language, spoke about it on similar occasions, and similarly thanked themselves for being a part of making it a reality in America. With many voices representing many different groups, in the second half of the nineteenth century the phrase "triumph of religious liberty" became so much a part of everyday conversation—in textbooks, magazine articles, newspapers, and correspondences—that it became meme-like and often was printed in quotation marks.[34] By the early twentieth century it was a universally recognized condensed linguistic symbol of Protestant thinking about religion in America. It was a phrase that fell so easily off the tongues of those who did not see the religious intolerance around them that it became a standard shorthand for a range of ideas about the progress of the nation toward meeting its goals, indeed, the nation's success in accomplishing those goals. And so deeply did the phrase as shorthand make its way into everyday discourse that it became a part not only of the language of a dominant Protestantism in America, but of the religious commentaries by some Catholic, Jewish, Mormon, and other oppressed groups as well. The power of that idea—the triumph of religious liberty—was so strong and so compelling, and the idea so interwoven into the religious views of late nineteenth-century white Americans, that even some of those suffering from intolerance were drawn to it. The transcript of a speech by Rabbi George Jacobs, who addressed a crowd of Philadelphians at the ninety-ninth birthday celebration of American independence, reported that the statue to be sponsored by B'nai B'rith "will represent 'the triumph of religious liberty' . . . since it is to place, in the light of open day, the greatest glory of the American nation. . . ."[35]

Religious liberty "is that which we have always believed to be our most precious possession," said the *New York Times.*[36] It was the "back-bone of democracy."[37] It was entwined with political liberty. "They stand or fall together," said the Seventh-day Adventist *Liberty.*[38] Early in the twentieth century, it was clear that "we love to boast of American freedom, especially American Religious Freedom and we claim that it is the backbone of American civilization."[39] The popular textbook *American Ideals Historically Traced, 1607–1907* professed that "the country has completely accepted a second noble ideal, that of religious toleration." Wisconsin minister Joseph Henry Crocker explained that religious freedom was a realized goal, not merely a hopeful direction: "Our fathers established, not simply universal toleration, but perfect religious equality, by making it unconstitutional for any state to make any law establishing an establishment of religion. . . . We have practically realized this secular ideal."[40] New Yorker Joseph Bondy, analyzing *How Religious Liberty Was Written into the American Constitution* (1927), was sure that "religious liberty is looked upon as an everyday affair; it is hard to conceive of a time when it did not exist."[41] Religious freedom, the "triumph of religious liberty," was for most a fact of everyday life, something breathed from the air, a commonplace.

Even for those who insisted on a historical perspective, there was a vast distance between the past and the present. In *Phases of Religion in America*, W. S. Crowe, a Universalist minister from New Jersey, wrote that "the triumph of religious liberty" was a matter of "the forward march" of time and an example of "the idea of *progress*." It was, specifically, a world apart from the Spanish Inquisition.[42] For Protestants eager to see the spread of their religion worldwide, it was, Crocker suggested, "this march of Christ's followers towards religious tolerance" that would make that possible.[43] The Rev. H. W. Thomas of the People's Church in Chicago thought similarly. He predicted (somewhat underinformedly) in 1890 that this "greatest triumph of religious liberty" would soon spread: "England, and Germany, and France, and Italy are preparing to follow our example."[44]

The historical record of religious intolerance, with the exception of occasional references to the Puritans, did not show up in nineteenth-century school textbooks. That was the conclusion of Ruth Miller Elson over fifty years ago, and it is also my conclusion.[45] The master narrative of American greatness and exceptionalism was sterilized of reports of failures to implement religious freedom. The history of intolerance was subjected to erasure, and the story of the triumph of religious liberty ever more enthusiastically fostered. Overweening enthusiasm for the triumph of religious liberty moreover amounted to a means of forgetting the trauma of religious violence, a fact too hard to remember.

The "triumph of religious liberty" presumed a victory over European legacies of intolerance, but it also took as a point of departure the early history of New England. The Baptists had Roger Williams for their own origin story about the struggle to establish religious freedom. Williams, it was said, defeated the Puritans. In the building of a nineteenth-century historical narrative of American progress and Protestant advance, the triumph of religious liberty included prominently the contributions of Williams. But a key theme was triumph over the intolerance of the founders of New England, the Puritans. That theme was appealing because Americans were drawn to the Puritans as much as they were repulsed by them. Americans saw themselves in the Puritans and also condemned the Puritans for their religious excesses and violence. In the context of that relationship, Americans played a deadly serious game of remembering and forgetting in their discussions of religious intolerance and Puritan blameworthiness.

American Protestant reflection on the sins of the Puritans was rooted in ambivalent feelings about John Calvin. As the historian Thomas J. Davis has shown, nineteenth-century American textbooks progressively pictured Calvin as un-American. Calvin was associated with intolerance in textbooks that were otherwise "aggressively Protestant in outlook." By mid-century, textbooks only "presented a few select facts that assured Calvin had a negative image."[46] Mentions of Calvin, developed from stereotypes common in European textbooks, blamed him for sectarian narrowness and incitement to religious violence. Early in the nineteenth century, Alexander Fraser Tytler, Lord Woodhouselee's *Elements of General History* (1809) set the tone by asserting that "the ablest advocates of Calvin will find it hard to vindicate him from the charge of intolerance and the spirit of persecution."[47] From there, textbook authors such as Emma Willard, George Park Fisher, Samuel Baxter Adams, and others offered bits and pieces of information about Calvin—such as that he burned Servetus[48]—meant to cast him in an unfavorable light.

Nineteenth-century writers tied the Puritans to Calvin. In most cases the consequences were less than salutary for the Puritans. Charles Francis Adams, in the course of condemning the New England Puritans for their religious intolerance, firmly established the historical argument for disapproval of them in linking them to Calvin: "The simple fact is that the Calvinistic, orthodox tenets of the seventeenth and eighteenth centuries constituted nothing more than an outrage on human nature productive in all probability of no beneficial results whatever."[49] James Truslow Adams, the Pulitzer-awarded (1922) historian of early New England, characterized the Puritan religious attitude as a "hard intolerance." He expanded: "The Puritan, at last, was no more a believer in the political rights of an individual as such, or in democracy, than in religious toleration, and the leaders of Massachusetts denounced both with equal vehemence. Calvin himself, who most fully represents the political philosophy of the movement," was inconsistent and confused in his thinking about it, but with the Puritans was culpable in "block[ing] the path to toleration."[50] Brooks Adams's *The Emancipation of Massachusetts* likewise viewed Puritan intolerance strongly in connection with its Calvinism, and other writers variously warned against Calvinistic attitudes that led to hatred, intolerance, and violence in early New England.[51]

The central problem with Calvinism, and the hereditable fault that befell the Puritans, was its sectarian character. Sectarianism was a central anxiety of Protestant Americans in their engagement with Catholics and Mormons in the nineteenth century, and awareness of it informed the American "paranoid style."[52] Americans viewed sectarianism, with its demands for purity and dominance, as a framework for secrecy and conspiracy, and especially as a home for undemocratic ideas and attitudes. Early twentieth-century sociological study "considers and describes early American Puritanism and its New England theocracy as the deeply medievalist and 'most totalitarian' subtype of an otherwise authoritarian Calvinism, and . . . the most repressive" movement in Christian history—alongside feudal Catholicism. New England Puritanism was the example of the Weberian "pure sect."[53]

The *Friends' Review* predictably cast its own vote with Weber that the Puritans were "the strictest" sect in New England.[54] More pointedly, Oscar S. Straus, in his speech to Yale alumni in 1896, reminded his audience that "the cradle of religious liberty has been rocked by the worst passions of mankind. Until comparatively recent times, every sect was intolerant from conviction," so that in the days of John Winthrop, "America was not an inviting country."[55] Albert Bushnell Hart lamented "the sectarian spirit of New England Puritanism,"[56] and for Protestant minister George Lorimer, writing in 1877, the "triumph of religious liberty" in America was a victory over "sectarian prejudice," preeminently visible in the struggles of Baptists against their fellow New Englanders.[57] Sydney George Fisher, author of the popular *Men, Women, and Manners in Colonial Times* (1898), proposed even how Cotton Mather had turned the table on Roger Williams, the figurehead of Baptist struggles against intolerance, in berating Williams for "the autocracy of that sectarian spirit" within Williams.[58]

The Puritans for all of their sectarian spirit and intolerance nevertheless were accorded some understanding by nineteenth-century writers. That did not mean that the complaints about Puritan intolerance ended. If anything, the rhetoric condemning it grew sharper. After mid-century, however, almost all who wrote about them in textbooks, journals, and magazines made accommodations to the Puritans, and spun their history in ways that were meant to save the Puritans from themselves. The influential historian George Bancroft, who seemed to hold back little in his condemnation of Puritan religious intolerance, opened the door for their rescue with the publication of his *History of the United States* in 1834. Others subsequently rushed in. Bancroft, as we have seen,[59] had sought to salvage the reputation of the Puritans by situating them in another time, and he explained that much consideration had to be given their imprisonment within the historical structures that conditioned that time. It was a time, he said, before progress had brought the principle of religious liberty to the forefront of political theory and social life. Bancroft also interpreted the Calvinistic influences as a mixture of undesirable sectarianism and a valuable emphasis on struggle against tyranny. Puritans were staunch advocates of freedom, said Bancroft, and Calvinistic or not, they were to be congratulated for that.

Bancroft's primary emphasis, and that of the great many writers who followed his lead, was that the Puritans were from another time. Because they were from another time and did not have the advantage of knowing that political liberty and religious tolerance were of the same cloth, they made a mistake.

The assignment of the New England Puritans to another historical period thought to differ greatly from the nineteenth century relocated them not only temporally, but spatially as well. To speak of the Puritans as part of a remote past was to speak of them as part of a faraway space. As Sergei Prozorov has argued in a recent discussion of spatiotemporal othering in international relations theory, "*every* gesture of othering is both spatial and temporal." For Prozorov, moreover, "the interdependence of spatial and temporal othering is not merely a contingent *empirical* fact rather a *transcendental* condition of every historical object that constitutes a political subject." The process often involves a deliberateness and a telos. "Temporal othering is a self-reflexive project of re-engaging with one's own history," and often amounts to a "project of self-transcendence, purging the traces of its past from its present and thus not letting it become its future."[60] To put it another way, "the past is a foreign country."[61] When nineteenth-century writers so decisively confined New England Puritanism to a clearly bounded past, they spatially othered the Puritans. The New England Puritans and the world they made became a foreign country.

Historians who recognized that the Puritans were intolerant but who wished to give them good account hastened to explain that things were different then, and that an "Old World," different from the "New World," shaped the thinking of Puritans. At mid-century, a Boston magazine commenting on the role of the Puritans in New England admitted that "they rather hated toleration." But "at that time religion everywhere was a matter of state regulation; everywhere the right of the state to control the faith of its subjects was fully conceded. The emigrants brought away with them from the Old World the doctrine of conformity in religion."[62] Charles Francis Adams in admonishing Puritans for intolerance likewise put it on their history: "Wherein did they differ in this respect from those of the established churches of the Old World against whose persecution they so loudly and so properly bore witness?"[63] In Philadelphia, a speaker discussing religious freedom and the role of early New Englanders couched it in more consolatory language: "a kind new mother could be found in the *new* world to replace the harsh old mother in the *old* world."[64]

The past that shaped the Puritans was a past of long ago and far away. Colonial America did not know what Americans knew in the nineteenth century. The *Chicago Daily Tribune*, in 1876, reviewing a book about New England history, wrote: "Much as we respect those old Puritan saints as founders of an Empire, they would not be agreeable people to live with in our day. What is now called religious freedom was then as unknown as the steamboat and the electric telegraph."[65] President Taft, speaking to a crowd at the 250th anniversary of Norwich, Connecticut, about the importance of religious freedom, made the usual remarks about the intolerance of the Puritans, but before he lost his New Englander audience added that "the truth is that in those days such a thing as freedom of religion was not understood." The president concluded—this was in 1909, as the second coming of the Ku Klux Klan was gestating—"We have passed beyond that now."[66] Other Connecticut observers of the history of New England, the editors of the Yale newspaper, got noticed by the *New York Times* for their own phrasing of the historical process. "College Newspaper Says the Pilgrim Fathers Learned Intolerance from Their Oppressors," ventured the *Times* headline. The *Times* then quoted the college paper: "From the intolerance of their oppressors they learned intolerance, and like them, had little sympathy for people of other persuasions."[67] That was the past, another time and another place. Puritans had lived in a place that did not know about religious freedom.

Nineteenth-century historians generally agreed that because of progress, Americans outgrew the Old World and the intolerance that it had bred in the Puritans. George Edward Ellis, president of the Massachusetts Historical Society, compared Puritans to "Papists and Prelatists" for their spirit of intolerance and their active persecution of religious others. But he characterized it as a phase: "These intolerant principles in the methods of all religion mark stages in the struggles of progressive liberty, light, and knowledge."[68] W. S. Crowe thought similarly, depicting "the triumph of religious liberty" overall in America as evidence of the march of progress away from the Spanish Inquisition. Puritans were other, as people living in a foreign land were other. At the same time they were the forefathers, the stock from whom many

Americans were descended, and crucial shapers of an American view of social and political order. Like Catholics and Mormons, they were imagined as foreigners, but at the same time, here they were.[69]

In the end, nineteenth- and early twentieth-century commentators on the intolerance of Puritans made compromises. In the end, it was Bancroft's claim that the Puritans were intolerant but also proponents of a principle of liberty that influenced the narrative about Puritan behavior. The *Christian Advocate* in 1886 translated that into religious images that its readership might be expected to understand. "The faithful pen of the historian shows," said the *Advocate*, "that as iron and clay were blended in the feet of Nebuchadnezzar's image, so was the clay of human passion, stern manners, and cruel intolerance mingled with the iron of Puritan courage, endurance, energy, educational zeal, and conscientious piety."[70]

For a readership that preferred a more academic approach, the commentary in *Life* magazine about the same time summarized the state of historical discussion of the Puritans. In a review of Harvard historian John Fiske's *The Beginnings of New England or, The Puritan Theocracy and Its Relations to Civil and Religious Liberty*,[71] the magazine summarized the book's argument:

> The author frankly confesses that "the story is full of instances of an intolerant and domineering spirit, especially on the part of Massachusetts, and now and then this spirit breaks forth in ugly acts of persecution." This was the point of view chosen by Brooks Adams in his caustic book on "The Emancipation of Massachusetts," which revealed the bigotry and fanaticism of the New England Puritans.
>
> Mr. Fiske claims in extenuation that with all its faults the Puritan theory of life contained within itself a curative principle—the principle of the equality and liberty of all men in the sight of God.[72]

It can be argued that "in the late nineteenth century, the place and meaning of Puritan were evoked in order to determine what America means," and that intense new scrutiny of the Puritans rested on "the delinking of Puritan ideals from theology."[73] That seems to have been Fiske's agenda. But all such projects aimed at salvaging something of the Puritan legacy were problematic. They required a certain amount of mental gymnastics, of separating some parts of the record from other parts, and of interweaving parts that hung together poorly. Because the Puritan past was a traumatic one, and because that trauma continued to influence the way Americans addressed the New England past, a certain amount of anxiety was always present in discussions of the Puritans, even in the late nineteenth century when a pragmatist approach to puritanism emerged in historical scholarship.

Historians were not unaware that their performances of saving the Puritans were problematic. Charles Francis Adams, tackling the question directly in his critical study of Massachusetts history and historiography, asserted that "there was almost no form of sophistry to which the founders of Massachusetts did not have recourse then." By the same token, "there is almost no form of sophistry to which the historians of Massachusetts have not had recourse since,— really deceiving themselves in their attempt to deceive others." Those who have tried to bring forward something positive about the Puritans "have, so to speak, wriggled and squirmed in the presence of the record."

A few years after the publication of Adams's book, the Tennessean Oliver Perry Temple argued that it was even harder to get a clear bead on the Puritans than Adams had proposed, and that there was a lot more squirming than even Adams had admitted. Commenting on the "narrowness, bigotry, superstition and crime . . . and cruelties against men" that took place in early Massachusetts, he cited Adams's remark that historians had "wriggled and squirmed" a good deal in addressing that history. He then upped the ante: "But I am not sure but that Mr. Adams 'wriggles' a little himself when he comes to explain the cause of this very extraordinary condition of things in Massachusetts under Puritan domination." Adams, said Temple, in fact "squirms, as he terms it, at their record, which he says they 'can not escape.'" The truth was that the Puritans had left "a gloomy record behind them," and that any attempt to save them from it required displacing them spatiotemporally: "The most and utmost that can be said in their defense is, that it was the fashion and the spirit of the age to persecute."[74] Adams, Temple, and other historians felt the trauma but did not name it.

One positive lesson that most writers attempted to extract from their research of the New England Puritans, at least as far as religion was concerned, was that religious liberty and political liberty were conjoined. The concept of the full interwovenness of those two kinds of liberty was, for example, fundamental to the highly visible early twentieth-century Seventh-day Adventist campaigns against Sunday laws. But for those whose Puritan studies undertook to explore "what America means,"[75] the engagement with Puritan history was very difficult. There was, indeed, much wriggling and squirming, much of what *Putnam's Monthly Magazine* called "an unconscious trial of the institutions and conduct of the past by the ideas of the present," in order to "make an estimate of the Puritan character, in reference to religious intolerance."[76] The Puritans appeared as complete strangers at times, as foreign as the people of Siam. At other times they were remembered as kin, as founders and models. The conscious and, more importantly, unconscious remembering of them could not escape that disjuncture.

A few Americans, finally, refused to believe that the Puritans were that much different from contemporary Americans who practiced religious intolerance and who promoted it in organizations and social movements. The Boston Unitarian minister Albert C. Dieffenbach was one of those. Dispirited by the rapid rise of Fundamentalism in the early twentieth century—because of its sectarian and autocratic spirit—Dieffenbach published *Religious Liberty: The Great American Illusion* in 1927. It was read and discussed in some circles, largely academic ones. He argued that "the battle between Modernists and Fundamentalists in our day has not created but only disclosed conditions that have controlled Protestant churches these four centuries."[77] There was no "triumph of religious liberty" in America. Fundamentalists within the Baptist and Presbyterian denominations were joining state to church and aimed to persecute those who did not get into line with their moral standards and social practices. For Dieffenbach, "Religious intolerance is to-day one of our controlling factors in daily life" and "religious liberty is the greatest illusion extant in this country."[78]

Some of Dieffenbach's anxiety about the rise of Fundamentalism was his association of it with the Ku Klux Klan—"the Fundamentalist Ku Kluxers"[79]—which, in its second coming, had grown rapidly after 1920 to claim over a million and a half members. His reading of the KKK as Fundamentalist was accurate. But more telling, in terms of the attitude of the Klan toward religious freedom, was the Klan's veneration of the Puritans as the agents of religious and political liberty. Alma White, an ordained Methodist bishop and founder of the Pillar of Fire Church that partnered with the Klan, wrote in *Klansmen: Guardians of Liberty* that the Puritans "did not come to America as mere sightseers or adventurers; they came to establish principles that would liberate the human race from the tyranny of the Old World." The United States, said White, "was founded on the principles of the Protestant faith." Those who threatened that legacy and those principles—Catholics, Jews, African Americans, and others—were not real Americans.[80]

White reinforced her portrayal of the Puritans by subtly de-othering them temporally (and thus spatially): Samuel Adams and Paul Revere, as well as George Washington, were Klansmen. As historian Lynn S. Neal observed, White stated her case in favor of the Puritans and their "principles" by "merging the American past and the Klan's present."[81] It was a present—and a past—to which Dieffenbach was opposed. It was a past about which academic historians squirmed when they tried to recoup it. But in the early twentieth century, it was a past—and a present—that many Americans, whether they were Fundamentalists, Klansmen, or others, embraced as populism gathered momentum nationally. In coordination with that project, writers and editors made great efforts to assert the power of Anglo-Saxon Protestantism, "this race of unequaled energy," as Rev. Josiah Strong wrote in *Our Country* (1885), that "had the largest liberty, the purest Christianity, the highest civilization" on earth.[82] Anti-Mormon, anti-Catholic, and racist, Strong, a leader of the Evangelical Alliance, looked forward to the global triumph of American Protestantism. He seemed untroubled by the problems of colonial New England, and perhaps, as was the case with White, he simplistically had conflated an idealized past with the present. His books depicted a future in which there ultimately were no foreign lands, only American Protestant power ruling an empire of fortunate souls rescued from superstition, priestcraft, and tyranny.

Forays into Internationalism

As Americans located Catholics, Jews, and Mormons overseas and put Puritans into a spatiotemporal box—a Pandora's box, in essence—that both remembered them and forgot them, they sharpened their gaze internationally. Politics and economics were centrally involved, and the muscular post–Civil War stature of the United States was crucial to the new discussions about America's role in the world. Religion also played a part in the growing internationalist perspective of Americans, its influence more powerfully felt in the corridors of power in Washington.

The failure of the South to construct an alliance with Great Britain during the Civil War contributed to the fall of the Confederacy. So too did the survival of the United States under one flag after 1865 bear on the failed ambitions of French ruler Napoleon III in Mexico, who, in a brazen attempt by an Old World power to recolonize the Americas, initiated a takeover of Mexico in late 1861. When the Mexicans collapsed that attempt to extend the French empire, and executed Emperor Maximilian I in 1867, part of the reason for the French defeat was the powerful reemergence of the United States from a Civil War that had prevented it from enforcing the Monroe Doctrine.

In the latter 1860s, a well-armed United States not only gave notice of its intent to protect the hemisphere from European interventions, but also demonstrated an interest in expanding its own territory with potential annexations in the Caribbean and Latin America. President Grant sought to annex Cuba, but Secretary of State Hamilton Fish (1869–1877) and Congress were not convinced that it was the right course for the nation at that time. William Seward, the previous secretary of state (1861–1869), and Nathaniel P. Banks, architect of the Alaska Purchase in 1867, had collaborated with Grant in a vision for U.S. expansion. One part of that plan, for Grant, was to acquire Venezuela. Another component of that vision called for the annexation of

Santo Domingo in 1870, but Grant's treaty implementing that action failed in a ratification vote. Aside from Alaska and the annexation of Midway (also in 1867), there was little to show for the aspirations of the Grant administration, and nothing as concerned territories to the south of the United States.

In subsequent administrations, there was periodic discussion about annexation, and especially regarding Cuba, which long had been of interest. There was a deep history of American interest in the island. President Jefferson thought Cuba could be annexed when he was presented with a proposal by a Cuban delegation. He remained positive about it, writing to President Monroe in 1823, "For certainly her (Cuba) addition to our Confederacy is exactly what is wanting to advance our power as a nation to a point of its utmost interest."[83] President Polk subsequently offered to buy Cuba from Spain for 100 million dollars, and the Ostend Manifesto, a secret diplomatic initiative concocted by parties wishing to see Cuba enter the Union as a slave state, offered 130 million dollars to Spain for the island in 1854, only to be refused. Other less formal but equally fruitless initiatives were hatched over the period of the Ten Years' War (1868–1878), a failed Cuban rebellion against Spain.

In spite of the interest in Cuba, Santo Domingo, and some other neighbors, American hemispheric interests in the nineteenth century had not been clarified. Ideas about the direction of foreign policy were shaped and reshaped by the constantly shifting currents of domestic politics and relations with European powers. The mismatch of vision with political will to implement plans of annexation was a characteristic feature of U.S. foreign policy for decades after the Civil War. There "emerged a dynamic that characterized the remainder of the nineteenth century," namely, that "assertive foreign policies would be formulated, if only partially achieved (if at all) in the face of domestic and foreign opposition, often to be abandoned, only then to resurface after a fallow period."[84]

While formal territorial expansion of the United States was minimal in the latter part of the nineteenth century—particularly in relation to the enormous enlargement of the British and French empires—the commercial interventions that Americans made grew steadily grander. Investors poured money into Mexico after the Civil War, and investments in Caribbean islands followed suit. In Cuba, a parade of former Confederate military leaders and prominent merchants built for themselves new lives on sugarcane plantations where slaves labored until the abolition of slavery in Cuba in 1886. Generals Jubal Early, John C. Breckinridge, Robert A. Toombs, Birkett T. Fry, John B. Magruder, Hamilton P. Bee, and William Preston were among those who decamped to Cuba after Appomattox.[85] Joined by many other former Confederates, some of the new arrivals stayed to establish vast plantation operations. The city of Cardenas became known as an "American city" on the north coast, and Havana was filled with American merchants and traders and cane growers. Americans introduced transformative technology, capital, and credit. At the end of the century, there were cases made for political intervention based solely on American economic interest in Cuba. The Spanish American War fought in 1898 accordingly was "the culmination of nearly half a century of commercial expansion into extracontinental areas."[86]

In the case of Cuba, American Protestant missionaries followed in the footsteps of the American investors. Some efforts had been undertaken before and during the Civil War, as the Protestant missionary societies began to lay plans for their evangelization of the world. Young men and women trained their sights more often on Asia and the Holy Land, orientalized places that were romantically depicted as waiting challenges for the Christian gospel, than on the Caribbean. Nevertheless, Protestants looked to Cuba as a mission field ripe for the taking from an intolerant Spanish Catholic regime that oppressed the spirit alongside the body. But the news that the early waves of missionaries sent back from Cuba in general was not good. Missionary Quakers complained in 1864 that intolerance was at its height, the mission enterprise arduous.[87] Subsequent reports largely confirmed that judgment for as long as Spain ruled the island. In 1869, an American journal outlined how "Cuba has no claim to the appellation of the 'Fortunate Isle,' nor her people to the title of 'The Blest.'" Under "the iron rule of Spanish intolerance," the scourge of "tyrannical misrule" in civil and religious matters, the people of Cuba struggled in vain in their "Unfortunate Isle."[88]

Speaking more directly to the point of Spanish Catholic domination of the island, the widely republished "Popish Intolerance in Cuba" addressed the problem in 1854 just as Lewis Cass was getting ready to challenge the U.S. Senate to protect the religious behavior of Americans overseas. Exemplifying the emergent interest of the U.S. government in looking after Americans in their activities in foreign lands, the article described the difficulties of an American Protestant in finding a burial place for his wife, who had died during their visit to Cuba. The case was about "the protection of American citizens and their enjoyment of their rights of conscience, and of religious worship, and to bury their dead." The claim made for American religious protections overseas was at the time starting to get traction in America alongside similar cases: "It is quite time that all the governments with which we have diplomatic relations, and to whose subjects the most perfect and civil liberty are granted and guaranteed when they come among us, should reciprocate the same."[89] The corpse of the wife had to be smuggled out of Cuba for burial in the United States, and there was no diplomatic resolution to that problem or the others that Protestants in Cuba encountered until the end of Spanish rule in 1898. Cuba, said Protestants, was intolerant.

The reluctance of the United States to intervene in Cuban affairs— whether it be to abolish slavery, protect the religious activities of American visitors, or manage the profitability of American investors there—was grounded in the circumstances of both domestic politics and international relations. Until the 1860s, there was much debate about admitting Cuba, with Southern states advocating its annexation as a slave state. That debate raised a host of peripheral issues having to do with trade, government, taxation, and ownership that acquired political gravity and undermined productive discussion for the rest of the century. At the same time, in the international arena, the United States was cautious in its relations with Spain, preferring diplomacy to military action, collaboration to conflict. The extent of that caution was measured in 1873 when Spain boarded the American gun-running vessel *Virginius* in international waters, brought the crew to Havana, and executed fifty-three of them for aiding the Cuban rebels. The United States protested, but weakly, and Hamilton Fish eventually settled for an $80,000 apology. The event was remembered in early 1898 when the USS *Maine* mysteriously exploded in Havana harbor, killing 256 American sailors.

During the period of time that the United States jousted with Spain over Cuba, the Monroe Doctrine increasingly became a tool enabling intervention. Invented as a "doctrine" in the 1840s by President James K. Polk, it drew its lifeblood from President James Monroe's State of the Union Address delivered in 1823. Written largely by then–Secretary of State John Quincy Adams, the position of the United States vis-à-vis European powers was set out in terms just clear enough to politely threaten but also susceptible of interpretation as a plea for the neutrality of the seas. Addressing European powers, Monroe stated that "we should consider any attempt on their part to extend their system to any portion of this hemisphere as dangerous to our peace and safety. . . . as the manifestation of an unfriendly disposition toward the United States." Implemented initially as a noninterventionist policy, the Monroe Doctrine by degrees was invoked for a lengthening list of interventions or threatened interventions, all in the name of the protection of fledgling American republics or resistance to European recolonization forays. Accordingly, "the Monroe Doctrine of 1823, which ruled out foreign interference in Latin American affairs, became the Monroe Doctrine of 1912, which justified unilateral U.S. intervention in those affairs."[90]

President Grant drew upon the Monroe Doctrine in framing his case for annexing Santo Domingo in 1870. That reasoning ironically owed something to Hamilton Fish, who made a formal effort that year to explain what the

Monroe Doctrine had to do with American recognition of the emerging South American republics. Referencing an assortment of nineteenth-century American confrontations with European powers, Fish recalled how the Monroe Doctrine "was at once invoked in consequence of the supposed peril of Cuba on the side of Europe; it was applied to a similar danger threatened [*sic*] Yucatan; it was embodied in the treaty of the United States and Great Britain as to Central America; it produced the successful opposition of the United States to the attempt of Great Britain to exercise domination in Nicaragua under the cover of the Mosquito Indians; and it operated in like manner to prevent the establishment of a European dynasty in Mexico." Nevertheless, said Fish, "This policy is not a policy of aggression; but it opposes the creation of European dominion in American soil. . . . it does not contemplate forcible intervention in any legitimate contest but it protests against permitting such a contest to result in the increase of European power." Fish in the end admitted that there was "an apparent change of foreign policy on our part," and that the cause for that was U.S. determination to recognize and protect the new South American republics. The United States and those republics were "necessarily dependent on each other," he said, and he listed them to drive home the point of the emerging reach of America international policy: Mexico, Guatemala, San Salvador, Honduras, Nicaragua, Costa Rica, Venezuela, Colombia, Ecuador, Peru, Chili, Bolivia, the Argentine republic, Uruguay, and Paraguay.[91] He could have added Brazil.

The repurposing of the Monroe Doctrine into a means by which to justify intervention was greatly advanced by President Theodore Roosevelt in 1904, when he cited it as justification for intervention in Santo Domingo.[92] That bold action came on the heels of what had been a long series of interventions over the previous half century in Latin American and Caribbean territories that had culminated in the Spanish American War. The war accordingly was not a departure from American policy but the product of a maturing view of American priorities in the Caribbean and Latin America. By the time of the Roosevelt Corollary, the frame had been set for a more forceful projection of American power. In concert with that development, there was emerging an additional rationale for intervention closely bound to American ideas of religion, and to Protestant Anglo-Saxon religion in particular.

Toward the end of the nineteenth century, the turning of foreign policy, underwritten by a reinterpreted Monroe Doctrine, a racial confidence in Anglo-Saxon Protestantism, and a growing determination to exploit the human and material resources of the hemisphere, was especially visible in relations with South America. Religion played a central role in American conceptualization of what those relations should be. During the nineteenth century, the United States made treaties of amity with many nations, including the republics that began springing up in South America in the wake of successful rebellions against Spain and Portugal. Those treaties included provisions for respect of religious worship and "liberty of conscience." Treaties signed with Ecuador (1839), Bolivia (1858), Paraguay (1859), and Nicaragua (1867) all contained the boilerplate language regarding protection of American citizens' religious activities in those new nations.[93] But such treaty language, it turned out, was not always implemented. According to many Protestant observers of the South American scene, those terms frequently were not honored. To those observers, it looked as if South America was a cesspool of intolerance, its inhabitants the victims of a ruthless and brutal Catholic regime that crushed all efforts to deviate from the ecclesiastical and theological orthodoxy of Spanish or Portuguese Catholicism. Even as the liberated territories coalesced as republics, that intolerance, said American Protestants, remained ingrained.

When Americans thought about South America in the nineteenth century, they fantasized about an exotic place, lush with greenery, snow-covered mountains, spectacular riverways, beautiful animals, and fascinating, unusual people. They also thought about it as a Roman Catholic stronghold, intolerant in the extreme and violent in its treatment of those who would not toe the Catholic line. Both of those ways of imagining South America were embedded in the prevailing notion that South America mirrored the United States. American observers of South America would not consciously admit that intolerance in South America was similar to the intolerance on display in the United States. But that sense of South America as a reflection of American problems, in the "squirming and wriggling" minds of Protestants who wrote about South America, nevertheless informed much American thinking about the twin continent. Americans projected onto South America the reality of intolerance at home. That does not mean that they did not actually discover incidences of intolerance in South America. There were enough stories of such intolerance to vividly animate the letters of American missionaries to their northerly relatives and colleagues. Rather, Protestant Americans built a theory about the religious predicament of South America out of a mixture of those reports of intolerant incidences and their ongoing displacement of the reality of religious intolerance that was taking place in the United States. All of that process was informed by repressed memory.

Rescuing the Twin

In order to appreciate the pattern of thinking that characterized Protestant estimations of South America, it is useful to bear in mind that Americans commonly imagined that continent in a peculiar but distinct relationship with North America. When Hamilton Fish asserted that the United States and South America were "mutually dependent," he was referencing not only the conjoined commercial, trade, and political interests of the involved parties but a more profound awareness of interwoven ideals and perhaps destinies. American professions of approval for the founding of republics in the former imperial territories of the European powers were as much expressions of a sense of kinship with South America (beginning with the fact that the United States similarly had freed itself from British rule) as they were signals to European powers that intrusions in those places would be unacceptable.

Louis Agassiz, the Harvard professor of zoology and geology, after visiting the Amazon River with his wife and comparing it to the Mississippi River basin, wrote with her in 1868 that it manifested "a further comparison between the twin continents of North and South America."[94] That phraseology was typical throughout the rest of the century, as more Americans related their experiences of visiting South America. By the early twentieth century, it occurred commonly even in writings that were meant to offer analyses of the political and social systems of the various nations of the continent. A writer for the *Chautauquian*, in commenting on American policy in South America, set his thinking in the context of "the twin continent," just as did the Rev. Francis E. Clark, an Andover graduate and founder of the enormous international Young People's Society of Christian Endeavor, who spoke of "our twin continent to the south."[95]

The *Baptist Missionary Magazine*, toward the end of the century, took to calling South American nations "sister republics."[96] William Taylor, in *Our South American Cousins*, spelled out in more detail what that meant: "The two Grand Divisions of the New World, discovered contemporaneously, their histories parallel in time, peopled by races derived from a common stock, having a family surname in common, and linked by a band of Nature's own making, may be regarded as Sister Continents." He emphasized the human commonality: "Their respective populations are kindred-cousins each to the other, in the great Race Family that is spread over the globe."[97] The people of the United States were kin to their neighbors in the twin continent to the south. Their histories and destinies were entwined.

Protestant writers hopeful of missionary progress in South America were particularly drawn to the idea of the kindred, the twin, the sister. The enthusiastic Harlan P. Beach and his fellow authors of *Protestant Missions in South America* (1906) explained the relationship in a section titled "Kinship with the United States in Physical Conditions and Resources.— The two Americas are twin continents." For Beach, the point was the urgency of "the mission now before the churches in our great southern twin-continent," and the importance of abetting that through "constant communication between the sister continents." That communication would enable "working on those masses of humanity . . . in kinship with the United States."[98]

South America was the twin of the United States because, as one Presbyterian writer said, "the priestly chains about the human intellect and conscience were violently broken and cast away." That writer, William Speer, had served as a missionary in China and perceived the connection with South America in very different terms than what he concluded about the American relationship with China. He professed that "South America was moved, by the contagion of civil and religious liberty in its twin continent of the North, to throw off the galling yoke of Spanish despotism and superstition."[99]

The belief that South America was in the process of escaping Catholic tyranny was echoed by many other Protestant writers, who played up scenes of intolerance under Catholic rule with depictions of torture, bloody executions, and lifelong imprisonment in subterranean dungeons. But beneath the surface of those protestations lurked a scary nagging question about the reflection of America in its twin. John Warner, a YMCA missionary in Brazil, wondered: "Woe to our beloved America if she should ever be caught in the toils of intolerance and bigotry as Brazil is today." The Rev. W. C. Porter, a missionary for forty years in Brazil, offered a more vivid picture of the problem, and it had to do specifically with the disjuncture between ideals and their implementation. Porter explained that the Brazilian constitution so closely followed that of the United States that it was considered by some to be a copy of it. The Brazilian constitution, like the American constitution, declared that "the State has no religion; that all creeds are free and equal in the sight of the law; that nobody shall be discriminated against because of his religious belief."[100]

The problem, said Porter, was that discrimination and violence were everywhere in a nation that had embraced the same principles regarding religion as did its sister nation to the north. Porter recounted the burning of Bibles in Pernambuco "by some friars, and the bishop did not say one word of condemnation." A Protestant church there recently had been burned down, and another just the previous month in the state of Espirito Santo. Religious minorities had problems with burials. Protestant marriages were not allowed. And candidates for public office fostered such intolerance, one promising that if elected he "would advocate the re-establishing of the state religion and would work for the Pope's supreme control in Brazil." Porter catalogued the problems in a Brazil that had copied the U.S. Constitution, and they were the same ones that were present in America, though he did not comment on that side of the equation. His South American twin was in fact more like the United States than he was able to admit.[101]

The stark mirroring of the situation in the United States—where Protestants dominated rather than Catholics—apparently was not Porter's intention, but his perception nevertheless concisely represented the dynamics at play in Protestant conceptualization of the twinning of the Americas. Harlan Beach to some extent saw it as well, but ever optimistic, he interpreted the similarities and differences in a way that allowed him to accept, at least in the short term, the reality of failures in "this regenerated Latin race." For Beach, "with the progressive evangelization of both Americas, there will be developed a *reflex action* between the two." That reflex action, he believed, would issue in progress.[102]

The American Protestant—largely evangelical—tendency to project onto other nations the failure to domestically implement the ideal of religious freedom became more visible as South America rose rapidly in importance as a Protestant mission field. That process of othering, which included the related phenomenon of the spatial othering of non-Protestant groups in America as themselves akin to foreign lands, was similar, for example, to how the Northern states of the United States conceptualized the Southern states in the twentieth century. In the United States, "the South long provided a mirror image for America's flaws and blemishes," a vessel for the frustration, guilt, defeat, and failure that the nation had experienced.[103] In the same way, South America was a mirror for the United States. As twin, sister, kin, it was a mirror that showed Americans their shortcomings as far as the realization of religious liberty and at the same time distracted Americans from having to come to terms concretely with those shortcomings on the domestic front. South America in its ongoing U.S. invention as a mission field was a mirror that reflected trauma in American identity, the American difficulty in addressing that trauma, and the unexpected ways in which it was, at times, remembered.

South America seen in this way as a mirror for the religious situation in the United States intersects with what some recent scholarly investigation of the Philippines and several other places characterizes as the history of U.S. effort to "export religious freedom" to other parts of the world. There is "American conflation of its national identity with the principle of religious liberty," and that "did not mean that they were only concerned with religious liberty at home but also with religious freedom abroad." In such a view, examination of the process of American attempts to export religious freedom discloses a history that serves "as a 'magic mirror' on which the evolving face of religious freedom in America is likewise reflected."[104] In short, as Americans struggled with implementing religious freedom domestically, they struggled even more explicitly and deliberately in defining it and implementing it in places like the Philippines.

In this book on religious intolerance, my primary interest is not in narrating what Americans accomplished—or failed to accomplish—internationally when they made the idea of religious liberty central to their global assertion of power. Nor do I offer an assessment of the realities of religious intolerance that existed in places such as South America, where Catholics did exercise power in a way that oppressed other groups. My interest is rather different from recent research by scholars who have taken that path in that I relate how American thinking about religion in other parts of the world reflects the reality of religious intolerance, not religious liberty, in America. While it is true that Americans attempted in various ways and with differing levels of success to export religious freedom, Americans also exported religious intolerance. That is, Americans projected their history onto other states, other peoples. While professedly engaged in a project of exporting the principle of religious freedom (that historically has met with mixed results), Americans were acting in coordination with deeper, affective, volatile impulses. America's projected national identity, constituted in part by memory of trauma involving religiously inspired genocides and reinforced by serial episodes of religious violence in nineteenth-century America, shone back from South America. Seen in the mirror of a South America invented in large part by missionary writing and reports, America was a place where intolerance still was strongly present and where a dominant religious group sought to suppress its competitors. But the mirror was inverted, so that Americans saw only their own "civil and religious freedom."

The starting point for Protestant missionary characterizations of South America was that the continent suffered terribly under the weight of a brutal Catholic repression of true religion. The ecclesiastical hierarchy that oversaw the religious policing of the inhabitants, the imported and fearsomely prosecuted Inquisition, the poisonous collusions between church and state, all informed by the strategic plotting of Rome for global hegemony, made South America a jungle of corruption. It was, in the letters of missionaries, a place where a slavery of the spirit stood out among all of the other problems of everyday life as the most pitiful and most enraging.

According to Protestants, the problem in South America was "due to the spirit of intolerance inherited from Spain" and from Portugal. That meant that there were vast numbers of persons who were "victims of religious intolerance and despotism,"[105] the conjoined evils of the Inquisition, exported from Europe to South America. For almost all writers, the painful legacy of

PROTECTIONS

the Inquisition remained deeply ingrained in the cultures of the South American republics even after their successful campaigns against European rule. James S. Dennis, the Princeton-educated Presbyterian missionary, surveying the course of Protestant missionizing in 1893, wrote in *Foreign Missions After a Century* that "the Spirit of the Inquisition still hides in the Papal system of South America. The blind intolerance of medieval Romanism still fights for supremacy."[106] The widely read ex-Confederate memoirist Rev. Randolph H. McKim pointed out that the influence of the Catholic Church in former Spanish and Portuguese colonies remained so strong that "her theologians to-day justify the intolerance of the dark ages" as a matter of course. In the latter part of the nineteenth century, U.S. writers evidenced that intolerance with reports of actions taken against Protestant missionaries in South America.[107]

One case that recurred often in religious publications was that of Francisco G. Penzotti, who was "of martyr stuff"[108] throughout his sufferings in Peru at the hands of Catholic authorities. Penzotti, a Methodist agent for the American Bible Society and founder of an evangelical church in Peru, in 1890 was imprisoned a short while for his preaching. As his case was taken up by the *New York Herald* and other newspapers, his reputation as a suffering hero and missionary exemplar spread among mission societies. His case often was used to illustrate the persecution of Protestants, and especially Protestant clergy, in South America. There was much drama in the descriptions of his confinement and his preaching to other prisoners while incarcerated. His story reinforced the message of the *Congregationalist* a few years later, in 1895, that "In South America, the Bible is a sealed book. Religion has lost its influence over the people, lying and deceit abound, crime is prevalent, conscience seems incapable of being awakened."[109]

In spite of the dramatic reports of attacks on Protestants in South America, Protestants expressed hope that a better future was on the horizon. At the same time that Americans complained about the ill treatment of missionaries and overall abuse of Protestants in South America, they voiced their trust that the situation was improving. That kind of hopefulness was standard among missionaries in the nineteenth and early twentieth centuries. In Asia and Africa, even in the aftermaths of local persecutions, missionaries wrote home encouragingly to potential recruits that there had been progress, both in converting persons and in affecting the attitude of local government officials about Protestantism itself. The missionary campaigns in South America were especially notable in their juxtaposing of outcries against oppression by the Catholic Church with claims that things were improving. Reports swung back and forth between those poles.

The same article in the *Congregationalist* that advised that "conscience seems incapable of being awakened" also exulted that "the country is open now as never before to evangelistic effort, for since the numerous republics have been established the tide of civil and religious liberty has steadily risen." And then, backtracking again, it added, "although instances of religious intolerance have recently occurred in Peru."[110] A few years later, the magazine, like many others, rushed to prospect the religious advances that would be made in the wake of the Spanish American War settlements, just as previous writers had predicted there would be a sea change in the South American situation following the founding of the republics there early in the century. "The stirring events of the last year," wrote the magazine in 1899, amounted to "the last struggle between the Middle Ages and the Declaration of Independence, between the Inquisition and the common school, between intolerance and tyranny. . . ."[111] A missionary writing from Santiago, Chile, in 1873 confessed that "It has required years to break through the thick crust of religion and intolerance," but the way was opening for all of those who "take on this anti-Papal work." Indeed, said the author, whose confidence—and analysis—were badly out of sync with the reality of Catholic power in Chile, the efforts of Protestant agitators had engendered "the perfect freedom which is now enjoyed."[112]

"Protestantism comes with its open Bible," said the *Christian Observer* in commenting on the South American republics. "It has had to encounter persecution. But such progress has been made that most of these States are divorced from the Church, and no longer support Romanism and its intolerance."[113] According to one analyst writing in 1901, "the spirit of intolerance is being wiped out."[114] But in Brazil, there was still "severe persecution," and, specifically for Baptists, ongoing "persecution and difficulties" in 1913. What one writer at one moment characterized as an open road to Protestant success was for another writer a difficult battle against entrenched Catholic intolerance with its concerted persecutions of Protestant missionaries and their congregations. Reports from the field typically boiled down to Edmund Merriam's wishful summary of the state of Baptist missions in Brazil: "The missions in Brazil are extraordinarily prosperous in spite of persecutions and difficulties."[115]

The persistence of Protestant belief that the people of South America continued to suffer under Catholic rule was redolent in the ongoing deployment of a series of heavily freighted terms in descriptions of the salvific goals of evangelical missions to the region. No matter how much missionary reports might highlight local successes, Protestants often portrayed their efforts as but a small fraction of the great effort that was needed. In 1895, an American writer asserted that "South America as a whole is almost untouched" by Protestantism.[116] A mission tour to South America in 1893 concluded: "Few lands challenge Christendom to-day with such imperative appeal as this neglected continent."[117] That meant, said an article on hemispheric evangelization, that Christians must rise to the challenge: "We must meet the facts squarely; American churches must evangelize Mexico and Central and South America, or the papal night of terrible darkness remain with all its superstition and vice. We cannot escape our duty."[118] The urgency of the task was repeated constantly in the religious press. A survey of missions in South America entreated in 1906: "Oh, that the American churches would open their eyes to the singular duty and opportunity that God has reserved for them in their own hemisphere."[119]

During the Spanish American War, the depiction of duty to evangelize was joined more concretely to the political mission of bringing the gospel of liberty to those oppressed by Spanish rule. The *Methodist Review*, keenly aware like other denominational publications that evangelical progress was dependent on noninterference by Catholic authorities in foreign lands, explained that "God has imposed on us the duty to see that religious intolerance in Cuba or the Philippines shall not repress the freedom of religious choice and work by anybody." But while Harlan Beach could define the evangelical mission to the South America in unflinchingly arrogant terms—"North America to the Rescue"[120]—there were the occasional voices of caution as well. Caspar Whitney, a journalist who had been embedded with the Rough Riders in Cuba, wrote of his expedition to South America in a way that likely would have put off evangelical missionaries: "We must give over the high-flown language of the big brother to the weakling, the patronizing air with which we proclaim the development of South Americans to be our 'right and duty.'"[121]

The presumptuousness of Protestant rhetoric regarding the spiritual state of South America and its need for redemption—the sort of rhetoric that Whitney cautioned against—was, as historians have noted, one part of a larger matrix of beliefs that included racial characterizations of Americans vis-à-vis their neighbors to the south. The broadcasting of announcements of evangelical duty to rescue South Americans from papal intolerance largely embraced the gospel that Anglo-Saxon blood was superior to South American blood. Oddly, evangelical writers, poorly informed about the demographics of South America, sometimes pointed out that the majority of the continent was descended from European blood, and that such a people accordingly were susceptible to some measure of civilizing if only the Anglo-Saxons would make an effort to bring that about. It was self-evident to many

American Protestants that the "liberty-loving Anglo-Saxon blood had established by ages of sublime sacrifice" a perfect civilization.[122] It was a platform for the fullest realization of Protestant ideals and a support for Protestant religious practice wherever it gained predominance. That claim, asserted by a 1905 Methodist report on "America as a World Power," was reinforced by other evangelical caricatures of cultural encounter. Another Methodist publication previously had filled in a few of the blanks in recklessly proclaiming that "the people of the United States are now reckoned to be of pure British origin. What a contrast this presents with the South American republics!" In Brazil, for example, "purity of blood is the exception, mongrel the rule."[123]

Just as Protestants in general had difficulty recognizing religious intolerance in the United States, some also experienced difficulties in understanding the racial makeup of the nation. That incompetency was translated to their understandings of South American demographics alongside their projection of the sin of religious intolerance in the United States to South American space.

The sense of urgency to convert South America came in part from a belief that American missionaries had gotten a late start in evangelizing the continent. In 1888, *Zion's Herald* framed the mission to South America this way: "To the religious public of the United States the Spanish peoples of the continent were long unknown. We know more of Europe, Asia, and Africa than of South America."[124] The mission to South America, wrote Harlan Beach in 1906, "is still in its infancy. It was long before evangelical Christians awoke to its needs and their responsibility to give to its people the pure gospel."[125] Writers commonly took the position that "as far as its missions are concerned, far less interest has been taken in its evangelization than in any other great division of the world."[126] But at the end of the nineteenth century, Protestants learned to rise enthusiastically to their duty to South America, because "God has opened the doors."[127] In that project the United States, as victor over Spain in 1898, had "been called to perform an important part. Through its instrumentality the intolerance of the Roman Catholic hierarchy has been broken down."[128]

The defeat of Spain propelled forward the initiatives that had been gaining momentum in the decade before the war, and the mission field of South America soon became a priority. While China remained the focal point for the visions of Protestant mission organizations—which increased greatly in number after 1890—South America drew more and more duty-minded Protestants to its Catholic towns and cities. It eventually became a leading site of American Protestantism's worldwide expansion, claiming over twenty percent of the population by the end of the twentieth century and causing changes within the Roman Catholic Church in most Latin American countries.[129] There may have been a late start to Protestant missionizing of the continent, but the resources committed by Protestants to rescuing the twin continent were enormous, and they were effective in accomplishing ambitious Protestant goals.[130] The Protestant evangelization of South America amounted to a "religious transformation."[131]

Civil and Religious Liberty in South America

Protestant missions, launched not only from the United States but also from England, organized their projects as efforts to "civilize" the populations they encountered. Missionaries worked to teach potential converts about Western traditions of morality, government, education, social life, and material culture. To an extent, American missionaries aimed to remake the host culture into something approximating an American community, as much as that could be effected within the constraints of local traditions. In approaching the mission field in such a way, they operated similarly to the Spanish Catholic missionaries who had preceded them in South Americas by centuries. The Spanish, who built mission villages and *reducciones*, likewise sought to impose Spanish traditions on South American indigenes, were more ambitious and demanding in erasing local culture in order to do so, and were more successful in achieving that outcome than were Protestants.

Protestants brought with them two gospels. One was rooted in their biblicism. The other was rooted in American ideas of government. They believed that those two gospels were interlocking parts of a great plan. They believed that "the principles contained in the Declaration of Independence and the Constitution" were a religious heritage, a scheme ordained by God. They believed that "providence provided that America should be free from the old-time curse of religious intolerance and have the inestimable uplift of perfect freedom of conscience and religious liberty."[132] The ubiquitous phrase "civil and religious liberty" expressed Protestant faith in the two gospels. In describing the task of missionizing South America, Protestants frequently declared that it included establishing civil and religious liberty in the communities that they adopted.

Because of their insistence on "both *civil* and *RELIGIOUS liberty* as the right of all," they committed themselves to persuading South Americans to claim their rights.[133] "So Protestantism comes with its open Bible, its right of individual judgment," said Presbyterian minister James H. McNeilly, a close friend of fellow Tennesseean President James K. Polk. "Its influence is recognized as being on the side of civil and religious liberty," and its interest in

Latin America was to bring both gospels to the masses there "and so rescue them from a soul-deadening spiritual tyranny."[134] Other writers racialized the mission specifically with regard to civil and religious liberty, which was construed as the unique product of Anglo-Saxon ingenuity. "The Anglo-Americans have shown themselves to possess a positive genius for establishing political and religious freedom," an author reminded his readers in 1900.[135] The civilization of Anglo-Saxons, transmitted through the energies of Protestant missionaries, would bring civil and religious liberty to South America through boots-on-the-ground everyday encounters with people who, it often was said, hungered and thirsted for God and for freedom.

The idea of merging civil and religious liberty as part of a comprehensive platform for personal freedom was promoted not only by missionaries. National leaders, both in the United States and in Latin America, spoke the same language as the missionaries. President Andrew Johnson sent an illustrative note to the governor of Connecticut, William A. Buckingham, who in June 1865 was presiding over a meeting of the National Council of Congregational Churches. The recently sworn-in president invoked the blessings of the Great Ruler, and concisely expressed his sense of official duty: "These duties I shall endeavor to discharge honestly and to the best of my judgment, with the conviction that the best interests of civil and religious liberty throughout the world will be preserved and promoted . . ."[136] Thirty-five years later, in 1900, President McKinley in his annual message to Congress remarked on the responsibilities of the nation to the Philippines. He began by pointing out that "its inhabitants, its churches and religious worship, its educational establishments, and its private property of all descriptions, are placed under the special safeguard of the faith and honor of the American army." Reinforcing his point, he added: "As high and sacred an obligation rests on the Government of the United States to give protection for property and life, civil and religious freedom, and wise, firm, and unselfish guidance."[137]

Such statements by McKinley and others were what might be called "religious freedom talk."[138] It was a kind of talk that included not only statements by American public officials and Protestant missionaries, but the public statements of persons active in many different areas, including commerce, banking, education, and diplomacy. By the middle of the nineteenth century, it already had made its way into the speech of Latin American leaders who wished to indicate their willingness to collaborate with the United States. Latin American republics had developed strong discourses about personal freedoms during the nineteenth century, and the American language that conflated civil and religious liberty became part of that. In his inaugural address in 1866, President José María Castro Madriz told his Costa Rican colleagues: "The civilization of the century has defined political and religious liberty and elevated them to the position of a dogma of peace and prosperity. I acknowledge them as such, and shall know now to respect and sustain them."[139] Such pronouncements reflected an awareness of "religious freedom talk" as it was carried on in the United States, but they also evidenced the influence of missionaries whose constant agitation in Catholic Latin America over time made government officials take notice.

Public declarations such as that by the president of Costa Rica also indicated a growing understanding on the part of government and business leaders in Central and South America that the linked gospels of freedom were potentially good for business. They understood what civil and religious liberty meant to missionaries and what it meant for a new nation in its prospective commercial relations with the United States. That connection between religious freedom and commercial expansion, frequently foregrounded in articles by missions boosters, was concisely stated in a report made by the organizers of a conference on Protestant missions in London in 1888. The spokesperson for the meeting summarized the salutary effects of Protestant evangelizing in terms that could not be mistaken: "I believe that the extension of civilization, the advancement of commerce, the increase of knowledge in art, sciences, and literature, the promotion of civil and religious liberty, the development of countries rich in undiscovered material and vegetable wealth, are all intimately identified with, and, to a much larger extent than most people are aware of, dependent upon the success of Christian Missions."[140]

The extent to which Protestant missionaries served as shock troops for imperial incursions has been the subject of much discussion among scholars. There is general agreement that missionaries played a key role.[141] Questions remain about the awareness of missionaries of what they were doing and their actual prioritizing of religious issues vis-à-vis civil issues. Methodist Bishop Thomas B. Neely of the Young People's Missionary Movement confidently expressed his opinion in 1909: "Political and religious liberty go together, and, where there is not religious liberty, there cannot be political liberty." His claim, which was repeated by missionaries in South America, was that religious liberty was the first step toward civil liberty, and that although the two were conjoined, the purpose of the missionary outreach was first of all to make a society safe for Protestant promotion of Bible-reading and participation in Protestant services and rituals (e.g., marriage). Speaking of the liberalization of South American political cultures that came along as part of that project, he said that many political observers "have recognized Protestantism as an aid in their movement, not that Protestant missions are political, for they are not."[142]

138   CHAPTER THREE

At the other end of the spectrum were critics of the missionary enterprise, who cast it as a collaborator with imperialism. "Today *imperialism* is welcomed by many preachers as a means of extending the influence of their religion," opined the *Arena* in 1900. That amounted to a duplicitous and malevolent agenda: "But, underlying the imperialist's efforts, is there not a lust for power and dominion, for additional territory, for enforcing upon others one's own social customs and habits of life, and last but not least a passion for religious propaganda—for compelling others to accept some divinely ordered religion?"[143] Such criticisms were infrequent in the nonreligious magazines and newspapers at the turn of the century and missing entirely from religious publications. But the complaint underscored the fact that the close relationship between civil and religious liberty, which missionaries said was implemented as a religious initiative first, with civil liberty to follow, might not have been as clearly conceived as the phraseology of "civil and religious liberty" suggested. Almost all writers assumed that the two kinds of liberty went together, but the extent to which they functioned as a means by which Protestantism could advance a goal of world domination was still to be debated. What was clear, in the meantime, was that the effort to establish religious liberty was part of a specifically Protestant design to advance its own interests, in South America and elsewhere.

U.S. Policy in South America

The translation of Protestant advocacy of civil and religious liberty into concrete policy took a favorable turn for the missionaries in the 1890s. Just as Secretary of State Lewis Cass was the right person at the right time with the right message in the early 1850s, so also Rev. John Lee, a Methodist minister serving in Cook County, Illinois, in the greater Chicago area, emerged as a leader in the discussion about U.S. policy regarding religion in South America. His efforts, like Cass's, led to diplomatic negotiations with South American countries and policy changes regarding religion in those countries. Lee's efforts came at a time when anti-Catholicism was again spiking, and religious intolerance of Mormons, Jews, and others likewise was widespread.

Lee became an activist for religious liberty for South America during a period of strong anti-Catholic feeling in Illinois. The sharp increase in the Catholic population of Chicago, the difficult situation between capital and immigrant labor, and the rise of organized midwestern anti-Catholic groups such as the American Protective Association (founded in 1887) all had contributed to the intensification of anti-Catholicism in Chicago. The APA, which claimed over two million members in the early 1890s, was part of a broader network of persons and groups that together constituted a renewed anti-Catholic crusade in the late nineteenth century. When Walter Sims, a leading figure in the APA, came to Chicago in 1894, a journal reported that "the hall was filled even to the galleries," and that Sims drew cheers for his claims that Jesuits had shot Lincoln and that President McKinley was a "a tool of the pope." It was, said the journal, a "revival of Knownothingism."[144]

A few years before Sims, the Methodist minister Justin D. Fulton, author of the anti-Catholic *The Fight With Rome* (1889), had visited Chicago. The crowd grew to such a size that "the city authorities, fearing a riot," moved the gathering into the cold outdoors in the interest of dispersing it, a tactic that did not work.[145] In the meantime "newsboys on the streets" of Chicago had no trouble selling the publications of the APA, and in nearby Peoria, according to *Forum*, "every candidate suspected of uncertainty on the Catholic question was strongly opposed, and the entire Board has A.P.A tendencies." Anti-Catholics showed strength at the polls, power in the streets, and a revitalized energy in their intolerance of Catholics in the Chicago area in the early 1890s.[146] It did not help that the Great Fire twenty years earlier had started in the barn of Patrick and Catherine O'Leary.

John Lee began his career with "inconspicuous pastoral appointments which he served with unpretentious fidelity."[147] But in 1894 he went to a lecture by the Methodist missionary John F. Thompson, who had been active in South America since 1870. Lee was moved by Thompson's description of the intolerance of Catholics in South America and soon found himself the chair of a committee to take up the cause of missionaries who labored under the difficult conditions that Thompson described. Flush with confidence that there was a bright future for Protestantism globally—the World Parliament of Religions had fostered such hopes during its meeting in Chicago the previous year—and angered by the seemingly unfettered exercise of Catholic power in South America, he threw himself into his work. He defined that work as a coordinated protest against the Catholic intolerance of Protestants in South America, and he began it by directly addressing the leadership of the Catholic Church in Rome, writing Pope Leo XIII, heads of state on three continents, ambassadors, secretaries of state, and other persons in high office in order to apprise them of oppressive Catholic rule in South America.

The campaign against Catholic intolerance in South America soon acquired visibility in the form of the Chicago Methodist Ministers Meeting. Its message became clearer and more focused. Lee and his associates were particularly perturbed by the fact that Protestant ministers reportedly were not allowed to marry persons in South America, and by reports that in some places couples married by Protestant clergy were not recognized as such by the civil authorities. Advancing under the motto "Between Romanism and Protestantism there can be no compromise,"[148] the Chicago Ministers Meeting became a political movement for a religious cause, supported not only by Protestants throughout the United States but by influential persons in Europe. For a decade it remained a topic in the religious press, in articles attracting the full spectrum of the Protestant readership, from journals such as the *Missionary Herald* to newspapers such as the *Heathen Woman's Friend*. Lee's account of the movement was carefully documented in his *Religious Liberty in South America* (1907), the preface to which announced that the book was a record of the activities in which the ministers engaged on the way to arriving at the point where "some definite results had been obtained."[149]

The Chicago Methodist Ministers campaign focused on South America in general but was particularly concerned with Peru, Bolivia, and Ecuador, the sites of reported stinging abuses by Catholic authorities, including interference with Protestant performances of marriage rituals. Much of Lee's book consisted of copies of letters of complaint he had sent to persons around the world and their written responses to those letters, together with extracts from different kinds of legal documents and official Roman Catholic proclamations. The string of documents began with a condemnation of "the Pope's denunciation of freedom of worship 'as an abominable act'" and the ways in which that opinion had affected Protestants in South America.[150] The case of Francis Penzotti served as a stepping-off point for Lee's protest.

The committee of Methodist ministers under Lee's supervision articulated their demands for religious liberty in South America by pointing out to Archbishop John Ireland (of St. Paul, Minnesota) that they wished the same religious liberty for South America as Catholics enjoyed in the United States. The request made its way up the ladder of Catholic authorities in Rome, who consistently responded by insisting that there was full religious liberty in South America. At that point Lee began to write celebrity Americans whom he believed might influence the State Department to apply pressure to South American countries to accede to the Protestant demands. He wrote to a wide range of persons, from Frances E. Willard, the president of the Women's Christian Temperance Movement, to various Catholic bishops and Protestant leaders, military figures, businessmen, and American presidents. He named his campaign "Agitation," and explained how, believing "in the wonderful efficacy of moral agitation, letters we addressed to leaders of thought in various parts of Christendom" would have the desired effect.[151] Eventually joining forces with the Evangelical Alliance, a powerful London-based organization with a long-standing interest in affronts to Protestants in

PROTECTIONS   141

foreign lands, he at last found himself in a position to expect a response from the White House.

In 1899, Lee's pleas to Presidents Cleveland and McKinley were answered when Secretary of State John Hay informed Lee that "copies of your letters have been communicated to the United States Ministers in Bolivia and Ecuador, with appropriate instructions."[152] The "appropriate instructions" are contained in Hay's letters sent at the same time to U.S. ministers George H. Bridgman in Bolivia, Archibald J. Sampson in Ecuador, and Irving B. Dudley in Peru. Hay instructed those three to urge their hosts "to advance in the path of tolerance which is trodden by modern states." In explaining what that meant, Hay copied from Lee's letter the three central goals of the Chicago Methodist Ministers Meeting that Lee had sent to President McKinley: "(1) To secure religious liberty for missionaries working in the republics of Peru, Ecuador, and Bolivia; (2) to secure religious liberty for native Christians who dissent from the Roman Catholic faith; (3) to secure in these South American republics the fullest civil liberty for American citizens and native-born Protestants, especially by the legalizations of marriages performed by others than clergy of the Roman Catholic Church."[153]

Peru, when initially challenged, already had begun to take steps to implement a broader conceptualization of religious liberty with passage of the Civil Marriage Bill in 1897. Lee took credit for that, detailing how his early letter to President McKinley had made its way to Assistant Secretary of State William Rufus Day, who then had intervened with Peru to press the government to change the marriage laws. Day wrote Lee, explaining that Lee's letter setting out the threefold agenda of the Chicago Methodist Ministers Meeting would be given to the legation in Peru with instructions to make an effort to see it through the Peruvian Congress. When Ecuador (1902) and finally Bolivia (1906) also fell into line, Lee declared his committee's work done, and he wrote his book to memorialize the Chicago Methodist Ministers Meeting's success in influencing the U.S. government to intervene in the religious affairs of South America. Lee included in his book much correspondence with State Department officials and his own group of clergy that evidenced the trail of the Methodist influence on the South American legislation. Taking a victory lap, Lee included a testimonial from John F. Thompson (whose speech originally had inspired Lee to act) that stated that Lee had "done more for the cause of religious liberty in South America" than anyone since the creation of the South American republics.[154]

The influence that the Chicago Methodist Ministers Meeting was able to exert upon U.S. foreign policy with regard to religion was significant. The denomination, once they recognized their agency, made it part of their vision for world Protestantism. The notes for the meetings of the Rock River Annual Conference, the ministerial association to which Lee belonged, evidence a long-standing interest in "civil and religious liberty," represented by a standing committee that reported on it at each meeting. But the effectiveness of Lee's campaign seems to have roused the Conference, which used it as a platform for voicing its belief in the duty of "the Anglo-Saxon race in the United States to develop and stand for the principles of civil and religious liberty." For the Chicago Methodists, "this movement has called out a large and sympathetic response on the part of a united Protestantism. But it is a significant fact that as of yet scarcely a word has appeared to show any real sympathy on the part of the Roman Catholic Church in the United States."[155] For the Methodist Rock River Association in 1902, the long-term payoff to Lee's efforts was a more politically empowered Anglo-Saxon Protestantism united against the tyranny of Roman Catholicism. It was Protestantism evidencing its power to project its agenda internationally.

The historian Andrew Preston, in an expansive study of religion and American foreign policy, wrote about the late nineteenth-century emergence of "religious freedom as a legitimate goal for American diplomacy." For Preston, the principle of religious freedom "quickly became official U.S. policy" under John Hay in 1899 through the agitation caused by Lee and his colleagues.[156] But Hay was acting under the influence of a developing view of American responsibility to protect Americans overseas that was grounded in the language of decades of treaties and defined more precisely by Lewis Cass's efforts as secretary of state in the 1850s. So, the turn in diplomacy was neither sudden nor experimental. Under Hay, we see the culmination of a process that had been engendered decades earlier and had been nourished by the steady growth in American talk about "civil and religious liberty" even as religious intolerance in America remained a serious problem. The ascent of religious freedom as an agendum of foreign policy was equally the Protestant response to the ongoing problem of Roman Catholics—and Mormons and others—as immigration brought more Catholics to American cities and the "revival of Knownothingism," as the *American Journal of Politics* characterized the late nineteenth century, began to coalesce.[157]

What was telling about the diplomatic scene at the turn of the century was the apparent ease with which the State Department lifted a principle of religious freedom from the everyday context of American religion that at the time was vexed by ingrained intolerance. Preston draws our attention to this with a telling remark about the extraction of an exportable principle of religious freedom from a complicated American setting of diverse and com-

PROTECTIONS   143

peting religious groups. For Preston, "the application of an abstraction" to U.S. discussions of foreign policy led to an "enduring principle." Specifically, Preston notes how in the late nineteenth century when that crucial process of abstraction from the domestic religious scene occurred, the U.S. government was itself at war with Mormons. And ironically, the issue was religious marriage. American diplomatic urging of the principle of religious liberty upon foreign governments "was a remarkable stance given the recent tensions over polygamy between the Latter-day Saints and the federal government." Those tensions included laws against the religious practice of polygamy, and they were one part of a broader and deeper set of restrictions, formal and informal, that were redolent in relations among Protestants, Catholics, Mormons, Jews, and others.[158]

For U.S. foreign policy to make a vow to promote religious freedom internationally meant that government officials chose to authorize as globally applicable a principle of religious freedom "abstracted" from the fraught social and political contexts of American religious life. Certainly the diplomats who undertook to promote religious freedom believed that it was a worthy principle, just as did John Lee and his Methodist colleagues in Chicago. The seemingly pristine language of law indeed gave the appearance of a principle free of its messy context and heavy cultural baggage. But in those discussions in the early twentieth century, the principle of religious freedom could not be fully abstracted from the backgrounds of religious intolerance in which it was embedded in America. Lee's campaign to bring religious liberty to South America was predicated on a fierce antipathy to what he believed to be Roman Catholic tyranny in South America, as well as a confidence in the Anglo-Saxon race, as a superior Protestant people, to triumph over its inferiors in foreign lands. When Lee was fighting religious opponents in Ecuador, he was also fighting them at home. He and his Chicago Methodist Ministers Meeting colleagues, along with Josiah Strong, the American Protective Association, editors of Protestant periodicals, and men and women in Protestant pews, were haunted by trauma about religious violence that was hardwired into American identity.

Protestants othered American Catholics, Mormons, and Jews as people who inhabited other places even though members of those groups actually lived in America. Protestants detected Catholic oppression overseas, but could not recognize Protestant intolerance of non-Protestant religions at home. Protestants identified as Americans who believed in religious liberty, but they also were Americans who had inherited the sin of the colonial fathers, and had failed to come to terms with it. They promoted a principle of religious freedom that was abstracted from the painfully conflicted world of their past and present. They offered that principle to the world as a representation of themselves, unable to acknowledge that what was visible in the mirror of other countries, in the intolerance of those nations, were their own failings.

Wilsonianism

In the summer of 1915, outside of Atlanta, a small mob lynched Leo Frank, a thirty-one-year-old Jew who recently had been convicted of murder on the barest of evidence.[159] Among the twenty-eight members of the mob known to historians were the ex-governor of Georgia, the future president of the Georgia Senate, county sheriffs, and prominent lawyers and businessmen. Thomas E. Watson, who served in the U.S. House of Representatives and the U.S. Senate, also played a role in the lynching, but indirectly, through *Watson's Magazine*, which inflamed public opinion against Frank. In the aftermath, Watson played another, possibly more consequential, role. A racist, anti-Catholic, anti-Jewish public figure of considerable influence, Watson used his power as editor to advocate for the white supremacist, Protestant worldview around which the Ku Klux Klan was coalescing in its renewed form in Stone Mountain, Georgia, just outside Atlanta.

In the same year that Frank was lynched, D. W. Griffith's *The Birth of a Nation* played to movie house audiences throughout the nation. The movie portrayed the post–Civil War KKK as a brave and determined movement serving a noble cause. Like Watson's publications, it stirred up a wave of enthusiasm for the Klan, which used it as a recruiting tool. Henry Ford's publication of *The Protocols of the Elders of Zion* likewise contributed to the growth of the Klan by marking Jews as seditious schemers. By the 1920s, the Klan, "a true mass movement,"[160] had organized itself not only in the South but in the Midwest and the West, and claimed four million members.[161] Its crusade for white Protestantism included women and children participants in festival-like gatherings and religious services, alongside the activities for which the Klan is best known, its cross-burnings, lynchings, racist intimidation, and inflammatory publications.[162] On a wet August day in 1925, some 30,000 Klansmen in robes marched down Pennsylvania Avenue in Washington, DC. The following day they burned an eighty-foot cross in nearby Arlington before a crowd of 75,000. Such dramas guaranteed the Klan national newspaper coverage and further platforms for the exposition of their beliefs and recruiting initiatives.

Mauritz A. Hallgren, a correspondent for *The Nation* and an important and influential public intellectual in the 1930s, paid particular attention to the

Klan in his *Landscape of Freedom: The Story of American Liberty and Bigotry* (1941). The book surveyed American attempts to create a free society and the difficulties and frustrations encountered in doing so. Hallgren referred to the 1920s as "the scandalous years" during which the Klan came to power and flourished throughout the nation, growing progressively bolder in its terrorizing of those it considered threats to white Protestant rule. While Klan violence against African Americans was brutal and widespread, the Klan was equally focused on doing battle with Catholics. According to Hallgren, "many Klansmen hated the Catholics even more than the Jews and the Negroes." The Klan built upon the sturdy nineteenth-century American foundations of anti-Catholicism an ambitious and fictionally rich plan to settle the score with the Knights of Columbus, the Catholic assassins of Lincoln, Garfield, and McKinley, and the Catholic armies that maintained secret armories in the large cathedrals throughout American cities. Hallgren observed: "In the north the Klan movement really was a full-blown revival of the Know-Nothingism of the nineteenth century, its energy and passion arising from the same deep and potent prejudice against papists."[163] In the South, the Klan targeted Catholics as well, but ritualized Klan violence against African Americans brought the white Anglo-Saxon aspect of Klan thinking to the forefront of the movement's activities there.

Hallgren compared the Klan's vision of America to the theocracy of the Puritans. Its defense of racial purity, female virtue, and "pure Americanism" were for him aspects of a Protestantism renewed by the spirit of the intolerant and uncompromising worldview of early New Englanders.[164] And it is clear that the Klan did imagine themselves as heroes on the order of the Puritans they revered. The Methodist bishop and outspoken anti-Catholic Alma White, as we have seen, drew explicit connections between the Klan and the Puritans. But at the bottom of the Klan's imitation of the Puritans lay a sense of victimhood, of having suffered for their beliefs as did the Puritans in England. Now, recognizing their Puritan heritage, the Klan believed they were duty-bound to organize a defense of their pure Protestant religion. The second coming of the Klan was the New World of the Puritans for those who joined it. For "its identity as the defender of Protestantism and America"[165] was rooted in a sense that American Protestants were under attack and that only a disciplined, concerted effort—one like that made by the Puritans—would guarantee that the nation survived as a public vessel of pure Christianity.[166]

Said to be four million strong and capable of intimidation on a large scale, but self-identifying as victims, Klan members pledged themselves to defend Protestantism from Catholic assault. That goal was interwoven with antisemitism and racism, but the Klan was fundamentally a religious movement, and it took its bearings from its relationship to its religious opponents. It defined itself in opposition to those opponents, and in so doing it frequently embraced the role of oppressed minority.

The Notre Dame College anti-KKK riot in 1924 brought that sense of victimhood to the forefront of the movement. South Bend, where Notre Dame is located, is in Indiana, which in the 1920s was one of the strongest Klan states in the nation and had recently elected a Klan member as governor. In the late spring, as Klan members began arriving in South Bend for a rally, inflammatory anti-Catholic Klan literature began circulating and one Klansman delivered a public lecture accusing Catholics of being disloyal to the United States. The students at the nearby Catholic college consequently traveled into town to confront the rally. They won a street battle with the assembled Klansmen, who seemed not to be expecting such resistance, and the rally left town. It later returned under the protection of deputized Klan members, but a standoff ensued and that rally also came to nothing.[167]

In the wake of the fracas in Indiana, Klan publications such as *Fiery Cross* complained loudly about the persecution of Protestants in America. They excoriated the Catholics from Notre Dame as lawless thugs and "presented the Klansmen as innocent victims." Such claims were rooted in Klan history. The Klan that emerged during Reconstruction had believed that whites were victims, and such a belief in white victimhood remained central to the movement's self-understanding. The anti-Catholic ideology that grew within the Klan and came to fruition in the Klan's 1920s reincarnation incorporated that sense of victimhood into a more specifically religious identity. The Klan ultimately alternated between a sense of victimization and a trust in their eventual dominance. They were "victims, defenders, and winners," roles that were entwined and that were articulated in clearer terms following the debacle at South Bend.[168]

The Klan was a forerunner of the assertions of victimhood that became one of the identifying marks of conservative evangelical Protestantism in the latter part of the century. But in the 1920s, such protestations can seem out of place to scholars trying to understand the place of the Klan in American life. At a time when Protestant power seemed at its peak, when Protestant missionary headman John Mott was forecasting "the evangelization of the world in this generation," when John Scopes was being convicted in the Dayton "monkey trial," and when recently immigrated Catholics and Jews formed a broad underclass, there would seem to be little reason for a Protestant group to imagine that it was the victim of plots engineered by its religious opponents. But white Protestant Americans were immersed in "the paranoid style" of politics, and the perception of being a victim emerged easily from the paranoid framing of the world. More importantly, the American identity of Protestants such as those who belonged to the Klan was shaped by the complex ingrained memory of events of early American colonial history. That memory framed for them the events of their present. Just as Puritans understood that they might "go native," absorbing by contact so much of Indian culture that they became Indian, so also did Protestants in the late nineteenth and early twentieth centuries imagine themselves in role reversals with Catholics. Protestants who were drawn to aspects of Catholicism put themselves in a position to understand themselves as victims because of the way that Catholics were treated in the Protestant culture of America at the time.

The phenomenon of Protestants experimenting with images of themselves as Catholics has been well documented. Research has shown how nineteenth-century Protestants were both repulsed by Catholicism and attracted to it. At times they longed for the spirituality that it represented and imagined themselves trading their own faith for what could appear to them as a rich tradition of exquisite religious feeling and gorgeous practice. "The Protestant American encounter with the estranged world of Catholicism provoked a characteristically conflicted response of repulsion and longing," resulting in "a fear of corruption and a hunger for communion."[169] That response undergirded a broad process of role-switching that was manifest in one way in the large numbers of Protestant conversions to Catholicism in the nineteenth century. More commonly that process resulted in instances in which Protestants would mentally try on what they believed it meant to be Catholic.

Whether it was through "Unconscious Influence," the title of Horace Bushnell's 1846 sermon in which he addressed the influence of Catholicism on Protestant life, or through a more deliberate and self-aware process, some Protestants slipped back and forth between their habitual religious identity and what they imagined as a Catholic one. For Bushnell there were "so many unconscious influences, ever streaming forth upon the people and back and forth against each other."[170] The paradoxical construction of nineteenth-century Protestant identity that emerged from unconscious influence mimicked the Puritan relationship with Indians, in which Puritans at times imagined themselves slipping into Native American life, becoming Indians in ways that assimilated them to the culture that they feared and decried. That same process, visible in the nineteenth-century Protestant trying-on of Catholicism, helped shape the perception by the Klan and other Protestants that *they*, not Catholics, were the persecuted minority. That perception reinforced their determination to strive for dominance and their chronic blindness to actual intolerance toward Catholics.

During the period of the reemergence of the Klan, Woodrow Wilson served as president (1913–1921). Much has been written about Wilson's religious sensibilities and how they influenced his thinking about foreign policy, particularly in the aftermath of World War I. Recent studies have been particularly useful for their careful setting of Wilson against a background of liberal Protestantism and its ideas about social and political order.[171] Wilson is best known in the fields of diplomatic history and international relations for his goal of a world "made safe for democracy," a phrase that he spoke to Congress in advocating war with Germany in 1917 and that recurred as shorthand for his subsequent international initiatives.[172] His thinking about how to reach that goal included establishing the League of Nations, among other institutional apparatus, and using the postwar stature and power of the United States to influence other nations to embrace democratic ideals and strengthen democratic institutions.

Wilson's worldview was profoundly shaped by his Calvinist Protestantism. "The religious heart of Wilson's sensibility cannot be denied," wrote Richard Striner, and that religion was reflected in much of what he attempted as president, both animating his plans and constraining them.[173] Equally important for Wilson's view of international relations was his racism. That racism came to the forefront of the national debate about race in 2016 when protesters at Princeton University, where Wilson served as professor and president, demanded that his name no longer be associated with the university. Princeton eventually chose to retain his name for its School of Public and International Affairs and for an undergraduate residential college. The publicity nevertheless acquainted Americans with what historians already were agreed upon, namely that Wilson, a Southerner who retained a fondness for the Lost Cause,[174] had a damaging record concerning race. He voiced racist views on a number of occasions, including his remark that "the domestic slaves, at any rate, and almost all who were much under the master's eye, were happy and well cared for."[175] More concretely, Wilson, in his first year as president in 1913, reversed the long-standing policy of racial integration in the federal civil service; he later played a role in defeating the Racial Equality Clause that Japan insisted be included in the founding documents of the League of Nations.[176]

Wilson's thinking about race and religion was framed by his belief that Anglo-Saxon Protestantism had created the highest civilization and that the extension of that civilization throughout the world was the most promising course for international relations. He was fully invested in the idea of American exceptionalism, of America as the providentially directed "city on the hill" that exemplified the highest ideals of morality, freedom, and democracy. That belief prompted Wilson to a grand vision of worldwide democracy and peace, but it also hamstrung his efforts to implement that vision. His "belief in God's providential mission for the United States in world history and his racial/ethnic identity profoundly limited the president's international vision and statecraft, which expressed a Eurocentric, particularly Anglo-American, bias and drew a global color line."[177]

Wilson's Anglo-Saxon Protestantism thoroughly informed his understanding of how societies work and nations flourish. It deeply colored—or, more accurately, un-colored—his understanding of American history. Unable to come to terms with race, he chose to ignore it when he could, a tactic that was well evidenced in his handling of the debate over the Racial Equality Clause, when he expressed his opinion, recorded by a stenographer: "My own interest, let me say, is to quiet discussion that raises national differences and racial prejudices. I would wish them, particularly at this juncture in the history of the relations of nations with one another, to be forced as much as possible into the background."[178] Phrased as if it were a tactic of cultural politeness, as it might be in any drawing room in Georgia or South Carolina where Wilson had lived, such a statement was in fact a refusal to recognize racial difference. Recognizing it would require addressing it with legal instruments designed to guarantee racial equality. "He was timid, cold, practically indifferent to questions of racial justice," and he was "incapable of summoning rhetoric that might inspire and transform racial problems."[179]

In fact, Wilson tended to avoid discussion not only of racial frictions but of religious intolerance. The record of those problems in America was not a history with which he was at all comfortable. He believed in a providentially guided America where abstract ideals of liberty and democracy were the hallmarks of progress. The realities of racial and religious conflict in America did not comport with that belief. The fact of religious intolerance in America was particularly challenging for him. In the five volumes of his *A History of the American People* (1902), there is one reference to religious intolerance. The same is true for the ten-volume edition published in 1918, in which, as one of his biographers wrote, Wilson "reaffirmed his commitment to white supremacy and his rejection of racial equality."[180] The reference to religious intolerance in the *History*, moreover, is to Thomas Jefferson's *First Inaugural Address*, in which Jefferson remarks on the nation "having banished from our land that religious intolerance under which mankind so long bled and suffered."[181] There are two throwaway references to religious persecution in the *History*, both outside the narrative, one in a caption to an illustration of

150 CHAPTER THREE

mistreatment of Quakers and the other in a photograph of the title page of a colonial-era publication.[182] Discussion of Mormons and the Mormon Wars likewise was conspicuously absent from the narrative.

When Marjorie L. Daniel wrote in 1934 that there were "evidences of a Protestant bias in Wilson's *History*,"[183] she articulated what was to become a central consideration for historians since. More recently, that bias has been succinctly stated: "Wilson's particular understanding of democracy . . . assumed the superiority and authority of white Protestants to *properly* lead."[184] Wilson, surrounded in the White House by a Cabinet of Southern Anglo-Saxon Protestants,[185] made determined efforts to order the world for that Anglo-Saxon Protestantism. Chief among his efforts was his active promotion of religious freedom internationally. It is only partially true that Wilson's internationalism took shape as "persistent attempts to remove religious persecution and intolerance as sources of war."[186] Certainly Wilson's initiative was focused on ending religious intolerance overseas. But he acted as he did for deeper cultural reasons than solely to avoid war. Following in the steps of previous presidents who had listened to the complaints of missionaries and to other Americans who reported their overseas religious predicaments, he continuously voiced his belief that an end to intolerance was essential to making the world safe. He advocated strenuously for a religious freedom clause to be added to the Covenant of the League of Nations, and he attempted a fallback position to reenter it when it was rejected. But his crusade disclosed his inability to come to terms with religious intolerance in the United States as much as it manifested an interest in establishing religious freedom elsewhere.

Wilson's internationalism emerged from the same background that shaped the thinking of people like John Lee and his tribe of evangelicals in South America. The missionaries understood their charge to be the dissemination of Anglo-Saxon Protestantism. Wilson packaged that as a "civilizing mission,"[187] where "the term *civilization* . . . served as a double-edged weapon for confirming the primacy of European (and later, North American) nations in the world order."[188] When Wilson historically "took the first step in offering transnational religious freedom as international law,"[189] he did so out of his concern that religious intolerance was making the world unsafe for white Anglo-Saxon Protestant democracy, and also because he projected American failings abroad. Like the Protestant missionaries who had been at work overseas for decades, he conceptually exported the religious intolerance he witnessed in America. From that flowed his remedy for religious intolerance, namely, religious freedom.

Wilson, it should be noted, was not the first official of the U.S. government to endeavor to make religious liberty a part of international negotiations. There were the many treaties of amity signed over the previous century as well as occasional direct diplomatic efforts, including the ones that were prompted by Lewis Cass and his allies. Additionally, in 1878, John A. Kasson, the minister to Austria-Hungary, and Bayard Taylor, the minister to Germany, attempted to intervene in the Congress of Berlin in 1878. As representatives of the various European nations involved labored to work out the shape of Europe and the Balkans in the aftermath of the Russo-Turkish War, Kasson and Taylor, who were in communication with Secretary of State William M. Evarts about their plans, proposed the following to the assembled delegates regarding Rumania: "That all citizens or subjects of any such foreign nationality shall, irrespective of race or religious belief, be entitled to equal rights and protection." Driving home the point in moral and characteristically American terms, they added: "To this extent, at least, it seems foreign governments would be justified by international law and the law of self-interest; while they would at the same time give effect to the humane instinct of all truly civilized and Christian nations."[190] The delegates did not oppose the intervention, and for a time the legal constitution of the affected states after the Russo-Turkish War included a profession of religious liberty. Wilson's initiative after World War I was more ambitious and should be recognized as a new stage of American foreign relations, but technically it was not the first American attempt to intervene in the religious affairs of foreign countries.

For one so concerned about religious intolerance internationally, and so certain that world peace required the end of that intolerance, Wilson's inability to see religious intolerance in the United States stands out. Wilson was haunted by the Civil War and Reconstruction, longed for a South composed of much of what it once was, and lived during a time when the most organized, purposeful, and widespread American campaign of religious intolerance against Catholics and Jews was at its peak. Wilson, a professional historian and thoughtful liberal, chose not to see that intolerance in the American past and present. He projected it eastward, to Europe and the Balkans. Like John Lee, he saw the problem, and it was someplace else.

The New Danger

The early twentieth-century American missionary projects in South America were carried forward by enthusiastic and dedicated American evangelicals whose purpose, first of all, was to convert. Like all mission enterprises that get traction on foreign soil, those initiatives could bear fruit in the form of schools, hospitals, and American-style marketplaces. The emergent liberal Protestantism of the nineteenth century and the first part of the twentieth century also sought conversions, but was more focused on institution-building. Those inculcated in the missionizing tradition that began at Andover, for example, while valuing conversions to Christianity, had almost from the beginning practiced their calling as a long-term effort to build religious infrastructure, on the assumption that the long haul for the success of Congregationalism would require it. That tendency eventually came to be recognized by liberal Protestant organizations as their core mission, practically speaking.

In 1932, the Harvard philosopher William Ernest Hocking, who began his career at Andover, published *Re-Thinking Missions: A Layman's Inquiry After One Hundred Years*, a book subsequently known as the Hocking Report. Hocking had visited and consulted with missionaries in China, and from those consultations he concluded that education and a concern for the physical welfare of persons should be acknowledged as the leading edge of missions, and that actual evangelization should follow from that. The report was much debated. Forthrightly evangelical Protestants, who had developed a tradition in South America that differed from Hocking's view, resisted. But the report influenced many subsequent mission campaigns, and especially in its proposal that missionaries cede control of their established communities to local authorities.[191]

The Hocking Report did not have the effect of undermining the notion of Protestant Anglo-Saxon agency as a crucial component in the Christianizing, and therefore civilizing, of people in other nations. In fact, those who promoted missions believed that a "world Protestantism" was more a possibility than ever. But by degrees over a period of time, missions became a matter of Americans learning to value the cultures in which they found themselves immersed. Liberal Protestants, and some evangelicals as well, felt themselves increasingly connected, on the ground, with the cultures they served. Although recruitment of missionaries still played on the exoticism and romance of distant places and people, the planning for missions took greater account of the importance of local cultures. Missionaries developed the kind of deep emotional bonds with host communities that led to a fuller appreciation for the ideas, values, and ways of life of their congregations. The idea of multiculturalism in fact was given a boost through the influence of men and women (the latter were the majority) who returned to America from their mission fields. The effect of American missions was in that sense clearly recursive.[192]

The deepening of attachments to overseas others was not enough to overcome long-established wariness about intolerance in foreign societies. For Protestants, fears of Catholic conspiracies remained, augmented, increasingly, by worries about Muslims. More importantly, the arrival of the Soviet

Union and China as global powers after World War II alarmed American Christians who believed that communists were intent on destroying Christianity, first within the borders of their own nations and then throughout the world. American Christians expressed a strong sympathetic connection with those who suffered intolerance in communist countries, but at the same time remained frightened by anything communist. There were Christian kin who needed saving in places such as China, but there was also the danger of opening the nation to communist infiltration through any connections with the Chinese. Resisting the Chinese (among other communist peoples) and at the same time sympathizing with them was a difficult enterprise for American Protestant missionaries and their supporters. During the Cold War era, that binary remained a problem that evangelicals could not solve.

4

Pursuits:
The Cold War and the Hunt for Intolerance

A World of Protestants

The American focus on religious intolerance outside the United States collaborated with a broader Protestant project to remake the world. By the mid-twentieth century, trust that white Anglo-Saxon Protestantism would redeem the world motivated the revitalized Protestant International, a centuries-long expansion of Protestantism from western Europe across the globe.[1] The Protestant International was grandly ambitious and exceptionally well organized. It built transnational structures upon which it rested its hopes to dominate the world. It was abetted by the development of print culture, migration, transformative ideas about social order, and the new institutions of civil government that coalesced after 1750. It was always an aspect of empire. As a global project it proved relentless and resilient. It envisioned a world of Protestants. At the beginning of the Cold War it was poised to realize its dreams.

World Christianity officially was celebrated as a historical and theological movement in America in 1945. In that year, Presbyterian clergyman and ecumenism advocate Henry van Dusen inaugurated the Henry Luce Professorship of World Christianity at Union Theological Seminary in New York. By that time, the term "world Christianity" had become well established in Protestant circles, and especially among the more liberal mainline denominations. The term had begun to circulate in the 1910s and 1920s and became more common as American Protestant missionary ventures grew and surpassed those mounted by Britain and other European countries. In terms of funding and the number of missionaries in the field, American Protestants built a robust and far-reaching campaign. Its goal, as its American figurehead John R. Mott stated it, was "the evangelization of the world in this generation."[2] Americans eventually dominated the mission field, and in so doing played a stronger hand in shaping the idea of world Christianity.

The idea of a world of Protestants had been an important component of American Protestant understanding of its evangelizing duty long before Mott. That idea crystallized, however, as the United States grew more powerful and became more involved in international affairs. Its energy was apparent in the *Andover Review* commentary on the activities of the American Board of Commissioners of Foreign Missions in 1885, when the *Review* reiterated the organization's commitment to "THE SPREAD OF THE GOSPEL and THE CONVERSION OF THE WORLD," a project that "has already begun to unite, the affections, prayers, and labors of the great family of Christians."[3]

That ABCFM sense of mission animated the landmark Edinburgh Missionary Conference of 1910, where Mott played a leading role in exhorting Protestant colleagues to proceed boldly and ecumenically in converting the world. It recurred repeatedly in the discussions and reports of various Protestant initiatives, influencing the Hocking Report of 1932 and then the Dulles Commission, a gathering of hundreds of Protestant ministers that convened in Ohio in 1942.[4] It underwrote the founding of the World Council of Churches in 1948 and, perhaps even more so, the founding of the National Association of Evangelicals in 1942.[5] The idea of world Christianity played a central role in the thinking of the influential Federal Council of Churches (f. 1908) and a letter sent to it by an allied organization, the Foreign Missions Conference, served as "a kind of charter for the Protestant International" in its emergent American form. The letter stressed that the "conditions for world government" lay not in treaties, World Courts, or the League of Nations, but in the Christianization of the world. Nevertheless, the U.S. emphasis on human rights and "religious freedom" that emerged during and after the war had much to do with the efforts of the Federal Council of Churches and its kindred organizations.[6]

On another front, the ecumenical project of the mostly mainline Protestants, while responsible for a number of important developments in how the United States conceptualized its role in human rights and international religious freedom, gradually lost momentum after mid-century. Evangelicals, who were less inclined to ecumenical religion, gained power and vigorously worked to reinforce the American Protestant hope for world Christianity. The fundamentalist Billy Graham, who preached a message of the need for conversion and the necessity of a conservative politics, mounted highly visible national crusades that he adapted to an international clientele in the 1950s. The news in the religious press about Graham's reception internationally was joyous.[7]

Inspired by Graham and having learned something from the previous ecumenical and liberal Protestant initiatives, conservative Protestants built an infrastructure for their own world project. They founded Fuller Theological Seminary in 1947, inaugurated or enlarged programs to train missionaries, and began putting large numbers of men and women into the field. Harold Cook of the Moody Bible Institute in Chicago, Robert Hall Glover of the China Inland Mission, and Harold Lindsell, the dean of Fuller, inspired their many print and lecture audiences with a vision of world Christianity close to being realized. An International Foreign Missions Association (IFMA) conference at the Moody Bible Institute in 1960 affirmed that "the total evangelization of the world may be achieved in this generation," while another meeting at nearby Wheaton several years later prospected more insistently, "the evangelization of the world in this generation, so help us God!"[8] Fuller established its School of World Mission in 1965, and three years after that the Association of Evangelical Professors of Missions began to meet. When evangelicals rallied at Lausanne in 1974 for an international planning session for missions, they already were riding high: 85 percent of American Protestant missionaries overseas were evangelical, and two-thirds of the funds for missions came from evangelical organizations.[9]

The recruitment of men and women to missionary initiatives rested on a vision of world Christianity that was rich in affect. Christianity from its beginnings had pictured itself as a community of persons who were knitted together in emotional bonds of care and loving attachment.[10] In the twentieth century, American Protestants drew relentlessly on that image of the extended Christian family in characterizing their international mission. For Protestants who were building a formidable missionary operation to bring their gospel to all parts of the world, the idea of Christian family was an especially useful one, allowing them a shorthand by which to explain how Christian converts from very different places around the globe fit into the Christian plan for history. Chinese, Africans, Bolivians, Pacific Islanders, Syrians, Burmese, Japanese, and every other population targeted by Protestant missionaries were imagined as family members. Differences rooted in millennia of cultural developments, including racial differences, theoretically were melted away by the acids of love brought by missionaries, aided by the hand of God. To be in a Christian family was to be like the American Protestants who had delivered the Christian gospel. The converted spoke a different language, looked different, had no blood relationship to Americans, married, worked, and died differently, and practiced a daily life different from that familiar to American Protestant missionaries, but they were kin. They were *felt* as kin.

American Protestants believed that converts all over the world were their family, and Americans enacted a complex emotional script in situating themselves alongside those whom they converted.[11] The feelings that they cultivated were those they believed were expected between family members. Early Christianity to some extent had pointed the direction for that strategy, and centuries of Christian missionizing had refined that conceptualization of Christian community. But Protestants in the twentieth century believed that they had arrived at a unique moment in Christian history, when space and time had compressed. The vast open space of the world was reduced to the measured "worldwide," and time was reduced to "this generation." It was possible to experience others as close in both space and time, and to feel other Christians on the other side of the world as kin. The world in that way was new for Protestant missionaries in the twentieth century.

The Archbishop of Canterbury William Temple had affirmed in 1942 that the global spread of Christianity was "the great new fact of our time."[12] Quoted widely, including in the U.S. Senate,[13] that phrase captured the long-lasting mood of the American Protestant effort to spread the gospel and build the worldwide family. References to the "worldwide Christian family" appeared everywhere, from *realpolitik* thinker Reinhold Niebuhr's journal *Christianity and Crisis* to the Methodist *Christian Advocate*, which reported in 1957 that "We are all members of one family, one Church worldwide, Christ's family, Christ's Church—whatever the color of our skin, wherever we live."[14]

In the worldwide family, Christians were brothers and sisters. Again, the terminology had deep roots in Christian history, but it was deployed anew after World War II in a way that emphasized both the geographical distribution of Christian siblings and the profound bonds that joined them. Over the next several decades, the terminology was progressively more decorated in the language of feeling. It was not just that Presbyterians could feel "the experiences of our Christian brothers and sisters in China," or that Methodists could recognize "our own neglected brothers and sisters" there.[15] It was, as testimony before Congress stated in 1981, "prayerful concern for our brothers and sisters" overseas.[16] It was, as the *American Baptist Woman* emphasized in 1986, a profound sense of connection: "Does learning to care mean learning to cry out on behalf of my sisters in South Africa and brothers in Latin America when they no longer have the energy to cry out for themselves?"[17] It was, in the language of a report published in the *Michigan Christian Advocate* as realization of the Cold War set in during the late 1940s, a feeling that crossed the boundaries of politics, and even the line that separated communism from the democratic West. Americans and their "fellow Christians in Russia" were "all made equally in God's image and are brothers of one another."[18] The kinship was mysterious but real. Protestant leaders of the worldwide Christianity campaign such as Van Dusen maintained "a continued faith in the unique, mystical power of Christianity. Even the sociologically-focused H. Richard Niebuhr . . . concluded his *Social Sources of Denominationalism* with a celebration of 'divine love' as a force that would unify Christians all over the globe if they would but cleave to it." There was a profound religiously framed "circulation of affect" that joined Americans to others throughout the world.[19]

The twentieth-century bonds of affection that tied Americans to their brothers and sisters in foreign lands were shaped by a specific aspect of the "worldwide" experience that Americans pursued. Americans considered themselves in a position to offer "sympathy" to people whose lives seemed difficult or whose political or material predicament seemed dire. Christians who thus approached their mission to the world with the expectation of feeling sympathy toward their local hosts were practicing a tradition that had been a part of American Christian missionizing since the Puritan migration to New England. Those Puritans fashioned a seal for the Massachusetts Bay colony around the image of a Native American who held in his mouth a banner unfurling to display the plea "Come over and help us," the New Testament language of Acts 16:9. But there was change over time in the meaning of those words.

Over the course of the nineteenth century and into the twentieth century, that theme of helplessness/helpfulness developed into a fresh conceptualization of the relation of the missionary to the host population. It was, in fact, a "paradigm shift" according to a Christian scholar of missions: "Evidently, then, a not-so-subtle shift had occurred in the original love motive; compassion and solidarity had been replaced by pity and condescension."[20] When Bishop Daniel Tuttle addressed the general convention of the Protestant Episcopal Church in St. Louis in 1916, he repeatedly drove home the theme of a conjoined helpfulness, sympathy, and brotherhood. The missionary, said Tuttle, "is there to show sympathy and goodwill, to give help and loving kindness." Tuttle emphasized further, "let our own work be steadily along the lines of goodwill and sympathy and allowance-making and patience and brotherly kindness and helpfulness."[21]

President Harry Truman brought together some of the themes of familial feeling in his radio remarks on the occasion of lighting the Christmas tree at the White House on Christmas Eve afternoon, 1949. "There are no ties like family ties," said Truman. "Those family ties reach out tonight to embrace the town, the State, the country, all of America—the whole world." Giving glory to God, the devout Baptist Truman then explained of Americans: "With all our strength we have always had a deep feeling of compassion—a human sympathy for the underdog, the oppressed of all lands, for all who bear heavy burdens. That is a part of the American spirit." Reflecting on the American settlement of the West, he added, as a footnote to his definition of a sturdy American spirit, that "we needed the strength of giants . . . to extend our frontiers."[22]

Historians for some time have discussed American Protestant missionizing as an aspect of colonialism and imperialism.[23] When we consider the affective dimensions of Protestant missionary projects within that framework of colonialism, the meanings of helpfulness and the centrality of pity are clearer. In missionary endeavors, "the gift of sympathy is also part of a certain economy of violence." In colonial contexts there is a "close linkage between civilization, sympathy, and colonization," and sympathy in such settings distanced the colonizer from the colonized even as it was performed in the interest of effacing difference.[24] Typically, "agendas motivated by 'compassion,' 'pity,' and 'empathy' motivated reformist zealots who swarmed . . . their colonial 'Other Worlds' overseas."[25] And those feelings ensured that colonialist status orders remained in place at the same time that they were taken as signs of the dismissal of status, even of difference.

Attention to the emotional data of American Protestant missionary work overseas enables recognition of the kinds of attachments that Americans experienced in localities in other parts of the world. It also helps conceptualize the vicarious experiences of Americans who were in contact with those missionaries as friends or family members, lecture audiences, readers, or church members who listened to sermons. Americans at home felt connected. They also recognized their difference. All of that was in keeping with the practice of colonialism. Colonial states "sought carefully to craft an appropriate distribution of affective attachment and detachment among colonized as well as colonizers."[26] Relationships between colonizer and colonized were thought to be most effective when there was some sense of mutuality, understood as a strong connection, alongside a sense of difference and distance. A Mennonite manual for missionaries in South Asia in 1963 urged readers to engage South Asians with "your imagination and sympathy," and that such an encounter should not be "based on giving only. The fellowship of brothers and sisters in Christ is a two-way communication."[27]

If the sympathy of the colonizer is a paradox, in that it involves "the necessary distance, and the imaginative bridging of it through a kind of identification—the double movement of the gaze of sympathetic power,"[28] then American Protestant attachment to the nations and peoples where mission work was in progress was in itself a paradox.[29] Protestant Americans who paid any attention to the world Christianity preached to them on Sundays defined themselves by their sympathetic attachments to the religious (and

160   CHAPTER FOUR

racial) others whom they targeted for missionary work. That paradoxical identification at the same time involved a cautious uncertainty of the other and a determination to maintain a precautionary distance.

Anti-Communism

The onset of the Cold War diminished the American Protestant ecumenical program for world Christianity.[30] But the evangelicals held on to their plans for converting the world and in fact flourished in the new global political order. They pushed ever harder for the realization of world Christianity, for the rescue of disadvantaged peoples with whom they sympathized. They also learned, contrastively and increasingly, to keep their distance. They learned a more acute fear of people in foreign lands, even more fear than they had felt for the Catholics in Rome, Spain, and South America. They learned above all that in the postwar world, the "great new fact" was not just world Christianity but communism and its intolerance of Christianity. The new American Protestant attachment to the foreigners who begged them to "come over and help us" was, like the attachment of Puritans to Indians, characterized by a sense of kinship alongside a composite feeling of fear, repulsion, and hostility. Protestants nurtured that dichotomous experience of international others through their writing, preaching, and behavior.

The complex emotional dynamics of the relationship between Americans and the nations whom they wished to Christianize took shape within a religio-political framework. The distinguishing feature of that framework was the American identification of the United States with Christianity. The joining of national identity with religion enabled the understanding of other nations as similarly constituted. In the case of the U.S.S.R and China (and at various times several other nations), that religion was atheism, which was conceptualized by Americans, and especially by evangelicals, as something akin to Christianity in certain structural ways, as an ideology and a practice. But it was a religion that existed in direct opposition to Christianity because it was Satanic, unethical, materialist, and evil. The "godless communist" Other was imagined a fervent unbeliever in the same nationalist way that Americans were zealous Christians.

The leads in conceptualizing the U.S.S.R. and other nations as "godless communism" were set by religious leaders from every faith. Billy Graham listened to reports of persons who had been in the U.S.S.R. and declared the Soviet nation "godless tyranny."[31] At the same time, he worried that the United Nations "bowed in deference to Russia," to "the Godless, atheistic Communists."[32] China was just as bad. That viewpoint overlapped with the Catholic position that a trip to China would be "an excursion into the incredible savagery of atheistic communism."[33] For one nun writing in 1953, "China today is not mere paganism, man's fumbling between right and wrong, guided only by his own middle brains." No, "this is Satanism, a superintelligent force of pure evil."[34]

Public officials followed the lead of the religious. The director of the Federal Bureau of Investigation, J. Edgar Hoover, wrote and spoke constantly of "communism for what it is—a materialistic, godless dogma dedicated to world domination." The "godless Communist conspiracy" was the core dynamic in the "struggle now raging between the camps of godless communism and human freedom."[35] For Harry Truman, what was crucial was gathering the "power of the free nations to overcome the conspiracy of godless communism."[36] Eisenhower was like-minded in recognizing "the implacable enemy of godless communism," and he affirmed the presumption of the popular Protestant view of "world Christianity" in declaring that religious "faith is the living source of all our spiritual strength. And this strength is our matchless armor in the world-wide struggle against the forces of godless tyranny and oppression."[37] Lyndon Johnson, who was impatient with evangelical theologizing of communism, was nevertheless sure that "we shall permit no godless 'ism' to bury America by force,"[38] and Ronald Reagan rarely lost an opportunity to make the common reference, as in his Easter and Passover radio address of 1983, in which he lamented "the brave Polish people" who struggled against "the oppression of a godless tyranny."[39]

Popular culture warned of godless communism in all manner of publications, including magazines, newspapers, and even comic books. The Catholic comic book *Treasure Chest*, which copied the look and some of the themes of the Marvel franchise, included a bonus comic in many of its 1961 issues. Called "This Godless Communism," the feature narrated the Soviet repression of religion in terms that cast the villains as purveyors of a perverted scientific and phony commonsense view of the world. In a typical frame, a pointer-wielding professor in a suit calmly but insidiously informed students in his classroom: "We have news for you students. You will no longer study religion. Since God does not exist there is no need for it."[40]

The point of public discussion of godless communism, for all of the deployment of the term throughout white American literary cultures, was that communism was not merely godless, it was itself a religion, and one that existed as the converse of the monotheistic religion that was familiar to Americans. Americans learned to think about communism, and to condemn it, by constructing it as a religion diametrically opposed to Christianity. The evangelical Protestant leader Carl Henry, speaking before the House

Un-American Activities Committee (HUAC) in 1956, urged the nation to awaken to the danger that beset it. Communism was not merely a godless political ideology but a powerful, motivating worldview that reached deep into the souls of men and women, posing an unprecedented threat to the West. He explained that "the modern crisis, in which the West itself is entangled more deeply than its leaders suspect, is therefore a religious crisis."[41]

Again, the overlap with some Catholic thinking was obvious. A Catholic writer in the 1960s spoke directly to the point: "When the tale is finally told, Communism emerges as a religion. A religion that has copied the methods of Christianity but has utterly corrupted its spirit."[42] In so characterizing communism, the author drew on a rich and familiar Catholic literature. As early as 1930, in the wake of the Vatican's instructions that Catholics were to pray at the end of every Sunday mass for the reconversion of Russia, the bishop of Baltimore was spelling out the predicament in unmistakable terms, commenting on "the unspeakable agonies of millions of believers—Catholic, Protestant, and Jewish—in the far-flung Russian area. A Godless nation is aborning. Atheism is the recognized State Religion."[43]

The communist state religion was evil. Billy James Hargis, a prominent evangelical who led the nationally popular electronic media ministry Christian Crusade in the 1950s and 1960s, told his followers that the fact of communism in Russia demanded that Christians make a decision. Hargis explained that "As God is totally good, Satan is totally evil. Whatever is good is of God, and whatever is evil is of Satan. Communism is satanic. It is anti-God, antichrist." Given that state of cosmic affairs, "Neutrality towards God is impossible. Neutrality towards Satan is also impossible. Neutrality towards communism is impossible."[44] To encourage Christians toward their decision, religious leaders cultivated affect by offering the figure of Joseph Stalin as the human embodiment of that evil. Communism was not merely an ideology, an abstraction, but human and hateable. The popular Christian lecturer Charles Lowery told HUAC in the aftermath of Stalin's death that "he was the devil in human and Soviet form," the incarnation of a "black, infernal wickedness." That character profile was passed along to Stalin's successor Nikita Khrushchev, in spite of Khrushchev's denunciations of Stalin.[45]

In American constructions of communism, fear of the enemy was joined to religious faith. It was a matter of one religion arrayed against another. In the context of postwar American foreign policy, "Soviet communism was especially evil because of its atheism and its enmity to all religious faith."[46] That sense of communism's evil designs on Christianity informed all public discussion about the Soviet Union and China, and it informed one of the most iconic political statements of the time, Ronald Reagan's reference to the "evil empire,"[47] a term that, once spoken, recurred throughout Reagan's presidency, whether he wished it to or not.

Anti-communist religious leaders kept fears about communism at a fever pitch. It may have been, as William G. McLoughlin argued in his book about Billy Graham, that fear of communism as a Satanic invention was good for an American revival of Protestant religion.[48] The influential publisher Henry Luce and Secretary of State John Foster Dulles, like Graham, certainly encouraged revival as a crucial component of American strategy for the Cold War.[49] It is possible also that what developed at mid-century was a pattern of thought in which communist nations served more generally as a condensed collective Other against which Americans could identify themselves.

Whether because revival was good for America during the Cold War or because communism made a good foe against which Americans could construct an identity more clearly, or both, clergy embraced the idea of the communist menace. They increasingly adorned their spoken antipathies to communism with language that presented the situation as extremely dangerous and urgent. One of the most forceful and influential of all the Christian statements about the problem was Billy Graham's "Satan's Religion," published in the *American Mercury*, a venerable journal founded by H. L. Mencken that had changed course after its sale at mid-century and become a conservative, antisemitic magazine. In a concise five-page article in 1954, Graham coalesced several key religious images of the communist threat, all built around the idea that communism was masterminded by Satan. Preaching that communism was "anti-Christian religion competing with Christianity for American souls," Graham articulated much of what subsequent evangelical preaching would take as its foundation for a discussion of communism.[50]

In 1960, when Billy James Hargis stated that "This battle against communism is Christ versus Anti-Christ; light versus darkness. It is not a political battle," he was channeling and refining Graham's vision of Christianity at war with communism.[51] The hard binary that evangelicals like Graham and Hargis and many others constructed boosted American willingness to conceptualize the battle between the two ideologies in martial terms. As Reuben Markham, of the American Council of Christian Laymen, wrote, "communism must crush Christianity or abdicate."[52] As Markham and others presumed, Christianity by the same token must crush communism or abdicate. In such discussions, the Amalekitish distinction between absolute good and absolute evil, and the understanding of victory as total annihilation of the other, jostled dialogically for discursive space with another idea, that all of humanity was a family, bonded to each other in the affection of kin.

As scholarship for some time has shown, American religious thinking about communism in the postwar era was diverse.[53] Liberal Protestantism had provided the inspiration and the energy for much American reflection on foreign policy before and during World War II, but in the 1950s, liberals began to lose power and influence and would continue to do so for the rest of the century. Truman attempted to get liberals and conservatives to work together and failed. An assortment of initiatives from the liberal side also failed, largely because the liberal impulse to ecumenism was unacceptable to confessionally preoccupied evangelicals. Protestant participation in the political culture of the Cold War accordingly included divergent views and discourses arising from contestation and competition.

Catholics in general, like Protestants, were opposed to communism. Moreover, they could claim a record of deeper and more forceful opposition to it. The Catholic Church had urged support of Francisco Franco during the Spanish Civil War in the 1930s because of his opposition to communism and secularity, the twin evils that the Church associated with the revolutionaries.[54] When Franco won, Catholics considered it a victory for the cause of their religion. It was an important moment for American Catholic *bona fides*, and U.S. Representative Peter Rodino in the 1960s was still officially congratulating Catholic Spain for its winning battle against "godless communism."[55] In prewar America, the Catholic program took shape when the Knights of Columbus (an organization that grew rapidly beginning just before mid-century) began their National Drive Against Communism, Atheism, and Home Destruction in 1937. They drummed up American support for the Spanish dictator Franco and launched a series of lectures on the "Perils of Communism." The Vatican extended its campaign against communism to the Soviet Union, becoming increasingly vocal about the threat that communism posed to Christianity. Catholic credentials accordingly would appear to be in order.

In some cases, however, Catholic efforts to stop the advance of communism led to complications in their relations with Protestants. Some Protestants thought that Catholics went too far, for instance, when American Catholics rallied to Franco, an effort that appeared to Protestants as support for a dictator opposed to democracy.[56] It took the efforts of the well-regarded television and radio personality Bishop Fulton J. Sheen, publicly praised by J. Edgar Hoover himself, to persuade Protestants not to suspect Catholics. Even then, his efforts followed upon the pro-fascist demagoguery of Father Coughlin, the prewar Detroit "radio priest," whose damage to Catholic standing nationally was severe and lasting. The fact that Catholics were the strongest supporters of Joseph McCarthy's hearings in Congress was little noticed at the time.[57] Problems remained for Catholics in spite of their displays of anti-communism.

American Jews, like Catholics, occupied uncertain social ground during the early period of the Cold War. A representative of the American Jewish Committee, testifying before HUAC, asserted that "Judaism and Communism are utterly incompatible."[58] Hoover, again, voiced confidence in Jews in his 1958 Cold War classic *Masters of Deceit*: "One of the most malicious myths that has developed in the United States is that persons of the Jewish faith and communists have something in common."[59] But Jews were disproportionately affected by the McCarthy witch hunts, and any hopes of forming a united patriotic front with Catholics and Protestants was hamstrung by not only Protestant and Catholic suspicions of Jews (including suspicions engendered by the virulently antisemitic outpourings of Father Coughlin in previous decades) but also an assortment of other issues having to do with ideas about authority and community.[60]

Evangelicals made an effort to build an institutional infrastructure for their own opposition to communism. Typical was the Methodist League Against Communism, Fascism, and Unpatriotic Pacifism, which was founded in 1936. Over several decades following that, as the idea of an evil communist conspiracy became commonplace, evangelical leaders made that idea the centerpiece of their preaching about America and its future. The evangelical view of other nations being both like and unlike America[61] remained strong. And as the evangelical anti-communist rhetoric grew more vivid, picturing "poor Russians" and "poor Chinese" as victims of a monstrous Satanic plot at the same time that it cast them as feared enemy soldiers, that rhetoric was exploited by political leaders in Washington. During this early Cold War period, "Protestant leaders failed to exercise a significant or determinative influence on the actual formation of American foreign policy."[62] Evangelicals nevertheless flourished, their thinking about the evil religion of communism continued to gain traction, and the linkages they made between spiritual/moral revival and American patriotism remained intact. They accomplished all of that while distancing themselves from both liberal Protestants and Roman Catholics. In fact, evangelicals remained strongly anti-Catholic. Even more importantly, their anti-communism was entwined with their anti-Catholicism.[63]

Intolerance

COMMUNISTS AND CULTS

In order to appreciate the ways in which Americans continued to project their religious intolerance to other parts of the world, it is necessary to understand the new forms that such intolerance took after World War II. Americans during the Cold War came to understand a more direct linkage between an assortment of new religious groups in America and certain religions overseas that they identified as dangerous. By creating narratives about communism as a religious cult engaged in a treacherous infiltration of America, Americans positioned themselves to see the religion of certain American groups as extensions of purportedly religious practices in the U.S.S.R., China, and other communist countries. Antipathy toward, and even violence against, such communist-related groups in America accordingly was conceptualized as a matter of the patriotic defense of democracy, not as religious intolerance.

Such imagining added to and reinforced the already well-established practice of repudiating American groups (such as Catholics and Mormons) that challenged Protestant hegemony. Fears about the communist threat led Americans to call for resistance to any religious group that could be associated with communism. Such groups were to be disowned, just as were Catholics and Mormons previously. At the same time, the new narratives about communism and religion ideologically built out the case for refusing to recognize actions taken against certain new religions as intolerant. Moreover, the excitement about communism engendered a clearer focus on it as an overseas culprit which, taken as a religion, ascended to prominence in Protestant thinking about overseas religious enemies. For Protestants, communism in timely fashion came to equal even Roman Catholicism as a threat.

The postwar era of anti-communist frenzy was manifest in religion in numerous ways. Communism was a competing religion, and it was evil. Communism also was a religion that used certain kinds of tactics in growing its membership that Americans, and especially American Christians, found abhorrent. Americans' discussion of communism as a competing religion drew upon a background of nervous American religious literature about new religions in eventually defining communism as a "cult." In understanding communism in that way, Americans additionally asserted that a key component of communist practice was to assimilate persons by brainwashing them.

The view that communism was a cult emerged against a background of American writing about cults more broadly. Some of that writing predated the war, and some emerged in the immediate postwar years and through the early decades of the Cold War. It focused on New Religious Movements (NRM) as a danger to Christianity and the nation. William C. Irvine's *Heresies Exposed* (1917), Charles Wright Ferguson's *Confusion of Tongues* (1928), and Jan Karel van Baalen's *The Chaos of Cults* (1938) all sounded the alarm about the dangers of religious movements that developed on the margins of Christianity and that remained differentiated from a supposed Christian mainstream by virtue of their deviant ideas and practices.

Irvine, a New Zealander who served as a missionary in India and later became a popular author in America, identified Mormons, Seventh-day Adventists, Jehovah's Witnesses, Theosophists, and Christian Scientists, among others, as groups that posed a serious threat to the integrity of Protestant Christianity and the nation. Mormons, who were "a terrible menace to America's welfare," were cast, like other NRMs, as frauds and liars whose doctrinal errors seeped into the mainstream of American Protestantism, polluting and undoing it by stealth.[64] Charles Wright Ferguson, a Texan and Methodist minister, considered similar NRMs, adding to the list the Ku Klux Klan, liberal Catholicism, and atheism, the last of which he believed proselytized more zealously than any other cult in America. His vivid portrayal of atheism as a powerful cult among others helped set the frame for American fears about godless communism twenty years later.[65]

The Chaos of Cults, van Baalen's survey, included additional groups, such as Bahaism, Unitarianism, Frank Buchman's Moral Re-Armament, and the Unity Church. The tone of the book was less alarmist than others of the time, with van Baalen making an effort to appear even-handed in his characterization of the fifteen cults he deemed most significant. But as a Christian Reformed minister who considered a cult "any religion regarded as unorthodox," he allowed ample room for criticism of every group he cited as fraudulent and dangerous. Moreover, the Princeton Seminary–educated van Baalen sought to give the appearance of scientific objectivity in his criticisms of groups he identified as cults, and typically made a case against each as he did against Mormons: "The book of Mormon is contradicted on every point by careful scientific investigation of early American anthropology." Cults, whatever their angle, all were "propagandists." The active propagandizing of the cults, moreover, was similar to that of the communists. Quoting H. Richard Niebuhr, van Baalen asserted that, in fact, the emotionally rich approach of cultist propaganda was something "they have learned from the communists."[66]

Communist propaganda succeeded, so said many Americans, because it brainwashed people into believing its doctrines. Reuben Markham, the influential author and anti-communist crusader who identified himself as "a rather aggressive Protestant," repeatedly emphasized that communism was a rival religion. In a series of books on communist influence in Eastern Europe after the war, he became more pointed in his characterizations of communism, referring to it frequently as a cult. In the Balkans, "Communistic Tito-worship" that was grounded in a "flaming emotional ideal" checked all the boxes. In addition to its dangerous emotionality and devotion to an authority figure, it had a "liturgy," he said. It was a "political conspiracy, called

Communism. The Communist cult. . . ."[67] Why did communism inspire the peasant masses of Eastern Europe? "The answer is that Communism in the Slav Balkan lands was a secular religion. . . . Communism was a cult."[68]

Christian writers filled out the picture of communism as a religious cult by including the various modifiers—Satanic, evil, anti-Christ—that were common in discussions of communism more generally. A study of "Hitler's totalitarianism and its communist offspring" explained that evil was consistent, that "the devil does not change, and because he is the ultimate author and life-giver to the Communist cult," the stories of Hitler and the U.S.S.R. were largely the same.[69] Academic analysts, for their part, added muscle to the view of communism as a religious cult. John Stephen Reshetar, writing under the auspices of the Foreign Policy Research Institute at the University of Pennsylvania, explained at length how the structure of the Communist Party in the Soviet Union was "ecclesial." Such views became constitutive of American thinking about communism and remained popular among conservatives and among religious Americans throughout the Cold War. In the 1980s, Senator Jesse Helms was still referring to "the pathologically anti-western communist cult which rules the Soviet Union."[70]

Americans believed that the communist cult assimilated people by brainwashing them. Testimony at Senate hearings in 1956 focused on "brainwashing, the fundamental strategy for international communism for expansion and control."[71] The highly regarded conservative author Russell Kirk, in *The American Cause* (1957), devoted a section of his book to "Communist Brainwashing," which he described as "clever political indoctrination, usually without physical intimidation," a characterization that rendered it all the more dangerous to Americans.[72] Kirk took his lead from recent publications about communist brainwashing techniques in North Korea, a growing literature based on debriefings of American military personnel who served time as POWs during the Korean War. The "North Korea brainwashing machine,"[73] as one writer referred to it, was a highly routinized and methodical program devised to overcome even the most stubborn resistance. The growing commentary about brainwashing reflected a conceptualization of it as an advanced scientific technology, a proven and near-irresistible means for changing the minds of persons.

The Anglophone "washing the brains" likely was coined by a writer in the UK in 1950 in an article on Chinese propagandizing.[74] The term was popularized, however, by Edward Hunter, author of *Brain-Washing in Red China* (1951). Hunter was an ambitious and adept self-promoter who wrote numerous books and articles about brainwashing, lectured widely, and appeared before Congress to testify about his findings regarding "the calculated destruction of men's minds" under communist regimes.[75] The term soon became standard in depictions of communist rule and found its way easily into the Christian clergy's preaching about communist cults. A delegate to the Assembly of God General Council gathering in Texas in 1959 spoke of how the best communist agents were deployed in America to places "wherever they can brainwash youth . . .—particularly in the Universities."[76]

The translation of fears about communist brainwashing to discussions about religious cults—and especially those on American university campuses—took place through the agency of a number of writers. One of those was Margaret Singer, a psychologist who studied the experiences of Korean War veterans alongside Robert Jay Lifton, a psychiatrist at Harvard and co-founder of the field of psychohistory. Her own research deviated from Lifton's in many ways, but her writings on brainwashing and cults in the 1960s and 1970s helped establish the idea of psychological coercion as a central consideration in the analysis of membership in religious cults. Her pronouncements on brainwashing, together with those of Hunter and several other purported specialists, merged with the religious literature on cults and the dangers they posed to the nation. Singer's thinking did not culminate in a comprehensive survey of the topic until the 1990s, when she published *Cults in Our Midst: The Hidden Menace in Our Everyday Lives*, but her theories were broadly accepted from the 1960s onward. Central among those theories was that religious cults were constituted by people who had been brainwashed and were kept in a condition of dependency by mind control methods that induced mental illness.[77]

The sociologists Anson D. Shupe and David C. Bromley, in surveying American fears about religious cults in the 1970s and the resistance of religious groups toward NRMs, concluded that "the brainwashing claim is . . . the essence of anticult theology."[78] The Christian Anticult Movement (CAM) that coalesced in opposition to NRMs accordingly sought to counter them by pointing out how they brainwashed their memberships but also by identifying, sometimes in great detail, the doctrinal errors or heresies that NRMs promoted. Typical of the CAM approach to countering religious cults was *The Kingdom of the Cults* (1965), a book by Baptist minister Walter Ralston Martin that detected the theological mistakes in the cults that had been identified by Christian writers prewar, as well as in the religions from Asia that had begun to attract Americans, and the groups that eventually came to be called New Age religions. For Martin, cults erred in distorting scripture and in replacing obedience to Jesus Christ with obedience to a human leader. Cult, communism, conspiracy, and brainwashing were interwoven in Martin's view of the changing religious landscape of the nation. Father Divine

(d. 1965), the founder of the International Peace Mission movement, for example, was the agent of a "communist conspiracy," a "glorified stooge" of communist plans to destroy the Christian West and replace it with atheistic totalitarianism. In general, "almost all systems of authority in cult organizations indoctrinate" their followers through brainwashing.[79]

American response to NRMs in the 1960s and the 1970s was uneven. The last vestiges of the ecumenical movement offered a framework for some measure of understanding. The creation of new cultural spaces in America arising from distinctions based on age, race, and gender at times also enabled pockets of tolerance for NRMs. But in general Americans distrusted NRMs. Perceived as enemies of freedom and conscience, and with seeming connections to communist methods and ideas, cults were openly threatened and frequently subjected to acts of violence. The violence against Jehovah's Witnesses in the 1940s, a nationwide anticult campaign that included physical assaults, the burning of their houses of worship, and other mob actions of various sorts, was directed anew at groups such as the Unification Church of Rev. Sun Myung Moon, whose Camp New Hope in Ulster County, New York, was partially destroyed by arson in 1980. Prior to the fire, the camp had been subjected to shootings and vandalism, and burned crosses had been left on the property. A KKK banner was found on the property after the fire.[80] Bombings took place at the Hare Krishna Temple in San Diego in 1979, at the organization's Philadelphia Temple in 1984, and at The Way College in 1981. Violence ranging from physical assault to arson and shootings took place at many other "cult" sites during the 1960s–1980s. Religious intolerance of NRMs was widespread and violent.

Attacks on cults varied in kind. By far the most common violence against cults was kidnapping, of which there were thousands of instances.[81] Taken by force from their religious communities and detained in grim environs, members of NRMs were subjected to "deprogramming," a spurious practice (supported by Margaret Singer, among others) intended to undo the brainwashing that was assumed to have taken place as the means of recruiting a person into the group. Such coercion, in a nation that prided itself on "freedom of conscience," spoke loudly about American inability to recognize domestic religious intolerance. Court rulings eventually put a stop to the anticult practices of kidnapping and deprogramming. But for several decades during the Cold War, those practices were legitimated by the Christian Anticult Movement, a network of mostly Protestant organizations—such as Walter Martin's Christian Research Institute—dedicated to the eradication of cults even if the means to that end was at odds with American ideals about religious liberty.

The mass suicide of hundreds of persons at the Peoples Temple in Jonestown in 1978, as well as several other tragic incidences, led to a public image of NRMs as "doomsday cults."[82] The debacle involving the Branch Davidian group at Waco in 1993, in which eighty-two members of the group died in a fire while besieged by federal agents and military, and the "Satanic panic" of the 1970s–1980s, reinforced that perception.[83] Although brainwashing theory and claims for the necessity of deprogramming were discredited by academic research in the 1980s, conservative religious organizations did not begin to turn away from the theory until the late 1990s, when Fuller Seminary professor Newton Malony presented a case against brainwashing that gained the attention of evangelicals who had been most concerned with cults.[84]

American anxieties about NRMs were intensified by the fact of the Asian origins of a number of highly visible religious movements during the 1960s–1980s. Cold War binary thinking for the most part lumped together Chinese, North Koreans, and North Vietnamese—all military adversaries—with Japanese and the populations of the Asian subcontinent and Tibet when it came to religious difference. In the middle part of the twentieth century, "many Americans did not ascertain the differences between Sikhs, Hindus, Muslims, and Indians as we understand them today. Lumping them together . . . suggests that religious distinctions mattered less to the majority of Americans than the population's foreign geographic origin, ethnicity, and broader culture."[85] All Asians were suspect for a number of reasons, but race braided with foreign religions was of particular concern to white American Christians struggling with the growing American pluralism. The problem was a matter of "racialized American civil religion."[86]

The national fears of a foreign conspiracy aimed at overthrowing the nation had been manifested in the internment of Japanese Americans during World War II. Those fears still flourished, animated in the 1960s by the war in Vietnam, and more precisely in the popularization of the "Domino Theory" of communist advance, a speculation that was deployed by successive administrations to justify American military interventions in southeast Asia. American antipathy to Asian religions moreover was constituted by unreformed attitudes underlying legal restriction of Asian immigration. From the Chinese Exclusion Act of 1882 through the formation of the activist Asiatic Exclusion League in 1905 and the federal Immigration Acts of 1917 and 1924, a view of the unfitness of Asians to behave responsibly in the American democracy had been codified in law. Discrimination against Asians over time expanded to include not only economic and political reasons—which formed the core of previous American opposition to Asians—but also worries that religion from Asia, which was becoming popular on college campuses, was a Trojan horse. Inside, it hid communists and other anti-Christian enemies.

172   CHAPTER FOUR

The turn to Asian religions among young Americans, which built upon American exposure to Asian traditions that were showcased at the Parliament of World's Religions in Chicago in 1893, took place through the agency of popular culture. The publicity surrounding the mid-1960s pilgrimage of the Beatles to India, the popular linkage of hallucinogenic drugs with spiritual awakening, the dissemination of the romantic theories of religion of Carl Jung and Joseph Campbell, and the easily digestible interpretations of Asian religion such as D. T. Suzuki's version of Zen were a few of the developments that provided a backdrop for the American attraction to Asian religions. Popular culture in fact was the central medium through which Asian religions were introduced to Americans during the Cold War era. The popular television show *Kung Fu* (1972–1975), for example, which was set in the historical American West, ended each episode with a lesson about the intermingling of martial arts violence with Asian wisdom and models of spirituality.[87]

The young Americans who journeyed from Christian and Jewish backgrounds into explorations of Asian religions, or into experimental versions of Christianity that incorporated Asian ideas and practices, were, editorialized the *Atlanta Constitution* in 1975, responding to the "failure of traditional Western religions." The pursuit of enlightenment through exploration of Asian traditions was, nevertheless, unlikely to end well: "Much of the youthful fiddling with exotic Eastern religions is probably immature, shallow and ephemeral."[88] The *New York Times*, citing Margaret Singer, proposed that the youthful American interest in religious cults was about drugs, macrobiotic diets, and "meditation and Chinese philosophy." Members were victims of hucksters who led such groups; they were young people who were "in the vulnerable periods between college and a job, or between careers or marriages."[89]

Fear that faith communities in America that drew upon Asian religions were part of a global conspiracy to undermine America and to diminish Christianity was reinforced by a few cases in which conspiracy to break American law actually was proven. The most widely publicized of those cases involved the Rev. Sun Myung Moon, the Korean founder of the Unification Church, which blended Christian and Korean traditions. A detailed U.S. House of Representatives report in 1978 iterated instances in which Moon had "secret meetings" with persons in the United States and that his organization was cover for "secret envoys of the Korean government." The report recommended a full investigation into Moon's role in the arms trade.[90] When suspicions about Moon eventuated in his conviction for income tax evasion and conspiracy in 1982, resulting in a fine and imprisonment, the news of his conviction was taken by some as a sign of broad Asian designs to subvert the country. For critics of Asian religions in America, that proof was made stronger still by the conviction of Ma Anand Sheela in 1985 for her role in a bioterror attack on an Oregon community near the Rajneeshpuram ashram that she codirected. Charged with attempted murder, assault, and forty-one separate acts of conspiracy, she was convicted of most charges and served a prison sentence.[91]

The growing number of Asian religious groups in America worried not only Christians of traditional and conservative mind, but persons occupying various positions on the political spectrum. Academic experts whose agenda differed markedly from that of conservative Christians were quick to criticize the Asian-influenced religious communities in America as superficial or outright fakes. Anthropologist Agehananda Bharati of Syracuse University was quoted dismissing "counterfeit Oriental cults" in America with the simple judgment "They're spurious."[92] Otherwise moderate newspaper editors complained constantly about Asian religious groups and especially about Moon and his Unification Church. *Napa Sentinel* writers Harry V. Martin and David Caul, who reported in detail on what they saw as brainwashing in cults, believed that Moon and his Unification Church were part of a "Right Wing Media Conspiracy" that controlled the *Washington Times*, the Christian Coalition, and the Republican Party.[93]

Some on the left also were critical. The Marxist and U.S. Labor Party founder Lyndon LaRouche (who improbably also shared some ground with the far right) ran a campaign for public office in 1980 in which his views were laid out in a booklet entitled *Stamp Out the Aquarian Conspiracy*. That title directly challenged the pitch of *The Aquarian Conspiracy* (1980),[94] a best-selling upbeat paean to the promise of eastern mysticism, Zen, and the nonrational. LaRouche, turning the tables, endorsed the idea that there was in fact a *dangerous* conspiracy of unreason, identified it as a problem rather than a promise, and blamed it on multinational corporations. "The population of the United States of America is being brainwashed," said the booklet. Business and financial leaders had enlisted an army of social psychologists to methodically change the way Americans thought about their society. The "Aquarian Penetration into the U.S. Government" was in fact an effort to bring about fuzzy-mindedness in the general population that would enable corporations to control them more easily.[95] Asian religions, with their mandalas, exotic spirituality, and seeming dismissal of science, were a tool in the broader corporate conspiracy to ruin the nation.

Fear of Asian religious communities in America translated into violence against them. Kidnappings were common, as family members and friends attempted to capture and deprogram young persons whom they believed to have been brainwashed by Asian manipulators. But arson, assault, and various

174 CHAPTER FOUR

kinds of discrimination also were a part of the intolerance toward NRMs that had some connection to Asian ideas or practices.[96] In 1983, when three American veterans burned down a Buddhist shrine in Massachusetts, the U.S. Commission on Civil Rights reported its concern about how the surge in "hate and hostility based on extremist concepts of racial purity or religious certitude leads to illegal acts of force and violence."[97] That concern was borne out in a growing number of violent acts against Asian religious groups. In Chicago in 1986, over a three-month stretch, Indian businesses were vandalized or otherwise attacked forty-seven times, while a street pamphlet, "The Traitor," informed readers that "Satan created all the gods of India." Hinduism, which was said to demand human sacrifice, was directed by demons on a mission to "rob your soul and take you to hell."[98] Various official reports published during the 1970s and 1980s included descriptions of violence against Asian religious groups and, in some cases, identified specific organizations, such as the KKK, as the perpetrators. But responsibility for violence was broader, concluded the Commission: "What is significant, however, is the fact that these groups advocate openly the racist and discriminatory beliefs that survive in individuals and institutions despite efforts at their eradication."[99]

Americans' Cold War–era enthusiasm for a worldwide family of Christians, in which Americans were joined through the mystical power of divine love with other brothers and sisters around the world, was one side of Christians' understanding of their relationship with a world of different peoples, religions, and ideas. Drawn to global others and keen on recognizing them as kin, Americans also were wary of them. Foreigners, howsoever much they might be the object of sympathy and tended to according to a religious ideal of care, were at the same time enemies to be feared. To reach out in international Christian missionary endeavors was also to allow an opening for communist, godless, or Asian evil to enter. American Christians to an extent made an effort to identify with members of their worldwide family outside the United States. At the same time, they policed boundaries that separated Asians and communists from America—another way of thinking about others and one that dominated the Cold War headlines.[100] The antipathy to NRMs and especially to those with an Asian component was rooted in a complex worldview that had as much to do with the international state of affairs as it did with the actual activities of emerging religious communities in the United States.

ANTI-CATHOLICISM

During the Cold War era, Protestant and Catholic Americans both looked suspiciously on Asian religions and on NRMs that they believed used Asian brainwashing tactics. But Protestants and Catholics were divided on much else. The long history of anti-Catholicism in America remained a central component in Protestant anxiety about the state of the nation and the future of the world. The mounting anti-Catholic bigotry in the late twentieth century was significant enough to be recognized as "the new anti-Catholicism."[101] In fact, anti-Catholicism had been strong in America throughout the Cold War but was an "ugly secret"[102] not usually acknowledged or recognized in the media. While the proceedings of the Second Vatican Council (1962–1965) were largely viewed favorably by non-Catholics in America, anti-Catholic sentiments in the 1940s–1950s, and then in resurgence after the 1970s, were an important part of religious self-understanding for many non-Catholics. The reinvigorated missionary enterprises of Catholics, especially in Africa and Asia, were viewed by evangelical Protestants in America as a direct threat to their hopes for the triumph of a Protestant International. The increased Catholic emphases on social services as the core of missions work were especially noted by Protestants who had been vigorously restructuring their own missionary activity around a similar agenda.[103]

Catholics appeared to Protestants as sect-like in their apparent devotion to a single leader, the Pope, and in their rigidly policed religious life and disciplined collective behavior.[104] In the complex American political world of the 1950s, Catholics, whose anti-communist fervor was well evidenced in publications and speeches, came to be equated with the totalitarian regimes of communist countries. Their modus operandi, said critics, duplicated that of the communist state.

Paul Blanshard, the general counsel for Americans United for Separation of Church and State, which was founded in 1948 initially to oppose government aid to Catholic schools, explained the problem in his influential *Communism, Democracy, and Catholic Power* (1951).[105] According to Blanshard, communism and Catholicism were structurally parallel systems. "The two patterns of power are as alike as the two poles of the earth," he wrote. "They occupy the opposite extremes of the moral universe, but they represent the same intellectual climate—the climate of authoritarian rule over the human mind." Both the Vatican and the Kremlin pursued grand designs for world domination, and "the theory of imperialist rights under which the two dictatorships operate is essentially the same." Their methods of propagandizing and controlling persons were alike, and their "strategies of penetration" included, for example, strong encouragement to couples to create large families that would change, by sheer numerical strength, the balance of power.[106]

Such Protestant construction of Catholicism as the opposite/twin of communism suggests again the well-practiced strategy of Protestant identity when it came to international relations. Protestants took themselves to be kin with Others whom they envisioned in China or Russia but equally believed that they were diametrically opposed to them. That in fact was exactly how some Protestants constructed American Catholics as communists/not-communists.

As the HUAC hearings began to come apart and their leader, Senator Joseph McCarthy, increasingly discredited, Catholics were criticized for their strong support of McCarthy. McCarthyite activists had voiced suspicion that liberal Protestants had been accommodating to communists, and HUAC in 1953 was on the verge of a full investigation of the National Council of Churches. Discussion of that possibility added a degree of difficulty to relations between Catholics and Protestants as far as theories and ideals of government were concerned.[107] However, it was not the Protestant-led National Council of Churches but the National Association of Evangelicals (NAE) that took the lead in opposing the Catholic Church.

Working with the organization Protestants and Other Americans United for Separation of Church and State (renamed Americans United for Separation of Church and State), the NAE built a campaign during the late 1940s and 1950s to oppose Catholic efforts to obtain tax money for parochial projects. Mailings, rallies, advertising, and even a film detailed Catholic refusals to acknowledge the separation of church and state and sounded the alarm about the threat of Roman rule in the United States posed by the presidential candidacy of John F. Kennedy. The NAE was not the only organization that voiced concerns about the religious implications of a Kennedy presidency. But, encouraged by evangelical leaders such as Carl Henry, James DeForest Murch, and NAE director of public affairs Clyde Taylor, evangelical Protestants articulated the fear that Catholics, operating like communists, were at work to destroy the separation of church and state. Moreover, intolerance toward Catholics did not diminish after the 1960 election. Historian Axel Schäfer's reading of the NAE archives of the period led him to conclude that "anti-Catholicism remained virulent in the NAE beyond the Kennedy election and the Second Vatican Council."[108] There were gesturings toward ecumenical cooperation on some level, but fear of Catholic conspiracy in America did not abate, and evangelical concern over Catholic intentions worldwide remained strong.

Anti-Catholicism in the NAE translated into greater efforts to establish the conditions for Protestant expansion abroad. Evangelicals pressured Washington to build relationships with foreign countries that would ensure the protection of Protestant missionaries who were competing with Catholics in mission fields in Africa, Asia, and South America. During this period, "the anti-Catholic campaigns were both a crucial means of mobilizing the evangelical constituency for the expansion of missionary activities abroad and of facilitating political re-engagement."[109] Those campaigns appeared to evangelicals early on to be paying off. Clyde Taylor, who would eventually become director of the NAE, boasted in 1949, "When world matters involving foreign missions are discussed by our Department of State we are invited."[110]

In subsequent decades, NAE influence only increased, as the NAE organized letter-writing campaigns to demand treaties with nations where Protestants wished to expand their missionary efforts. Like his predecessors in the nineteenth century, Taylor and his religious allies—including groups beyond the NAE—aimed at shaping treaties to include protections for U.S. citizens abroad. A "core campaign" for the NAE increasingly was characterized by Taylor as a matter of promoting religious liberty worldwide. The overt anti-Catholicism of the NAE and other evangelical groups lessened over time as evangelicals shifted their agenda from pushing back against what they viewed as oppressive Catholic regimes (such as in South America) to a more politically pragmatic promotion of "religious liberty" for all regardless of faith community or denomination. Taylor eventually described NAE efforts to influence foreign policy as an initiative "not made because they are Christians but because they are U.S. citizens and hence our government has certain basic obligations to protect and guarantee their freedoms. Usually the basis of such a defense is the treaty of 'peace, friendship and navigation' signed between the countries involved."[111] The evangelical effort, which began as an anti-communist and anti-Catholic assignment, ended up "in the long term, phrasing evangelical interests as a religious freedom issue."[112]

Religious intolerance of Asians, NRMs, and Catholics during the Cold War involved fear of communism and suspicion that those groups were extremely authoritarian, even totalitarian, in their organization of collective religious life. As such, those groups gave the appearance of being dangers to American democracy. In the case of Asians, racism also was involved, but Asians generally were conceptually linked—by Americans who feared them—with communism and "devil religion." The case of intolerance toward African American religious groups was different.

AFRICAN AMERICAN CHURCHES

Intolerance of African American religious groups in the latter part of the twentieth century had less to do with communism or Catholicism and more to do with race. African Americans, especially in the South, tended to be Baptists, Methodists, Pentecostals, or otherwise Protestant, although Catho-

178   CHAPTER FOUR

lic communities also existed. Intolerance toward them, much of which was manifested as the destruction of African American churches, had a long history. It was dramatically evidenced anew during the years of the Civil Rights movement, and was predicated on the perception that the church was the central institution of African American life. Intolerance of African American religious groups had little to do with differences in doctrine or religious practice. But it was intolerance nonetheless, and a violent strain of intolerance. In attacking black churches, intolerant persons and groups sought to destroy the religious expressions of black collective identity.

While individual civil rights religious leaders and their followers—most notably Martin Luther King Jr.—were shockingly assaulted or murdered, the burning of black churches was one of the most consistent and dramatic expressions of religio-racial intolerance in America after mid-century. In the years following *Brown v. Board of Education* (1954), which disallowed the segregation of public schools, there were hundreds of attacks or attempted attacks on black churches in the South. One of the most tragic and most remembered of those occurrences was the bombing of the 16th Street Baptist Church in Birmingham, Alabama, in September 1963, in which four girls died. Attacks on churches had spiked previously during Reconstruction and during the second coming of the KKK in the 1920s. The period of the Civil Rights movement was a time of particular violence, however. The church bombings and arsons came in clusters across the South, affecting as many as three hundred churches.[113] During just the twelve weeks surrounding the signing of the Civil Rights Act (1964), thirty-four black churches burned.[114]

In order to understand the full context of overseas projection of American religious intolerance that typified the evangelical-led campaign for international religious freedom in the 1990s, it is necessary to consider the so-called "fourth wave" of black church burnings that took place during that decade. Over an eighteen-month period in 1995–1996, authorities investigated at least sixty-four[115] arsons of black churches. Not all of those finally were deemed arson, and once authorities began to investigate, they concluded that about a third were clearly hate crimes, although many of the burnings were left unsolved. Moreover, a number of white churches burned during the same period (but proportionately far less than black churches). As statistics were compiled, the fact remained that a large number of black churches were destroyed by white arsonists. In some cases, such as in Greeleyville, South Carolina, the KKK was involved.[116]

The media response to the burnings was excited and unrelenting once investigators detected a pattern of hate-crime arson[117] in several clusters of cases in the Carolinas and an area of Tennessee/Alabama. National discussion turned from other problems facing the nation to the black church burnings, with commentators nationwide expressing their outrage in newspaper columns and television editorials. The issue shot to the top of the domestic agenda for President Bill Clinton, who visited the site of the ruined church in Greeleyville and condemned the "rash of church burnings" breaking out across the South.[118] Clinton urged Congress to pass legislation, eventually called the Church Arson Prevention Act, which he signed in July 1996. The nation was preoccupied with the arsons for over a year, intense feelings were expressed, and the problem of racial-religious intolerance was given maximum visibility.

Virtually every religious organization in the United States spoke out against the church arsons and offered a statement of support for the eventual legislation that aimed to prevent arson and support the rebuilding of burned churches. Over the course of several years, however, it became clear which religious organizations were willing to prioritize ongoing active lobbying for the Act and take on responsibility for coordinating rebuilding efforts. At the forefront were the Congress of National Black Churches and, especially, the National Council of Churches (NCC). When President Clinton spoke publicly a few days after the passage of the Act in July 1996 to thank those who had created the legislation, he included by name Joan Campbell of the NCC alongside a half-dozen members of Congress whom he also thanked. The NCC was prominently acknowledged for the next several years in the annual reports of the National Church Arson Task Force, and especially for its ongoing partnership with the government in rebuilding churches and discouraging arson of religious buildings. The National Association of Evangelicals was not mentioned by Clinton in his speech, nor was the NAE acknowledged in the annual Task Force reports as an involved participant in the rebuilding and in the campaign to stop church arson. The NAE, instead, was looking overseas for religious intolerance.[119]

For a nation that historically has had difficulty coming to terms with domestic religious intolerance, the passage of the Church Arson Prevention Act seemed to signal a possible turn in the nation's willingness to confront religious intolerance head-on. But much remained the same. A large American Christian community that historically had responded to spikes in religious intolerance in the United States by projecting it elsewhere embarked again in 1996 on an intensive campaign to direct the nation's attention to religious intolerance in other countries. That campaign resulted in legislative victories that were trumpeted by evangelicals and their allies for the next twenty years.

180   CHAPTER FOUR

The International Religious Freedom Act (1998), created in the immediate aftermath of the black church burnings, was the culmination of a project started decades earlier.

Human Rights and Religious Persecution

In 1996, the NAE issued its *Statement of Conscience*, a condemnation of "worldwide religious persecution," in which it listed, as a primary crime, "church burnings." The locations of persecution listed were "many Islamic countries" and nations ruled by "communist regimes" that persecuted persons of "Christian faith." Issued on January 23, ten days after new fires burned two African American churches in Boligee, Alabama,[120] the document made no mention of the United States among the offenders and no mention of church burnings in America. There was much feeling in the document, which spoke out against "reigns of terror," and their "practice of torture," "demonization of powerless Christian scapegoats," "murder of Christian converts and their children," and "unpunished mob violence." Islam was the only religion mentioned besides Christianity, and Muslims were cast as persecutors.[121]

The NAE statement can be understood partially in its connections to the development of human rights activism in America. During the 1930s and 1940s the international human rights movement began to coalesce, and Social Gospel ideas, including those of the American Baptist Walter Rauschenbusch (d. 1918), played a role.[122] The outlines of that movement gradually were becoming clearer in America through a series of statements by government leaders and non-governmental organizations (NGOs). Several events were of particular importance. In early 1941, President Roosevelt articulated the "Four Freedoms" in a closing to a major policy address. The second of those freedoms he defined as the "freedom of every person to worship God in his own way everywhere in the world."[123] The emphasis in the "Four Freedoms" on the universal rights of the person subsequently shaped the Atlantic Charter of August 1941. The Atlantic Charter did not specifically address freedom of worship but in general drew upon the language and spirit of the Four Freedoms.[124] The Declaration by the United Nations in early 1942 to fight the Axis powers explicitly acknowledged its indebtedness to the ideas in the Atlantic Charter and pledged the signatory nations specifically to defend religious freedom (a step further than the language of the Atlantic Charter) and preserve human rights.[125]

On the heels of government action, religious groups and religious writers formulated their own statements about freedom of religion as a human right. In 1943, John Foster Dulles, a Presbyterian elder and director of the

Commission to Study the Bases of a Just and Durable Peace, presented the organization's *Six Pillars of Peace* during a luncheon meeting in New York. The short statement, which subsequently was published in the *New York Times*,[126] asserted "the right of spiritual and intellectual liberty."[127] The statement became a popular topic in the media, and during 1943 Dulles and other commission members visited over a hundred cities, where they met with local church and community groups to discuss the *Six Pillars*.[128] The next year the American Jewish Committee issued its own *Declaration of Human Rights*, which grounded its vision of a "new world," post-Hitler, in the "dignity and inviolability of the person" and "basic human rights." The roster of signatories included eighty-one Christian church leaders alongside 236 rabbis, and 172 government officials. The American Jewish Committee promoted the statement as "approved by Roosevelt."[129] The Catholic Association for International Peace, founded by activist priest John A. Ryan in 1927, was involved in the conversation about human rights as well. A report by the organization in 1941 included Rev. Wilfred Parsons's "International Bill of Rights" and other discussion of the "rights of man" that placed religion squarely at the center of the emergent human rights movement.[130]

The end of the war brought more reports and statements. The Federal Council of Churches and the Foreign Missions Conference of North America collaborated in forming the Joint Committee on Religious Liberty (JCRL). In 1945, M. Searle Bates published *Religious Liberty: An Inquiry*, a collection of JCRL writings issued as a report on the worldwide challenges to religious freedom. Bates, like a growing number of writers at the time, cast the problem as a matter of human nature and rights: "Liberty is the nature of man. . . . The need for religious liberty has not to be argued. It leaps out from the world situation."[131] Bates identified the Soviet Union, Spain, and places under Muslim rule as the most challenging cases of religious oppression. In Russia, atheists sought to end religion; in Spain, Catholic rule under Franco oppressed religious minorities; and in Muslim countries, as later writers were to reiterate, religious freedom was nonexistent. The tone of the report "oscillated between viewing religious freedom as a predominantly Protestant idea, and, at the same time, acknowledging the prospect for a broader religious coalition against the forces threatening it."[132] *Religious Liberty*, understood against the background of the previous hundred years of American religious history, was an updated expression of the ideas that informed most American discussion of religion in international relations. Protestant missions served as the animating spirit of the report (the actual publisher of the book was the International Missionary Council), Catholics were cast as dangerous competitors,[133] and communist secularism was the looming menace.

The United Nations Charter (1945) and the Universal Statement of Human Rights subsequently adopted by the United Nations (1948) further advanced the interests of various American religious constituencies. More importantly, the role played by religious groups, and especially Protestants, in defining religious freedom as a human right in those documents evidenced the influence of religious groups on official thinking about international relations.[134] John Foster Dulles, not yet secretary of state but already an important national figure in 1945, remarked on the Charter: "It was the religious people who took the lead in seeking that the organization should be dedicated not merely to a peaceful but to a just order. It was they who sought that reliance should be placed upon the moral forces" of the General Assembly and the Economic and Social Council, rather than upon "the power of a few militarily strong nations" comprising the Security Council.[135]

The promotion of the idea of religious freedom was part of the promotion of human rights during the Cold War, and both were animated by "affectually driven politics."[136] A "new global affect" emerged during the Cold War, and there was a "transformation of global structure and affect that shaped the era's human rights advocacy." A new "transnational politics of human rights" emerged grounded in feeling and a new view of international order.[137] There was first of all the emergence of terms such as "global humanity" and "global economy." Those terms and similar ones were indications of a new view of Earth, which, for historian Benjamin Lazier, was represented by and partially inspired by the vision of the "Blue Marble" rising over the horizon of the moon as photographed from the *Apollo* spacecraft in 1968.[138] And, with regard to the "affectual politics" involved, there was the emergence of the "public testimonial in which a regard for the authenticity of experience and concern with the psyche, the therapeutic, and the emotions became as important as detached analytical research and statistical measure in making truth claims."[139]

The human rights movement built cases for reform based on the testimonials of witnesses who related their experiences, and especially their suffering, in public displays that appealed affectively to audiences who listened to them. Mark Philip Bradley explained how first-person accounts of detention and torture, of witnessing brutality, executions, and disappearances, became the truth that grounded reports of human rights violations. Truth was an affectual truth, part, again, of the "circulation of affect,"[140] as stories rich in feeling made their way from the mouths of witnesses to the ears of persons distal to the suffering itself. Media were especially important in this process, as conveyors not only of words but of images and sounds that contributed to the credibility of the testimony.[141]

The coalescence of the American human rights movement, through the emergence of a global view joined with affectual politics, took place in the 1970s. When the role of religion is taken seriously, however, it is clear that the movement had deep roots in the Protestant campaign to locate and decry religious intolerance overseas. The American Protestant view of "world Christianity" that became the standard after 1945 arose out of a century of Protestant commitment to the promotion of Christianity in foreign lands. From the early nineteenth century onward, Protestants were constantly made aware of places beyond the borders of the United States, places on the other side of the world where natives hungered for the gospel. Ministers preached sermons about missions; organizations formed to collect money, men, and women for missions; and reports about the struggles of missionaries all over the globe made their way regularly into the papers or into best-selling books. Protestants read those publications, wrote about them in their letters to each other, and discussed them in social gatherings. They accordingly developed a keen awareness of a certain "global humanity," which they called "worldwide Christianity."

The reports of challenges faced by missionaries and their converts, of their suffering at the hands of intolerant governments and local cultures, were central to Protestant designs for fostering worldwide Christianity. Decades before groups such as Amnesty International learned to craft reform projects that relied upon testimony of witnesses to torture and murder, Protestants who grasped the notion of "worldwide Christianity" already had learned to promote their cause in just such a fashion. In the nineteenth century, dissemination of persecution stories was minimally organized. Consumers of those stories found them in many places, in religious publications, conversations, and sermons. Over time, the stories were deployed more deliberately, however, in service to Protestant interest in influencing treaties with other nations where guarantees of protection of missionaries were sought. As Protestants became more aware of their power in influencing relations between the United States and other nations with regard to religious issues—Dulles's boast that "it was the religious people who took the lead"—they became more systematic in their use of persecution stories.

After 1945, the political tactic of reliance on stories of brutality against Christians was common in Protestant circles. Catholics also circulated persecution stories, and schoolchildren routinely were taught them as part of religious training in parochial schools.[142] Horrific stories of the Holocaust, with their deep pathos and intrinsic demand for reckoning, set the tone. Among politically engaged Protestants, the methodical retelling of stories about persecution of Christians during the Cold War accordingly aimed for maximal affective appeal. One example of that is the American discussion of the cases of several East Asian clergy who came to America to talk about persecution in their homelands. In March 1959, five Protestant church leaders testified before HUAC: Peter Chu Pong was from Hong Kong; Shih-Ping Wang, Tsin-tsai Liu, and Samuel W. S. Cheng were from Taiwan; and Kyung Rai Kim was from Seoul. All were witnesses to persecution, in either Red China or North Korea. Each gave extensive answers to the questions of the panelists who interviewed them.

Peter Chu Pong related his experiences in China after the communists gained power there in 1949. He spoke specifically of "brainwashing" by communists aimed at inculcating in the populace three specific points: "1. denial of a living God; the teaching of creation through evolution. 2. Denial of Christ as God. . . . 3. Christianity is a 'religious instrument of foreign imperialists' to poison the Chinese people. . . .'" Those points—including the oddly emphasized but coincidentally hot evangelical topic of evolution—were repeated for years in subsequent testimony. They set the frame for the reports of suffering, which were extensive, detailed, and pathetic. "They slapped our faces, kicked our bodies, and poured cold water on our heads," said Pong. "They made my children stand and watch. If they cried the Communists beat them." Condemned for his Christian beliefs, he was told to confess to crimes he had not committed. Pong explained that "if I had confessed they would have killed me immediately." Pong reported being beaten with sticks, and jailed for weeks with one meal per day. Released from prison, he escaped to Hong Kong, but his wife remained in prison, where she was tortured in order to force her to divorce her husband (which reportedly she did not).[143]

Tsin-tsai Liu recounted similar suffering after the Chinese "began wholesale persecution of Protestant churches in 1950." He described in detail one torture that Christians endured that would return as a topic of debate in America a half century later: "They stop the noses of the people and pour water in their mouths. Every time the person breathes he swallows water. After he swallows enough water his stomach swells, and then they stand on it. Then they use 24-hour questioning."[144] Samuel W. S. Cheng provided further detail, describing the murder of his Christian sister-in-law: "They used five horses. One horse was tied to her neck and the other horses were tied to her arms and legs and they went in all directions. The biggest horse ran and it just tore her body into pieces. The blood streamed all over the public square, and the people shut their eyes and cried."[145] All five of the witnesses over the course of the interview gave such compelling testimony about the suffering they and other Christians had endured under communist regimes.

PURSUITS 185

The stories Pong and his colleagues told were highly publicized and were repeated for years in Christian publications. The *New York Times* informed a wide audience of the testimonies in an article, "Asian Christians Bare Red Terror," published in mid-1959.[146] From there the story circulated to all kinds of publications. The conservative evangelical *American Mercury*, which published some of Billy Graham's most emotional warnings about communist evil, was one of the first to pick up the story. In 1959 it framed Pong's experiences as typical of Christians behind the Iron Curtain.[147] In 1960 Pong's persecution, featuring the story of waterboarding, together with Cheng's story appeared prominently in *The Cross and the Flag*, a far-right magazine created by *Christian Nationalist Crusade* founder Gerald L. K. Smith.[148] Also in 1960 the five persecuted ministers were brought before HUAC for another round of questioning. The committee director, Richard Arens, described the scene as an occasion "to confer with five persons who have experienced in their own lives the impact of communism in action—raw, ruthless terrorism as practiced by the perpetrators of the most monstrous conspiracy against humanity in all recorded history." Pong began by repeating the three points, but on this occasion he enlarged the point about evolution: "They told the people the whole universe was created through evolution."[149]

In 1962, Pong's testimony appeared in *Message for America: A Handbook for Those Who Will Defend Freedom*, by Robert D. Dilley, chairman of the Iowa Conservative Party. It also was presented that year in Billy James Hargis's *The Facts About Communism and Our Churches*. In 1963, Forrest Davis, a fiercely anti-communist journalist who had made his reputation covering the Scopes trial in 1925, gave Pong a voice. In *The Red China Lobby*, Davis put his own spin on the issue of evolution in stating the first of Pong's three points: "Denial of a living God and the starkly scientific hypothesis of creation through evolutionary processes." Herman J. Otten's *Baal or God* discussed Pong in 1965, and Hargis returned to Pong in 1968, in the *Christian Crusade Weekly*.[150] Over the next two decades, the stories of Pong and Cheng and the others solidified in Christian circles as touchstones for persecution, and set the tone for arguments for protection of Christians overseas. Like the human rights campaigns of the 1970s that were drenched in affect arising from personal testimony of suffering, the religious effort to secure U.S. government involvement in the protection of Christians overseas was built from cases in which emotional engagement with the mediated experiences of persecuted persons formed the core of the project. The stories had strong emotional impact among American Christians who believed they were mystically joined with other Christians worldwide in a transcendent brotherhood—such as

186   CHAPTER FOUR

those who ascribed to the NAE founding *Statement of Faith* (1942), which included among its seven short points "We believe in the spiritual unity of believers in our Lord Jesus Christ."[151]

During the 1980s and 1990s, as religious organizations discovered more effective ways in which to influence the political process and shape policy, the issue of persecution of Christians in communist countries remained lively. Periodic hearings, such as one on *Religious Persecution Behind the Iron Curtain* that took place in the Senate in 1985, built out the case against Soviet, Chinese, and North Korean persecutors. In that hearing, several American groups were singled out as examples of persecution overseas: evangelical Christians were the first, followed by Seventh-day Adventists, Mennonites, Baptists, and Pentecostals.[152] When African American churches burned in 1995–1996 and Americans turned away from that to look overseas for instances of religious persecution, they were well prepared to find it in places such as Russia and China, even though the Cold War had ended. And they made their case for the protection of religion in well-practiced fashion, leading with stories of suffering and following with explanations for why an end to intolerance around the world was both an ideal and a practical good. The United States, the exceptional nation, was not considered part of that worldwide problem.

Religious Freedom Legislation

Thomas F. Farr, who served as the first director of the State Department's Office of International Religious Freedom (1999–2003), observed that three issues bearing on religion were conjoined during the Cold War and its immediate aftermath: human rights, anti-communism, and persecution.[153] It was against that background that the National Association of Evangelicals issued their *Statement of Conscience* in 1996, with its complaints about communist "reigns of terror" and the persecution of Christians. That official announcement of the Statement took place at a summit meeting on worldwide persecution held at the Mayflower Hotel in Washington, DC, in January. The meeting was organized by Michael Horowitz, a Jew who studied tort reform at the Hudson Institute, whose *Wall Street Journal* op-ed in 1995 raised interest about Muslim persecution of Christians (e.g., "torturing him and plucking out his eyes") in Ethiopia, Sudan, Egypt, Iran, and Pakistan.[154] Horowitz and Nina Shea, a Catholic human rights activist, together with evangelical leaders such as Chuck Colson, Richard Land, Gary Bauer, and other Christian Right figures, prodded the House Human Rights Committee to meet the following month to discuss, in witness Nina Shea's words, "the persecution of Christians throughout the world."[155] The hearing, entitled "Persecution of Christians Worldwide," focused on discussion of persecution in the communist countries of China, North Korea, and Vietnam, which were deemed the "worst" persecutors.[156]

The initial discussion of religious persecution in the House translated to a Horowitz draft of the "Freedom from Religious Persecution Act," otherwise known as the Wolf–Specter bill for its sponsors, Senator Arlen Specter and Representative Frank Wolf, who introduced it in September 1997. An assortment of witnesses testified at the hearings for the bill, including representatives of Amnesty International and the U.S. Catholic Conference as well as a number of prominent evangelicals, including the Southern Baptist leader Richard Land, Donald Argue, president of the NAE, and Donald Hodel, president of the Christian Coalition, among others. Also testifying were Atilio Okot John and Tsultrim Dolma, persons who had experienced persecution. John, the first witness called, recounted violence against Christians in Sudan, where "churches have been burned . . . even pastors of the churches are thrown into the burning churches."[157]

Testimony given at the Wolf–Specter hearings was vivid in detail and rich in affect. Discussion revolved around the stories of persecution, not only in the testimonies of John and Dolma but through reference to accounts published by Christian writers in books that were at the time claiming a large Christian readership. Two of those books, introduced into the hearing by Argue, were Paul Marshall's just-published *Their Blood Cries Out* (1997) and Nina Shea's *In the Lion's Den* (1997).[158] Both were collections of stories of suffering. Marshall's collection consisted of a series of scenes of extreme violence related to him by his informants, including the rape of women followed by their disemboweling, children beheaded, the slow roasting of Christians, mass murder, mutilations, starvations, beatings with hammers, and other tortures. Shea's book also offered blood and suffering.

The aims of Wolf–Specter were constructed directly out of the fury generated by reports of the terrible suffering of persons published in books and periodicals and summarized in the hearings. Wolf–Specter was devised as a means of punishing nations for their brutal treatment of Christians. Anger toward those who persecuted Christians was channeled into a proposed scheme that would accord extraordinary power to an administrator located in the White House, not the State Department. The person in that White House office would oversee machinery constructed to identify persecuting nations and punish them severely with economic sanctions. The bill was written in

188 CHAPTER FOUR

such a way that the sanctions were all but automatic once the office discovered crimes. The process, described by Farr, was in essence "to denounce persecutors and threaten them with punitive actions."[159]

Support for Wolf–Specter included some Catholics and Jews, but the majority came from evangelicals. The bill itself privileged the persecution of Christians but also made brief mention of Tibetans, Buddhists, and Iranian Baha'is. As Farr writes, "the default focus was on Christians" and "there was little doubt that Christians were intended to be the centerpiece of the effort."[160] The power behind the bill, its driving force, was a network of evangelicals on the Christian Right. The journalist Ira Rivkin recalled that "I was at the initial news conference in the Capitol building when Wolf–Specter was introduced. And it is my clear recollection that . . . this Act was then perceived as a bill that came out of the Religious Right and was for the protection of Christians."[161] When the bill passed the House in May 1998 by a vote of 375–41, there was rejoicing among conservative evangelicals: "For the Religious Right, this was their bill, and since they considered their motives and purposes pure, the bill was immaculate. It was an emotional issue for them, and they mobilized support through their radio programs."[162]

The bill in fact turned out not to be immaculate. It was opposed by a strong coalition of business interests as well as some human rights and religious organizations. A group of the nation's largest exporters formed USA*Engage to combat the bill, arguing that its sanctions process was flawed and would have a severely detrimental effect on trade. The Clinton White House in 1996 already had rebuffed an attempt by the evangelical Christian Legal Society to withdraw Most Favored Nation trading status with China because of religious persecution of Christians there.[163] Human rights organizations likewise believed that the power given to the overseer of the sanctions process, and the terms defining that process, would ruin relations between human rights organizations and countries punished summarily for persecution. The National Council of Churches spoke loudly against the bill for its starkly punitive approach and circumvention of diplomacy.[164] It was clear that Wolf–Specter would not pass the Senate.

Unbeknownst to Horowitz, a group in the Senate was framing a similar bill that would soften the sharply punitive focus of Wolf–Specter and include diplomacy. The alternative bill, proposed by Senator Don Nickles and Representative Chris Smith, incorporated language about the promotion of religious freedom, and attempted to give the impression of a more constructive agenda than that implied in Wolf–Specter. The International Religious Freedom Act (IRFA), however, could not escape the ethos of Wolf–Specter. It remained focused on discovering and confronting religious persecution, especially of Christians, and offered no blueprint for how religious freedom was to be promoted. It "paid rhetorical homage to religious freedom," but in the end, as Farr wrote, "although IRFA proponents claimed they sought religious freedom, what they really sought was a U.S. effort to reduce religious persecution."[165] The bill passed the Senate 98–0 just weeks before the 1998 elections. Subsequently, from their office hidden away in a corner of the State Department, the staff of IRFA soon discovered that their role was much less than supporters of the original bill had envisioned.

With the passage of IRFA, American Christians acquired a powerful tool for characterizing the "rest of the world" as a place plagued by persecution of Christians. In effect the granting of a charter stipulating official U.S. concern about persecution overseas, the passage of IRFA was the culmination of years of effort on the part of American Christians, and especially Protestant evangelicals. It reified overseas persecution beyond what previous diplomacy had done, defined a legal framework for addressing it, and gave the appearance of positioning it prominently in U.S. foreign policy. It did not matter that the State Department Office of International Religious Freedom had little actual power and was subject always to auxiliary status in the context of larger diplomatic initiatives. What mattered was the official recognition of the problem of religious persecution in the world—the world outside the United States.

The inability of evangelicals on the Religious Right to admit the broad cultural implications of dozens of African American churches being burned during the years leading up to IRFA, and their refusal in general to see religious intolerance in America, instead projecting it overseas, reached a crucial point in 1998. Evangelicals were emboldened like never before, and were never more sure of themselves as patriotic Americans. The NAE, expressing that feeling a few years later, urged: "Never before has God given American evangelicals such an awesome opportunity to shape public policy in ways that could contribute to the well-being of the entire world."[166] And for evangelicals and others who saw in IRFA the beginning of a new chapter in American foreign policy, the powerful notion of America as an exceptional nation remained central to their thinking. The opening section of IRFA in fact "sets up an American exceptionalism" and suggests the imposing on other states of an American vision regarding religion. The first line of IRFA, "The right to freedom of religion undergirds the very origin and existence of the United States," which is a "prized legacy" of American heritage, positioned America as the historical shining city on a hill with a message to a world thought to desperately need it.[167]

One of the strongest supporters of the initiative had been the evangelical Gary Bauer, then president of the Family Research Council and a leading light of the Religious Right. As Wolf–Specter was being debated in Congress, Bauer read a *New York Times* article about human rights violations in China in which Boeing CEO Philip Condit was asked what thoughts he had about those violations. Said Condit: "They are the same ones that I have about human rights violations in the United States . . . I happened to be in China during the Rodney King beating. Now, there is a whole bunch of background that goes along with that. But watching that on CNN in China, their perspective was, 'What was that about?'" Bauer reported a strong emotional response to reading that statement: "I almost fell out of my chair when I read that. It's a viciously anti-American statement." For Bauer and his allies, racial persecution, like religious persecution — or both together during the church burning season of the mid-1990s — did not, could not, exist in America.[168]

At the beginning of the Cold War, American Christians had set out to dominate the world. They imagined a future in which Christian brothers and sisters were joined by transcendent spiritual bonds in one worldwide family. All were kin, tied together by deep emotions that included, notably, sympathy. But performances of sympathy expressed both the human connection of Christians to others and the profound cultural distance separating them. During the Cold War era, the threat of communism was palpable daily, and thinking about people in other parts of the world remained framed by the remnants of colonialist assumptions about superiority/inferiority. American Christians, in spite of their trust in divinely engineered family ties, nevertheless felt themselves to be different from their distant kin in China, Korea, and the Soviet Union. Like early Americans who had felt themselves both drawn to Indians and repelled by them, who wished to annihilate Indians as Amalekites and at the same time save them, so did Americans at the end of the twentieth century project both sides of that ingrained national trauma internationally. The desire to annihilate was projected alongside the trust in kinship. Chinese and Russians, among others, were a clear and present danger even as they were needy humans who were felt as family.

During the Cold War, there was overt intolerance of Catholics, New Religious Movements, and Asian American religious communities, as well as ongoing resentment toward African American churches. And a vicious animus toward Muslims began to show itself toward the end of the era. The United States remained a nation where the ideal of religious freedom was incompletely implemented. Many Americans tried to unsee that flaw. They renewed their focus on the mistreatment of Christians overseas, and especially in communist countries. Their IRFA was not about spreading religious freedom, but about locating and punishing intolerance, and almost all of the resources of IRFA were devoted to finding out and publicizing religious persecutions.[169]

Evangelicalism grew strong as a political and social force during the Cold War. Looking away from intolerance at home, evangelicals and some other Christians, identifying as highly patriotic Americans, improved greatly upon their decades-old project of finding intolerance in other parts of the world. In the style of activism typically associated with human rights campaigns of the 1970s–1990s, evangelicals made a calculated emotional pitch to the nation—as they had been doing on a smaller scale for the better part of a century—that relied on witness testimony to achieve legislative movement on policy issues. Evangelicals, the driving force behind IRFA, built out of emotional materials a campaign to combat religious intolerance. Sympathy remained important, but it was allied with sorrow, anger, and a deeply felt insistence on punitive justice.

The sincere effort to feel the experiences of persecuted persons from other parts of the world sank deeply into evangelical self-understanding during the latter part of the twentieth century. In the next century, the depths of that feeling would lead to a reversal as evangelicals learned to feel themselves as the victims of persecution. The buried trauma that shaped American under-standings of nation and international relations would emerge dramatically not as an impulse to forget and look away, but as one to remember, or, more appropriately, to misremember.

5

Persecutions:
The Importation of Intolerance in
the Twenty-First Century

White American Christians

In the aftermath of *Obergefell v. Hodges* (2015), which upheld the right of same-sex couples to marry, James Dobson declared, "We lost the culture war." Dobson, the high-profile evangelical leader and founder of Focus on the Family, like many conservative Christians in America was crestfallen at the decision. A wave of lament passed through the conservative religious community, reinforced by a multitude of public admissions that Dobson was right. Conservative author Rod Dreher had anticipated the decision by a few weeks, and already had announced in the *American Conservative*, "Yes, we lost the culture war." But in the weeks and months following *Obergefell*, as the full reality took hold, conservative Christians, led by evangelicals, poured out their grief. Surveying the mood of defeat, the *Christian Research Journal* concluded, "The culture war is over. We (the Christian Right) lost." Many Christians were shocked that a nation they believed was founded on biblical Christianity could have taken a cultural turn deemed so sinful. *Renew America* protested, "70% of Americans say they're Christians. Even with that huge number we lost the culture war." The *Christian Index* soberly observed, "Most social commentators have pronounced that the Judeo-Christian traditionalists lost the culture war when the Supreme Court voted 5–4 in favor of gay marriage."[1]

The news did not improve for the traditionalists. In 2016, the Public Religion Research Institute (PRRI), collaborating with the Brookings Institution, reported that a majority 57 percent of Americans believed that the United States was no longer or never had been a Christian nation. Even more telling was the proportion of white evangelical Protestants who believed that the United States was no longer a Christian nation. From 2012 to 2016, that percentage increased from 48 percent to 59 percent.[2] At the same time, Robert P.

Jones, the founder of PRRI, published *The End of White Christian America*, a data-rich story of decline. Jones reported that 51 percent of Americans identified as white Protestants in 1993, but that by 2014 only 32 percent identified similarly. Moreover, because white Christians were disproportionately older Americans, and because younger white Americans were not affiliating, the outlook for white Christian America (WCA) was one of further regression. Jones argued that *Obergefell* had prompted a "profound identity crisis" in WCA, that historical WCA resistance to civil rights had produced a backlash, and that WCA as a result of its losses felt isolated and disoriented because they were no longer "America's default faith." Moreover, Jones proposed that if current trends held, unaffiliated Americans would comprise as large a percentage of the population as Protestants by 2051.[3] In 2017, PRRI officially declared white Christians (in total for all denominations) a minority after analyzing a large sample of survey respondents (101,000) in which 43 percent identified as white Christians. In a religion poll in 1976, 81 percent had identified as such.[4]

White American Christians, and especially evangelicals, responded to their experience of loss by embracing the idea that they were a persecuted group. In 2016, three out of four Republicans and supporters of Donald Trump said that discrimination against Christians was as serious as discrimination against any other group.[5] In a poll conducted in 2017, white evangelicals, specifically, registered the opinion that Christians in America suffered more discrimination than American Muslims.[6] A surge of publications promoting the idea that Christians in America were persecuted included Mary Eberstadt's *It's Dangerous to Believe: Religious Freedom and Its Enemies* (2016) and Rod Dreher's *The Benedict Option: A Strategy for Christians in a Post-Christian Nation* (2017). Both aimed at a broad Christian audience (Catholics and Orthodox as well as Protestants), claiming that there had been a rise in discrimination against Christians in America and that secularists and nefarious others were to blame. Christian moviemakers responded as well, producing a raft of pictures like the highly successful *God's Not Dead*. A wishful and at the same time mournful story of the triumph of Christian students against an "atheist" professor, it made thirty-two times its shoestring budget at the box office.[7]

The post-*Obergefell* gloominess of white Christians was not the product of a sudden realization that they had lost ground in competition with other groups and ideologies. Rather, it took shape as a clarified awareness of a pattern of cultural change begun decades earlier with the *Roe v. Wade* (1973) decision legalizing abortion. But for all of the disheartening change, white Christian churches, and especially evangelicals, at the same time in fact were gaining political power. That power was dramatically evidenced in the surprising victory of Donald Trump in the presidential election of 2016. And in the aftermath of the Trump victory, the thinking of conservative American Christians about their social place became vastly more complicated. Even as they grieved over having lost the "culture war," conservative Christians rejoiced that they had gained an exceptionally strong position in the new federal and state administrations. They creatively leveraged both of those public roles—as winners and as losers—to advocate for policies that they believed would restore them to cultural dominance. Presenting themselves as a persecuted religious group, but holding greater power in government than any of their competitors, they endeavored to restore a world they had feared was lost.

American Christians in the late twentieth century had begun thinking seriously about their own perceived predicament in America in conjunction with their recognition of the extent of anti-Christian persecution abroad. Christians had been aware of persecutions behind the Iron Curtain for over fifty years. But as long as that seemingly impermeable Curtain remained, and as long as the persecuted remained behind it, American Christian religious groups remained doubtful about their capability to challenge it effectively. For all of the Cold War–era congressional hearings and media coverage regarding persecution in communist countries, Christians were inclined to picture change in terms of an apocalyptic reckoning rather than a concerted diplomatic program aimed at relieving victims of their suffering. After the fall of the Iron Curtain and the accompanying changes to the global political scene, American Christians became emboldened to call out and politically organize against persecution of Christians in places such as China, Russia, Rumania, Albania, and elsewhere. The apocalyptic imagery remained, but a practical program took root. Just as American Christians could define themselves as both winners and losers in the cultural-political battles of the period, so also they complexly imagined a future in terms of both a radical eschatology and the progressive historical elimination of Christian persecution.

In the late twentieth century, Americans became more aware of the extent of the persecution of Christians globally. The growth of missions, which put many more feet on the ground in far-off places, prompted that awareness. The end of the Cold War inspired an enormous effort by evangelicals to missionize in places where they previously had been unable or unwilling to stake a claim. The events of 1989 proved a boon to evangelical missions: "Evangelicals poured into Eastern Europe to proselytize the liberated peoples of the Soviet bloc. Meanwhile, their numbers in the global south were way up; conversions in Latin America and Africa, in particular, were creating millions of new believers. In 1989, evangelical leaders around the world began to remap their global dreams."[8] Those dreams included nightmares in the form of discoveries of persecutions, which missions organizers narrated for Americans back home. Statistics loomed larger as key parts of those narratives. As evangelicals across the board, liberals as well as conservatives, became more concerned and more involved, they produced studies that increasingly blended sad stories with statistics that brought a wide-angle view to the problem. The passage and initial implementation of IRFA in the late 1990s was informed by that awareness, which came about partially through publications such as Paul Marshall's *Their Blood Cries Out*. That book early on set the parameters for subsequent discussion with a claim that 200 million Christians suffered under regimes that persecuted them and hundreds of millions more lived in countries that impeded Christian practice.[9]

Subsequent studies, large and small, by a wide range of groups, including Voice of the Martyrs (VOM), Amnesty International, Human Rights Watch, Puebla Institute, the Religion and State Project, and the Pew Research Center, began to flesh out the numbers proposed by Marshall, using legal records, observations, interviews, diplomatic testimonies, and other detective work to bring greater precision to the data. They followed the lead of the Dutch-founded organization Open Doors (including Open Doors USA since mid-century), which began publishing in the 1990s its annual *World Watch List* of the fifty worst countries for the persecution of Christians. The *World Watch List* progressively developed a scoring system that blended qualitative and quantitative data.[10] The 2018 list reported that 215 million Christians worldwide suffered persecution and identified North Korea as the worst offender.[11] The various reporting organizations formed a consensus that Christians are the most persecuted religious group in the world, and have been for much of the twenty-first century.[12] That opinion acquired international legitimacy when German chancellor Angela Merkel declared in 2012 that Christianity is "the most persecuted religion in the world."[13] That global view, as stated cogently by Merkel, was widely reported in media and embraced by politicians, religious leaders, and human rights activists.

Many white American Christians who became aware of the global persecution of Christians responded with efforts aimed at overcoming it. The evangelical magazine *Christianity Today* laid the groundwork for that campaign in 1992, with a cover story entitled "They Shoot Christians, Don't They?"[14] The article depicted the twentieth century as "a century marked by unprecedented religious persecution" and warned of "an ongoing battle in the communist world."[15] The "*religious* zealotry" of a "resurgent Islam" likewise posed a threat to Christians. The evidence of persecution in "scores of countries" made it a "worldwide" problem. Christians, said the magazine, should "not hesitate to involve ourselves in the widest range of ways to help our suffering fellow believers."[16] Recognition of Christian suffering, a sense of obligation to send help, hope for the rescue of victims, and designs for a robust program of involvement in a wide world together formed the core of the emergent Christian conceptualization of the battle against persecution.

In the fall of 1996, Americans rallied to participate in the International Day of Prayer for the Persecuted Church. An event promoted by the National Association of Evangelicals, together with other evangelical organizations such as Campus Crusade for Christ and Prison Fellowship, it was conceived as a way of bringing visibility to the problem.[17] It was followed over the next two decades by hundreds of other forums and events that likewise sought to galvanize discussion of anti-Christian animus globally. In 1997, a series of articles in the *New York Times* by A. M. Rosenthal and Jeffrey Goldberg[18] addressed the global problem, while the Pew Charitable Trusts–funded *Freedom and Religious Belief: A World Report* announced itself as a study that "exposes persecution and discrimination in virtually all world regions."[19] Those publications contributed to the crystallizing of the idea that Christian persecution was a pervasive global problem, not merely a matter of outliers, not merely prejudice against Christians in certain countries.

By 2005, there were numerous news services, denominational associations, church organizations, policy groups, blogs, and legal societies devoted to the discovery and condemnation of persecution around the world. Oklahoma Wesleyan University established an undergraduate degree in "Persecuted Church Ministry." Seminary and Bible college curricula soon followed that lead. Such enterprises formed a network of "Christian activism in the global arena."[20] And, as distress about Christian persecutions overseas grew, Christians began to voice their concerns about prejudice against Christians at home.

In 2003, David Limbaugh, the brother of radio entertainer Rush Limbaugh, published a book castigating the U.S. government, the media, Hollywood, and assorted others for attempting to tear the nation away from "America's Christian roots." *Persecution: How Liberals Are Waging War Against Christianity* was a complaint about "secularism" in America. The first line of the book, "This book chronicles discrimination against Christians in American society," was followed by assorted angry narrations of instances in which Limbaugh believed "liberals" were intolerant of Christians. Like much similar protesting that was to follow from other writers over the next fifteen years, the book was compromised by exaggerations, highly selective presentation of information, flawed reasoning, and blinding rage at left-of-center politics. But it resonated with the Religious Right and the conservative media, sold well, and helped set a frame for subsequent conservative discussion of the persecution of Christians in America.[21] It led to Texas pastor and anti-gay activist Rick Scarborough—who deemed the book a "must-read for those concerned with rescuing our drowning culture"—organizing "The War on Christians" conference in Washington, DC, in March 2006.[22] That meeting brought together Gary Bauer, Phyllis Schlafly, Sam Brownback, and other public officials and religious celebrities. The goal was to explore the implications of a Fox News poll several months earlier that showed that 59 percent of Americans polled believed that "Christianity is under attack" in the United States.[23] The "war on Christians" subsequently became a rallying cry voiced by media figures, politicians, clergy, and activist laypersons concerned about the future of Christianity in America.[24]

Provoked by a growing body of alarmist literature, such as Janet L. Folger's *The Criminalization of Christianity: Read This Before It Becomes Illegal* (2005),[25] evangelicals, joined by some other Christians, began to organize against what they believed was a growing problem of persecution of Christians in America. During 2005–2006, a series of Family Research Council "Justice Sunday" events brought Christians together to protest the "war on Christians" by an allegedly activist judiciary. Organizations such as Seeds of Persecution published a running tab on perceived infringements on the religious freedom of Christians.[26] Media personalities fashioned lucrative public images discussing claims of persecution on radio and television. On Fox News, a rebounding[27] Todd Starnes spoke to his national audience about specific occurrences of perceived intolerance, effectively utilizing the practice of cultivating emotional response by digging deep into the suffering of Christian individuals he believed were wronged in some way. Some of those narratives were collected in his *God Less America: Real Stories from the Front Lines of the Attack on Traditional Values* (2014).[28] Americans eagerly consumed such literature—the book was a million-seller—and the Religious Right behaved as if it had internalized the book's message. Many white evangelicals came to believe, as conservative religious columnist Fay Voshell argued in 2015, that "It's not just 'over there.'"[29] Franklin Graham, the inheritor of his father's evangelical ministry and accordingly one of the most influential evangelicals in America, confessed his own fears in 2015, thus legitimating the nascent narrative for his millions of followers. Speaking with Todd Starnes on Fox News, he wondered, "Is there going to be discriminations against churches, against organizations like the one I represent . . . will we be discriminated against by the government?"[30]

Identifying with the Persecuted

Evangelicals over the course of several generations had been taught to identify with the victims of persecution overseas. They learned that lesson well, so well that they became the persecuted. The evangelical investments in (1) the idea of a world Christianity led by Protestants, (2) the tragic narrative of persecution of Christians overseas, (3) the practice of cultivation of feelings for those so persecuted, (4) and the extended Christian family united mystically by bonds of Christian love together set the table for American Christians' changing self-understanding of their own status.

Religious leaders at the end of the twentieth century more energetically promoted the idea that it was spiritually advantageous and morally necessary to identify with those Christian family members who were persecuted in other countries.[31] The idea was cogently articulated in 1998 by Amy Wierman, who led a prayer group in Pennsylvania once a week. She explained that "All Christians everywhere, the body of Christ, are really one body, so if one part is feeling pain, we should all be feeling pain." She pointed out that "The Christian woman raped in Egypt, that is my sister. The guy shot in Pakistan, that is my brother."[32] Religious organizations devised a full suite of psychological and physical exercises, the purpose of which was to encourage identifying with the persecuted. Those projects were national and local, large and small. Voice of the Martyrs inaugurated a national program called "Exile Night," an overnight vigil for individuals and groups that was "an opportunity for churches, youth groups and student groups to identify with their persecuted family members in a tangible way, experiencing a small piece of what displaced believers face every day."[33] The Baptist Cascade Church in Monroe, Washington, gathered for a "Wear Orange Sunday" to assert "the value of identifying with persecuted Christians." Church members donned orange T-shirts because the Christians beheaded by ISIS on a beach in 2015 wore orange jumpsuits.[34]

Pastor Gregory C. Cochran, a pastor and faculty member at California Baptist University, told his cohort "why it is important to identify with the persecuted church." Cochran exhorted that "The New Testament calls for us to close the gap in the body of Christ by identifying in united fashion with the persecuted. We can't do that if we separate ourselves into 'those over there' who suffer persecution and 'us over here' who do not. That is an artificial, unbiblical distinction." Cochran, seeking to provoke effort from his followers, made an argumentative turn that changed the playing field by legitimating name-calling as torture: "Those who wish to make a distinction between torture and name calling are correct in so doing with regard to the severity of the crime . . . nevertheless . . . the difference is in degree of persecution—not in whether or not persecution was suffered."[35]

The practice of identifying with the persecuted has a long and complex Christian history. That history begins with the core mythos of Christianity, the suffering of Jesus as a sacrifice for the sins of humanity. The followers of Jesus early on came to understand themselves as imitators of the example of Jesus. Imagining themselves likewise as innocent victims, they identified with the suffering of Jesus, so that "from the very beginning, victimhood was hardwired into the Christian psyche."[36]

The victim model of Christian discipleship was reinforced in the early church, and was bolstered by the circulation of stories about the persecution of early Christians that cast them as martyrs, and praised them as saints.[37] Those stories, among other psychological framings of victimhood that became a part of the Christian tradition, were constitutive of American Christianity since colonial times.[38] Additionally, Americans typically have understood that a key goal of their Christian practice was to "empty themselves of self," as the nineteenth-century American Adventist prophet Ellen G. White put it.[39] Christians who hoped for an inflow of divine grace prepared themselves for that by making space within. They sought to empty themselves through devotional exercises, prayer, suffering, and identifying with a Jesus who "emptied himself" (Phil. 2:7). To be a victim was to give up the self, to be made ready to receive saving grace, as a martyr. The movie *The Passion of the Christ* (2004), a graphic depiction of the exsanguination of Jesus—he was emptied of his blood—set a box-office record[40] partly because of the large numbers of Christians who were bused to it by their churches. In the process, it encouraged its audiences to identify with the bleeding Jesus and vividly reinforced the idea of Christian victimhood.

The durability and authority of the Christian model of victimhood was evidenced in its interwovenness with Americans' trepidation about their own persecution in the twenty-first century. Even as they were registering their fears that persecution was underway, Christians spoke of embracing the opportunity to endure difficulties in imitation of Jesus. Johnnette Benkovic, a popular Catholic writer and media personality, advised her readers that the persecution of Christians in America was in fact an opportunity. She recommended "reading the lives of the saints and especially the martyr saints," and urged Christians to "Be joyful. There is a certain joy that accompanies struggle and challenge."[41] That approach to struggle applied to the community as much as the individual. As a member of a Presbyterian church near Denver observed in discussing persecution in America, when "blood is spilled, that's when we grow . . . That's very true in Christendom."[42]

The narrative of Christian martyrdom and victimhood has appeared in various forms in diverse cultural and historical settings. In the recent past, in the decades since the human rights movement began to acquire momentum, the figure of the victim has played a central role in international efforts to address injustice. The effectiveness of the strategy of foregrounding the victim in a tale of suffering[43] made victimhood a distinguishing feature of the politics of human rights. The utility of keying on the victim, whether in human rights campaigns or in American Christian conceptualizations of their persecution, was the same: it provided a starting point for debate that bestowed advantages on those claiming to be victims.

Invocation of victimhood has a way of appearing to cut through the assumption that "everything is political" by establishing what appears to be non-political space. That is, "victimhood can be a prime way of suspending or attempting to suspend the political through an appeal to something non-agentive and 'beyond' or 'before' politics, such as poverty or suffering." The claim of victimhood does not erase politics, but rather "victimhood establishes a space for a specific kind of politics" because "it poses itself as the neutral or indisputable starting point from which discussion, debates, and action—in a word, politics—can and must proceed."[44] Put another way, claims of victimhood leverage "unjust suffering as cultural capital."[45]

In some instances, groups claim "underdog status" even if they hold power. In Israel, right-wing groups in power appropriate the human rights rhetoric and tactics of weak and oppressed groups in order to characterize themselves as victims. Depicting themselves, paradoxically, as oppressed by the state, such groups endeavor to insulate themselves from claims that they are acting from purely political motives. Claiming victimhood, such groups attempt to pressure state authorities to "fully exercise their powers against disadvantaged groups" in such a way as to advance conservative interests.[46] The Religious Right in America operates in a similar way in that "the language of liberation and rights loses its anchoring in the historical narratives of the dispossessed and disenfranchised," so that "we are left with the Christian persecution complex—a discursive entity impervious to critique."[47]

Reeling from losses incurred in battles over same-sex marriage, school prayer, sexual ethics, the roles of women, and other issues, conservative Christians working through the Republican Party nevertheless managed to extend their control of statehouses and the federal government in the second decade of the twenty-first century. During those years, they also built a rhetorical and organizational platform for advertising their claim that they were a weak and persecuted minority. The strong investment in politics included a turnout in force to elect President Donald Trump, whom Liberty University president Jerry Falwell Jr. described as evangelicals' "dream president."[48]

In spite of their seeming investments (and indisputable victories) in the day-to-day business of influencing national policy, and notwithstanding their announcements of long-term campaigns to vanquish liberals and nonbelievers from positions of power, evangelicals remained deeply engaged with an eschatology that forecasted the end of the world. American evangelicalism is replete with examples of how actors ranging from Billy Graham, to author Hal Lindsey (*The Late, Great Planet Earth* [1970]), activist Tim LaHaye, *Christianity Today*, and Fuller Theological Seminary produced a forceful "revival of apocalypticism" in the latter part of the twentieth century.[49] In the early twenty-first century, that worldview was well in evidence, beginning with anxieties about Y2K—the forecasted crisis of computer technology when the calendar turned to 2000—and proceeding from there to a series of nationally broadcasted predictions of the end.[50]

After 2000, clergy in large and small churches continued to warn their local congregations of the imminent but unpredictable end, and some who enjoyed national pulpits offered more specific information. The popular Family Radio host Harold Camping had predicted that the end would take place in 1994, but later recalculated and began in early 2011 to assert that the correct date was May 21, 2011. His prediction, which included a detailed description of a series of events that would take place, garnered continuous national coverage, and various phrasings of the "May 21 Movement" topped searches on Yahoo and Google.[51] Other evangelical leaders, including Ronald Weinland and John Hagee, subsequently made new predictions.[52] Most of the seven in ten evangelicals who identified as some form of millennialist (according to the NAE[53]), however, remained watchful and wary but unpersuaded of a specific date for the end.

Evangelical forays into shaping national and foreign policy during and after the Cold War were partly framed by eschatological considerations.[54] Evangelical ideas about American relations with Israel, for example, were fully grounded in an apocalyptic worldview. So also were other campaigns, ranging from advocacy for nuclear weapons buildups to opposition to abortion. Christian groups on the fringes, such as Christian Identity groups that aggressively preached white supremacy, were particularly liable to articulate their visions for a Christian order within an apocalyptic worldview. White supremacist groups, by positioning themselves within apocalyptic discourse about the coming of a New Order, replaced the historical Jews-as-victims with Aryans-as-victims. In other words, those groups argued that there had been a Holocaust of whites, not Jews.[55] The same millennialist pattern of thinking held true for the pro-life movement. The profoundly millennialist orientation of the anti-abortion group Operation Rescue illustrates how "in millennialism, there is a thin line between the tendency to empathize or identify with enslaved and persecuted people and the tendency to see oneself as enslaved or persecuted." The tactics of such persons evidence how they "not only identify with the unborn as a persecuted group but they then identify themselves as a persecuted minority."[56]

Millennialism—and typically the "dispensationalist" variety that many evangelicals embraced—set a temporal frame that made possible intellectual and emotional exercises that would have been more difficult to perform within a conventional view of history. By deconstructing the notion of history as open-ended, linear, and unpredictable, and replacing it with a view of history as orderly, harmonious, and teleological,[57] apocalyptic temporality enabled a sense of profound connections between bodies in distal spatial locations. The "spatial-temporal collapse that is characteristic of most apocalyptic" folded both time and space. The past, present, and future were harmonized. Space was similarly collapsed so that, in the apocalyptic imaginary, what was happening "over there" was at the same time happening "here."[58] The millennialism of evangelicals accordingly played a part in their capability to imagine themselves joined with overseas others in suffering persecution. It enabled them to cross the "thin line" between sympathizing with others and fully identifying with them.

When white supremacist Christian Identity members identified with Jews as victims of the Holocaust in order to claim victimhood themselves, they clearly remained apart from Jews, believing themselves in fact to be the opposite of Jews. But in the complex steps of their dance of identification, they took on the victim status imagining that they had not acquired the unwanted baggage of Jewishness. Pro-lifers, as Carol Mason writes, accomplished a similar turn, identifying with fetuses that were in physical terms different from them, and in certain ways physically other (e.g., the fetus does not breathe air), but at the same time fully imagining themselves as fetus-as-victim. Such paradoxical instances of identification recall the complex dynamics of colonial American identification with Indians. Early Americans saw Indians as other but at the same time identified with them. Later, during the Cold War, American Christians categorically feared communists behind the Iron Curtain and Asians in China, Vietnam, and elsewhere. They constructed their American identity as the opposite of those peoples. Yet they identified with those peoples for the way they were denied the Christian gospel or were persecuted for embracing it. The dynamic, again, was paradoxical, but grounded in aspects of American identity that had been established centuries earlier.

Stages of Persecution

Not all American Christians believed that they were persecuted. Alan Noble, a professor at Oklahoma Baptist University, detailed the "evangelical persecution complex" in 2014. Asserting that "Christians with a global perspective on their faith rightly identify themselves as part of a persecuted people in the 21st century," Noble admitted that it was not unrealistic for Christians to anticipate some "restrictions to religious liberty in the future." But in thinking about what those restrictions might be, "it is easy to imagine, wrongly, that they are already here." Warning "that believers can come to see victimhood as an essential part of their identity," he concluded that "for most of U.S. history, Christians haven't been persecuted—at least not in comparison to early believers or what Christians in places like Iraq face today."[59]

Jason Wiedel, a preacher from Virginia, was more pointed in his remarks: "Viewing ourselves as the persecuted minority is ironic, because much of the broader culture see Christians, especially conservative evangelicals, as the oppressive majority." He warned that "the perception of American Christians regarding persecution is completely out of line with the cultural reality. We have embraced a delusion—the persecution complex."[60] The *Concordia Journal* of the conservative Missouri Synod of Lutherans provided a similar viewpoint, explaining that "rather than being persecuted, Christianity is losing the rather absolute predominance it once held in America."[61]

Commentators who wrote from perspectives that were not Christian asserted that Christians had badly overplayed their hand. Political watchdog groups accused Christians of crying wolf, arguing that they had created "myths" for the purpose of "reframing political losses as religious oppression," and set out to debunk the stories told by Christian television and radio personalities.[62] Numerous writers pointed out how white evangelicals held power and how their persecutors—sometimes identified by Christians as "secular" atheists and the nonaffiliated—were vastly underrepresented in government, numbering only one person in Congress in 2017.[63] After the election of Donald Trump and the consequent appointments of numerous conservative evangelicals in cabinet, agency, and judiciary positions, the Christian complaint looked even more untenable.

Christians who claimed that they were persecuted did not ignore criticisms that they had exaggerated their predicament. While some Christians continued to deploy an extreme characterization of their persecution in America, many on the Religious Right sought a position from which they could repel criticisms and yet continue to protest about their status as victims. They found that position in the idea of "stages" of persecution, a standpoint that allowed them cover for insisting that they were persecuted but that differentiated their situation from that of Christians in places such as Iraq and Sudan. The idea of stages moreover leveraged a religious eschatology that collapsed the future into the present by signaling that the various stages all shared a common signifier—serious suffering—even if the form of persecution (e.g., Americans endured no physical torture) differed.

The theory that persecution advanced according to a set of clearly defined stages did not become a part of twenty-first-century Christian discourse about America all at once. It arose piecemeal, as various religious leaders, media figures, and writers experimented with language and ideas that would convey their belief that American Christians indeed were persecuted, even if not by the same means as in other parts of the world. In 2006, about the time of the "War On Christians" conference in Washington, Chris Matthews, host of the MSNBC television news program *Hardball*, interviewed Tony Perkins, the president of the conservative Christian policy group the Family Research Council. Matthews asked Perkins: "Do you believe, Tony, that you feel under attack? Or is this a clever marketing tool?" Perkins responded: "Well, I agree, there's none being thrown to the lions today, but I'm not allowing those cubs to become adult lions. And that's what we're talking about addressing those issues."[64]

Perkins's statement, vague but oddly pointed, typified the discussion carried on by other evangelicals. While seemingly evasive, it signaled positively to Christians who already believed that they were being persecuted. Similarly, Kelly Shackelford, founder of the First Liberty Institute, could convey her meanings to insiders by commenting on perceived hostility toward Christians by saying: "Religious hostility is the red light on the dashboard that tells us we have a problem and that violence will come next if not fixed."[65] One writer might call attention to the "process leading to persecution," while another advocated a "broader understanding of persecution."[66] A quotation that was passed around widely on the internet captured some of the idea of the expected progression: "I expect to die in bed, my successor will die in prison, and his successor will die a martyr in the public square."[67]

Forays into explaining a "broader understanding of persecution," which was a rhetorical means of claiming solidarity and, in the long term, identity with Christians being tortured and murdered in other countries, gradually acquired heft as they coalesced into a theory. Within the Christian community, that theory took on the authority of a settled principle of social interaction, a transhistorical and omnilocative law of society, as it was repeatedly referenced by those who believed they were persecuted in America. As a theory of the "stages" of persecution, it was not the first attempt to temporally organize intolerance as a process of advancing brutality. The Methodist pastor Jesse Lyman Hurlbut, for example, in 1918 had drawn on academic scholarship in detailing the "stages of persecution" in the early Christian church, tracking them from 98 to 313 CE.[68] The starting point for most American Christians in thinking about stages of persecution was not the early church, however. It was the Holocaust. And in the rich eschatological context of American Christianity, the focus of the new discussion of stages was less a matter of chronological progress through a series of periods than an emphasis on themes, a delineation of "types" of persecution that characterized each stage of the Holocaust and, by extension, American Christianity.

Christians in America who believed they were persecuted made an effort to draw an equivalence to the persecution of Jews by the Nazis. Robert Jeffress, the pastor of a large Baptist church in Texas and eventual evangelical spiritual advisor to President Trump, stated in 2015: "I want to remind people that, you know, the Nazis weren't able to take the Jews to the crematoriums immediately. The German people wouldn't have allowed it. Instead, the Nazis had to change public opinion. They marginalized the Jewish people, disparaged them, and made them objects of contempt." Whenever that happens, said Jeffress, "the taking away of further rights will be very easy."[69] Former U.S. Senator Rick Santorum expressed a similar concern. Discussing how the Nazis murdered the Jews, Santorum asked why the Jews did not heed the signs: "Why didn't the Jews see this, and move?" He continued: "Same thing here," warning Christians that the scenario where "your lives are really in danger becomes a possibility down the road."[70] Popular Christian writers such as Thomas Horn and Jeff King, among many others, had been constant in their complaining about the "isolation" and "marginalization" of Christians, and that shared understanding—that a public dislike for conservative Christians was the harbinger of a terrible approaching reckoning—served as the foundation for further elaboration of stages.

Christians' articulation of stages of persecution from "marginalization" to murder was indebted to an extensive academic scholarship on the Holocaust that attempted to historically order the progression of Nazi persecution of the Jews. In 1961, Raul Hilberg, in an interpretation that was to shape subsequent historical analyses of the Holocaust, proposed that it proceeded in stages from 1933 to 1945. Nazi persecution of Jews began through social and political discrimination that marginalized Jews, developed through their isolation and ghettoization, and ended in their annihilation.[71] Christian writers learned the lesson of that scholarship. They proposed a similar model in their characterizations of the persecution of Christians. Vernon J. Sterk, in a dissertation written at the School of World Missions of Fuller Theological Seminary in 1992, gave a detailed analysis, complete with charts, of the stages of persecution of Christian mission communities based on missionary testimonies from overseas. Sterk wrote about the "threats and warnings stage" and its progression to "fines and penalties," imprisonment, and expulsion.[72]

Subsequent commentators elaborated on the defining characteristics of the various stages. Finnish clergyman Johan Candelin, head of the World Evangelical Alliance Religious Liberties Commission, subsequently proposed three distinct but progressive stages: *disinformation*, which begins in the media; *discrimination*, which assigns Christians to second-class status as citizens; and *persecution*, from the state, mobs, other religious groups, and organizations.[73] At the same time, the American Don McAlvany published *Storm Warning: The Coming Persecution of Christians and Traditionalists in America* (1999), which defined five stages of persecution.[74] American evangelicals Jim Cunningham and Paul Estabrooks drew directly on Candelin and on an eight-stage outline proposed in 1996 by Gregory H. Stanton,[75] the president of Genocide Watch, in their *Standing Strong Through the Storm* (2004). Estabrooks originally proposed a three-stage model similar to Candelin's but later added a fourth stage, in the following sequence: opposition, disinformation, injustice, and mistreatment.[76]

Conservative Christian discussion of persecution in America developed over the course of a decade or so from occasional explanation of the themes that were discussed by writers such as Estabrooks to full embrace of a theory of stages. In 2001, Thomas Horn, the influential author of Christian apocalyptic novels, had warned that "even a casual observance of the facts reveals growing isolation of Christians as a people group," as non-Christians "mockingly stereotype Christians as an unenlightened fringe."[77] By 2016, when the American organization International Christian Concern issued its "Hall of Shame Report," mockery of Christians was read as a wake-up call. The report asserted that "Christians in the U.S. are facing constant attacks in the media, where they are portrayed as bigoted, racist, sexist, and close-minded" and "are being marginalized through law."[78] The strident tone was grounded in the deepening trust by some Christians that there was a model that predicted the future. For an apocalyptically minded community, who were committed to searching the Bible and the skies for signs of the end, trust in a theory of stages leading to terrible tribulation corresponded with Christian belief in a step-by-step apocalyptic scheme of history ordained by God and visible—with the right set of eyes—in inerrant scripture.[79]

Thinking about the stages of Christian persecution in America was condensed into doctrine through the agency of several writers during 2009–2012. Joseph M. Esper, a Catholic priest from Michigan, published *Spiritual Dangers of the 21st Century* (2009), in which he repeated and augmented with anecdotes McAlvany's five stages: stereotyping, marginalization, vilification, criminalization, and persecution. Esper believed that the progress toward persecution was "moving into stage four."[80] That scheme was directly appropriated by Johnnette Benkovic, the Catholic founder of Women of Grace, in 2011.[81] Subsequently, Monsignor Charles Pope of Washington, DC, drew from Benkovic in a blog post addressing the problems faced by "Catholics and Bible-believing Christians" in America. He argued that there were five stages of persecution, just as did Esper and Benkovic, but he transposed stages two and three, so that the order was: stereotyping, vilifying, marginalizing, criminalizing, and "persecuting the targeted group outright."[82] Finally, the Protestant writer Fay Voshell in 2015 demonstrated how reliance on the model could enable Christians in America to understand the urgency of their predicament, linking the discussion of stages in America to stages witnessed overseas, in a demonstration that "It's not just 'over there.'"[83]

After 2015, claims that Christians were persecuted in America increasingly were framed within the context of the "stages of persecution." Christians invoked the idea as if it were a law of history. Those who were concerned that the persecution process had commenced in America also spoke out about how dangerous it was and how it must be addressed. Typical was an analysis of the stages of persecution that compared them to the five stages of cancer. Just as the first stage of cancer was easier to treat than the fifth stage, so also persecution had to be stopped in its early stages. There were other similarities, such as: "One thing that is important in assessing the stage of a cancer is whether or not the lymph system has become involved. The lymph system can enable cancer to travel throughout the body. Our court system is doing something similar."[84]

Alongside such carcinogenic speculations was a project that presented itself as more concrete and more consequential: the identification of those who sought to persecute Christians in America. And while secularists, liberals, atheists, and the unaffiliated remained oft-mentioned culprits, the discussion turned increasingly to Muslims and their allies. Additionally, not only were Muslims thought to be behind a conspiracy to persecute American Christians, but they were suspected of a plot aimed at achieving political control of the United States. "I keep hearing about Muslims wanting to take over the United States," said Republican candidate for Senate Sharron Angle in 2010. "I saw that they are taking over a city in Michigan."[85] Another Muslim-watcher that year proposed how that takeover in the United States would occur. The short primer "4 Stages of Islamic Conquest" outlined the process as follows: (1) infiltration, (2) consolidation of power, (3) open war with leadership and culture, and (4) totalitarian Islamic theocracy.[86] The stages of Christian persecution and the stages of Muslim takeover were roughly conjoined.

American expressions of concern about Christian persecution overseas since the mid-twentieth century had been framed largely as condemnation of the practices of communist and Muslim nations. The various lists that were created regularly by religious groups such as Open Doors and International Christian Concern, the testimonies of Christian writers such as Nina Shea and Paul Marshall, and the annual spring reports of the U.S. Commission on International Religious Freedom focused overwhelmingly on communist/ formerly communist states and Muslim countries. After 9/11, the emphasis on Muslim intolerance by Christian watchdog groups grew and the focus on communism, which remained strong, gradually was rephrased as "Marxism." The two enemies, moreover, increasingly were conceptualized as collaborators. *WorldNetDaily* asked in 2017: "Downfall coming through coalition of Islamists and Marxists?" to which it argued that such a coalition "is working to destroy the United States."[87] Another Christian media outlet offered a more precise statement of the danger: "Marxist [*sic*] and Muslims Have United to Bring Down America and Persecute Christians and Conservatives."[88]

American Christian identification with like-minded believers persecuted in other countries entailed imagining—feeling—oneself as persecuted. American Christians imported, as it were, the sufferings of others into America, and that identification was so far-reaching that American Christians came to believe that they themselves were in fact the victims of persecution in the United States. At the same time that Americans imported the victim, moreover, they imported the persecutors, those who enabled that claim of victimhood. In the early twenty-first century, American Christians who believed they were persecuted increasingly blamed communists and especially Muslims for their difficulties. A U.S. foreign policy that set out to identify persecutors of Christians in other countries had repeatedly cast Muslims and communists as the enemies of "religious freedom," and had created a powerful discourse about the intolerant nations in which they operated. Now, rebounding back to the United States, that official view took hold in a new way. It was one kind of example of the "recursive" consequences of foreign policy, and an illustration of the model of the mutually reinforcing relationship between the domestic and the foreign, under the canopy of national identity.

Conservative American Christians did not think merely that Christianity in America might be endangered. They believed the nation itself, which for them was above all a Christian nation, was under actual attack. The nation, in fact, had been attacked on 9/11 and threatened by a number of terrorist events in the aftermath of 9/11. There was reason to be wary of terrorists. But American nationalism, which always has been deeply informed by a Christian mythos regarding the nation's exceptional status, was for many an essential extension and public expression of their Christianity. Accordingly, many Americans took the Muslim threat as they did the communist threat: it was a battle between nations in which countries such as Iraq and Iran, alongside China and Russia, were arrayed against a Christian America. It was often conceptualized as a battle of nations and was informed above all by national identity. More specifically, it was informed by a national identification that was rooted in a complex of ideas and feelings regarding religion, the trauma of the national past, the misremembering of that past, and the projection of the nation's failings overseas from where it had in the end rebounded back to America.

One way in which a conjoined American Christian nationalism and sense of persecution came to be expressed was in the opposition to President Barack Obama, who was elected to the first of his two terms in 2008. Critics, and most vocally Donald Trump, claimed that Obama was not an American citizen, that he had been born in Kenya, that he secretly was a Muslim (his middle name, Hussein, was offered as proof), and that his mission was part of a great worldwide conspiracy to establish Shari'a (Islamic jurisprudence) in America. Additionally, he was criticized as a Marxist whose healthcare initiative, among others, was a slippery slope to a full-out Marxist state, and whose education at elite schools had made him a thorough secularist who sought to erase the religious aspect of American national identity—although this last criticism was difficult to square with the claim that he wished to enact Islamic law in America. Obama, the first African American president, proved to be a lightning rod for white racist anger but equally so represented for many the means for the descent of the United States from Christian nationhood to Christian persecution under Muslim/communist rule.

The fear that America was becoming a place where Christians would be persecuted by Muslims—just as Christians were persecuted in Muslim nations abroad—found powerful expression in campaigns undertaken to prevent the practice of Shari'a in the United States. By 2015, over thirty states had enacted laws officially disallowing Shari'a in court cases. By 2017, 201 anti-Shari'a bills had been introduced into the legislatures of forty-three states. Promoted nationally by groups such as the American Freedom Law Center, such legislation played to what a careful observer of religious hatred in the United States called the "mass hysteria surrounding the so-called threat of 'Sharia law' in the United States."[89] It did not matter to those claiming victimhood that Obama had produced his birth certificate evidencing his American birth, nor did it matter that he was raised as a Christian and attended a Christian church in Washington, DC. It likewise did not matter, as the evangelical Christian Coalition of Alabama director Randy Brinson said in a moment of realism, that "Sharia law is not going to be implemented in Alabama, it just isn't. . . ."[90] What did matter was the imagination of American Christians, which fostered a view of the world and of America in the world that placed them in the shoes of persecuted Christians overseas, and then brought that persecution, including the persecutors, to American shores.

Islamophobia, which had deep roots in America, including the depiction of Mormons as Muslim Amalekites, was vividly expressed in the campaigns against Shari'a after Obama's election, and was significantly advanced during the presidency of Donald Trump. Trump was elected on an anti-immigrant platform that included a "Muslim ban," a promise to bar the entry of Muslims into the United States. He tried several ways in which to implement his ideas about immigration, and was rebuffed by the courts several times. He eventually settled on a program that would restrict visa waivers for persons because of their national citizenship rather than because of the potential immigrant's religious affiliation. The seven[91] countries initially identified all were majority Muslim states, and the "travel ban" regarding them was upheld by the Supreme Court in June 2018. While the naming of Muslim countries was partly a product of legal roadblocks to initial efforts to restrict Muslims as a group, it made sense to white evangelicals, 76 percent of whom approved of the ban of persons from specific Muslim countries.[92] The lists and reports tracking persecution of Christians had, after all, always identified places of persecution by country. And white evangelical Christians identified themselves by country as Americans, with all of the religious meaning that term could bear. The ban was about one country arrayed against others. It was a matter of international relations, a Christian state versus Muslim states.

Religious Intolerance and Post-Christian America

For those who had believed that the United States was a Christian nation, the fact that America by the time of Trump's presidency was no longer a majority white Christian state was confusing. It led to the inclination "to double down on a form of white Christian nationalism, which treats racial and religious identity as markers and defends a shrinking demographic with increasingly autocratic assertions of power."[93] But there was another, related, way that a formerly white Christian majority reacted to their diminished stature. One writer remarked that "many of them have come to feel like foreigners in their own country." As one disheartened American said, "things have changed so much that I often feel like a stranger in my own country," a view shared by half of the predominantly Christian white working-class demographic.[94] America, for many white Christians, indeed had become a foreign country.

The development of American foreign policy in the nineteenth and twentieth centuries, with its increasing focus on the protection of Christians abroad, bore consequences for how Christians identified themselves as Americans. But the ramifications of that historical process, as important as they were, did not alone lead directly to the disenchantment of white Christians in the twenty-first century. The losses suffered by the Religious Right in battles about sex and procreation, school prayer, women's roles, and in other arenas played a central part in eliciting the feelings of deflation experienced by white Christians. Nevertheless, the generations-deep practice of methodically imagining oneself in the shoes of fellow Christians suffering persecution, and the ongoing, successful effort to gain official state recognition of the need for overseas protections, played determinative long-term roles in American religious history. American Christians came to feel that they were living in a foreign land because they had practiced that identity in manifold ways, in the emotional connections that they cultivated with other religious "family" members in a worldwide Christianity. To feel defeated in battles to protect what they believed to be crucial American Christian social traditions was one thing; to conceive of oneself as a foreigner, as a stranger in a strange land,[95] was a significant enlargement of that feeling and the invention of a new perspective. Against a background of ideas about time, destiny, and suffering, the experience of loss and a sense of fellow suffering with Christians worldwide combined to form a newly adapted worldview for many white Christians, and especially for white evangelicals.

The historical failure of the Protestant majority to see religious intolerance in America propelled their efforts to see it elsewhere. They looked overseas because they could not face the trauma, which they had tried to forget, that came with recognizing it in America. When they finally did see intolerance, it was through a circuitous process of having displaced it overseas, and then imported it back into America. In one crucial sense, intolerance for them still did not exist in America, because America had become a foreign country, and the persecution of Christians in America was imagined as intrinsically joined to difficulties experienced by Christians globally. Facing an American future in which Christians would be a shrinking minority, those who had been unable to come to terms with their historical persecution of other Americans remained unable to do so. Characterizing themselves as persecuted, declaring themselves to be victims, but at the same time depicting the nation as having abandoned its Christian foundations, Christians positioned themselves to continue to believe that a Christian America was not guilty of intolerance. But a post-Christian America was.

Acknowledgments

Many different persons and organizations have helped me with this project. Fellowships courtesy of the National Humanities Center and the American Council of Learned Societies made possible research and writing. An appointment to the Institute for Religion, Culture, and Public Life at Columbia University provided me with a quiet study, excellent research resources, and a cluster of generous engaged scholars who listened to my ideas and offered valuable criticisms. I am especially thankful to my Religion Department colleagues there, Courtney Bender and Josef Sorett, and to Jack Lewis Snyder in International Relations, for their willingness to think with me about various parts of this project.

My current graduate students and research assistants at Florida State University as always were terrific conversational partners, offering suggestions for elaborations of my arguments and making welcome demands for clarifications. I thank Tucker Adkins, Nicholas Austin, Timothy Burnside, Kevin Burton, Taylor Wilson Dean, Andrew Gardner, Haley Iliff, Jesse Lee, Robert Lee, Andy McKee, Michael McLaughlin, Sher Afgan Tareen, Dan Wells, and Nico Wrobel.

I am grateful to colleagues who took the time to read my prose and who responded so generously to my queries. Charlie McCrary read a piece of the draft treating religious freedom scholarship and provided excellent critical insight. Cara Burnidge likewise provided guidance about the roles played by Woodrow Wilson. Mike Ashcraft applied his keen eye to a chapter that discussed twentieth-century New Religious Movements and the anticult scare. David Kirkpatrick consulted about the section on South America. Thanks also to Paul Harvey. Above all, I am indebted to Heather Curtis and Melani McAlister, who read the entire manuscript and offered pages upon pages of detailed criticism of arguments, requests for clarifications, and suggestions for further research. I could not have imagined two better readers of this book and count myself immensely lucky to have had the benefit of their knowledge and critical insight. They are model colleagues, and the gift they made of their expertise made the book much better than it otherwise would have been.

Alan Thomas and Tim Mennel at the University of Chicago Press encouraged this work and expertly managed the transition from manuscript to book. I thank them both and especially Tim for his several readings of the manuscript and point-on suggestions for improving it. Marianne Tatom did a brilliant job of copyediting the manuscript, from fact-checking to word choice. Adam Sweatman made a great index. Susan Karani kept everything moving smoothly through production.

My department chairs at Florida State University, John Kelsay and Aline Kalbian, made everything work smoothly as I transitioned in and out of residence over a few years. I thank them for supporting me and making it easy.

It is a pleasure to acknowledge in the dedication Ben Ray, who was my faculty colleague at the University of Virginia, and whose recent meticulous study of the Salem witch trials brilliantly models how careful, judicious scholarship can transform historical interpretation. His unfailing generosity toward a young scholar, his constant encouragements, and his wise perspective on scholarly endeavor remain with me as proof of how academic collegiality is, at its best, a matter of friends thinking together.

Notes

Introduction

1. James Madison, *A Memorial and Remonstrance on the Religious Rights of Man* (Washington, DC: S. C. Ustick, 1828), 8; and *Memorial and Remonstrance Against Religious Assessments in the Writings of James Madison*, ed. Gaillard Hunt, vol. 2 of 10 (New York: G. P. Putnam's Sons, 1901), 189.

2. There are many kinds of American Protestants, and they think in many different ways about faith, society, and politics. The same is true for Catholics. Moreover, Protestants and Catholics have occasionally agreed in their thinking, and have even acted together at times to address social and political issues affecting them. While recognizing such diversity and the risks of generalizing about those two groups and others, the historical analyses made in this book attend to broad patternings of historical events and directions of historical change. One of those patterns is the historically continuous friction between Protestants and Catholics, and the alignments of those two groups into opposite camps in moments of severe cultural strain or crisis.

3. Harold G. Brown recently has written of a similar process in France from the sixteenth to nineteenth centuries. For Brown, the visual and textual representations of mass violence—largely having to do with religious wars—led to intense cultivation of empathy by those who engaged such depictions. That empathy with others' suffering—built out of responses to *mediations* of that suffering over many years—led to collective trauma (*Mass Violence and the Self: From the French Wars of Religion to the Paris Commune* [Ithaca, NY: Cornell University Press, 2018]). An overview of the category of collective trauma is on pp. 14–18.

4. Philip Gleason, "Identifying Identity: A Semantic History," *Journal of American History* 69 (1983): 910. Gleason warned that "responsible use of the term demands a lively sensitivity to the intrinsic complexities of the subject matter with which it deals, and careful attention to the need for precision and consistency in its application. But of course its enormous popularization has had just the opposite effect: as identity became more and more a cliché, its meaning grew progressively more diffuse, thereby encouraging increasingly loose and irresponsible usage" (931).

5. Sacvan Bercovitch, *The Puritan Origins of the American Self* (New Haven, CT: Yale University Press, 1975), ix, 94.

6. The discussion of the meaning of national identity in the field of international relations, as well as in history and the social sciences, has advanced in tandem with discussion about

216   NOTES TO PAGE 7

nationalism itself. During the 1980s–1990s, the first major, cross-disciplinary stage of the discussion featured a range of theories that have been revised, extended, and debated since then. Some theories focused on ancient roots of religion, language, blood, or shared ritual life. Other research emphasized how dominant groups or elites created, deployed, and altered identities as they exercised power in the interest of achieving certain goals. A number of theories stressed collective agreement about rights, proprieties, values, and the means and ends of politics. Representative writings of approaches articulated during this period of time are collected in *Nationalism*, ed. John Hutchinson and Anthony D. Smith (Oxford: Oxford University Press, 1994). A useful typology of approaches is in Anthony D. Smith, *Myths and Memories of the Nation* (Oxford: Oxford University Press, 1999), 3–9. Smith organizes theoretical approaches into four clusters: primordialists (Pierre van den Berghe, Edward Shils, Clifford Geertz); perennialists (Tadeusz Wałek-Czarnecki, Mario Attilio Levi); modernists (Eric Hobsbawm, Ernest Gellner, Elie Kedourie, Benedict Anderson); and ethno-symbolists (John Armstrong, John Hutchinson, Anthony D. Smith). In recognizing differences among theories, Duncan S. A. Bell nevertheless observes that "The construction of stories about identity, origins, history, and community" is common to the processes explicated by all the various kinds of theories. "Representation and discourse should therefore be seen as a constitutive feature of nationalism. We are all constructivists in this sense" ("Mythscapes: Memory, Mythology, and National Memory," *British Journal of Sociology* 54 [2003]: 69).

7. The cultural turn in the related scholarship of international history/diplomatic history/international relations has developed with particular emphases on culture, identity, memory, and trauma, and increasingly has incorporated race and gender, among other topics. As Patrick Finney has observed of the cultural turn in the field, "The origins of the turn to culture are complicated and, as with most such shifts, lie both in perceived changes in real world international relations and in the realm of ideas," but that "in not much more than a decade it has vastly expanded the horizons of international history, and through the deployment of new source materials and new methodologies has generated an enormously fertile literature" (Patrick Finney, "Introduction: What Is International History?," in Finney, ed., *Palgrave Advances in International History* [Houndmills: Palgrave Macmillan, 2005], 18). See also Finney, *Remembering the Road to World War Two: International History, National Identity, Collective Memory* (London: Routledge, 2010); and, on "national memory cultures," see the essays in Finney, ed., *Remembering the Second World War* (New York: Routledge, 2018). Andrew Rotter discusses "Culture" in Finney, ed., *Palgrave Advances in International History*, 267–99. Useful overviews are Akira Iriye, "Culture and International History," in *Explaining the History of American Foreign Relations*, ed. Michael J. Hogan and Thomas G. Paterson (Cambridge: Cambridge University Press, 2004), 241–56; and Anders Stephanson, "Commentary: Considerations on Culture and Theory," *Diplomatic History* 18 (1994): 107–19.

The focus on identity in the cultural turn of the field, in addition to the samples cited above, also is central to Stefan Berger, *The Search for Normality: National Identity and Historical Consciousness in Germany since 1800* (Oxford: Berghahn, 1997); William E. Connolly, *Identity/Difference: Democratic Negotiations of Political Paradox* (Ithaca, NY: Cornell University Press, 1991), including the discussion of religious intolerance, identity, and difference in relation to New Spain (41–46); R. B. J. Walker, *Inside/Outside: International Relations as Political Theory* (Cambridge: Cambridge University Press, 1993); David Campbell, *Writing Security: United States Foreign Policy and the Politics of Identity* (Minneapolis: University of Minnesota Press, 1998); Matthew Jacobson, *Barbarian Virtues: The United States Encounters Foreign Peoples at*

Home and Abroad, 1876–1917 (2000); and Albert Mathias, David Jacobsen, and Yosef Lapid, eds., *Identities, Borders, Orders: Rethinking International Relations Theory* (Minneapolis: University of Minnesota Press, 2001).

Examples of the focus on gender within this approach to analyzing U.S. foreign policy are in Andrew Rotter, "Gender Relations, Foreign Relations: The United States and South Asia, 1947–1964," *Journal of American History* 81 (1994): 518–42; and Michelle Mart, "Tough Guys and American Cold War Policy: Images of Israel, 1948–1960," *Diplomatic History* 20 (1996): 357–80. On race, see Alexander DeConde, *Ethnicity, Race and American Foreign Policy* (Boston: Northeastern University Press, 1992); Penny von Eschen, *Race Against Empire: Black Americans and Anticolonialism, 1937–1957* (Ithaca, NY: Cornell University Press, 1997); Thomas Borstalmann, *The Cold War and the Color Line: American Race Relations in the Global Arena* (Cambridge, MA: Harvard University Press, 2001); and Melani McAlister, *Epic Encounters: Culture, Media, and U.S. Interests in the Middle East since 1945* (Berkeley: University of California Press, 2001). Christina Klein draws on Edward Said in *Cold War Orientalism: Asia in the Middlebrow Imagination, 1945–1961* (Berkeley: University of California Press, 2003). The intersectionality of race and gender hierarchies is discussed in Mary Renda, *Taking Haiti: Military Occupation and the Culture of U.S. Imperialism, 1915–1940* (Chapel Hill: University of North Carolina Press, 2001).

The large literature on trauma and memory in international relations also is part of the cultural turn. Examples are Jenny Adkins, *Trauma and the Memory of Politics* (Cambridge: Cambridge University Press, 2003); and Dan Stone, *Constructing the Holocaust* (London: Vallentine Mitchell, 2003). One approach to identity and trauma is in Bernhard Giesen, "National Identity as Trauma: The German Case," in *Myth and Memory in the Construction of Community: Historical Patterns in Europe and Beyond*, ed. Bo Strath (Bruxelles: Lang, 2000), 227–47.

8. Benedict Anderson writes that nations are products of the imagination "because the members of even the smallest nation will never know most of their fellow-members, meet them, or even hear of them, yet in the minds of each lives the image of their communion." What Anderson called "print capitalism" fostered the dissemination of ideas and values that underwrote a population of individuals that, in fact, "is imagined as a community, because, regardless of the actual inequality and exploitation that may prevail," the nation "is always conceived as a deep, horizontal comradeship." The personal feelings involved in belonging to the imagined community are a manifestation of "the *attachment* that peoples feel for the inventions of their imaginations." Nationality and nationalism are "cultural artefacts of a particular kind" that "command such profound emotional legitimacy." Anderson undertook as a key part of his study of national communities the "attempt to show why these particular cultural artefacts have aroused such deep attachments" (Benedict Anderson, *Imagined Communities: Reflections on the Origin and Spread of Nationalism*, rev. ed. [London: Verso, 1991], 6, 7, 141, 4; originally published 1983). See the related discussion of national identity in Ernest Gellner, *Nations and Nationalism* (Ithaca, NY; London: Cornell University Press, 1983); and in Eric Hobsbawm and Terence Ranger, eds., *The Invention of Tradition* (Cambridge: Cambridge University Press, 1983); and the discussion of national identity and emotion in Ronald Grigor Suny, "Why We Hate You: The Passions of National Identity and Ethnic Violence," Berkeley Program in Soviet and Post-Soviet Studies Working Paper Series (2004), http://iseees.berkeley.edu/sites/default/files/u4/bps_/publications_/2004_01-suny.pdf, accessed December 5, 2017.

9. "L'essence d'une nation est que tous les individus aient beaucoup de choses en commun, et aussi que tous aient oublié bien des choses." Ernest Renan, "Qu'est-ce qu'une nation?," in *Oeuvres Complètes*, vol. 1 of 10 (Paris: Calmann Lévy, 1947–1961), 892.

10. Anderson was particularly interested in remembering and forgetting. In a pregnant chapter on the topic in the second edition of *Imagined Communities*, he began by citing Renan: "Every French citizen must have forgotten St. Bartholomew's, the Provence massacres in the 13th century." Anderson analyzed the passage by pointing out that, "In effect, Renan's readers were being told to have 'already forgotten' what Renan's own words assumed that they naturally remembered!" How did the French both remember and forget those "colossal religious conflicts" in European history? "How," asked Anderson, "are we to make sense of this paradox?" Drawing a rough comparison between the psychodynamics of the individual person and the collective behavior of the population of a state, Anderson argued that national meaning-making was grounded in the process of remembering/forgetting. A "systematic historiographical campaign," mounted in the schools, executes that agenda. Offering the example of America, he asserted that there is a "vast pedagogical industry," present in America as well as in France and elsewhere, that "works ceaselessly to oblige young Americans to remember/forget the hostilities of 1861–5 as a great 'civil' war between brothers rather than between—as they briefly were—two sovereign nation-states." In other words, the construction of a national narrative that defines community advances—in this American case—on the premise of fratricide. The violent contestations between rival groups, North and South, are conceptualized as clashes between two groups that are related as kin. Additionally, Anderson noted that the relationship of dominant whites with enslaved blacks and Native Americans in North America was exceptionally riven, more so than relations between groups in Europe. Nevertheless, white Americans engaged in those relations imagined fraternity as they practiced a broader racially inflected fratricide, and to an extent unmatched in Europe. "In the United States of America," wrote Anderson, "this paradox is particularly well exemplified." As is apparent in the next chapter of this book, this instance is analogous to the paradox of New England colonists and Indians sensing a strong connectedness even as they cast each other as enemy others (Anderson, *Imagined Communities*, 199–200, 202, 205).

11. Some recent discussion of the role of affect in national politics and the shaping of national identity builds on the research of scholars such as Brian Massumi (*Parables for the Virtual: Movement, Affect, Sensation* [Durham, NC: Duke University Press, 2002]) and Sara Ahmed (*The Cultural Politics of Emotion* [London: Routledge, 2004]). There are a range of approaches to the topic, however, and there is no consensus about how affect and national identity specifically are related. See Carol Vogler, "Social Identity and Emotion: The Meeting of Psychoanalysis and Sociology," *Sociological Review* 48 (2000): 19–42; W. Russell Neuman, George E. Marcus, Michael MacKuen, and Ann M. Crigler, *The Affect Effect: Dynamics of Emotion in Political Thinking and Behavior* (Chicago: University of Chicago Press, 2007); Christopher Weber, "Emotions, Campaigns, and Political Participation," *Political Research Quarterly* 66 (2012): 414–28; Carol Johnson, "The Politics of Affective Citizenship: From Blair to Obama," *Citizenship Studies* 14 (2005): 495–509; and Ali Mashuri and Esti Zaduqisti, "National Identification and Collective Emotions as Predictors of Pro-Social Attitudes Towards Islamic Minority Groups in Indonesia," *Europe's Journal of Psychology* 10 (2014), doi:10.5964/ejop.v10i2.707.

12. Drawing like many other twentieth-century historians on the psychoanalytic writing of theorists such as Erik Erikson, international relations theorist William Bloom articulated a view of national identity and foreign policy that incorporated what he referred to as "identification theory." Bloom like Anderson conducted his analysis of international relations with an eye to mass psychological processes. Bloom was much more detailed, explicit, and insistent than Anderson in explaining the gravity of a "national identity," represented by "the symbols of the

NOTES TO PAGE 8

nation," that prompts people to "act as one psychological group." But the problems of extrapolating a collective psychology of the state, a national identity, from theories arising from research on personal psychology aside, Bloom offered an additional insight. The ongoing project of national identity construction and maintenance, when threatened by domestic political processes, "can overspill into international conflict." For studies that draw upon Bloom's thinking, international relations theoretically is captive to the shifting ground of national identity. See William Bloom, *Personal Identity, National Identity, and International Relations* (Cambridge University Press, 1990), 29, 51–52, 61, 120, 151–52, 49, 116, 156. Scholarship that critically addresses the idea of national remembering and forgetting in specific historical contexts, and in ways that foreground important theoretical considerations, includes: Consuelo Cruz, "Identity and Persuasion: How Nations Remember Their Pasts and Make Their Futures," *World Politics* 52 (2000): 275–312; Priya Kumar, "Testimonies of Loss and Memory: Partition and the Haunting of a Nation," *Interventions: International Journal of Colonial Studies* 1 (1999): 201–15; Marek Tamm, "History as Cultural Memory: Mnemohistory and the Construction of the Estonian Nation," *Journal of Baltic Studies* 39 (2008): 499–515; Karen E. Till, *The New Berlin: Memory, Politics, Place* (Minneapolis: University of Minnesota Press, 2005); and Sneja Gunew, *Haunted Nations: The Colonial Dimensions of Multiculturalisms* (London: Routledge, 2013).

There is a deep scholarly literature that addresses the topics of "the feeling of forgetting," the haunted perpetrator, and collective memory. I list here some of the research that has helped me frame my ideas about those topics. For discussion of the affective residues of what is "forgotten," see Santiago Arango-Munoz, "The Nature of Epistemic Feelings," *Philosophical Psychology* 27 (2014): 193–211; "Metacognitive Feelings, Self-Ascriptions, and Mental Actions," *Philosophical Inquiries* 2 (2014): 145–62; and "Scaffolded Memory and Metacognitive Feelings," *Review of Philosophy and Psychology* 4 (2013): 135–52; as well as Sven Bernecker, "Remembering Without Knowing," in Bernecker, *Memory: A Philosophical Study* (New York: Oxford University Press, 2009), 65–103; Paul Connerton, "Seven Types of Forgetting," *Memory Studies* 1 (2008): 59–71; Jérôme Dokic and Jean-Rémy Martin, "Felt Reality and the Opacity of Perception," *Topoi* 36 (2017): 299–309; Michael E. Harkim, "Feeling and Thinking in Memory and Forgetting," *Ethnohistory* 50 (2003): 261–84; Leon Litwinski, "Hatred and Forgetting," *Journal of General Psychology* 33 (1945): 85–109; C. B. Martin and M. Deutscher, "Remembering," *Philosophical Review* 75 (1966): 161–96; Kourken Michaelian, Dorothea Debus, and Denis Perrin, eds., *New Directions in the Philosophy of Memory* (London: Routledge, 2018), "Part III: The Affective Dimension of Memory," 137–78; Anne Meylan, "Epistemic Emotions: A Natural Kind?," *Philosophical Inquiries* 2 (2014), 173–90; E. Mizrak and I. Oztekin, "The Relationship Between Emotion and Forgetting," *Emotion* 16 (2016): 33–42; Michael F. O'Reilly, "Postcolonial Haunting: Anxiety, Affect, and the Situated Encounter," *Postcolonial Text* 3 (2007): 1–15; B. Kenneth Payne and Elizabeth Corrigan, "Emotional Constraints on Intentional Forgetting," *Journal of Experimental Social Psychology* 43 (2007): 780–86; Paul Ricouer, *Memory, History, Forgetting*, trans. Kathleen Blamey and David Pellauer (Chicago: University of Chicago Press, 2004); and Ali I. Tekcan and M. Aktürk, "Are You Sure You Forgot? Feeling of Knowing in Directed Forgetting," *Journal of Experimental Psychology* 27 (2001): 1487–90.

For examples of analysis of haunting and history, see Jessica Auchter, *The Politics of Haunting and Memory in International Relations* (London: Routledge, 2014); Renée L. Bergland, *The National Uncanny: Indian Ghosts and American Subjects* (Hanover, NH: Dartmouth College / University Press of New England, 2000); Jose Colmeiro, "A Nation of Ghosts: Haunting, Historical Memory, and Forgetting in Post-Franco Spain," *452 F: Revista de Teoría de la Litera-*

tura y Literatura Comparada 4 (2011): 17–34; Jill Lepore, *The Name of War: King Philip's War and the Origins of American Identity* (New York: Vintage, 1999); Anna Thiemann, *Rewriting the American Soul: Trauma, Neuroscience, and the Contemporary Literary Imagination* (London: Routledge, 2017); and Ban Wang, *Illuminations from the Past: Trauma, Memory, and History in Modern China* (Stanford, CA: Stanford University Press, 2004).

On collective memory and feeling, see also Alan Confino, "Collective Memory and Cultural History," *American Historical Review* 102 (1997): 1386–1403; Eric Halperin, Daphna Canetti-Nisim, and Sivan Hirsch-Hoefler, "The Central Role of Group-Based Hatred as an Emotional Antecedent of Political Intolerance: Evidence from Israel," *Political Psychology* 30 (2009): 93–123; and William Hirst and Alin Coman, "Building a Collective Memory: The Case for Collective Forgetting," *Current Opinions in Psychology* 23 (2018): 88–92.

On trauma and especially perpetrator trauma, see Cathy Caruth, "Unclaimed Experience: Trauma and the Possibility of History," *Yale French Studies* 79 (1991): 181–92; Ron Eyerman, "Perpetrator Trauma and Collective Guilt," in Eyerman, *Memory, Trauma, and Identity* (Cham: Springer, 2019), 167–94; Bernhard Giesen, "The Trauma of Perpetrators: The Holocaust as the Traumatic Reference of German National Identity," in *Cultural Trauma and Collective Identity*, ed. Jeffrey Alexander, Ronald Eyerman, Bernhard Giessen, Neil Smelser, and Piotr Sztompka (Berkeley: University of California Press, 2004), 112–54; L. M. MacNair, *Perpetration-Induced Traumatic Stress: The Psychological Consequences of Killing* (Westport, CT: Praeger, 2002); Alex Pillen, "Language, Translation, Trauma," *Annual Review of Anthropology* 45 (2016): 95–111; Saira Mohamed, "Of Monsters and Men: Perpetrator Trauma and Mass Atrocity," *Columbia Law Review* 115 (2015): 1157–1216; Raya Morag, *Waltzing with Bashir: Perpetrator Trauma and Cinema* (New York and London: I. B. Tauris, 2013); Petar Ramadanovic, "From Haunting to Trauma," *Postmodern Culture* 11 (2001), doi:10.1353/pmc.2001.0005; and Geoffrey White, "Violent Memories/Memory Violence," *Reviews in Anthropology* 46 (2017): 19–34.

13. Discussing this point, Anderson proposes that "as with modern persons so it is with nations" (*Imagined Communities*, 205). That statement, however, should not be misunderstood as trust in a thoroughgoing correspondence between the two.

14. Benedict Anderson and Sigmund Freud, among many others, have shaped thinking about collective feeling and collective identity. Building on such theories, other scholars have focused on the *negotiation* of identities in encounters with others and across national boundaries. Sara Ahmed questions whether "collective feelings are feelings that the collective 'has,' as if the collective was a subject. Rather the collective is an effect of the impressions left by others. . . ." For Ahmed, it is the encounter with others that brings forward the affective response that is read as an expression of collective identity, and that is "how feelings make the collective appear as if it were a body . . ." ("Collective Feelings, Or, the Impressions Left by Others," *Theory, Culture & Society* 21 [2004]: 27). Sujata Moorti discusses how perceived transnational kinships are crucial in the forging of transnational community identities for populations in diaspora ("Desperately Seeking an Identity: Diasporic Cinema and the Articulation of Transnational Kinship," *International Journal of Cultural Studies* 6 [2003]: 355–76). I draw selectively on the insights redolent in such research in framing American collective identity and collective feeling in relation to encounters with other nations.

15. Where Erikson and Freud predominated in studies such as William Bloom's, it is Hegel, Bakhtin, Kristeva, and Levinas, among others, whose thinking about "others" has framed discussions of national identity that take seriously the roles of opponent states in the construction of national identity. Iver B. Neumann, drawing on such thinking, observed that "the nation

NOTES TO PAGES 8–9

as an 'imagined community' . . . is only a starting point." The process for Neumann is more manifestly social than the psychological approach of Bloom and like-minded writers. Oftentimes, that process is cast as severely dialectical, with clearly defined and precisely represented opponents sharpening each other's image as they frictively engage. See Iver B. Neumann, "Self and Other in International Relations," *European Journal of International Relations* 2 (1996): 143.

16. Anne Norton argued that ambiguities of national identities were crucial: "Individual and collective identities are created not simply in the difference between the self and other but in those moments of ambiguity where one is other to oneself, and in the recognition of the other as like." For Norton, "representation, both political and semiotic, is created in the paradox of simultaneous presence and absence" (*Reflections on Political Identity* [Baltimore: Johns Hopkins University Press, 1988], 7). The process as she describes it can be violent. Iver B. Neumann extended Norton's insight into a broader conceptualization of self and other in international relations. It is especially "the ambiguity of strangers" that is important for the relation of self and other for Neumann, who draws from Levinas: "The relationship with the other is not an idyllic and harmonious relationship with communion, or a sympathy through which we put ourselves in the other's place; we recognize the other as resembling us, but exterior to us" (Iver B. Neumann, "Self and Other in International Relations," *European Journal of International Relations* 2 [1996]: 143). The constructivist theorist Alexander Wendt proposed that "social identities and interests always are in process during interaction" between states. For Wendt, identification "is a continuum from negative to positive—from conceiving the other as anathema to the self to conceiving it as an extension of the self." For Wendt and others, the relationship is fundamentally a matter of symbolic interaction (Alexander Wendt, "Collective Identity Formation and the International State," *American Political Science Review* 88 [1994]: 386).

Such a notion of relationship to the other underlay, for example, Tzvetan Todorov's historical depiction of relations between Europeans and Native Americans in sixteenth-century New Spain. Todorov described that encounter as a complex of simultaneous interrelated processes involving embrace of the other, rejection of the other, judgment of the other, and ignorance of the other (*The Conquest of America* [New York: Harper and Row, 1984]). A view of the state in accord with such a view sees the state engaging the other in multiple ways that sometimes differ because of the moments and places of encounter and the immediate interests at stake.

17. Edward W. Said, *Orientalism* (New York: Pantheon, 1978), 95.

18. Critical dismissals of Said's *Orientalism* are plentiful, and especially since 9/11. Examples are Bernard Lewis, *Islam and the West* (New York: Oxford University Press, 1993), 99–118; Robert Irwin, *For Lust of Knowing: The Orientalists and Their Enemies* (London: Penguin, 2007); and Daniel Martin Varisco, *Reading Orientalism: Said and the Unsaid* (Seattle: University of Washington Press, 2007).

19. Andrew J. Rotter, "Saidism Without Said: Orientalism and U.S. Diplomatic History," *American Historical Review* 105 (2000): 1210.

20. Valerie Kennedy, *Edward Said: A Critical Introduction* (Cambridge: Polity Press, 2000), 30; and Robert J. C. Young, *White Mythologies: Writing History and the West*, 2nd ed. (London: Routledge, 2004), 179. While the East is constructed as exotic, Said's analysis also means "in effect, that the East becomes the repository or projection of those aspects of themselves which Westerners do not choose to acknowledge (cruelty, sensuality, decadence, laziness, and so on)" (Peter Barry, *Beginning Theory: An Introduction to Literary and Cultural Theory* [New York: Oxford University Press, 2017], 195). Western texts about "other" places "were not accounts of different peoples and societies, but a projection of European fears and desires masquerading as

scientific/'objective' knowledges. Said's *Orientalism* examines the process by which this discursive formation emerges" (Ensieh Shabanirad and Seyed Mohammad Marandi, "Edward Said's *Orientalism* and the Representation of Oriental Women in George Orwell's *Burmese Days*," *International Letters in Social and Humanistic Sciences* 60 [2015]: 26). Colonialism projects onto the colonized "the settler's own anxieties and negative self-images" (Abdul R. JanMohamed, *Manichean Aesthetics: The Politics of Literature in Colonial Africa* [Amherst: University of Massachusetts Press, 1988], 3). The idea that the content of the projection is not only a kind of inventory of negative traits but that it also is animated by repressed fears enables a clearer understanding of how national identity, memory, forgetting, and especially trauma can be involved in international relations.

21. For scholars such as those cited in the previous footnote, the Orient took shape in Western imaginations partly as a mirror image of the flaws and ugly conceits of the West. An inversion, it became the opposite of the West, against which the West appeared enlightened, rational, and superior. The West constructed itself in a dialectics with colonized nations that involved the transference of disagreeable or villainous aspects of Western identity to them. That projected material included fears and desires. To a certain extent, national identity can be understood as a similar case: a nation symbolically situating itself in relation to other states or regions, projecting its ideals, cultural mores, and hopes onto the host state ("they are like us"), but at the same time *unadmittedly* projecting—and sometimes in greater degree—its failings, fears, and traumas ("they are not like us").

While Said's *Orientalism* is a recent prompt to recognizing the possibility of Western projection eastward, discussion of the idea of projection significantly predates Said's writing. Giambattista Vico, Ludwig Feuerbach, and Sigmund Freud, among others, made projection central to their understandings of culture.

22. The American sociologist Jeffrey C. Alexander proposed that "cultural trauma occurs when members of a collectivity feel they have been subjected to a horrendous event that leaves indelible marks upon their group consciousness, marking their memories forever and changing their future identity in fundamental and irrevocable ways" (Jeffrey C. Alexander, "Toward a Theory of Cultural Trauma," in *Cultural Trauma and Collective Identity*, ed. Jeffrey C. Alexander, Ron Eyerman, Bernard Giesen, Neil J. Smelser, and Piotr Sztompka [Berkeley: University of California Press, 2004], 1).

23. Neil J. Smelser has written, for example, about the "unwillingness to remember" in West Germany immediately after the Holocaust (Neil J. Smelser, "Psychological and Cultural Trauma," in *Cultural Trauma and Collective Identity*, 51).

24. Erica Resende and Dovile Budryte, "Introduction," in Erica Resende and Dovile Budryte, eds., *Memory and Trauma in International Relations: Theories, Cases and Debates* (Abingdon, UK: Routledge, 2014), 3. Discussing how the traumatic event is never fully assimilated, Resende and Budryte depict trauma as "the experience of unbearable affect," something outside of normative experience and beyond the limits of writing. Nations as "emotional communities" invent memories in the shadows of traumas. In its acute emotionality, trauma is sensed as instability of culture, as collective life ungrounded and accidental (2, 8). Julia Kristeva wrote that "traumatic memories . . . are not repressed but constantly evoked as the denial of negation prevents the work of repression . . ." (*Black Sun: Depression and Melancholia* [New York: Columbia University Press, 1989], 46).

25. For an example of ontological insecurity in Kosovo, see Brent J. Steele, *Ontological Security in International Relations: Self-Identity and the IR State* (Abingdon, UK: Routledge, 2008),

NOTES TO PAGE 10

114–48; Jennifer Mitzen, "Ontological Security in World Politics: State Identity and the Security Dilemma," *European Journal of International Relations* 12 (2006); and Richard Ned Lebow, *National Identities and International Relations* (Cambridge: Cambridge University Press, 2016).

26. If, as collective memory pioneer Maurice Halbwachs argued, "the past is not preserved but constructed on the basis of the present," then memory, and the memory of trauma, especially, is always a process. It is a part of what Duncan S. A. Bell calls the "national mythscape," an ongoing mingling of remembering, forgetting, and mythologization. See Maurice Halbwachs, *On Collective Memory*, ed. and trans. Lewis A. Coser (Chicago: University of Chicago Press, 1992), 40; Duncan S. A. Bell, "Mythscapes: Memory, Mythology, and National Memory," *British Journal of Sociology* 54 (2003): 75–78; and Bell, ed., *Trauma, Memory, and World Politics: Reflections on the Relationship Between Past and Present* (New York: Palgrave Macmillan, 2006).

27. Walter L. Hixson expresses this idea in writing that there is a "mutually reinforcing relationship between the domestic and the foreign, under the canopy of national identity" (Walter L. Hixson, *The Myth of American Diplomacy: National Identity and U.S. Foreign Policy* [New Haven, CT: Yale University Press, 2008], 8). He argued that the myth of America as a "providentially destined 'beacon of liberty'" determinatively influenced the course of American foreign policy. In his view, the myth led regularly to war rather than to a cooperative internationalism (1). The power of that myth and its embeddedness as a part of national identity made it difficult to dislodge. Moreover, it historically has informed a hawkish foreign policy that in turn has rebounded back upon the domestic state, exerting influence over the state with a renewed authority and capability. The national myth, projected as foreign policy and to some extent objectified in that way, returns in force to bolster and reinvigorate the trunk from which it was born. Hixson concludes that "foreign policy plays a profoundly significant role in the process of creating, affirming, and disciplining conceptions of national identity." For Hixson, it is only "by analyzing the mutually reinforcing relationship between the domestic and the foreign, under the canopy of national identity," that it is possible to understand power within the state and in international relations (8).

28. For Richard Ned Lebow, national "identity construction is dialectical in that the seemingly opposed process of distancing oneself from another actor or actors can occur at the same time one draws closer to them" (Richard Ned Lebow, *National Identities and International Relations* [Cambridge: Cambridge University Press, 2016], 62). National identity projected internationally returns to the state in some form to influence the ongoing process of identity construction so that "the relationship is recursive" (11, 5). That line of argument refines and interprets a claim previously made by David Campbell that the identity of the state is itself an "effect" of the discourses that make up foreign policy (Campbell, *Writing Security*, 56). For Campbell, those discourses of foreign policy have largely to do with security concerns that prompt ongoing constructions and reconstructions of community boundaries. For related discussion on how a specifically "European" identity "shapes and is increasingly incorporated into national identities," see Michael E. Smith, "Implementation: Making the European Union's International Relations Work," in Christopher Hill, Michael E. Smith, and Sophie Vanhoonacker, eds., *International Relations and the European Union*, 3rd ed. (Oxford: Oxford University Press, 2017), 161.

As the importance of understanding the interrelationship between national identity and foreign policy became clearer, and scholars attempted to analyze more precisely what national identity implies and how it is relationally constituted with foreign policy, Lebow offered a clarification. He contributed to scholarly discussion of national identity by articulating more precisely the theory that just as national identities guide foreign policy, so also does foreign policy

224   NOTES TO PAGES 11–14

influence national identities. Lebow observed, as have other scholars, that the state is not the same as a person and the psychological processes we might describe with regard to a person do not always translate to the state. But, drawing qualifiedly on ideas redolent in personal identity theory and putting them in conversation with broader analyses of the state, Lebow advanced discussion of the idea of state identity as a matter of process. But what is crucial to Lebow's understanding is this: external actors impose identity upon the state, and are able to do so because the state recognizes the closeness of that actor to itself—even as it sees it as other.

One way to think about national identity is to theorize it as a composite of national myths, and to acknowledge that the power of those distinct myths rises and falls in the shifting relationships of the myths to each other. Lebow preferred to talk of a state with multiple identities, or multiple "identifications." Those identifications can at any given moment be in collaboration, at odds, or in the process of change as each affects the others. "They interact," he wrote, "and changes in one are likely to prompt, even require, changes in the other." For Lebow, national identity, in the end, is a misleading concept unless we recognize that it is an amalgam, made up of a range of different myths or identifications dynamically related one to the other (21, 11).

29. This is discussed fully in chapter five.

30. For discussion of the ways in which that process involved affect, see John Corrigan, *Emptiness: Feeling Christian in America* (Chicago: University of Chicago Press, 2015).

31. David Sehat, *The Myth of American Religious Freedom* (New York: Oxford University Press, 2011), viii.

32. John Corrigan and Lynn Neal, *Religious Intolerance in America: A Documentary History* (Chapel Hill: University of North Carolina Press, 2010).

33. Jeffrey Andrew Barash writes that collective memory "draws on the sedimented and stratified passive reservoir from which group dispositions and habitual activities are spontaneously reenacted" (*Collective Memory and the Historical Past* [Chicago: University of Chicago Press, 2016], 90). He proposes that a "passive" mechanics of collective memory forms "group experience without necessarily occasioning explicit notice or reflection" (171). The American memory of trauma is such a collective memory, one that looms on the edges of what is noticed. Barash cogently summarizes the early psychoanalytic influence on thinking about collective memory and historical trauma (20–26).

34. Andrew Preston, *Sword of the Spirit, Shield of Faith: Religion in American War and Diplomacy* (New York: Anchor Books, 2012); Melani McAlister, *The Kingdom of God Has No Borders: A Global History of American Evangelicals* (New York: Oxford University Press, 2018); Walter A. McDougall, *The Tragedy of U.S. Foreign Policy: How America's Civil Religion Betrayed the National Interest* (New Haven, CT: Yale University Press, 2016), and *Promised Land, Crusader State: The American Encounter with the World Since 1776* (Boston: Houghton Mifflin, 1997); Heather D. Curtis, *Holy Humanitarians: American Evangelicals and Global Aid* (Cambridge, MA: Harvard University Press, 2018); and Jack Lewis Snyder, ed., *Religion and International Relations Theory* (New York: Columbia University Press, 2011).

35. An example of the "cure" approach is the scholarship of John T. Noonan Jr., who, promoting the idea of American exceptionalism, claimed that France, Japan, and Russia had followed the American example, adopting religious freedom as it had been modeled in the United States in order to overcome their problems with religious frictions. Regarding his approach to the issue of religious freedom in America, he wrote: "For my part, I approach this most difficult and fundamental of subjects not without diffidence and doubt but with the belief that religion is a projection (for who could deny the freight of human desires that every religion has born?),

NOTES TO PAGE 14 225

and that religion is also a response to another, an other who is not a human being, an other who must have an intelligence and a will to be, analogously, a person. Heart speaks to heart, says Newman with poignant lucidity. There is a heart not known, responding to our own. Such is human experience. Religion is ineradicable because of this other and greater to whom we relate and respond" (*The Lustre of Our Country: The American Experience of Religious Freedom* [Berkeley: University of California Press, 1998], 1–2). The admittedly theological approach of Noonan was joined with his confidence in identifying the exceptional American remedy for religious problems in other nations.

There is an extensive literature on the topic of religious freedom in the United States, including a cluster of recent studies on U.S. efforts to foster American-style religious freedom internationally. Some of the current research on the international aspect assumes very broad definitions of religion and religious freedom, on the assumption that the transferability of the American legal ideal of religious freedom to other countries—if it even is possible—requires fluidity in identifying what is religious. Such an approach anticipates a program fraught with challenges: cultural differences leading to divergent understandings of what religion is, misapprehensions of the applicability of First Amendment language to foreign societies, and American arrogance stemming from an exceptionalistic view of the United States and its vaunted exemplary religious history. Some research concludes that the American mission to bring religious freedom to other countries is misplaced. A share of that research is conducted within an analytical frame influenced by the aims and methods of legal history and legal interpretation and from allied concerns about what is meant by "religion" that have developed over time within critical discourses germane to the field of religious studies. For decades religious studies scholars have struggled over how to identify the subject matter of their field, and the recent interest in legal definitions of religious freedom—including the futility of trying to define it—is a collaboration with that long-standing religious studies quandary. That collaboration is reinforced by coincident attention within legal studies and international relations as to how human rights (which sometimes are said to include religion) are to be defined.

Some attempts to wrestle with such problems involving the definition of religion and religious freedom are Saba Mahmood, *Religious Difference in a Secular Age: A Minority Report* (Princeton, NJ: Princeton University Press, 2015); Elizabeth Shakman Hurd, *Beyond Religious Freedom: The New Global Politics of Religion* (Princeton, NJ: Princeton University Press, 2015); Winnifred Fallers Sullivan, *The Impossibility of Religious Freedom* (Princeton, NJ: Princeton University Press, 2007); and Elizabeth Shakman Hurd, Saba Mahmood, Winnifred Fallers Sullivan, and Peter G. Danchin, eds., *Politics of Religious Freedom* (Chicago: University of Chicago Press, 2015). The introduction to a recent journal theme issue on religious freedom roughly summarizes that viewpoint in its reporting that "what is meant by religious freedom has never been stable and continues to change, both in the United States and elsewhere" (Elizabeth Shakman Hurd and Winnifred Fallers Sullivan, "Editor's Introduction," *Journal of Law and Religion* 29 [2014]: 358). Some of that scholarship takes off in step with Talal Asad's theories (*Genealogies of Religion: Discipline and Reasons of Power in Christianity and Islam* [Baltimore: Johns Hopkins University Press, 1993] and *Formations of the Secular: Christianity, Islam, Modernity* [Stanford, CA: Stanford University Press, 2003]) to argue that the category of religion as a modernist construction narrows human experience and social behavior in ways that obscure the enmeshment of what is called religious with ideas and behaviors deemed specifically political, racial, ethnic, gendered, or class-specific, with consequent implications for how power is constituted and projected. That criticism concludes that familiar definitions of religion are neither objective nor

226   NOTES TO PAGES 15–19

neutral, that they conceal more than they reveal, and that they intrinsically enable judgments of value, that is, the distinguishing of good religion from bad religion—a binary that is rejected as unproductive. For such reasons, attempts to define religion for purposes of constructing foreign policy are suspect. Studies by Tisa Wenger (*Religious Freedom: The Contested History of an American Ideal* [Chapel Hill: University of North Carolina Press, 2017]) and Anna Su (*Exporting Freedom: Religious Liberty and American Power* [Cambridge, MA: Harvard University Press, 2016]) are less directly concerned with the definition of religion, but their research intersects with that of scholars who are engaged in the debate about secularity and religion.

The starting point for this book is not to engage in debates about the definition of religion. It is not to substantively engage the arguments of scholars who have written about religious freedom, which is approached as a legal ideal (workable or not) in much current scholarship. Such scholarship in general has set a course that rests upon the trust that religion is ambiguous—including, for some, because it is special, for others because it is not, and for others because it is both—and that any attempt to legally enforce religious freedom is vexed by many problems. This book sets off from another direction. When members of one religious group rejoice in burning down the house of worship of another, there is little room, no matter how religion is defined, to deny that such an act was a matter of religious violence. Such an act could be intersectioned, as it were, with race, ethnicity, gender, class, or other factors. But a burning church, temple, or mosque is still a building on fire. The point is not to explain how an ideal of religious freedom can solve intolerance, or to prescribe what that tolerance should look like, but to demonstrate how religious intolerance survives amid an American population that claims a commitment to the ideal of religious freedom. Rather than discussing how American ideas of religious freedom have been cast in law, been variously interpreted, collaborated with imperial aspirations, evolved, or been unevenly applied, the task at hand is to address how Americans practiced forgetting the fact that the nation has a long, deep history of religious *intolerance*. And that they *exported* their own religious intolerance—in a feat of spatial projection—regardless of whether they nevertheless claimed to be "exporting freedom" (Su, *Exporting Freedom*, passim).

36. Chapter one discusses the divine directive to remember the Amalekites at the same time as forgetting them.

37. "World Protestantism" was also a popular movement in England.

38. Americans denounced Asian religions in racial terms even though a large percentage of Americans who claimed affiliation with those religions were non-Asians.

Chapter One

1. John Cotton, "Master John Cotton's Answer to Master Roger Williams," reprinted in *The Complete Writings of Roger Williams*, ed. Perry Miller, vol. 2 of 7 (New York: Russell & Russell, 1963), 47; Alfred Cave, "Canaanites in a Promised Land: The American Indian and the Providential Theory of Empire," *American Indian Quarterly* 12 (1988): 277–97.

2. Roger Williams, "Roger Williams to Major John Mason, June 22, 1670," in *Letters of Roger Williams, 1632–1682*, ed. John Russell Bartlett (Printed for the Narragansett Club: Providence, 1874), 342, 343.

3. For various perspectives on the matter of genocide and the Pequot, see Ronald Dale Karr, "'Why Should You Be So Furious?': The Violence of the Pequot War," *Journal of American History* 85 (1998): 876–909; Andrew Lipman, "'A meanes to knitt them togeather': The Exchange of Body Parts in the Pequot War," *William and Mary Quarterly* 65 (2008): 3–28; Michael Freeman,

NOTES TO PAGES 20–23 227

"Puritans and Pequots: The Question of Genocide," *New England Quarterly* 68 (1995): 278–93; Steven T. Katz, "The Pequot War Reconsidered," *New England Quarterly* 64 (1991): 217–20; Andrea Robertson Cremer, "Possession: Indian Bodies, Cultural Control, and Colonialism in the Pequot War," *Early American Studies* 6 (2008): 295–34 ; and Jeffrey Ostler, *Surviving Genocide: Native Nations and the United States from the American Revolution to Bleeding Kansas* (New Haven, CT: Yale University Press, 2019).

4. Captain John Mason, "Brief History of the Pequot War," in Charles Orr, ed., *History of the Pequot War* (Cleveland, OH: Helman-Taylor, 1897), 29.

5. Mason, "Brief History of the Pequot War," 30.

6. Mason, "Brief History of the Pequot War," 44–45.

7. Bernard Bailyn, *The Barbarous Years: The Peopling of North America: The Conflict of Civilizations, 1600–1675* (New York: Alfred A. Knopf, 2012), 443–48.

8. Thomas Shepard, *The Autobiography of Thomas Shepard* (Boston: Pierce and Parker, 1832), 62.

9. Captain John Underhill, "Newes From America," in *History of the Pequot War*, 81.

10. Underhill, "Newes From America," 84.

11. Underhill, "Newes From America," 81.

12. Mason, "Brief History of the Pequot War," 35.

13. Mason, "Brief History of the Pequot War," 44.

14. Philip Vincent, "A True Relation of the Late Battell Fought in New England," in *History of the Pequot War*, 107.

15. Charles Orr, ed., *History of the Pequot War*, vii.

16. Williams wrote of Indian understandings of boundary: "The natives are very exact and punctual in the bounds of their lands, belonging to this or that Prince or People, (even to a River, Brooke,) &c. And I have known them to make bargain and sale amongst themselves for a small piece or quantity of ground" (*A Key into the Language of America*, ed. John J. Teunissen and Evelyn J. Hinz [Detroit: Wayne State University Press, 1973], 167).

17. Underhill, "Newes From America," 82, 80.

18. Jessica Stern, "*A Key* into *The Bloudy Tenent of Persecution*: Roger Williams, The Pequot War, and the Origins of Toleration in America," *Early American Studies* (2011): 576. Stern observed of British colonists in New England that "the settlers embraced violence with religious fervor" (578).

19. Jill Lepore, *The Name of War: King Philip's War and the Origins of American Identity* (New York: Vintage, 1998), 175, 23. See also the discussion about memory and identity on pp. 173–90.

20. Cotton Mather, *Magnalia Christi Americana* (London: Thomas Parkhurst, 1702), bk. 6, p. 35.

21. Among the many interpretations of Rowlandson's experiences, a range of perspectives are in Mitchell Robert Breitwieser, *American Puritanism and the Defense of Mourning: Religion, Grief, and Ethnology in Mary White Rowlandson's Captivity Narrative* (Madison: University of Wisconsin Press, 1991); Teresa A. Toulouse, *The Captive's Position: Female Narrative, Male Identity, and Royal Authority in Colonial New England* (Philadelphia: University of Pennsylvania Press, 2013), 21–45; and Christopher Castiglia, *Bound and Determined: Captivity, Culture Crossing, and White Womanhood from Mary Rowlandson to Patty Hearst* (Chicago: University of Chicago Press, 1996), 45–52.

22. John McWilliams identifies a number of other crises in addition to the wars (*New England's Crises and Cultural Memory* [New York: Cambridge University Press, 2004]).

23. Benjamin Tompson, *New England's Crisis* (Boston: John Foster, 1676), 10.

228   NOTES TO PAGES 23–27

24. Richard Slotkin, *Regeneration Through Violence: The Mythology of the American Frontier* (Middletown, CT: Wesleyan University Press, 1973), 21.

25. Slotkin, *Regeneration Through Violence*, 57.

26. Karen Kupperman, *Indians and English: Facing Off in America* (Ithaca, NY: Cornell University Press, 2000), 20, 30, 19. Kupperman's apt term "face off" captures something of the way in which encounter eroded identity for both parties even as the encounter itself remained strong and compelling.

27. Lepore, *The Name of War*, xiii.

28. Lepore, *The Name of War*, 8, 5–8, 26ff.

29. John McWilliams, *New England's Crises and Cultural Memory*, 11.

30. Joyce G. MacDonald, "Imitation and Forgetting in Benjamin Thomson's New England Pastorals," *Early American Literature* 46 (2011): 208, 212.

31. A contemporary example of this global framework for thinking about race is the racially charged American conceptualization of the nation's relation to the world fostered by the Donald Trump administration. See for example the discussion of Donald Trump's depiction of African and Caribbean countries in his comments January 11, 2018, in Patrick Wintour, Jason Burke, and Anna Livsey, "UN Condemns Donald Trump's 'Shithole' Remarks as Racist," *The Guardian*, January 12, 2018, https://www.theguardian.com/us-news/2018/jan/12/unkind-divisive-elitist -international-outcry-over-trumps-shithole-countries-remark, accessed January 12, 2018.

32. Linford D. Fisher, "'Why shal wee have peace to bee made slaves': Indian Surrenderers During and After King Philip's War," *Ethnohistory* 64 (2017): 91–114.

33. Slotkin takes this process as fundamental to American search for identity as the frontier moved westward. Some examples of his articulation of the New England beginnings of this are on pp. 58, 69ff. For a recent discussion, see Sylvester Johnson, *African American Religions, 1500–2000: Colonialism, Democracy, and Freedom* (New York: Cambridge University Press, 2015).

34. For a discussion of how race came to be constructed in the colonial period, and specifically among Puritans, see Richard A. Bailey, *Race and Redemption in Puritan New England* (New York: Oxford University Press, 2011).

35. Lepore, *The Name of War*, 191–226.

36. Rev. William Apess, *Eulogy on King Philip*, 2nd ed. (Boston: Author, 1837), 12, 6.

37. John Augustus Stone, *Metamora; or, the Last of the Wampanoags* (New York: Feedback Theatrebooks & Prospero Press, 1996), 40, 14; and B. Donald Grose, "Edwin Forrest, 'Metamora,' and the Indian Removal Act of 1830," *Theatre Journal* 37 (1985): 181–91.

38. Lydia Maria Child, *The First Settlers of New England* (Boston; Author and Munroe and Francis, 1829), 13.

39. Child, *The First Settlers of New England*, iii–iv.

40. Salma Hale, *History of the United States* (New York: N & J White, 1835), 34.

41. Timothy Dwight, *Travels in New-England and New-York*, vol. 3 of 4 (London: William Baynes and Son, 1828), 3. Originally published in 1821–1822.

42. Catharine Maria Sedgwick, *Hope Leslie, or, Early Times in the Massachusetts* (New York: White, Gallaher, and White, 1827), 92.

43. Philip Gould, "Catharine Sedgwick's 'Recital' of the Pequot War," *American Literature* 66 (1994): 649, 651. For Gould, gender, as well as race and republicanism, was key to Sedgwick's representation of the war and its aftermaths. For Gould, the Pequot in Sedgwick's telling are both "satanic savage and vigilant republican," and as such serve as "an ideal of citizenship and a foil for civilization." Sedgwick, in defining the practice of republicanism, "inverts the equivalence

NOTES TO PAGES 27–31

her own culture drew between Puritan and Pequot valor," so as to picture republicanism as a "savage code" of civic behavior.

44. Benjamin Franklin, *A Narrative of the Late Massacres* (1764), in *The Paxton Papers*, ed. John R. Dunbar (The Hague: Martinus Nijhoff, 1957), 71, 72.

45. John Corrigan and Lynn Neal, *Religious Intolerance in America: A Documentary History* (Chapel Hill: University of North Carolina Press, 2010). A discussion of the fluidity in colonial American thinking about religious difference is in Susan Juster, *Sacred Violence in Early America* (Philadelphia: University of Pennsylvania Press, 2015).

46. Congregationalists' complaints about the religious intolerance of Church of England leaders and their allies were interwoven with ideas about the process of politics and the good of society in colonial New England clergy such as Jonathan Mayhew and Charles Chauncy. See John Corrigan, *The Hidden Balance: Religion and the Social Theories of Charles Chauncy and Jonathan Mayhew* (New York: Cambridge University Press, 1987).

47. Charles Inglis, "Letters of Papinian" (New York: Hugh Gaine, 1779), 123. The juxtaposing of tolerant Tories with intolerant Puritans was well established in the eighteenth century and was repeated by many North American writers, such as the Canadian Egerton Ryerson (*The Loyalists of America and Their Times: From 1620 to 1816*, vol. 1 of 2 [New York: Haskell House Publishers, 1970 (original publication 1880), 132]).

48. Hannah Adams, *A Summary History of New England* (Dedham, MA: H. Mann and J. H. Adams, 1799), 93. Adams cited Thomas Hutchinson's *History of Massachusetts Bay*, vol. 1, for authenticity of the story.

49. Adams, *A Summary History of New England*, 52.

50. Edmund Burke, *An Account of the European Settlements in America*, 5th ed., vol. 2 of 2 (London: J. Dodsley, 1770), 146.

51. Thomas Loraine McKenney, *History of the Indian Tribes of North America* (Philadelphia: D. Rice and A. N. Hart, 1855), 184.

52. B. B. Cahoon, "Americanizing the Catholic Church," *American Journal of Politics* (April 1893): 382.

53. Review of *Lays of the Scottish Cavaliers*, by William Edmondstoune Aytoun, *North British Review* (May 1850): 7.

54. "Art. II," *Quarterly Review*, vol. 150 (July/October 1880) (London: John Murray, 1880), 68.

55. "A Page of the Past and a Shadow of the Future," *Catholic World* (September 1871): 766.

56. Robert G. Ingersoll, "The Christian Religion: Part II," *North American Review* (November 1881): 521–22.

57. Ron Eyerman, *Cultural Trauma: Slavery and the Formation of African American Identity* (New York: Cambridge University Press, 2002), 130. Eyerman proposed that black American collective identity that coalesced during the period of the Depression and World War II was a matter of some forgetting, and some remembering. There was active, sometimes ironic dialogue between the two.

58. Lepore's phrasing, borrowed here, is not intended to define a simple process, because identity is not simple or even stable.

59. The earliest biography reporting this utterance as part of Jackson's deathbed pronouncements appears to be John Stilwell Jenkins, *The Life of General Andrew Jackson* (Albany, NY: Derby, 1947), 186–87.

60. In characterizing dysfunctional attachment among social groups as a condition arising in part from trauma, I extrapolate from a large body of psychological literature that addresses

230   NOTES TO PAGES 32–35

the attachment problems of individuals. Some of the earliest research is in John Bowlby, *Attachment and Loss: Vol. 1: Attachment* (New York: Basic Books, 1969); *Attachment and Loss: Vol. 3: Loss, Sadness and Depression* (New York: Basic, 1980); and "Attachment Theory and Its Therapeutic Implications," in S. C. Feinstein and P. Giovacchini, eds., *Adolescent Psychiatry: Developmental and Clinical Studies*, vol. 6 (Chicago: University of Chicago Press, 1978), 5–23; and Victoria A. Fitton, "Attachment Theory: History, Research, and Practice," *Psychoanalytic Social Work* 19 (2012): 121–43. A more recent suggestive study is Daniel K. Lapsley, Nicole M. Varshney, and Matthew C. Aalsma, "Pathological Attachment and Attachment Style in Late Adolescence," *Journal of Adolescence* 23 (2000): 137–55.

61. Perry Miller, "The Garden of Eden and the Deacon's Meadow," *American Heritage* 7 (1955): 54. See also Abraham I. Katsh, *The Biblical Heritage of American Democracy* (New York: KTAV, 1977), and especially chapter 7, "The Influence of the Hebrew Bible on the Literature of England and America" (139–64). On the widespread influence of the Bible in America, see Nathan O. Hatch and Mark A. Noll, eds., *The Bible in America: Essays in Cultural History* (New York: Oxford University Press, 1982); James Turner Johnson, ed., *The Bible in American Law, Politics, and Political Rhetoric* (Philadelphia: Fortress Press, 1985); and Ernest R. Sandeen, ed., *The Bible and Social Reform* (Philadelphia: Fortress Press, 1982).

62. John Corrigan, "New Israel, New Amalek: Biblical Exhortations to Religious Violence," in *From Jeremiah to Jihad: Religion, Violence, and America*, ed. Jonathan Ebel and John Carlson (University of California Press, 2012), 111–27; "Amalek and the Rhetoric of Extermination," in *The First Prejudice: Religious Tolerance and Religious Intolerance in the Making of America*, ed. Chris Beneke and Chris Grenda (University of Pennsylvania Press, 2011), 53–72; and "Religious Diversity in the 1790s," *Cambridge History of Religions in America*, vol. 2, ed. Stephen Stein (New York: Cambridge University Press, 2012), 3–25.

63. Exodus 17:8, 17:14; Numbers 24:20; Deuteronomy 25:17–19.

64. 1 Samuel 15:2–3.

65. On this aspect of the Amalekite story as an example of the "ban" (h rem, the destruction of all life in Old Testament holy war), see Susan Niditch, *War in the Hebrew Bible: A Study in the Ethics of Violence* (New York: Oxford University Press, 1993). See also Roland H. Bainton, *Christian Attitudes Toward War and Peace: A Historical Survey and Critical Evaluation* (New York: Abingdon, 1960), 151ff, 168ff; Avi Sagi, "The Punishment of Amalek in Jewish Tradition: Coping with the Moral Problem," *Harvard Theological Review* 87 (1994): 32–46; Joel S. Kaminsky, "Did Election Imply the Mistreatment of Non-Israelites?," *Harvard Theological Review* 96 (2003): 397–425; and Shalom Carmey, "The Origin of Nations and the Shadow of Violence: Theological Perspectives on Canaan and Amalek," *Tradition: A Journal of Orthodox Jewish Thought* 39 (2006): 57–88. Gerald Cromer discusses the ways in which comparison to Amalek has been used over time to stigmatize foes, including the Gentile other, the Jewish other, and the other self ("Amalek as Other, Other as Amalek," *Qualitative Sociology* 24 [2001]: 191–202).

66. Exodus 17:14.

67. Deuteronomy 25:17–19.

68. See Corrigan, "Amalek and the Rhetoric of Extermination."

69. John Winthrop, *A Modell of Christian Charity* (1630), *Collections of the Massachusetts Historical Society*, 3rd series 7 (1838), 46. Useful background is in Susan Niditch, *War in the Hebrew Bible.*

70. Jonathan Edwards, *A History of the Work of Redemption* (New York, 1786), 95. The project was based on a series of sermons that he preached in 1739.

NOTES TO PAGES 35–38

71. Charles G. Finney, "Attributes of Love," *Lectures on Systematic Theology* (London, 1851), vol. 20, 15.

72. Alexander Campbell, *Popular Lectures and Addresses* (Philadelphia: James Challen and Son, 1863), 334, 335.

73. Ellen Gould Harmon White, *The Spirit of Prophecy: The Great Controversy Between Christ and His Angels and Satan and His Angels*, vol. 1 of 3 (Battle Creek, MI: Steam Press of the Seventh-day Adventist Publishing Association, 1870), 362.

74. Mary White Rowlandson, *The Sovereignty and Goodness of God . . . Being a Narrative of the Captivity and Restauration of Mrs. Mary Rowlandson*, originally published in 1682. Cited material is from Carla Munford, ed., *Early American Writings* (New York, Oxford University Press, 2002), 325.

75. Cotton Mather, *A Discourse Delivered unto Some Part of the Forces Engaged in a Just War of New England* (Boston, 1689), title page, 37, 28.

76. Alden T. Vaughan, *Roots of American Racism: Essays on the Colonial Experience* (New York: Oxford University Press, 1995), 44–49; Kupperman, *Indians and English*, 27–30, 31. Quote from Kupperman, 31.

77. Sabine MacCormack, "Limits of Understanding: Perceptions of Greco-Roman and Amerindian Paganism in Early Modern Europe," in *America in European Consciousness, 1493–1750*, edited by Karen Ordahl Kupperman (Chapel Hill: University of North Carolina Press, 1995), 96, 98, 106, 80.

78. Luca Codignola, "The Holy See and the Conversion of the Indians in French and British North America, 1486–1760," in Kupperman, *America in European Consciousness, 1493–1750*, 196 (emphasis mine); Bobé, *Mémoire sur la découverte de la Mer de l'Quest* (1718), 53, 72–75, quoted in Cornelius J. Jaenen, "'Les Sauvages Ameriquains': Persistence into the 18th Century of Traditional French Concepts and Constructs for Understanding Indians," *Ethnohistory* 29 (1982): 52.

79. Alden T. Vaughan thought that the ten tribes model "encouraged colonists to 'uplift' rather than enslave or exterminate" the Indians. I contend that it provided the means by which to see Indians as religious kindred and thus to deploy against them the full rhetoric of Amalekite enmity. Menasseh ben Israel, quoted in Vaughan, *Roots of American Racism*, 49; John White, *The Planter's Plea* (London, 1760); Robert Wauchope, *Lost Tribes and Sunken Continents: Myth and Method in the Study of American Indians* (Chicago: University of Chicago Press, 1962), 3. A useful discussion of Hugo Grotius's statement of the theory, *De Origine Gentium Americanarum dissertatio* (Amsterdam, 1642), including important Spanish precedents and critical opposition to the theory, is in Joan-Pau Rubiés, "Hugo Grotius's Dissertation on the Origin of the American Peoples and the Use of Comparative Methods," *Journal of the History of Ideas* 52 (1991): 221–44.

80. Quoted in Vaughan, *Roots of American Racism*, 51.

81. Cotton Mather, *The Mystery of Israel's Salvation Opened* (London, 1669), 96. Mather seems to have had second thoughts about the theory at a later time, judging by the tone of his remarks about Eliot's embrace of the theory of Indians as the ten tribes (*Magnalia Christia Americana*, bk. 3, 192–93). Discussion of Williams, Penn, and Sewall and others is in Vaughan, *Roots of American Racism*, 50ff and 274n58, 63, 67. Jonathan Edwards, *A History of the Work of Redemption* (transcr. and ed. John F. Wilson [New Haven, CT: Yale University Press, 1989], 155–56); and Gerald R. McDermott, "Jonathan Edwards and the American Indians: The Devil Sucks Their Blood," *New England Quarterly* 72 (1999): 539–57.

82. Charles Crawford, esq., *Essay Upon the Propagation of the Gospel* (Philadelphia, 1799); James Adair, *Adair's History of the American Indians*, ed. Samuel Cole Williams (Johnson City,

TN: Watauga Press, 1930); William Apess, "The Indians: The Ten Lost Tribes," appendix to *The Increase of the Kingdom of Christ* (1831), in *On Our Own Ground: The Complete Writings of William Apess, A Pequot*, ed. Barry O'Connell (Amherst: University of Massachusetts Press, 1991).

83. Vaughan, *Roots of American Racism*, 52–53.

84. David S. Lovejoy, "Satanizing the American Indians," *New England Quarterly* 67 (1994): 604.

85. "Report of Commissioner of Indian Affairs," *North American Review* 99 (October 1864): 449.

86. Cited in John Gorham Palfrey, *History of New England*, vol. 2 (Boston, 1860), 225.

87. Thomas Symmes, *Historical Memoirs of the Late Fight at Piggwacket, with a Sermon Occasion'd by the Fall of the Brave Capt John Lovewell* (Boston, 1725), i (also paginated as "Front Matter 1").

88. Symmes, *Historical Memoirs of the Late Fight at Piggwacket*, 1. Symmes theorized, in jeremiad-like tones, that God was not yet ready to deliver Indians into the hands of the English. Thomas S. Kidd has proposed that the publication of such accounts was abetted by the maturing cosmopolitanism of New England, which supplied to authors "an interest in figures such as Indian fighters and brave heroes of the sea" (175). Thomas S. Kidd, "'The Devil and Father Ralle': The Narration of Father Rale's War in Provincial Massachusetts," *Historical Journal of Massachusetts* 30 (2002): 159–80.

89. Cited by Frederick D. Huntington in *Celebration of the Two Hundredth Anniversary of the Settlement of Hadley, Massachusetts* (Northampton, 1859), 31. Christine M. DeLucia discusses the caricaturing of Native Americans as victims in *Memory Lands: King Philip's War and the Place of Violence in the Northeast* (New Haven, CT: Yale University Press, 2010).

90. Robert L. Dabney, *A Defence of Virginia, and Through Her, of the South* (New York, 1867), 33.

91. Robert L. Dabney, *True Courage: A Discourse Commemorative of Lieut. General Thomas J. Jackson*, (Richmond, VA, 1863), 15.

92. "History, as Expounded by the Supreme Court," *Putnam's Monthly Magazine of American Literature, Science, and Art* 9 (1857): 543; George Bancroft, *History of the United States*, vol. 3 of 10 (Boston, 1837–1874), 408; and F. A. Walker, "The Indian Question," *North American Review* 116 (1873): 330.

93. Edward Eggleston, *Century Illustrated Magazine* 26 (1883): 717; *The Living Age* 111 (1871): 462; and Frederick D. Huntington, *In Celebration of the Two Hundredth Anniversary of the Settlement of Hadley, Massachusetts* (Northampton, 1859), 31.

94. Rev. James M. Whiton, "Moral Defects in Recent Sunday School Teaching," *New Englander and Yale Review* 43 (1884): 240–41.

95. "Indian Hating," *Western Monthly Magazine and Literary Journal* 2 (1833): 403.

96. George W. Manypenny, cited in George E. Tinker, *Missionary Conquest: The Gospel and Native American Cultural Genocide* (Minneapolis: Fortress Press, 1993), 98.

97. A. B. Greenwood, cited in Lynwood Carranco and Estle Beard, *Genocide and Vendetta: The Round Valley Wars of Northern California* (Norman: University of Oklahoma Press, 1981), 104.

98. *Humboldt Times*, May 23, 1863, cited in Jack Norton, *Genocide in Northwestern California: When Our Worlds Cried* (San Francisco: Indian Historian Press, 1979), 128.

99. *Chico Courant*, July 28, 1866, cited in Clifford E. Trafzer and Joel R. Hyer, *Exterminate Them: Written Accounts of the Murder, Rape, and Slavery of Native Americans During the California Gold Rush, 1848–1868* (East Lansing: Michigan State University Press, 1999), 1.

NOTES TO PAGES 42–45

100. Psalm 51:9: "Hide thy face from my sins, and blot out all mine iniquities."

101. *The Confession of Faith, Together with the Larger Catechism* (Boston, 1723), 94.

102. John Hale, *A Modest Inquiry Into the Nature of Witchcraft* (Boston, 1702), 168.

103. *The Ladies Repository and Gatherings of the West* 5 (1845): 9; S. G. Goodrich, *A History of All Nations*, vol. 1 (New York, 1864), 159.

104. William Henry Green, "The Perpetual Authority of the Old Testament," *Presbyterian Quarterly and Princeton Review* 22 (1877): 222.

105. Susan B. Anthony, "Diary of Susan Brownell Anthony, 1861," in *The Life and Work of Susan B. Anthony*, vol. 1 (Indianapolis: Bowen Merrill, 1898), 216.

106. Sylvester Johnson, *The Myth of Ham in Nineteenth-Century American Christianity: Race, Heathens, and the People of God* (New York: Palgrave Macmillan, 2004).

107. C. A. Bartol, "Our Sacrifices," in *Sermons on Slavery and the Civil War* (Boston, 1861), 4; Rev. J. P. Cleaveland, *A Discourse Delivered at the Twenty-First Anniversary of the Society for the Promotion of Collegiate and Theological Education at the West* (New York, 1865), 10–11; Eben Conant to Abraham Lincoln, January 11, 1865, Abraham Lincoln Papers, Library of Congress. Discussion of references to Old Testament heroes, including Saul, in Confederate thinking about the war is in Kurt O. Berends, "'Wholesome Reading Purifies and Elevates the Man': The Religious Military Press in the Confederacy," in *Religion and the American Civil War*, ed. Randall Miller, Harry S. Stout, and Charles Reagan Wilson (New York: Oxford, 1998), 148.

108. "Indian Hating," *Western Monthly Magazine and Literary Journal* 2 (1833): 403–8.

109. From General Choke's American rantings about the Watertoast Association, witnessed by young Martin Chuzzlewit in Dickens's 1844 novel—"Down with it! Away with it! Don't hear of it! Burn its records! Pull the room down! Blot it out of human memory!"—to Mark Twain's reflections on "blotting out remembrance" in "A Cure for the Blues" in 1906, Americans read about "blotting out memory" in various fiction and nonfiction publications (Charles Dickens, *The Life and Adventures of Martin Chuzzlewit* [New York, 1884], 366). The words are those of Choke's listeners responding to his cry to dissolve the association. Mark Twain, "A Cure for the Blues," in *The $30,000 Bequest and Other Stories* (New York: Harper and Brothers, 1917 [originally published 1903], 99–122). The notion was well-enough established by mid-century for Ashabel Davis, in his history of New Amsterdam, to complain to his readers: "Blot out the fields of memory, and what do you accomplish, but to quench the lights of history?" (Ashabel Davis, *History of New Amsterdam* [New York, 1853], 93). By the end of the century, defenders of religious tolerance in America could in their own way complain that anti-Catholic rhetoric sought notoriously to "blot out from memory such Catholic patriots as General Sheridan and . . . Chief Justice of the United States, Roger Taney" (George P. Lathrop, "Hostility to Roman Catholics," *North American Review* 158 [1894]: 569).

110. The literature on English and American anti-Catholicism has grown in recent years. Most scholarship has developed out of the groundbreaking work by Ray Allen Billington, *The Protestant Crusade, 1800–1860: A Study of the Origins of American Nativism* (New York: Macmillan, 1952); and John Higham, *Strangers in the Land: Patterns of American Nativism, 1860–1925* (New Brunswick, NJ: Rutgers University Press, 1955). Subsequent useful studies are Jenny Franchot, *Roads to Rome: The Antebellum Protestant Encounter with Catholicism* (Berkeley: University of California Press, 1994); Francis D. Cogliano, *No King, No Popery: Anti-Catholicism in Revolutionary New England* (Westport, CT: Greenwood Press, 1995); and Jody Roy, *Rhetorical Campaigns of the 19th Century Anti-Catholics and Catholics in America* (Lewiston, NY: Edwin Mellen Press, 2000). Two studies that focus on the relations between immigrant status and

234 NOTES TO PAGES 46–50

Catholicism are Matthew Frye Jacobson, *Whiteness of a Different Color: European Immigrants and the Alchemy of Race* (Cambridge, MA: Harvard University Press, 1998); and Joseph P. Cosco, *Imagining Italians: The Clash of Romance and Race in American Perceptions, 1880–1910* (Albany: State University of New York Press, 2003). See also *U.S. Catholic Historian* 21 (2003), an issue on American anti-Catholicism edited by Christopher Kauffman.

111. James West Davidson, *The Logic of Millennial Thought: Eighteenth-Century New England* (New Haven, CT: Yale University Press, 1977).

112. Nathan Stone, *Two Discourses Delivered at Southborough, October 9, 1760, Occasioned by the Entire Reduction of Canada* (Boston: S. Kneeland, 1761), 2.

113. "Extermination," *Times and Seasons* 5 (1844): 624. The publication is Mormon.

114. Joseph F. Berg, *Farewell Words to the First German Reformed Church, Race Street, Philadelphia. Delivered March 14, 1852* (Philadelphia, 1852), 21; and *Lectures on Romanism* (Philadelphia, 1840), 23, 24.

115. Heinrich H. Maurer, "The Problems of a National Church before 1860," *American Journal of Sociology* 30 (1925): 534; George Parsons Lathrop, "Hostility to Roman Catholics," *North American Review* 158 (1894): 569; William Barry, "'Americanism,' True and False," *North American Review* 169 (1899): 39; "The Secret Oath of the American Protective Association, October 31, 1893," in Michael Williams, *The Shadow of the Pope* (New York: McGraw-Hill Book Company, 1932), 103–4; and *Methodist Review* 3 (1887): 939.

116. These streams were progressively enriched through incorporation of anti-Catholic streams of intolerance brought to North America from non-Anglophone countries.

117. Jack Tager, *Boston Riots: Three Centuries of Social Violence* (Boston: Northeastern University Press, 2001), 15, 41–51; Dirk Hoerder, "Boston Leaders and Boston Crowds, 1765–1776," in Alfred Young, ed., *The American Revolution* (Dekalb: Northern Illinois University Press, 1976), 239–45; Alfred Young, "Pope's Day, Tar and Feathers, and 'Cornet Joyce, jun.,': From Ritual to Rebellion in Boston 1745–1775," unpublished paper cited in Gary Nash, *The Urban Crucible* (Cambridge, MA: Harvard University Press, 1986), 165.

118. Bibliographies listing books that address this aspect of the history of the Church of Jesus Christ of Latter-Day Saints are in Douglas James Davies, *An Introduction to Mormonism* (New York: Cambridge University Press, 2003); and in Terryl L. Givens's *The Latter-Day Saint Experience in America* (Greenwood, CT: Greenwood Publishing, 2004). See also Kenneth H. Wynn, *Exiles in a Land of Liberty: Mormons in America 1830–1846* (Chapel Hill: University of North Carolina Press, 1989), 268–76.

119. B. H. Roberts, *A Comprehensive History of the Church of Jesus Christ of Latter-Day Saints* (Provo, UT: Brigham Young University Press, 1965), 1: 441.

120. Wynn reconstructed this speech by Joseph Smith from several sources. See Kenneth H. Wynn, *Exiles in a Land of Liberty: Mormons in America 1830–1846* (Chapel Hill: University of North Carolina Press, 1989), 140, 231nn35–6.

121. Joseph Smith, *History of the Church of Jesus Christ of Latter-Day Saints*, 2nd ed. (Salt Lake City, UT: Deseret, 1973), 3:183–86.

122. Jan Shipps, *Mormonism: The Story of a New Religious Tradition* (Urbana: University of Illinois Press, 1987), x.

123. "The Mormons and Their Religion," *Scribner's Monthly* 3 (February 1872): 401; and "Christian Missions," *Charleston Gospel Messenger and Protestant Episcopal Register* 23 (March 1847): 370.

124. "Miscellany: Mormon War," *The Liberator*, July 5, 1844, p. 108.

NOTES TO PAGES 50–54

125. *Messenger and Advocate* (July 1836): 347–48.

126. "The Mormon War," *Atkinson's Saturday Evening Post*, November 24, 1838, p. 3.

127. "A Traveler's Views," *New York Times*, June 26, 1871, p. 8.

128. "Steps to Blot Out Mormonism," *New York Times*, January 22, 1882, p. 7.

129. "Truth Will Prevail," *Times and Seasons*, April 15, 1845.

130. Joel Shoemaker, "A Co-operative Commonwealth," *The Arena* 27 (February 1902): 169.

131. Orestes A. Brownson, *Christianity and the Church Identical* (New York, 1857), 344.

132. "Proclamation by the Governor," broadside, September 15, 1857, signed by Brigham Young. Reproduced in Nels Anderson, *Desert Saints: The Mormon Frontier in Utah* (Chicago: University of Chicago Press, 1942), 173; Height quoted in Juanita Brooks, *The Mountain Meadows Massacre* (Norman: University of Oklahoma, 1991), 52.

133. The "oath of vengeance" came even more visibly to the forefront of public debate about Mormonism during the crisis surrounding the seating of U.S. Senator Reed Smoot in 1903. See Kathleen Flake, *The Politics of American Religious Identity: The Seating of Senator Reed Smoot, Mormon Apostle* (Chapel Hill: University of North Carolina Press, 2004). On the oath (and its relation to Smoot), see David John Buerger, *Mysteries of Godliness: A History of Mormon Temple Worship* (San Francisco: Smith Research Associates, 1994), 133–36.

134. Mark Twain, *Roughing It*, vol. 2 (New York: Harper Bros, 1904 [originally published 1871]), 350; and Will Bagley, *Blood of the Prophets: Brigham Young and the Massacre at Mountain Meadows* (Norman: University of Oklahoma Press, 2002).

135. John D. Lee, *Mormonism Unveiled; or the Life and Confessions of the Late Mormon Bishop John D. Lee* (St. Louis, 1877), 234. The most thorough discussion of the event is in Ronald W. Walker, Richard E. Turley Jr., and Glen M. Leonard, *Massacre at Mountain Meadows* (New York: Oxford University Press, 2008).

136. *Christian Pamphlet*, vol. 5 [United States: s.n. 1864–1882], 9.

137. J. H. Beadle, "The Mormon Theocracy," *Scribner's Monthly* (July 1877): 393.

138. Mrs. Frank Leslie, *California: A Pleasure Trip from Gotham to the Golden Gate* (New York, 1877), 73.

139. "A Way to End the Mormon War," *Littell's Living Age* 20 (February 10, 1858): 494.

140. Book of Mormon, Alma 43:6; 21:2–3; 43:13.

141. William W. Clapp, *A Record of the Boston Stage* (Boston, 1853), 374.

142. "Syria," *Littell's Living Age* 143[?] (November 1, 1879): 301.

143. Bruce Kinney, *Mormonism: The Islam of America* (New York: Fleming H. Revell, 1912). Discussed in Givens, *The Viper on the Hearth*, 130.

144. See for example Edward Rigley, "The Aspects of Mormonism (Letter the Second)," *New York Observer* 35 (September 10, 1857): 292.

145. Deuteronomy 25:17–19.

146. Discussions of some examples are in subsequent chapters of this book.

147. Erica Resende and Dovile Budryte, "Introduction," 2–3.

148. Americans, said the American historian Richard Hofstadter, are a people obsessed with conspiracies. Writing during the Cold War, Hofstadter tracked that obsession through the nineteenth and twentieth centuries. He described how Americans participated in a politics of paranoia, how they feared that enemies constantly hatched conspiracies against them, how they feared that duplicity abounded, and how dangerous secrets were everywhere hidden from view. Hofstadter emphasized that the "distinguishing thing about the paranoid style is not that its exponents see conspiracies or plots here and there in history, but that they regard a 'vast' or

236   NOTES TO PAGES 57–60

'gigantic' conspiracy as the motive force in historical events." Belief that the national history was formed and forecasted by secrets, by what was hidden, and that hidden information, motive, and power were always at work directing the course of the nation formed the central doctrine of the paranoid worldview. Americans imagined that "history is a conspiracy, set in motion by demonic forces of almost transcendent power, and what is felt to be needed to defeat it is not the usual methods of political give-and-take, but an all-out crusade. The paranoid spokesman sees the fate of this conspiracy in apocalyptic terms—he traffics in the birth and death of whole worlds, whole political orders, whole systems of human values." A religious view of the world involving evil, Satan, eschatology, and apocalypse was central to Hofstadter's depiction of the American paranoid style. So also was the history of fictive relations between religious groups in America. See Richard Hofstadter, *The Paranoid Style in American Politics and Other Essays* (Cambridge, CA: Harvard University Press, 1964; originally published 1952), 29.

Chapter Two

1. *Niles' Weekly Register*, fourth series, vol. 38, July 24, 1830. The speech was made at a gathering in South Carolina.

2. "Final Triumph of Religious Freedom," *Baptist Memorial and Monthly Record*, vol. 6 (New York: E. Hutchinson, 1848), 45–46.

3. Donald L. Drakeman discusses how the book proved important in the thinking of Chief Justice of the Supreme Court Morrison Waite regarding religious liberty (*Church, State, and Intent* [New York: Cambridge University Press, 2010], 49–53).

4. Robert R. Howison, *A History of Virginia: From Its Discovery and Settlement by Europeans to the Present Time*, vol. 2 of 2 (Richmond: Drinker and Morris, 1848), 186.

5. Joshua Lawrence, *A Patriotic Discourse* (Tarborough, NC: Free Press, 1830), 10.

6. W. E. D., "Correspondence," *Christian Examiner*, November 26, 1853, 3. On Mayhew, see John Corrigan, *The Hidden Balance: Religion and the Social Theories of Charles Chauncy and Jonathan Mayhew* (New York: Cambridge University Press, 1987).

7. Andrew W. Young (Andrew White), *Introduction to the Science of Government* (Warsaw, NY: Author, 1836), 290, 23.

8. William H. McGuffey, *McGuffey's New Fifth Eclectic Reader* (Cincinnati: Sargent, Wilson, and Hinkle, 1857), 248, 152.

9. John McCaffrey, *Oration Delivered at the Commemoration of the Landing of the Pilgrims of Maryland* (Gettysburg: H. C. Neinstedt, 1842), 6.

10. Edward Rigley, "The Aspects of Mormonism," in *New York Observer*, ed. Sidney E. Morse and Richard Morse, vol. 35 (New York, September 10, 1857), p. 209.

11. William Adams, *A Discourse Delivered at New-London, October 23d. A.D. 1760* (New London, CT, 1761), 8; John M. Lowrie, "War with Amalek," in *The Hebrew Lawgiver*, vol. 1 (Philadelphia, 1865), 276. Manly openness or boldness, as a kind of manly "pluck," was crucial to male identity in the years that Lowrie was writing. See John Corrigan, *Business of the Heart: Religion and Emotion in the Nineteenth Century* (Berkeley: University of California Press, 2002), 128–62, 186–206.

12. David Brion Davis, "Some Ideological Functions of Prejudice in Ante-Bellum America," *American Quarterly* 15 (1963): 116, 118.

13. Rev. Lewis Cheeseman, *Differences Between Old and New School Presbyterians* (Rochester, 1849), 156–59; Thomas J. Vaiden, *Rational Religion and Morals* (New York, 1852), 245–46; *The*

NOTES TO PAGES 60–63

Olive Branch; Or an Earnest Appeal in Behalf of Religion, the Supremacy of Law, and Social Order (Philadelphia, 1844), 11–21. *The Olive Branch* is an example of one way in which a newspaper article or journal essay occasionally narrated the role of dominant groups in causing religious violence. Such publications typically called upon both sides in a religious dispute to admit their failings and endeavor to work together rather than against each other.

14. Kees W. Bolle, ed., *Secrecy in Religion*, Studies in the History of Religion, Supplements to *Numen* 49 (Leiden: E. J. Brill, 1987).

15. "Gnosticism," *Mercersburg Review* (October 1858): 526.

16. *The Harbinger: Devoted to Social and Political Progress* 7 (May 27, 1848): 27.

17. *The Friend; a Religious and Literary Journal* 20 (January 23, 1847): 139; "Secret Societies in China," *Littell's Living Age* 131 (November 18, 1876): 445; and "History and Religious Opinions of the Druses," *Biblical Repertory* 5 (January 1, 1829): 210.

18. "The Asian Mystery," *North American Review* 93 (October 1861): 344.

19. Cornelius C. Blatchly, "The Aim of Antimasons and of the Working Man," *Working-man's Advocate* 1 (December 12, 1829): 1; and "Freemason, Jesuits, and Jews of Portugal," *The Amaranth; or Masonic Garland* 1 (October 1828): 196, 199.

20. Review of *The Works of Jacob Behmen* [Boehme], *the Teutonic Philosopher*, in *Christian Review* 19 (July 1854): 446.

21. "The Civil War. A Sermon by Rev. E. H. Sears," *Monthly Religious Magazine* 25 (June 1861): 376.

22. Edward Beecher, *The Papal Conspiracy Exposed and Protestantism Defended* (Cincinnati, 1855), 29; Lyman Beecher, *A Plea for the West* (Boston, 1835); and Samuel B. Morse, *The Foreign Conspiracy Against the Liberties of the United States* (New York, 1835).

23. "Account of a Prevailing and Dangerous Sect of Heretics," *Evangelical Intelligencer* 2 (August 1808): 396; and Scipio de Ricci, *Female Convents: Secrets of Nunneries Disclosed* (New York, 1834), 94. Gladden's remarks are reprinted from a *Harper's Weekly* article in "Are We on the Verge of Another Papal Panic?," *Current Opinion* 62 (September 1914): 190; Gladden, "The Anti-Catholic Crusade: A Rejoinder," *The Century* 48 (July 1894): 473.

24. Rector of Oldenwold, *The Cloven Foot, on Popery, Aiming at Political Supremacy in the United States* (Boston: Wentworth and Company, 1857), 118.

25. George Peck, ed., *The Methodist Quarterly Review*, third series, vol. 27 (New York: G. Lane and C. B. Tippett, 1845), 95; Anna Ella Carroll, *The Great American Battle; or, the Contest Between Christianity and Political Romanism* (New York and Auburn: Miller, Orton, and Mulligan, 1856), 257; and "Jesuitical Forgery," *The Protestant* (October 30, 1830): 348.

26. Background discussion is in Michael Fitzgibbon Holt, *The Political Crisis of the 1850s* (New York: Norton, 1978).

27. "The Catholic Question," *Western Monthly Magazine, and Literary Journal* 3 (June 1835): 377.

28. Billington, *Protestant Crusade*, 319. Historian John Loughery comments that "New York newspapers were . . . filled with accounts of brawls that got out of hand" (*Dagger John: Archbishop John Hughes and the Making of Irish America* [Ithaca, NY: Cornell University Press, 2018], 241).

29. A more sweeping psychoanalytic perspective on this issue could lead to the conclusion that Protestants' secret, their repressed memory of colonial-era genocide, was as troublesome as the supposed secrets of Catholic rebels. To complain about Catholic conspiracy was to complain as well about the pain involved in a weightier conspiracy to bury a terrible past. The "passive"

238   NOTES TO PAGES 63–65

dynamics of collective memory, including trauma, remain a powerful component of collective memory (see introduction, note 33, above referencing Barash, *Collective Memory and the Historical Past*).

30. The central role of trauma and forgetting in the history of slavery in America is discussed in Marc Howard Ross, *Slavery in the North: Forgetting History and Recovering Memory* (Philadelphia: University of Pennsylvania Press, 2018).

31. Nancy Lusignan Schultz, *Fire and Roses: The Burning of the Charlestown Convent, 1834* (New York: Free Press, 2000); Jody M. Roy, *Rhetorical Campaigns of the Nineteenth-Century Anti-Catholics and Catholics in America* (Lewiston, NY: Edwin Mellen Press, 2000), 55–56; Ray Allen Billington, "The Burning of the Charlestown Convent," *New England Quarterly* 10 (1937): 4–24, and *The Protestant Crusade, 1800–1860: A Study of the Origins of American Nativism* (New York: Macmillan, 1938); Jenny Franchot, *Roads to Rome; The Antebellum Protestant Encounter with Catholicism* (Berkeley: University of California Press, 1994); Jeanne Hamilton, "The Nunnery as Menace: The Burning of the Charlestown Convent, 1834," *U.S. Catholic Historian* 14 (1996): 35–65; Tracy Fessenden, *Culture and Redemption: Religion, the Secular, and American Literature* (Princeton, NJ: Princeton University Press, 2006); *Awful Disclosures of Maria Monk* (Princeton, 1834); William Nevins, *Thoughts on Popery* (New York: John S. Taylor, 1836); and Richard Baxter, *Jesuit Juggling: Forty Popish Frauds Detected and Disclosed* (New York: Craighead and Allen, 1835).

32. I apply here the phrase from Hofstadter, "The Paranoid Style in American Politics," 6. See also Roy, *Rhetorical Campaigns*, 71ff.

33. Quoted in Billington, "The Burning of the Charlestown Convent," 9.

34. "The Anti-Catholic Riots in Philadelphia in 1844," *American Catholic Historical Researches* 13 (1896): 50–64; "The Philadelphia Anti-Catholic Riots in Philadelphia in 1844," *American Catholic Historical Researches*, New Series 7 (1911): 231–34; John E. Buschman, "The Upper Class and Blacks in the Philadelphia Anti-Catholic Riots of 1844," *Records of the American Catholic Historical Society of Philadelphia* 99 (1988): 1–16; Amanda Beyer-Purvis, "The Philadelphia Bible Riots of 1844: Contest over the Rights of Citizens," *Pennsylvania History* 83 (Summer 2016): 366–93; Fessenden, *Culture and Redemption*, 60–73; Elizabeth M. Geffen, "Violence in Pennsylvania in the 1840's and 1850's," *Pennsylvania History* 36 (1969): 381–410; Michael Feldberg, *The Philadelphia Riots of 1844: A Study of Ethnic Conflict* (Westport, CT: Greenwood, 1975); Vincent P. Lannie and Bernard C. Diethorn, "For the Honor and Glory of God: The Philadelphia Bible Riots of 1840," *History of Education Quarterly* 8 (1968): 44–106; Kenneth W. Milano, *The Philadelphia Nativist Riots: Irish Kensington Erupts* (Stroud, UK: History Press, 2013); and David Montgomery, "The Shuttle and the Cross: Weavers and Artisans in the Kensington Riots of 1844," *Journal of Social History* 5 (1972): 411–46. Tracy Fessenden discusses the conflict in Philadelphia alongside early twenty-first-century debate about the placement of the Ten Commandments in a government building in "The Nineteenth-Century Bible Wars and the Separation of Church and State," *Church History* 74 (2005): 784–811.

35. Douglas G. Jacobsen, *An Unprov'd Experiment; Religious Diversity in Colonial New Jersey* (Brooklyn, NY: Carlson Publishing, 1991). For a view of the ways in which religious and cultural differences in the middle colonies led to frictions, see Randall Balmer, *A Perfect Babel of Confusion: Dutch Religion and English Culture in the Middle Colonies*, 2nd ed. (New York: Oxford University Press, 2002 [originally published 1989]).

36. Thomas Jefferson to Dr. Thomas Cooper, November 2, 1822, in *Thomas Jefferson: Writings: Autobiography / Notes on the State of Virginia / Public and Private Papers / Addresses / Letters*, ed. Merrill D. Peterson (New York: Library of America, 1984), 1463.

NOTES TO PAGES 66–70

37. *Princeton Review* 4 (1840): 469.

38. *Friends' Intelligencer* 2 (August 9, 1845): 148.

39. *Friends' Intelligencer* 2 (October 11, 1845): 221.

40. *The Truth Unveiled; or, a True and Impartial Exposition of the . . . Terrible Riots in Philadelphia . . . by a Protestant and Native Philadelphian* (Philadelphia: M. Fithian, 1844), 17, 22.

41. *American Catholic Historical Researches* 8 (1891): 90. Historians Sam Bass Warner and Gary B. Nash have pointed out how rioting was a particular problem in Philadelphia in the 1830s and 1840s. The militia was ineffective, and city leaders were unable to form the city's population into political coalitions that could be leveraged in the interest of keeping order. Warner and Nash viewed the events of 1844 as arising primarily from economic problems. Sam Bass Warner, *The Private City: Philadelphia in Three Periods of Its Growth* (Philadelphia: University of Pennsylvania Press, 1968), 125–57; Gary B. Nash, *First City: Philadelphia and the Forging of Historical Memory* (Philadelphia: University of Pennsylvania Press, 2002), 170–75, 212–13.

42. *A Philadelphia Perspective: The Diary of Sydney George Foster Covering the Years 1834–1871*, ed. Nicholas B. Wainwright (Philadelphia: Historical Society of Philadelphia, 1967), May 12, 1844, and July 24, 1844, pp. 166, 175.

43. Edwin H. Chapin, *A Discourse Preached in the Universalist Church, Charlestown, on Sunday May 12, 1844* (Boston: A Tompkins, 1844), 5; and C. Collins, "Letter from the South," *Zion's Herald and Wesleyan Journal* 19 (May 3, 1848), 70.

44. Andrew Jackson Davis, *The Principles of Nature, Her Divine Relations, and a Voice to Mankind* (New York, 1852), 716; Lauren P. Hickok, *Empirical Psychology* (Schenectady, NY, 1855), 227; William Ellery Channing, *A Selection from the Works of William E. Channing, D. D.* (Boston, 1855), 228; Washington Irving, *The Works of Washington Irving*, vol. 13, *Mahomet and His Successors* (New York, 1861), 359; Frederick Jackson Turner, *The Frontier in American History* (New York, 1920), 165; *Home Evangelization: A View of the Wants and Prospects of Our Country* (New York: American Tract Society, 1850), 18; "Not opposed to revivals," *Trumpet and Universalist Magazine* 19 (March 27, 1847): 162; Vaiden, *Rational Religion and Morals*, 310; and "About a Red Hat," *Christian Union* 11 (May 17, 1875): 226. See also "Sectarian Intolerance," *Religious Intelligencer* 12 (June 9, 1827): 25ff.

45. M. Michelet, *Spiritual Direction, and Auricular Confession; Their History, Theory, and Consequences: Being a Translation of* "Du Prétre, de la Femme, de la Famille" (Philadelphia: James M. Campbell, 1845).

46. See "The Catholic Question," *Western Monthly Magazine and Literary Journal* 3 (June 1835): 599–604.

47. "Auricular Confession in the Protestant Episcopal Church," *Literary World* (January 26, 1850): 84; *Brownson's Quarterly Review* (October 1850): 448ff; and "The Confessional," *The Aldine, the Art Journal of America* (March 1, 1877): 260.

48. Rev. R. F. Clarke, S.J., "The Practice of Confession in the Catholic Church," *North American Review* 169 (December 1899): 829; "The Roman Catholic Faith," *New Englander and Yale Review* 2 (October 1844): 578; Ezra C. Seaman, *Essays on the Progress of Nations* (New York, 1853), 68; Richard W. Thompson, *The Papacy and Civil Power* (New York, 1876), 189; "Catholic Testament," *Evangelical Magazine and Gospel Advocate* (August 2, 1834): 243; *The Living Age* 17 (April 1, 1848): 20; and R. L. Delisser, *Pope, or President? Startling Disclosures of Romanism* (New York, 1959), 23.

49. Charles Bulkley, "A Short and Candid View of Popery, in a Sermon Preached at the Old Jewry December 3, 1754," *Methodist Magazine* 1 (December 1818): 452; P. A. Browne, *Upon the*

Subject of Romanism and the Pope. Addressed to the people of the United States (Philadelphia, 1846), 5. Commentary that addresses the issue with respect to the long history of the Inquisition and the impulse to "exterminate" opponents can be found in "Catholic Propagandism in the United States," *Baltimore Literary and Religious Magazine* 5 (May 1837): 211; "Art. XXVII: The Cathari or Albigenses," *Universalist Quarterly and General Review* 7 (October 1850): 364; "Schmidt's History of the Albigenses," *North American Review* 70 (April 1850): 458; "Papistry of the XIX. Century, in the United States," *Baltimore Literary and Religious Magazine* 5 (June 1839): 286; and "The Spanish Inquisition in History," *The Dial* 45 (November 1, 1908): 294. The view that Catholic hatred drove their plan for dominance was widespread: "Catholics must hate heretics, philosophers, reformers, and republicans of all sorts and shape. . . . They will form a community of hatred which daily will increase and strongly bind them one to the other" ("Ten Years in Rome," *The Galaxy* 10 [September 1870]: 363).

50. Theodore W. Curtis, "A Word for the Mormons," *The Arena* 21 (June 1899): 716; *Scientific American* 1 (October 2, 1845): 3; "Christian Missions," *Charleston Gospel Messenger and Protestant Episcopal Register* 23 (March 1847): 370; and "Prevalence of Evangelical Truth," *The Liberator* 14 (January 5, 1844): 4. On the similarity of charges against Mormons to those leveled against Catholics, see Gary L. Bunker and Davis Bittor, *The Mormon Graphic Image, 1834–1914* (Salt Lake City: University of Utah Press, 1983), 82.

51. Catholics, whom Protestants sometimes compared to Mormons as equally authoritarian, corrupt, and anti-American, could be highly critical of Mormons in antebellum America. See Matthew J. Grow, "The Whore of Babylon and the Abomination of Abominations: Nineteenth-Century Catholic and Mormon Mutual Perceptions and Religious Identity," *Church History* 73 (2004): 139–67.

52. C. C. Goodwin, "The Political Attitude of the Mormons," *North American Review* 132 (March 1881): 283. On race, and especially the construction of Mormons as "Asiatics," see Bruce Burgett, "On the Mormon Question: Race, Sex, and Polygamy in the 1850s and the 1990s," *American Quarterly* 57 (March 2005): 75–102.

53. "The Mormon Theocracy," *Scribner's Monthly* 14 (July 1877): 392.

54. Jefferson, quoted by Mordecai M. Noah, in *A Discourse of the Restoration of the Jews* (New York: Harper & Brothers, 1845), v.

55. James Madison, *A Memorial and Remonstrance on the Religious Rights of Man* (Washington, DC: S. C. Ustick, 1828), 8; and *Memorial and Remonstrance Against Religious Assessments in the Writings of James Madison*, ed. Gaillard Hunt, vol. 2 of 10 (New York: G. P. Putnam's Sons, 1901), 189.

56. Christine Heyrman, *American Apostles: When Evangelicals Entered the World of Islam* (New York: Hill and Wang, 2015), 71–96.

57. Emily Conroy-Krutz, *Christian Imperialism: Converting the World in the Early American Republic* (Ithaca, NY: Cornell University Press, 2015).

58. Lydia Maria Child, *Good Wives* (Boston, 1833), 246.

59. Amanda Porterfield, *Mary Lyon and the Mount Holyoke Missionaries* (New York: Oxford University Press, 1997), 56.

60. Laura Rogers Levens, "Leaving Home and Finding Home: Theology and Practice of Ann Hasseltine Judson and the American Baptist Mission to Burma, 1812–1826" (PhD diss., Duke University, 2015).

61. Quoted in Levens, "Leaving Home and Finding Home," 93.

62. "The War in Burma," *Religious Intelligencer*, February 19, 1825, p. 595.

NOTES TO PAGES 74–79   241

63. Adoniram Judson's Journal, May 11, May 27–28, and June 21–22, 1819, in Ann Judson, *Account of the American Baptist Mission to Burmah*, 165, 170–71, quoted in Levens, "Leaving Home and Finding Home," 216.

64. For a related discussion of the nineteenth-century Middle East, see Ussama Makdisi, *Artillery of Heaven: American Missionaries and the Failed Conversion of the Middle East* (Ithaca, NY: Cornell University Press, 2008). Makdisi challenges the interpretive paradigm of a "clash of civilizations" in assessing the history of American Protestant missionary engagement in Lebanon.

65. "Religious Intolerance of the Chinese Government," *The Missionary Herald, Containing the Proceedings of the American Board of Commissioners for Foreign Missions* (April 1833), 145.

66. Alexander Burnes, *Travels into Bokhara* (Philadelphia: Carey and Hart, 1835), 87.

67. David O. Allen, D.D., *India: Ancient and Modern* (Boston: John P. Jewett, 1856), 42, 58.

68. "Foreign," *New York Observer and Chronicle* (January 23, 1851): 31.

69. Daniel McGilvary, D.D., *A Half Century Among the Siamese and the Lao: An Autobiography* (New York: Fleming A. Revell, 1912), 109, 204.

70. "Isenberg and Krapf's Travels in Abyssinia," *Eclectic Magazine of Foreign Literature* (July 1844): 236.

71. "The Anniversaries: American Board of Foreign Missions Statement," *New York Evangelist* (May 21, 1857): 168; "Foreign Missionary Meeting," *Christian Observer* (May 28, 1841): 86.

72. "Extract from a Communication, Headed, WOODEN GOD," *Reformer* (February 1, 1822): 45; *A History of Baptist Missions in Asia, Africa, Europe, and North America* (Boston: Gould, Kendall and Lincoln, 1849), 284.

73. "Foreign Religious Intelligence. Italy," *The Independent* (December 9, 1858): 2.

74. George Smith, *A Narrative of an Exploratory Visit to Each of the Consular Cities of China* (New York: Harper, 1847), 62.

75. Smith, *A Narrative*, 61.

76. W. W. Wood, *Sketches of China* (Philadelphia: Carey and Lea, 1830), 23.

77. "The French in the South Seas," *Littell's Living Age* (September 3, 1853): 599.

78. "The Foreign Missionary for June . . . ," *Christian Statesman* (August 7, 1879): 578.

79. "Foreign Relations Intelligence," *The Independent* (October 28, 1858): 3.

80. "View of Publick Affairs: Europe, Asia, Africa, America," *Christian Advo*cate (September 1, 1828): 429, 431.

81. George Wilkins Kendall, *Narrative of the Texan Santa Fé Expedition* (New York: Harper and Brothers, 1847), 551.

82. Fitch W. Taylor, *The Broad Pennant; or, a Cruise in the United States Flag Ship of the Gulf Squadron* (New York: Leavitt, Trow, 1848), 135.

83. Lorenzo de Zavala, "Sketch of Education in the Republic of Mexico," *American Annals of Education* (September 1834): 395, 389.

84. "Syria: Extracts from a Communication," *Missionary Herald* (November 1834): 414.

85. "Mr Buckingham's Lectures: Lecture VII," *New York Evangelist* (December 16, 1837): 205.

86. "Syria: Extracts from a Communication," 411.

87. "Mission to Persia," *Religious Intelligencer* (September 13, 1834): 244.

88. Henry Stuart Foote, *Texas and the Texans; or, Advance of the Anglo-Americans to the South-West* (Philadelphia: Cowperthwait and Company, 1841), 79.

89. "One Curse Removed!!!," *Religious Intelligencer* (November 8, 1834): 382.

90. "Europe. No. VI.: Spain," *New-England Magazine* (November 1834): 385.

91. Samuel F. B. Morse, "Foreign Conspiracy Against the Liberty of the United States. No. V," *Christian Secretary* (October 25, 1834): 162. Reprinted from the *New York Observer*.

92. Brutus, "Foreign Conspiracy Against the Liberties of the United States. Number XII," *Christian Advocate and Journal* (December 26, 1834): 65.

93. Discussion of some transatlantic background is in Jonathan Den Hartog, "Trans-Atlantic Anti-Jacobinism: Reaction and Religion," *Early American Studies* 11 (2013): 133–45. Also useful is Bryan Waterman, "The Bavarian Illuminati, the Early American Novel, and Histories of the Public Sphere," *William and Mary Quarterly* 62 (January 2005): 9–30. An important source is John Robison, *Proofs of a Conspiracy against All the Religions and Governments of Europe, Carried on in the Secret Meetings of the Free Masons, Illuminati, and Reading Societies* (Philadelphia: T. Dobson & W. Cobbett, 1798).

94. "Intolerance," *Boston Recorder* (October 17, 1834): 166.

95. G., "Letter from France," *New York Observer and Chronicle* (December 20, 1834): 202.

96. Benedict J. Fenwick, "Memoranda of the Diocess [*sic*] of Boston from the Arrival of Bishop Fenwick or rather from the day of his Consecration," handwritten ms. in Archives, Archdiocese of Boston, p. 27, cited in Hamilton, "The Nunnery as Menace," 39.

97. *Christian Watchman*, August 15, 1834; *Western Christian Advocate*, August 29, 1834; and *Christian Examiner*, 17 (September 1834): 13. See also the *American Protestant Vindicator*, August 27, 1834.

98. *New York Observer*, August 30, 1834.

99. A Catholic Layman, "Address to the Public. No. 6: On Religious Intolerance and Persecution," *The Jesuit; or, Catholic Sentinel* (November 1, 1834): 345. The author likely was Mathew Carey of Philadelphia.

100. B. Fenwick, "The Dawn of Religious Persecution in America," *United States Catholic Miscellany* (August 23, 1834): 62.

101. A Catholic Layman, "Address to the Public. No. IV," *The Jesuit; or, Catholic Sentinel* (October 11, 1834): 114.

102. George Bancroft, *History of the United States of America, From the Discovery of the Continent*, vol. 1 of 6 (New York: D. Appleton and Co., 1888), 322, 320.

103. Bancroft, *History of the United States of America*, vol 1, 311, 317. A useful contextualizing discussion is in Dean C. Hammer, "The Puritans as Founders: The Quest for Identity in Early Whig Rhetoric," *Religion and American Culture: A Journal of Interpretation* 6 (1996): 161–94.

104. The magazine's publisher, Robert Walsh Jr. (1784–1859), was of Pennsylvania Quaker and Irish Catholic descent. His opinions about religion, religious freedom, and liberty changed a number of times over the course of his professional life as a political writer. He was sensitive to intolerance, but at the same time a vocal supporter of the idea that Americans, not the British, had established true religious and political freedom. An overview of his transformations as a thinker is in Joseph Eaton, "From Anglophile to Nationalist: Robert Walsh's 'An Appeal from the Judgments of Great Britain,'" *Pennsylvania Magazine of History and Biography* 132 (2008): 141–71.

105. "Art. IV.—A History of the United States," *American Quarterly Review* (September 1, 1834): 202, 203, 204, 205. The author of the review is not identified.

106. "Tribute to John Calvin," *New York Evangelist* (December 6, 1834): 194.

107. Rebecca Gratz, "Letter from Rebecca Gratz to Benjamin Gratz, July 11, 1844," in *The American Jewish Woman: A Documentary History*, ed. Jacob R. Marcus (New York: KTAV, 1981), 102.

NOTES TO PAGES 84–87

108. Samuel Augustus Mitchell, *An Accompaniment to Mitchell's Map of the World* (Philadelphia: S. A. Mitchell, 1845), 288. Mitchell, a Philadelphian, was a geographer and enthusiastic promoter of Protestant missionary activity overseas.

109. "General Intelligence: Summary of Foreign News," *Christian Advocate and Journal* (December 18, 1844): 75.

110. Josiah Gregg, *Scenes and Incidents in the Western Prairies* (Philadelphia: J. W. Moore, 1844), 218–19. Gregg's discussion included comments about race and the mixed blood of races. Although there was much written about race in connection with missionary work overseas, there was comparatively less attention to race and ethnicity in newspapers, magazines, and books that commented on the Philadelphia riots. Ethnic difference was a more common but still not a leading topic. A useful overview of ethnic issues is Michael Feldberg, *The Philadelphia Riots of 1844: A Study of Ethnic Conflict* (Westport, CT: Greenwood, 1975).

111. "Romish Intolerance," *Christian Register* (July 27, 1844): 118.

112. "Legislating for the Church," *Christian Observer* (November 22, 1844): 2.

113. *Rome's Policy Toward the Bible; or, Papal Efforts to Suppress the Scriptures*, by "An American" (Philadelphia: James M. Campbell, 1844), 96. See also the advertisement for the book in the *Episcopal Recorder* (July 25, 1844): 75.

114. "Romish Intolerance in the City of the Pope," *Christian Register* (June 22, 1844): 96.

115. Views about the rise of the market as an unwelcome disrupter of agrarian life versus its fashioning by persons in ways that improved the common good are in John Lauritz Larson, *The Market Revolution in America: Liberty, Ambition, and the Eclipse of the Common Good* (New York: Cambridge University Press, 2010); and in Charles Grier Sellers, *The Market Revolution: Jacksonian America, 1815–1846* (New York: Oxford University Press, 1991). Daniel Walker Howe has argued that the market as historians typically refer to it had coalesced by the end of the eighteenth century (Daniel Walker Howe, "Charles Sellers, the Market Revolution, and the Shaping of Identity in Whig-Jacksonian America," in Mark Noll, ed., *God and Mammon: Protestants, Money, and the Market: 1790–1860* [New York: Oxford University Press, 2001], 54–74).

116. "The Progress of Christianity-Hindrances-Prospect," *Christian Advocate and Journal* (October 30, 1844): 46.

117. Mitchell, *An Accompaniment to Mitchell's Map*, 288.

118. Levin was arrested and charged with inciting the highly destructive riot that took place in Philadelphia in early July. One religious newspaper said that he was charged specifically with "having used language" in his newspaper "*exciting riot and treason*" ("Article 5," *Christian Observer* [July 19, 1844]: 115). He was never tried for that charge. His nativism, among other of his political views, is discussed in John A. Forman, "Lewis Charles Levin: Portrait of an American Demagogue," *American Jewish Archives* 12 (1960): 150–94. The fact that Levin was a Jew who identified with the Protestant majority, and who defended American Protestant power against the perceived schemes of Catholics, illustrates the fluidity of thinking about religious opponents and the ambiguities arising from the intersections of politics, economics, and religion. Levin appears to have had strong, enduring friendships with Catholic families in Philadelphia in spite of his anti-Catholic oratory, but ideologically he identified with the Protestant majority which, he believed, embodied the spirit of an enlightened democratic capitalism.

119. Lewis C. Levin, "The National Policy of the Native Americans," *Daily Sun* (September 11, 1844): 1.

120. Related discussion is in John Corrigan, *Business of the Heart: Religion and Emotion in the Nineteenth Century* (Berkeley: University of California Press, 2001); and *The Business Turn*

244   NOTES TO PAGES 87–92

in American Religious History, ed. Amanda Porterfield, John Corrigan, and Darren Grem (New York: Oxford University Press, 2017).

121. "Commerce as a Liberal Pursuit," *Merchants' Magazine and Commercial Review* (January 1, 1840): 9, 13, 12, 11, 10.

122. "Commerce and Commercial Character," *Merchants' Magazine and Commercial Review* (February 1, 1841): 129, 135, 136.

123. Joseph R. Underwood, *Speech of Mr. Underwood, of Kentucky, on the War with Mexico. Delivered in the Senate of the United States, February 10, 1848* (Washington, DC: Towers, 1848[?]), 4, 5, 6. Underwood's opposition to annexation lay in the fact that he believed the resulting diversity of people—"Anglo-Saxons, Aztecs, Negroes, and Spaniards"—would make for an overly "heterogenous nation" that would prove impossible to govern. Differences of language and culture would make national unity all but impossible (5).

124. Joseph R. Underwood, "Stipulated Arbitration: A Report Made to the Senate of the United States, February 23, 1853," *Advocate of Peace* 10 (April 1853): 257.

125. Joseph R. Underwood, "Report of the Committee on Foreign Relations," 32nd Cong. 2d Sess. (1853), Sen. Rep. Com. 418, 14–16.

126. Adelaide Rosalia Hasse, *A List of Correspondences Relating to Foreign Affairs*, vol. 1 of 3 (Washington, DC: Carnegie Institution of Washington, 1914–1921), 39–40.

127. Arthur Schlesinger Jr., "Human Rights and the American Tradition," *Foreign Affairs* 57 (1978): 503–26.

128. Hillary Rodham Clinton, "Remarks at the Release of the 2011 International Religious Freedom Report," Washington, DC, July 30, 2012, https://2009-2017.state.gov/secretary/20092013clinton/rm/2012/07/195782.htm, accessed June 12, 2017.

129. Cass appears to have held some deistical views and, like Jefferson, recognized in the Bible useful moral teachings.

130. Willard Carl Klunder, *Lewis Cass and the Politics of Moderation* (Kent, OH: Kent State University Press, 1996), 45; William T. Young, *Sketch of the Life and Public Services of General Lewis Cass* (Detroit: Markham & Elwood, 1852), 98; and Andrew C. McLaughlin, *Lewis Cass* (Boston and New York: Houghton, Mifflin and Company, 1899), 305. McLaughlin cited the *Congressional Globe*, 30, 556 (36th Congress).

131. Schlesinger, "Human Rights and the American Tradition," 509.

132. *Diplomatic Relations with Austria, Speech of Hon. R. M. T. Hunter of Virginia, in the Senate of the United States, January 31, 1850* (Washington, DC: Congressional Globe Office, 1850), 1.

133. *Lewis Cass, Diplomatic Relations with Austria: Speech of Hon. Lewis Cass, of Michigan, in the Senate of the United States, Friday, January 4, 1870* (Washington, DC: Congressional Globe Office, 1850[?]), 6. Nicole M. Phelps points out that a severance of relations between nations considered Great Powers was not uncommon, but nevertheless a serious action (*U.S.–Habsburg Relations from 1815 to the Paris Peace Conference* [New York: Cambridge University Press, 2013], 57).

134. "New national policy" was a term Cass adopted from Archbishop Hughes's letter regarding Cass's initial proposal for protection of Americans overseas. Cass, in presenting his case against religious intolerance overseas, hoped for a world in which relations between states would be more visible. Blessing the international progress of democracy and inveighing against religious intolerance, Cass summed up the situation at mid-century: "Government cannot now do deeds of darkness darkly." The plottings of Catholic powers would be exposed, the schemes of oppressive governments opened to critical observation. There would be a campaign to "reclaim

NOTES TO PAGES 93–95

the human family from political and religious thralldom." Cass believed that "the world is watching, judging, and approving, or condemning." And it was becoming clear that "no system of despotism can close its boundaries to the access of this mighty engine." The undertone was that invisible conspiracies remained, at home and abroad. In the habit of thinking about religious others as enemies relentlessly plotting the overthrow of the social and political order, Americans exercising their "paranoid style" assumed that much was hidden and that what was hidden was dangerous. Lewis Cass, *Speech of Mr. Cass, of Michigan, delivered in the Senate of the United States, May 15, 1854, on the Subject of the Religious Rights of American Citizens Residing or Traveling in Foreign Countries* (Washington, DC: Congressional Globe Office, 1854), 8, 13, 15, 16, 19, 20, 21, 5.

135. "General Cass' Speech in the Senate," *The Christian World* (New York: The Union, 1854), 298.

136. Elizabeth Emma Stuart, "Letter from Elizabeth Emma Stuart to William Chapman Baker, June 1, 1854," in *Stuart Letters of Robert and Elizabeth Sullivan Stuart and Their Children 1819–1864: With an Undated Letter Prior to July 21, 1813*, vol. 2 (New York: Privately published, 1961), 615.

137. Christine Heyrman discusses how King's performance of a muscular Christianity before Muslims was partly an effort to exemplify Christian manliness for an American audience that he believed had become too feminized (*American Apostles: When Evangelicals Entered the World of Islam* [New York: Hill and Wang, 2015], 191–250).

138. Angelo Repousis, "'The Devil's Apostle': Jonas King's Trial against the Greek Hierarchy in 1852 and the Pressure to Extend U.S. Protection for American Missionaries Overseas," *Diplomatic History* 33 (2009): 807–37. King returned to Greece and died in Athens in 1869.

139. The "Young America" movement is discussed in Yonatan Eyal, *Young America and the Transformation of the Democratic Party, 1828–1867* (New York: Cambridge University Press, 2007); and Edward L. Widmer, *Young America: The Flowering of Democracy in New York City* (New York: Oxford University Press, 1999). See also Repousis, "'The Devil's Apostle.'"

140. "The Mob Spirit—Religious Intolerance," *National Era* (March 11, 1852).

141. "Our Foreign Relations," *National Era* (January 6, 1853).

142. "Foreign Relations—Non-Intervention," *National Era* (January 15, 1852).

143. The *National Era* at mid-century was fully engaged in reiterating warnings about papal plots to undermine Protestantism, advising such as "The Pope may re-establish the Inquisition in Spain, and make bonfires of Protestant books in Italy, and suppress Protestant worship in Rome, but his friends in this country must be admonished that we live under a different dispensation" ("The Mob Spirit—Religious Intolerance").

144. Anne Lohrli, "The Madiai: A Forgotten Chapter of Church History," *Victorian Studies* 33 (1989): 30.

145. Father Patrick Moran, "The Madiai Controversy," *Newark Daily Advertiser*, February 11, 1853.

146. Archbishop John Hughes, "Open Letter," *New York Freeman's Journal* (December 15, 1853). I have relied on republication of the letter in the *National Era* (December 25, 1851), 206. Some of the politics that framed the letter are discussed in John Hassard, *Life of the Most Reverend John Hughes, First Archbishop of New York* (New York: Cosimo, 2008; originally published 1868), 260–70.

147. Hughes in turn responded to Cass's speech: *Archbishop Hughes in Reply to General Cass and in Self-Vindication* (New York: Edward Dunigan & Brother, 1854).

246   NOTES TO PAGES 96–103

148. *Complete Works of the Most Rev. John Hughes, Archbishop on New York*, ed. Lawrence Kehoe (New York: Lawrence Kehoe, 1866), 478. Hughes's speech with the phrase "a new national policy has been broached" was widely republished in the Catholic and Protestant press.

149. "Our Foreign Relations," *National Era* (January 6, 1853).

150. On "manifest destiny" and the Young America movement, see Widmer, *Young America.*

151. "Treaty of Peace and Amity, Concluded Between the United States of America and the Dey and Regency of Algiers," signed December 22 and 23, 1816. The text of this treaty and many others are in the *United States Treaties and International Agreements: 1776–1949* (sometimes referred to as the Bevans collection) of the Library of Congress, https://www.loc.gov/law/help/us-treaties/bevans.php. The text of the Algiers treaty is located at https://www.loc.gov/law/help/us-treaties/bevans/b-alg-ust000005-0051.pdf, and the cited language is on p. 54 of that text.

152. "Treaty of Amity, Commerce, and Navigation, December 12, 1828." For the text of the Brazil treaty (and the others cited here), see the Avalon site located at Yale: http://avalon.law.yale.edu/19th_century/brazil01.asp, accessed December 4, 2017.

153. "Treaty of Peace, Friendship, Navigation and Commerce Between the United States and Venezuela, May 31, 1836," http://avalon.law.yale.edu/19th_century/venez_001.asp, accessed February 14, 2018.

154. Quoted in Natalie Isser, "Diplomatic Intervention and Human Rights: The Swiss Question, 1852–1864," *Journal of Church and State* 35 (1993): 581.

155. Isser, "Diplomatic Intervention and Human Rights," 581.

156. President Millard Fillmore's opposition is stated in "To the Senate of the United States, February 13, 1851," in James D. Richardson, ed., *A Compilation of the Messages and Papers of the Presidents* (New York: Bureau of National Literature, 1908), 2634–35.

157. This is discussed in chapter five.

158. "Peace, Friendship, Limits, and Settlement (Treaty of Guadalupe Hidalgo)," in the Bevans collection, https://www.loc.gov/law/help/us-treaties/bevans/b-mx-ust000009-0791.pdf, accessed February 14, 2018. The language was added by the United States to the original treaty draft. See p. 797n11.

159. "Peace, Friendship, Limits, and Settlement (Treaty of Guadalupe Hidalgo)."

Chapter Three

1. The term "internal orientalism" here draws upon Louisa Schein, "Gender and Internal Orientalism in China," *Modern China* 23 (1997): 70.

2. Anssi Paasi, *Territories, Boundaries, and Consciousness: The Changing Geographies of the Finnish-Russian Border* (Chichester, UK: John Wiley and Sons, 1996), 13.

3. David R. Jansson, "Internal Orientalism in America: W. J. Cash's *The Mind of the South* and the Spatial Construction of American National Identity," *Political Geography* 22 (2003): 296, 297.

4. Jansson, "Internal Orientalism in America," 297. Jansson's analysis is predominantly focused on white Southerners as an "other" to white Northerners.

5. "Critical geopolitics analyzes how geographical assertions, assumptions, and metaphors construct relationships between political communities. It attempts to de-naturalize the common sense these geographies contain." See Ethan Yorgason and Chiung Hwang Chen, "Kingdom Come: Representing Mormonism Through a Geopolitical Frame," *Political Geography* 27 (2008): 479.

NOTES TO PAGES 104–109

6. Margaret McGuinness, "Catholicism in the United States," in *The Oxford Research Encyclopedia of American History*, ed. Jon Butler, Online Publication Date: July 2016, doi:10.1093/acrefore/9780199329175.013.319.

7. "Classified Ad 2—No Title," *New York Daily Times* (November 10, 1854), 5.

8. "Syllabus of Errors, Pius IX," items 77, 55, http://digihum.mcgill.ca/~matthew.milner/teaching/resources/docs/piusix-syllabus.pdf, p. 9, accessed October 12, 2017.

9. No bibliographies are complete, but a recent one that includes a good sampling of relevant studies is in Kenneth C. Barnes, *Anti-Catholicism in Arkansas: How Politicians, the Press, the Klan, and Religious Leaders Imagined an Enemy, 1910–1960* (Fayetteville: University of Arkansas Press, 2016), 145–54.

10. Thomas A. Tweed, *Our Lady of the Exile: Diasporic Religion at a Cuban Catholic Shrine in Miami* (New York: Oxford University Press, 1997), 131.

11. John L. Brandt, *America or Rome, Christ or the Pope* (Toledo: Loyal Publishing Co., 1895), 515, 396.

12. W. C. Brownlee, *Popery: An Enemy to Civil and Religious Liberty, and Dangerous to Our Republic* (New York: Bowne and Wisher, 1835), 6; and Joseph van Dyke, *Popery, the Foe of the Church, and of the Republic* (Philadelphia: People's Publishing, 1872), 142.

13. William H. Van Nortwick, *The Anti-Papal Manual: A Book of Ready Reference for American Protestants* (New York: Holt Brothers, 1876), 97.

14. *The Menace* in each issue reported its weekly readership. It averaged over a million, and at times as much as 1.5 million. That accounting was not badly overstated, according to scholars. Some contextualizing discussion of the paper is in Higham, *Strangers in the Land,* 180–84.

15. "A Slave Seeks Freedom," *The Menace* (December 11, 1915): 1.

16. "Independent Territory," *The Menace* (August 21, 1915): 1.

17. "Where Rome Rules Supreme!," *The Menace* (January 24, 1914): 1.

18. "Buffalo Romanists Hunt for John Doe," *The Menace* (March 7, 1914): 1.

19. Stanley Frost, "Alien Piety in Chicago: A Protestant Report of the Eucharistic Congress," *Forum* 76 (September 1926): 343, 345, 361.

20. David Paul Nord, "Reading the Newspaper: Strategies and Politics of Reader Response, Chicago, 1912–1917," *Journal of Communication* 54 (1995): 74. Nord specifically discusses the case of *The Menace.*

21. Twentieth-century evidence for the enduring spatial characterization of Mormonism as a separate kingdom is in Yorgason and Chen, "Kingdom Come."

22. C. P Lyford, *The Mormon Problem: An Appeal to the American People* (New York: Phillips and Hunt, 1866), 188.

23. Hugh Latimer Burleson, *The Conquest of the Continent* (New York: Domestic and Foreign Missionary Society, 1911), 122.

24. Joseph Nimmo, *The Mormon Usurpation: An Open Letter Addressed to the Committee on the Judiciary of the House of Representatives* (Huntington, NY: "The Long-Islander" print, 1886), 52.

25. George Ticknor Curtis, *A Plea for Religious Liberty and the Rights of Conscience* (Washington, DC: Gibson Bros., 1886), 35.

26. Leo P. Ribuffo, "Henry Ford and 'The International Jew,'" *American Jewish History* 69 (1980): 437.

27. *The International Jew: The World's Foremost Problem* (Dearborn, MI: Dearborn Publishing Company, 1920), 107.

28. *The International Jew.* The book asked more specifically, "Has it a 'foreign policy' with regard to Gentiles? Has it a department which is executing that foreign policy?" (90).

29. Samuel Howard Ford, "Centennial Address," *Ford's Christian Repository and Home Circle* 47 (1889): 430.

30. Rev. P. S. Evans, "Liberty and Toleration," *Baptist Quarterly Review* 5 (1883): 161.

31. Titus Mooney Merriman, *Welcome, Englishmen,* 2nd ed. (Boston: Arena Publishing Company, 1896), 206.

32. *Celebration of the One Hundredth Anniversary of the First Baptist Church, Meriden, Conn. October 7, 1886* (Meriden, CT: Republican Book Dept., 1887), 42.

33. T. S Dunaway, "Baptist Principles Vindicated," *Baptist Quarterly Review* 4 (July 1, 1882): 293. Many Protestant groups stressed the "constitutional principle" of religious liberty as the key to its success. Seventh-day Adventist Charles M. Snow's *Religious Liberty in America* (Washington, DC: Review and Herald Publishing Association, 1914) nevertheless complained that even that principle could be endangered by those who did not wish to see church and state fully separated.

34. An example is Carroll Frey and the Penn Mutual Life Insurance Company, *The Independence Square Neighborhood* (Philadelphia: Penn Mutual Life Insurance Company, 1926), 79.

35. George Jacobs, *Celebration of the Ninety-Ninth Birthday of American Independence* (Philadelphia: King and Baird, 1875), 32.

36. "Religious Liberty," *New York Times,* December 18, 1927, BR10. The article reviewed a book by Albert C. Dieffenbach challenging religious freedom as an achieved goal. Dieffenbach's argument is mentioned below.

37. Martin Zielonka, *Is Religious Liberty the Great American Illusion?* (El Paso, TX: Temple Mt. Sinai, [19–]), 6. The author likewise reviews Dieffenbach's book (see previous footnote).

38. Editor, "The Termination and Achievements of the Great War," *Liberty* 14 (1919): 3. Joseph Henry Crocker used similar language in discussing religious freedom and political freedom: "The emancipation of society from tyranny and the deliverance of the spirit of man from human authority imposed from without run parallel in history" (*The Winning of Religious Liberty* [Boston and Chicago: Pilgrim Press, 1918], ix).

39. Zielonka, *Is Religious Liberty the Great American Illusion?,* 1–2.

40. Joseph Henry Crocker, *Problems in American Society: Some Social Studies* (Boston: George H. Ellis, 1889), 207.

41. Joseph Bondy, *How Religious Liberty Was Written into the American Constitution* (Syracuse, NY: Author, 1927), 7.

42. W. S. Crowe, *Phases of Religion in America: A Course of Lectures* (Newark, NJ: Ward and Tichenor, 1893), 124.

43. Crocker, *The Winning of Religious Liberty,* viii.

44. H. W. Thomas, "Change and Progress," *Christian Register* 5 (January 1890): 5.

45. Ruth Miller Elson, in the most expansive study of nineteenth-century American history textbooks, found that lessons about colonial America did include rare references to intolerance, but examples of intolerance that took place after independence were missing from later nineteenth-century textbooks. Examples of toleration instead were often included in textbooks (*Guardians of Tradition: American Schoolbooks of the Nineteenth Century* [Lincoln: University of Nebraska Press, 1964], 56–60, 171). Margaret A. Nash discusses how early American textbooks, in fashioning a "moral history" of the nation, did not refrain from identifying religious intolerance in early Massachusetts ("Contested Identities: Nationalism, Regionalism, and Patriotism in Early American Textbooks," *History of Education Quarterly* 49 [2009]: 437–38).

NOTES TO PAGES 114–118

46. Thomas J. Davis, "John Calvin in Nineteenth-Century History Textbooks," *Church History* 65 (1996): 235, 236.

47. Alexander Fraser Tytler, Lord Woodhouselee, *Elements of General History, Ancient and Modern* (New York: E. Duyckinck, 1819), 240. The first American edition was published in Philadelphia in 1809, and the original in Edinburgh in 1801.

48. Calvin's role in the burning is debated by historians.

49. Charles Francis Adams, *Massachusetts: Its Historians and Its History. An Object Lesson* (Boston and New York: Houghton Mifflin and Company, 1893), 84.

50. James Truslow Adams, *The History of New England*, vol. 3 (Boston: Little, Brown, 1926), 79, 84, 148.

51. Brooks Adams, *The Emancipation of Massachusetts* (Boston: Houghton, Mifflin, 1886).

52. See chapter two.

53. Milan Zafirovski, "The Most Cherished Myth: Puritanism and Liberty Reconsidered and Revised," *American Sociologist* 38 (2007): 37. See also Zafirovski, "The Sociological Core vs. the Historical Component of the Weber Thesis: Some Deviant Cases Revisited," in *Social Theories of History and Histories of Social Theory*, ed. Harry F. Dahms (London: Emerald, 2013), 75–128. Zafirovski exegetes Weber, Tawney, and other twentieth-century sociological and historical writers who studied Puritans.

54. "The Puritans and Quakers in New England," *Friends' Review*, June 30, 1892, 772.

55. Oscar S. Straus, *Religious Liberty in the United States* (New York: P. Cowen, 1896), 4, 2.

56. Albert Bushnell Hart, ed., *The American Nation: A History* (New York: Harper and Brothers, 1904), 303–4.

57. George C. Lorimer, *The Great Conflict: A Discourse Concerning Baptists, and Religious Liberty* (Boston: Lee and Shepard, 1877), 99–100, 90.

58. Sydney George Fisher, *Men, Women, and Manners in Colonial Times* (Philadelphia: J. B. Lippincott, 1898), 147. A mid-nineteenth-century edition of the *Magnalia* has "autocatacritic" instead of Fisher's "autocracy" (*Magnalia Christi Americana*, ed. Thomas Robbins, vol. 2 of 2 [Hartford, CT: Silas Andrus and Son, 1853], 498).

59. See chapter two.

60. Sergei Prozorov, "The Other as Past and Present: Beyond the Logic of 'Temporal Othering' in IR Theory," *Review of International Studies* 37 (2011): 1275, 1276.

61. David Lowenthal, ed., *The Past Is a Foreign Country* (Cambridge: Cambridge University Press, 1985).

62. L. A. J., "The Intolerance of the Puritan Church of New England," *Universalist Quarterly and General Review* 15 (1858): 161.

63. Adams, *Massachusetts: Its Historians and Its History*, 19.

64. Jacobs, *Celebration of the Ninety-Ninth Anniversary*, 31–32.

65. "Literature: The Fourth Volume of Palfrey's *History of New England*," *Chicago Daily Tribune* (March 25, 1876): 9.

66. "Free Religion Urged by Taft: President Raps the Intolerance of Puritans," *Atlanta Constitution* (July 6, 1909): 2.

67. "Yale Blames Puritans for Play Censorships," *New York Times*, March 15, 1925, E1.

68. George Edward Ellis, *The Puritan Age and Rule in the Colony of Massachusetts Bay, 1629–1685* (Boston: Houghton Mifflin, 1888), 544.

69. Crowe, *Phases of Religion*, 124.

70. "The Puritan and His Creed," *Christian Advocate* (March 25, 1886): 183.

71. John Fiske, *The Beginnings of New England or, The Puritan Theocracy and Its Relations to Civil and Religious Liberty* (Cambridge, MA: Riverside Press, 1889). Fiske's interpretation followed Bancroft's in condemning the Puritans for intolerance but attributing to them an ideal that eventually wore down their theocratic model and led to a "strengthening of the spirit of liberty" (153).

72. "Bookishness: Mr. John Fiske on the 'Puritan Theocracy,'" *Life* (July 11, 1889): 20. Brooks Adams was Fiske's former student. The cited material in the quote is from Fiske, *The Beginnings of New England*, 153.

73. M. Gail Hamner, *American Pragmatism: A Religious Genealogy* (New York: Oxford University Press, 2003), 16, 17.

74. Oliver Perry Temple, *The Covenanter, the Cavalier, and the Puritan* (Cincinnati: Robert Clarke Company, 1897), 190, 195, 196, 197, 198.

75. Hamner, *American Pragmatism*, 16.

76. "Curiosities of Puritan History: Toleration," *Putnam's Monthly Magazine of American Literature, Science, and Art* 5 (1855): 369.

77. Albert Charles Dieffenbach, "Religious Liberty—The Great American Illusion," *The Independent*, January 8, 1927, p. 36.

78. Albert Charles Dieffenbach, *Religious Liberty: The Great American Illusion* (New York: W. W. Morrow and Company, 1927), 119, 39.

79. Dieffenbach, "Religious Liberty," 37.

80. Alma White, *Klansmen: Guardians of Liberty* (Zarephath, NJ: Good Citizen, 1927), 42, 62.

81. Lynn S. Neal, "Christianizing the Klan: Alma White, Branford Clarke, and the Art of Religious Intolerance," *Church History* 78 (2009): 371.

82. Josiah Strong, *Our Country* (London: Saxon, 1889).

83. Thomas Jefferson to James Madison, January 23, 1823, quoted in "Continental Policy of the United States—The Acquisition of Cuba," *United States Democratic Review* (April 1859): 1.

84. Jay Sexton, "The Civil War and U.S. World Power," in *American Civil Wars: The United States, Latin America, Europe, and the Crisis of the 1860s*, ed. Don H. Doyle (Chapel Hill: University of North Carolina Press, 2017), 25–26.

85. Louis A. Pérez, *Cuba and the United States: Ties of Singular Intimacy* (Athens: University of Georgia, 2003), 19, 20.

86. Walter LaFeber, *The New Empire: An Interpretation of American Expansion, 1860–1898* (Ithaca, NY: Cornell University Press, 1963), 285.

87. "Descriptive Aspects from Letters," *Friends' Intelligencer* (May 11, 1864): 150.

88. "The Unfortunate Isle," *The Round Table* (April 3, 1869): 211.

89. "Popish Intolerance in Cuba," *Christian Advocate and Journal* (May 9, 1854): 37.

90. William Earl Weeks, *The New Cambridge History of American Foreign Relations*, vol. 1, *Dimensions of Early American Empire, 1754–1865* (New York: Cambridge University Press, 2013), 56.

91. "Correspondence in Relation to the Condition of the Commercial Relations between the United States and the Spanish American States and Brazil," *United States Department of State/ Executive Documents Printed by Order of the House of Representatives* (1870–1871), 257, 256, 254.

92. For elaboration of this process of change, see the clarifying discussion in Jay Sexton, *The Monroe Doctrine: Empire and Nation in Nineteenth-Century America* (New York: Hill and Wang, 2011).

93. "Treaty of Friendship, Commerce and Navigation, Between the United States of America

NOTES TO PAGES 127–133

and the Republic of Nicaragua," signed at Managua, June 21, 1867, Article XII; "Treaty of Friendship, Navigation, and Commerce, Between the United States of America and the Republic of Ecuador," signed June 13, 1839, Article XIV; "Treaty of Peace, Friendship, Commerce and Navigation, Between the United States of America and the Republic of Bolivia," signed May 13, 1858, Article XIV; and "Treaty of Friendship, Commerce and Navigation, Between the United States of America and the Republic of Paraguay," signed February 4, 1859, Article XIV. Treaties are available at *United States Treaties and International Agreements: 1776–1949*, Library of Congress, https://www.loc.gov/law/help/us-treaties/bevans.php.

94. Professor and Mrs. Louis Agassiz, *A Journey in Brazil* (Boston: Ticknor and Fields, 1868), 409.

95. George B. Waldron, "Our 'Dog in the Manger' Policy in South America," *The Chautauquian: A Weekly Newsmagazine* (February 1902): 469; Rev. Francis E. Clark, D.D., "The Individuality of the South American Republics," *North American Review* (December 1909): 786.

96. "Our Sister Republics," *Baptist Missionary Magazine* (December 1889): 449.

97. William Taylor, *Our South American Cousins* (New York: Phillips and Hunt, 1881), 3.

98. Harlan P. Beach et al., *Protestant Missions in South America* (New York: Student Volunteer Movement for Foreign Missions, 1906), 198, 212, 190, 246.

99. William Speer, *The Great Revival of 1800* (Philadelphia: Presbyterian Board of Education, 1872), 71.

100. Rev. W. C. Porter, "Romanism and Republics," *Christian Observer* (April 28, 1909): 5–6.

101. Porter, "Romanism and Republics," 6.

102. Beach, *Protestant Missions in South America*, 214.

103. Fred Hobson, *Tell About the South: The Southern Rage to Explain* (Baton Rouge: Louisiana State University Press, 1983), 16.

104. Anna Su, *Exporting Freedom: Religious Liberty and American Power* (Cambridge, MA: Harvard University Press, 2016), 40, 2, 7.

105. J. M. Spangler, "Is Democracy a Failure in the Spanish-American Republics?," *Methodist Review* (November 1900): 934, 935.

106. James S. Dennis, *Foreign Missions After a Century* (New York: Fleming H. Revell, 1893), 134.

107. Rev. Randolph H. McKim, "Religious Reconstruction in Our New Possessions," *Outlook* (October 28, 1899): 505.

108. Edward C. Millard, *South America, the Neglected Continent* (New York: F. H. Revell Co., 1894), 93.

109. "Progress of the Kingdom: South America—A Neglected Continent," *The Congregationalist* (June 6, 1895): 887.

110. "Progress of the Kingdom," 888.

111. "The C. H. M. S. at Hartford: Annual Rally in Center Church," *The Congregationalist* (June 1899): 802.

112. "Monthly Concert for August: Chili and Spanish American Evangelization," *New York Evangelist* (July 31, 1873): 6.

113. James H. McNeilly, "Latin America," *Christian Observer* (August 21, 1901): 8.

114. "Items of Interest," *Congregationalist and Christian World* (July 20, 1901): 103.

115. Edmund Merriam, *A History of American Baptist Missions* (n.p., 1913), 64, 270.

116. "Progress of the Kingdom," 887.

117. Millard, *South America: The Neglected Continent*, 170.

252   NOTES TO PAGES 133–137

118. "Mexican Evangelization," *Christian Advocate* (February 20, 1873): 58.

119. Beach, *Protestant Missions in South America*, 210.

120. Beach, *Protestant Missions in South America*, 210.

121. Caspar Whitney, "The View-Point," *Outing Magazine* (February 1907): 670.

122. "America as a World Power," *Methodist Review* (March 1905): 5.

123. Spangler, "Is Democracy a Failure in the Spanish-American Republics?," 931.

124. A., "The Reformation in Spanish America," *Zion's Herald* (October 10, 1888): 324.

125. Beach, *Protestant Missions in South America*, 188.

126. "Progress of the Kingdom," 887.

127. "The World Open to the Gospel," *Christian Observer* (August 17, 1898): 1.

128. "Two Million Dollars for Educational Institutions and Hospitals in Our Foreign Missions," *Zion's Herald* (June 28, 1899): 806.

129. Todd Hartch, *The Rebirth of Latin American Christianity* (New York: Oxford University Press, 2014).

130. Stephen C. Dove, "Historical Protestantism in Latin America," *Cambridge History of Religions in Latin America*, ed. Virginia Garrard-Burnett, P. Freston, and Stephen C. Dove (Cambridge: Cambridge University Press, 2014), 286–303. On the relation of capitalism and imperialism to Protestant evangelizing, see José Bonino, "The Protestant Churches in America Since 1930," *Cambridge History of Latin America*, vol. 6 (Cambridge: Cambridge University Press, 1995), 583–604.

131. Joseph E. Potter, Ernesto F. L. Amaral, and Robert D. Woodberry, "The Growth of Protestantism in Brazil and Its Impact on Male Earnings, 1970–2000," *Social Forces* 93 (2014): 125.

132. "America as a World Power," 5.

133. "The Religious Reformation in Mexico," *Baptist Missionary Magazine* (October, 1870): 395.

134. McNeilly, "Latin America," 8, 9.

135. Spangler, "Is Democracy a Failure in the Spanish-American Republics?," 930.

136. "President Johnson to the Congregational Convention," *Hartford Daily Courant* (June 21, 1865): 3.

137. William McKinley, "Annual Message of the President," in *Papers Relating to the Foreign Relations of the United States, with the Annual Message of the President Transmitted to Congress December 3, 1900* (U.S. Department of State, 1900), xl.

138. Tisa Wenger broaches the term in her discussion of the Philippines (*Religious Freedom: The Contested History of an American Ideal* [Chapel Hill: University of North Carolina Press, 2016]).

139. J. M. Castro, "Inaugural Address of President J. M. Castro to the Legislative Chambers [translation]," *Executive Documents Printed by Order of the House of Representatives during the Second Session of the Thirty-Ninth Congress, 1866–'67* (U.S. Department of State, 1866–1867), 438.

140. James Johnston, *Report of the Centenary Conference on the Protestant Missions of the World* (London: James Nisbet and Co., 1888), 329.

141. There is much recent work on missionaries, and a thorough review of that literature is not the aim of this chapter. The current literature is characterized by the variety of viewpoints it takes and the disparate themes that it explores. Emily Conroy-Krutz discusses the ways in which American Protestant missionary enterprises carried forward an American political and ideological agenda in *Christian Imperialism: Converting the World in the Early American Republic* (Ithaca, NY: Cornell University Press, 2015). Kevin Grant explains how missionaries

NOTES TO PAGES 137–144

played a role in resistance to the African slave trade in *A Civilised Savagery: Britain and the New Slaveries in Africa, 1884–1926* (London: Routledge, 2005). Ussama Makdisi, in *Artillery of Heaven: American Missionaries and the Failed Conversion of the Middle East* (Ithaca, NY: Cornell University Press, 2008), details the complex social and political worlds that framed a "locally rooted ecumenical humanism and a secularized evangelical sensibility" in Lebanon (187). David Kirkpatrick traces the development of a Protestant Social Christianity in Latin America and its worldwide exportation in *A Gospel for the Poor: Global Social Christianity and the Latin American Evangelical Left* (Philadelphia: University of Pennsylvania Press, 2019). Among the cluster of recent studies of foreign missionaries to the United States is Rebecca Y. Kim, *The Spirit Moves West: Korean Missionaries in America* (New York: Oxford University Press, 2015). A study of the manner in which humanitarian efforts conjoined with American missionary projects were promoted in the evangelical press is Heather Curtis, *Holy Humanitarians: American Evangelicals and Global Aid* (Cambridge, MA: Harvard University Press, 2018).

142. Thomas B. Neely, *South America: Its Missionary Problems* (New York: Young People's Missionary Movement of the United States and Canada, 1909), 144, 283–84.

143. "Evolution vs. Imperialism," *The Arena* 23 (February 1900): 1–2, 4.

144. Charles Robinson, "The Threatened Revival of Knownothingism," *American Journal of Politics* (November 1894): 504–5.

145. "Article 3," *Christian Union* (March 22, 1888): 358–59.

146. E. M. Winston, "The Threatening Conflict with Romanism," *Forum* (June 1894): 425, 426.

147. "John Lee, Liberator," *Christian Advocate* (February 23, 1922): 221. This obituary credited Lee as the source of changes to law regarding religion in South American countries.

148. John Lee, *Religious Liberty in South America* (Cincinnati: Jennings and Graham, 1907), 6.

149. Lee, *Religious Liberty in South America*, vi.

150. Lee, *Religious Liberty in South America*, 14.

151. Lee, *Religious Liberty in South America*, 119.

152. Lee, *Religious Liberty in South America*, 150.

153. "Mr. Hay to Mr. Bridgman, September 1, 1899," in *A Digest of International Law*, ed. John Bassett Moore, vol. 2 of 8 (Washington, DC: Government Printing Office, 1906), 180.

154. Lee, *Religious Liberty in South America*, 213.

155. "Minutes of the Rock River Annual Conference of the Methodist Episcopal Church, October 8–15, 1902, Chicago, Illinois" (The Conference, 1902), 85. Lee was honored as having "done more for civil and religious liberty in South America than any other living man" (85).

156. Andrew Preston, *Sword of the Spirit, Shield of Faith: Religion in American War and Diplomacy* (New York: Knopf, 2012), 189.

157. As discussed above and cited in footnote 144 (Charles Robinson, "The Threatened Revival of Knownothingism," 504).

158. Preston, *Sword of the Spirit*, 188, 189.

159. Frank was pardoned posthumously, in 1986.

160. David Harry Bennett, *The Party of Fear: From Nativist Movements to the New Right in American History* (Chapel Hill: University of North Carolina Press, 1988), 223.

161. Kathleen M. Blee, *Women of the Klan: Racism and Gender in the 1920s* (Berkeley: University of California Press, 2011), 17.

162. Kelly J. Baker, *Gospel According to the Klan: The KKK's Appeal to Protestant America,*

1915–1930 (Lawrence: University Press of Kansas, 2011); and Lynn S. Neal, "Christianizing the Klan: Alma White, Branford Clarke, and the Art of Religious Intolerance," *Church History* 78 (2009): 350–78.

163. Mauritz A. Hallgren, *Landscape of Freedom: The Story of American Liberty and Bigotry* (New York: Howell, Soskin and Company, 1941), 385.

164. Hallgren, *Landscape of Freedom*, 380.

165. Neal, "Christianizing the Klan," 357.

166. See also Barnes, *Anti-Catholicism in Arkansas*.

167. Baker, *Gospel According to the Klan*, 198–225.

168. Baker, *Gospel According to the Klan*, 212, 7, 33, 242.

169. Franchot, *Roads to Rome*, xxiii.

170. Horace Bushnell, *Unconscious Influence: A Sermon* (London: Partridge and Oakley, 1852), 32.

171. David Ambrosius, *Woodrow Wilson and American Internationalism* (New York: Cambridge University Press, 2017); Cara Lea Burnidge, *A Peaceful Conquest: Woodrow Wilson, Religion, and the New World Order* (Chicago: University of Chicago Press, 2016); and A. Scott Berg, *Wilson* (G. P. Putnam's Sons, 2013).

172. The exact phrasing is: "The world must be made safe for democracy" (Woodrow Wilson, "Request for Declaration of War," April 2, 1917, Sixty-Fifth Congress, 1 Session, Senate Document No. 5).

173. Richard Striner, *Woodrow Wilson and World War I* (Lanham, MD: Rowman and Littlefield, 2014), 177.

174. Historians generally recognize Wilson's attraction to the Lost Cause (see Ambrosius, *Woodrow Wilson and American Internationalism*, 90). The first reference that I can locate of an American historian suggesting it is in Frederick Jackson Turner's remark that "the most significant thesis of President Wilson (himself of Southern antecedents)" in Wilson's *History of the American People* has to do with states' rights. See Turner's review of Woodrow Wilson, *A History of the American People* (*American Historical Review* 8 [1903]: 764).

175. Woodrow Wilson, "States Rights," chapter 31 in *The Cambridge Modern History*, vol. 7, ed. Sir Adolphus William Ward, George Walter Prothero, and Sir Stanley Mordaunt Leathes (New York: Macmillan, 1903), 441.

176. A survey of Wilson's support for the Jim Crow status of African Americans is in Eric S. Yellin, *Racism in the Nation's Service: Government Workers and the Color Line in Woodrow Wilson's America* (Chapel Hill: University of North Carolina Press, 2013).

177. Ambrosius, *Woodrow Wilson and American Internationalism*, 1.

178. David Hunter Miller, *The Drafting of the Covenant* (New York: G. P. Putnam and Sons, 1928), 462. Arthur Stanley Link believes the statement to be un-Wilsonian and that it may have been the product of Wilson's fatigue or the result of poor stenography (*The Papers of Woodrow Wilson*, vol. 57 [Princeton, NJ: Princeton University Press, 1987], 268).

179. Gary Gerstle, "Race and Nation in the Thought and Politics of Woodrow Wilson," in J. M. Cooper, ed., *Reconsidering Woodrow Wilson: Progressivism, Internationalism, War, and Peace* (Baltimore: Johns Hopkins University Press, 2008), 93–94.

180. Ambrosius, *Woodrow Wilson and American Internationalism*, 90.

181. Thomas Jefferson, quoted in Woodrow Wilson, *A History of the American People*, vol. 3 of 5 (New York: Harper Brothers, 1902), 168. The same reference to the same quote can be seen in the expanded version of the history published as the nation entered the war. See *A History of*

the American People, Enlarged by the Addition of Original Sources, vol. 6 of 10 (New York: Harper Brothers, 1918), 54.

182. The title page of the book is photographically reproduced in Wilson, *History*, vol 2. of 10 (1918), 40. The book is *New England's Spirit of Persecution Transmitted to Pennsylvania* (New York: William Bradford, 1693). The caption refers to the persecution of Quakers and is in the same volume of the *History*, p. 40.

183. Marjorie L. Daniel, "Woodrow Wilson—Historian," *Mississippi Valley Historical Review* 21 (1934): 362n3.

184. Burnidge, *A Peaceful Conquest*, 99.

185. Berg, *Wilson*, 266–67.

186. Su identifies this as her core argument regarding Wilson's role in promoting religious freedom internationally. See Anna Su, "Woodrow Wilson and the Origins of the International Law of Religious Freedom," *Journal of the History of International Law* 15 (2013): 237. While I am in agreement with Su to some extent, the reasons for Wilson's advocacy of religious freedom internationally were more complex than Su's discussion admits.

187. See Frank Ninkovich, *Global Dawn: The Cultural Foundation of American Internationalism, 1865–1890* (Cambridge, MA: Harvard University Press, 2009).

188. Patrick Manning, *Navigating World History: Historians Create a Global Past* (New York: Palgrave Macmillan, 2003), 31.

189. Su, "Woodrow Wilson," 240.

190. Quoted in I. Naamani Tarkow, "Foreign Intercession on Behalf of Justice by the United States in the 19th Century," *Indiana Law Journal* 18 (1943): 105.

191. William Ernest Hocking, *Re-Thinking Missions: A Layman's Inquiry After One Hundred Years* (New York: Harper and Brothers, 1932).

192. David Hollinger, *Protestants Abroad: How Missionaries Tried to Change the World but Changed America* (Princeton, NJ: Princeton University Press, 2017).

Chapter Four

1. A concise overview of the modern Protestant International is in Christopher Clark and Michael Ledger-Lomas, "The Protestant International," in *Religious Internationals in the Modern Age: Globalization and Faith Communities Since 1750*, ed. Abigail Green and Vincent Viaene (Basingstoke: Palgrave Macmillan, 2012), 23–52. A view that focuses on theological aspects of the Protestant International as World Christianity is in Dale T. Irvin, "World Christianity: An Introduction," *Journal of World Christianity* 1 (2008): 1–26.

2. John R. Mott, *The Evangelization of the World in This Generation* (New York: Student Volunteer Movement for Foreign Missions, 1900).

3. *Andover Review* 4 (1885): 356.

4. The awkward role of Dulles himself in the meeting is discussed in Mark G. Toulouse, *The Transformation of John Foster Dulles: From Prophet of Realism to Priest of Nationalism* (Macon, GA: Mercer University Press, 1985), 145–50.

5. James Strasburg, "Creating, Practicing, and Researching a Global Faith: Conceptualizations of World Christianity in the American Protestant Pastorate and Seminary Classroom, 1893 to the Present," *Journal of World Christianity* 6 (2016): 217–36. Strasburg observes: "Overall, usage of world Christianity as a worldwide ecumenical reality crescendoed through World War II and reached fortississimo in anticipation of the founding of the World Council of Churches" (225).

256 NOTES TO PAGES 155–159

6. See the discussion of the ecumenically inflected side of the Protestant effort to engender World Christianity in Hollinger, *Protestants Abroad*, 94–116. Quoted material is from Hollinger, *Protestants Abroad*, 100.

7. Discussion of Graham and other "world Christianity" activists is in John Corrigan and Frank Hinkelmann, eds., *Return to Sender: American Evangelical Missions to Europe in the Twentieth Century* (Münster: LIT-Verlag, 2018).

8. Quoted material is from Gerald H. Anderson, "American Protestants in Pursuit of Mission: 1886–1986," *International Bulletin of Missionary Research* 12 (1988): 110.

9. Anderson, "American Protestants in Pursuit of Mission," 111.

10. Amanda Porterfield, *Corporate Spirit: Religion and the Rise of the Modern Corporation* (New York: Oxford University Press, 2018).

11. Klein demonstrates the centrality of the idea of "adoption" of foreigners into an American family in *Cold War Orientalism*.

12. William Temple, quoted in David J. Bosch, "An Emerging Paradigm for Missions," *Missiology: An International Review* 11 (1983): 486.

13. Temple's phrase was widely quoted, including in the U.S. Senate (*Judicial Review: Hearings before the Subcommittee on Constitutional Rights of the Committee on the Judiciary, United States Senate, Eighty-Ninth Congress, second session, on S. 2097* [Washington, DC: U.S.G.P.O., 1966], 777).

14. *Christian Advocate* 57 (1957): 240; and *Christianity and Crisis: A Bi-weekly Journal of Christian Opinion* 25 (1965): 284.

15. George Thompson Brown, *Christianity in the People's Republic of China* (Louisville: John Knox Press, 1983), 198; and *The Methodist Woman*, vol. 23 (Cincinnati: Joint Commission on Education, Cultivation, Board of Missions of the United Methodist Church, 1962), 37.

16. *Implementation of the Taiwan Relations Act: Hearings before the Subcommittee on Asian and Pacific Affairs of the Committee on Foreign Affairs, House of Representatives, Ninety-Sixth Congress, second session, June 11, 17 and July 1980, Volume 4* (Washington, DC: U.S.G.P.O, 1981), 81.

17. *American Baptist Woman* 30 (1986): 7.

18. *Michigan Christian Advocate*, vol. 76 (Adrian: Michigan Christian Advocate Publishing Company, 1949), 66.

19. Hollinger, *Protestants Abroad*, 109. For discussions of affect, including proposals about how it "circulates," see Sara Ahmed, "Affective Economies," *Social Text* 22 (2004): 17–39; *The Promise of Happiness* (Durham, NC: Duke University Press, 2010); and *The Cultural Politics of Emotion*; as well as Brian Massumi, *The Politics of Affect* (Cambridge: Polity, 2015). For a more specific view of affect and religion, see John Corrigan, ed., *Feeling Religion* (Durham, NC: Duke University Press, 2017), 1–21, 200–221, 242–59. For a discussion of affect and American Protestant overseas enterprises, see McAlister, *The Kingdom of God Has No Borders*, "Part Three: Emotion," 195–265.

20. David J. Bosch, *Transforming Mission: Paradigm Shifts in Theology of Mission* (New York: Orbis, 1991), 296. Bosch discusses how the plea to "come and help us" was repeated in missions publications of the late nineteenth and early twentieth centuries (296).

21. Daniel S. Tuttle, "Sermon," in *Journal of the General Convention of the Protestant Episcopal Church* (Printed for the Convention, 1917), 397.

22. Harry S. Truman, "Radio Remarks on the Occasion of the Lighting of the Community Christmas Tree on the White House Grounds, December 24, 1948," in *Public Papers of the Presidents of the United States* (Washington, DC: Government Printing Office, 1964), 287.

NOTES TO PAGES 159–161

23. Most recently Conroy-Krutz, *Christian Imperialism.*

24. Amit Rai, *Rule of Sympathy: Sentiment, Race, and Power* (New York: Palgrave, 2002), 53, 129, 99.

25. Ann Laura Stoler, *Along the Archival Grain: Epistemic Anxieties and Colonial Common Sense* (Princeton, NJ: Princeton University Press, 2009), 61, 62, 53. Stoler has analyzed the colonial setting for its "discursive density around issues of sentiments and their subversive tendencies . . . and their beneficent and dangerous political effects" (62). In focusing on the Dutch colonial state, she makes a strong argument that such feelings "were not a metaphor for something else." For Stoler, the "attachments and affections—tender, veiled, violent, or otherwise . . . make vivid the dislocations and distresses of empire" and should not be translated as epiphenomena or made subject to reductive analyses that disclose the true "'rational' categories 'behind'" those feelings (53). Stoler makes the point that the cultivation of feelings at times were useful in attempts to cope with the stresses of the colonial setting.

26. Karen Vallgårda, *Imperial Childhoods and Christian Mission* (New York: Springer, 2014).

27. Jan Gleysteen, illustrator, *God Builds the Church in South Asia: A Resource Book* (Harrisonburg, VA: Herald Press, 1963), 147.

28. Amit Rai, *Rule of Sympathy*, 73.

29. Cheryl E. Matias observes: "By attaching oneself to the Other, the White colonizer feels defined by his juxtaposition to Blackness" (*Feeling White: Whiteness, Emotionality, and Education* [New York: Springer, 2014], 91).

30. Justin M. Reynolds, "Against the World: International Protestantism and the Ecumenical Movement between Secularization and Politics, 1900–1952" (PhD diss., Columbia University, 2016).

31. Billy Graham, "Foreword," in John Noble and Glenn D. Everett, *I Found God in Soviet Russia* (New York: St. Martin Press, 1959), 10.

32. Billy Graham, quoted in William G. McLoughlin, *Billy Graham: Revivalist in a Secular Age* (New York: Ronald Press, 1960), 116.

33. Msgr. Thomas J. Cawley, review of Jean Monsterleet, *Martyrs in China* (Regnery, 1957), in the Catholic magazine *Best Sellers: The Semi-Monthly Book Review* 16 (March 15, 1957): 415.

34. Sister Mary Victoria, *Nun in Red China* (New York: McGraw-Hill, 1953), 117.

35. J. Edgar Hoover, "Keys to Freedom," *Law Enforcement Bulletin* 33 (1964): 23; "Message from Director J. Edgar Hoover," *Law Enforcement Bulletin* (1964): 2; and "The Faith of Free Men," *Law Enforcement Bulletin* 34 (1965): 24.

36. Harry S. Truman, "Radio and Television Remarks on Election Eve, November 3, 1952," in *Harry S. Truman: 1952–53: Containing the Public Messages, Speeches, and Statements of the President, January 1, 1952, to January 20, 1953* (Washington, DC: Office of the Federal Register, National Archives and Records Service, General Services Administration, 1966), 324.

37. Dwight D. Eisenhower, "Address at the Annual Luncheon of the Associated Press, New York City, April 25, 1955," in *Dwight D. Eisenhower: 1955: Containing the Public Messages, Speeches, and Statements of the President, January 1 to December 31, 1955* (Washington, DC: Office of the Federal Register, National Archives and Records Service, General Services Administration, 1959), 419; and "Message to National Co-Chairmen, Commission on Religious Organizations, National Conference of Christians and Jews, July 9, 1953," in *Dwight D. Eisenhower: 1953: Containing the Public Messages, Speeches, and Statements of the President, January 20 to December 31, 1953* (Washington, DC: Office of the Federal Register, National Archives and Records Service, General Services Administration, 1960), 489.

38. Lyndon B. Johnson, "Remarks at the Municipal Park, South Gate, California, October 11,

1964," in *Lyndon B. Johnson: 1963–64: Containing the Public Messages, Speeches, and Statements of the President* [book 2 of 2 books] (Washington, DC: Office of the Federal Register, National Archives and Records Service, General Services Administration, 1965), 1291.

39. Ronald Reagan, "Radio Address to the Nation on the Observance of Easter and Passover, April 2, 1983," in *Ronald Reagan: 1983* [book 1 of 2 books] (Washington, DC: Office of the Federal Register, National Archives and Records Service, General Services Administration, 1984–1985), 488.

40. "This Godless Communism" was published by the Catholic Guild in 1961. The issues are available online at https://www.historyonthenet.com/authentichistory/1946-1960/4 -cwhomefront/7-comics/tcgodless/This_Godless_Communism_1961.html, accessed June 19, 2019. The quote is from p. 22 of an early issue, but issues are not identified by number on the site.

41. Carl Henry, "The Fragility of Freedom in the West," in *Soviet Total War: Historic Mission of Violence and Deceit,* vol. 1, September 23, 1956, 85th Congress, 1st Session, House Document No. 227, Part 1 (Washington, DC: U.S. Government Printing Office, 1956), 50.

42. Cawley, *Best Sellers: The Semi-Monthly Book Review,* 416.

43. Anti-communism as a religion is a theme in some historical scholarship about the Cold War, and is discussed in the context of political and social issues in Richard Gid Powers, *Not Without Honor: The History of American Anticommunism* (New Haven, CT: Yale University Press, 1988). The quote is from p. 110.

44. Billy James Hargis, *Communism, The Total Lie* (Tulsa, OK: Christian Crusade, 1963), 27.

45. Charles Lowry, "The Ultimate Ungodliness," in *Soviet Total War: Historic Mission of Violence and Deceit,* vol. 1, September 23, 1956, 85th Congress, 1st Session, House Document No. 227, Part 1 (Washington, DC: U.S. Government Printing Office, 1956), 41, 42.

46. William Inboden, *Religion and American Foreign Policy, 1945–1960: The Soul of Containment* (New York: Cambridge University Press, 2008), i.

47. Reagan was asked at a news conference in 1987, "You have described in the past the Soviet Union as an evil empire. . . . Do you still feel that way?" He answered: "with regard to the evil empire, I meant it when I said it." See "Remarks and a Question-and-Answer Session with News Editors and Broadcasters, December 11, 1987," in *Ronald Reagan: 1987* [book 2 of 2 books] (Washington, DC: Office of the Federal Register, National Archives and Records Service, 1989), 1508, 1509.

48. McLoughlin, *Billy Graham,* 139–46.

49. Dianne Kirby, "John Foster Dulles: Moralism and Anti-Communism," *Journal of Transatlantic Studies* 6 (2008): 279–89.

50. Billy Graham, "Satan's Religion," *American Mercury* (August 1954): 42. The dualism and Satan's "masterminding" of communism that Graham insisted upon in his depictions of "Christianism vs. Communism" (the title of a 1957 radio sermon available at https://billygraham.org/ audio/christianism-vs-communism/) is discussed in a number of essays in Andrew S. Finstuen, Anne Blue Wills, and Grant Wacker, eds., *Billy Graham: American Pilgrim* (New York: Oxford University Press, 2017). See especially chapter 4, by Michael S. Hamilton, "From Desire to Decision: The Evangelistic Preaching of Billy Graham," 43–53.

51. Billy James Hargis, *Communist America—Must It Be?* (Tulsa, OK: 1960), 7.

52. Reuben Henry Markham, *Let Us Protestants Awake!* (Madison, WI: American Council of Christian Laymen, 1950), 37.

53. Recent studies that are useful in understanding that diversity and the politics in postwar

NOTES TO PAGES 164–168

American religion are Jonathan P. Herzog, *The Spiritual-Industrial Complex: America's Religious Battle Against Communism in the Early Cold War* (New York: Oxford University Press, 2011); Kevin Schultz, *Tri-Faith America: How Catholics and Jews Held Postwar America to Its Protestant Promise* (New York: Oxford University Press, 2011); Joshua M. Zeitz, *White Ethnic New York: Jews, Catholics, and the Shaping of Postwar Politics* (Chapel Hill: University of North Carolina Press, 2007); Angela Lahr, *Millennial Dreams and Apocalyptic Nightmares* (New York: Oxford University Press, 2007); Andrew S. Finstuen, *Original Sin and Everyday Protestants: The Theology of Reinhold Niebuhr, Billy Graham, and Paul Tillich* (Chapel Hill: University of North Carolina Press, 2009); Mark Silk, *Spiritual Politics: Religion and America Since World War II* (New York: Simon and Schuster, 1988); and Darren Dochuk, *From Bible Belt to Sunbelt: Plain-Folk Religion, Grassroots Politics, and the Rise of Evangelical Religion* (New York: Norton, 2010). See also Robert Fuller, *Naming the Antichrist: The History of an American Obsession* (New York: Oxford University Press, 1996).

54. Giuliana Chamedes, "The Vatican, Nazi-Fascism, and the Making of Transnational Anti-Communism in the 1930s," *Journal of Contemporary History* 51 (2016): 261–90.

55. Peter Rodino, July 18, 1962, *Congressional Record: Proceedings and Debates of the 87th Congress, Second Session*, vol. 108:120–24 (Washington, DC: Supt. of Documents, U.S. Government Printing Office, 1962), 13080.

56. Powers, *Not Without Honor*, 134–36.

57. Donald F. Crosby, S.J., *God, Church, and Flag: Senator Joseph R. McCarthy and the Catholic Church, 1950–1957* (Chapel Hill: University of North Carolina Press, 1978), 228–51.

58. Cited in Edward S. Shapiro, *A Time for Healing: American Jewry Since World War II* (Baltimore: Johns Hopkins University Press, 1992), 36.

59. J. Edgar Hoover, *Masters of Deceit: The Story of Communism in America and How to Fight It* (New York: Henry Holt and Company, 1958), 255. The chapter is entitled "The Communist Attack on Judaism."

60. Zeitz, *White Ethnic New York*.

61. America remained the "exceptional" nation in that troubled logic.

62. Inboden, *Religion and American Foreign Policy*, 101.

63. Axel Schäfer, *Piety and Public Funding: Evangelicals and the State in Modern America* (Philadelphia: University of Pennsylvania Press, 2012).

64. William C. Irvine, *Heresies Exposed: A Brief Critical Examination in the Light of the Holy Scriptures of Some of the Prevailing Heresies and False Teachings of Today* (Glasgow: Pickering and Inglis, 1930), 100. The book appeared originally in 1917, published by Pickering and Inglis in Glasgow, under the title *Timely Warnings*. Its subsequent American publications, with a number of different publishers, were prompted by American interest in the specific groups that Irvine warned against, almost all of which were of American origin.

65. Charles Wright Ferguson, *The Confusion of Tongues: A Review of Modern Isms* (New York: Doubleday, Doran, 1929). The relevant discussion of atheism in on pp. 427–40.

66. Jan Karel van Baalen, *The Chaos of Cults: A Study of Present-Day Isms*, 2nd ed. (Grand Rapids, MI: Eerdman's, 1952), 335, 166, 327. Mormonism was one of the most ambitiously "propagandist" cults (144).

67. Reuben H. Markham, *Rumania Under the Soviet Yoke* (Boston: Meador Publishing, 1949), 236, 237.

68. Reuben H. Markham, *Tito's Imperial Communism* (Chapel Hill: University of North Carolina Press, 1947), 61.

260   NOTES TO PAGES 168–171

69. J. Horton Barrett, *Communism's Prophet: A Study of Hitler's Totalitarianism and Its Communist Offspring: Materialism Amock [sic] in the Modern World. A Christian Analysis and a Christian Answer* (New York: Greenwich Book Publishers, 1957), 5.

70. "Nuclear Arms Reductions," Senate Reports Nos. 485–509, 97th Cong., 2d Sess., January 25–December 21, 1982 (Washington, DC: U.S. Government Printing Office, 1983), 75.

71. *Communist Interrogation, Indoctrination and Exploitation of American Military and Civilian Prisoners: Hearings Before the United States Senate Committee on Government Operations, Permanent Subcommittee on Investigation, Eighty-Fourth Congress, Second Session, on June 19, 20, 26, 27, 1956* (U.S. Government Printing Office, 1956), 66.

72. Russell Kirk, *The American Cause* (Chicago: H. Regnery Co., 1957), 4.

73. A. J. W. Taylor, "Good Will Attracts Troubled Inmates and Inspires Confidence," *Federal Probation* 27 (1963): 13.

74. Marcia Holmes, "Edward Hunter and the Origins of 'Brainwashing,'" *Hidden Persuaders* blog, May 26, 2017, http://www.bbk.ac.uk/hiddenpersuaders/blog/hunter-origins-of-brainwashing/, accessed April 15, 2018.

75. Edward Hunter, *Brain-Washing in Red China: The Calculated Destruction of Men's Minds* (New York: Vanguard, 1951).

76. J. Robert Ashcroft, quoted in Hargis, *Communist America—Must It Be?*, 54.

77. Margaret Singer and Janja Lalich, *Cults in Our Midst: The Hidden Menace in Our Everyday Lives* (San Francisco: Jossey-Bass, 1995). Singer argued, for example, that chanting, meditation, and yoga changed body chemistry through hyperventilation and other physical exercises, and that those changes led to psychic breakdown.

78. Anson D. Shupe and David C. Bromley, *Strange Gods: The Great American Cult Scare* (Boston: Beacon, 1981), 95.

79. Walter Ralston Martin, *The Kingdom of the Cults* (Grand Rapids, MI: Zondervan Publishing House, 1965), 215, 220, 25.

80. The collection of documents from the FBI and the Unification Church, along with reports of local authorities that include additional instances of intolerance, is at https://www.tparents.org/Moon-Books/SunMyungMoon-FBI/SunMyungMoon-830601.pdf, accessed April 20, 2018.

81. J. Gordon Melton, *Encyclopedic Handbook of Cults in America* (New York: Garland, 1992), 369. Protestants historically knew something about kidnapping. Protestant presses over the course of a century and a half had published fabulous new and reprint accounts of girls kidnapped and held hostage in Catholic convents.

82. Philip Jenkins, *Mystics and Messiahs: Cults and New Religions in American History* (New York: Oxford University Press, 2000), 5, 208–11, 215–26.

83. W. Michael Ashcraft, *A Historical Introduction to New Religious Movements* (New York: Routledge, 2018), 13.

84. Thomas Robbins and Dick Anthony, "The Limits of 'Coercive Persuasion' as an Explanation for Conversion to Authoritarian Sects," *Political Psychology* 2 (Summer 1980): 22–37. See also Dick Anthony, "Religious Movements and 'Brainwashing' Litigation: Evaluating Key Testimony," in Thomas Robbins and Dick Anthony, eds., *In Gods We Trust: New Patterns of Religious Pluralism in America*, 2nd ed. (New Brunswick, NJ: Transaction Press, 1989), 295–344. Newton Malony, a professor at Fuller Theological Seminary, was invited to deliver Fuller's annual Integration Lectures in 1996. He chose as his subject "Brainwashing and Religion."

85. Anne M. Blankenship, "Asian American Religions from Chinese Exclusion to 1965," in

The Oxford Handbook of Religion and Race in American History, ed. Kathryn Gin Lum and Paul Harvey (New York: Oxford University Press, 2018), 449.

86. Thu Thanh Khuc, "The Afterlives of the Vietnam War: Race, Religion, and the Politics of Meaning" (PhD diss., University of California–Santa Barbara, 2012), vii.

87. Jane Naomi Iwamura, *Virtual Orientalism: Asian Religions and American Popular Culture* (New York: Oxford University Press, 2011).

88. "Imperfect Master?," *Atlanta Constitution*, April 10, 1975, 4A.

89. John M. Crewdson, "How California Has Become Home for a Plethora of Cults," *New York Times*, November 30, 1978, A18.

90. *Investigation of Korean-American Relations: Report of the Subcommittee on International Organizations of the Committee on International Relations, U.SW. House of Representatives* (Washington, DC: U.S. Government Printing Office, 1978), 355, 358, 392.

91. Lewis F. Carter, *Charisma and Control in Rajneeshpuram: A Community Without Shared Values* (New York: Cambridge University Press, 1990), 236.

92. "Asian Cults Counterfeited in America," *Atlanta Constitution*, March 5, 1974, 7B.

93. Harry V. Martin and David Caul, "The Moonies: Who They Are, How They Work," *Napa Sentinel*, 1995, http://www.perkel.com/politics/moonies/1earth4.htm, accessed March 5, 2018. See also Harry V. Martin and David Caul, "Mind Control," *Napa Sentinel*, Aug./Sept./Oct./Nov. 1991, http://centerforaninformedamerica.com/wp-content/uploads/2015/12/MK-ULTRA.pdf, accessed March 5, 2018. Martin edited the *Sentinel*.

94. Marilyn Ferguson, *The Aquarian Conspiracy: Personal and Social Transformation in the 1980s* (New York: J. P. Tarcher, 1980).

95. Citizens for LaRouche, *Stamp Out the Aquarian Conspiracy* (1980), 4, 41, http://wlym.com/archive/oakland/brutish/Aquarian.pdf, accessed March 21, 2018. Gordon Arnold points out that the act was not only a matter of religion but blended race, religion, and memories of war (*The Afterlife of America's War in Vietnam: Changing Visions in Politics and Onscreen* [Jefferson, NC: McFarland, 2006], 80).

96. White middle-class American embrace of religions such as Buddhism and Hinduism often was a matter of innovation on the part of the adopters. Americans were selective in what they took from Asian traditions, and they sometimes blended those elements with others taken from additional traditions, resulting in makeshift versions of the tradition as it was practiced in India or Japan.

97. U.S. Commission on Civil Rights, *Intimidation and Violence: Racial and Religious Bigotry in America* (Washington, DC: Author, 1983), 3.

98. Quoted material is from *The State of Asian Pacific America: A Public Policy Report* (Los Angeles: LEAP Asian Pacific American Public Policy Institute and UCLA Asian American Studies Center, 1993), 297.

99. U.S. Commission on Civil Rights, *Intimidation and Violence*, 7; Los Angeles County Commission on Human Relations, *The New Asian Peril: Report of a Hearing in Rising Asian Bigotry* (Los Angeles: Author, 1984).

100. Christians were not the only group opposed to Asian religions and NRMs. Non-Christians and non-believers also sometimes voiced their opposition.

101. Philip Jenkins, *The New Anti-Catholicism: The Last Acceptable Prejudice* (New York: Oxford University Press, 2003).

102. Andrew Greeley, *An Ugly Little Secret* (Kansas City, MO: Sheed, Andrews, and McMeel, 1977).

262   NOTES TO PAGES 175–179

103. A discussion of increased Catholic missionary activities in Africa in the latter part of the twentieth century, and the focus on social services there, is in Barbra Mann Wall, *Into Africa: A Transnational History of Catholic Medical Missions and Social Change* (New Brunswick, NJ: Rutgers University Press, 2015).

104. Jenkins, *The New Anti-Catholicism*, 42.

105. Protestant clergyman and political figure Chuck Colson complained over a half century later that in the twentieth century "many Protestants accepted" Blanchard's views set out in the book (Chuck Colson, "The New Anti-Catholic Bigotry," *Townhall*, April 27, 2007, n.p., https://townhall.com/columnists/chuckcolson/2007/04/27/the-new-anti-catholic-bigotry-n1379839, accessed March 21, 2018).

106. Paul Blanshard, *Communism, Democracy, and Catholic Power* (Boston: Beacon Press, 1951), 287, 288, 263.

107. Philip Jenkins, *The Cold War at Home: The Red Scare in Pennsylvania, 1945–1960* (Chapel Hill: University of North Carolina Press, 1999), 181.

108. Schäfer, *Piety and Public Funding*, 136–37. Schäfer's discussion of the NAE's anti-Catholicism is based on his extensive reading of the NAE archives.

109. Schäfer, *Piety and Public Funding*, 100.

110. Schäfer, *Piety and Public Funding*, 100.

111. Schäfer, *Piety and Public Funding*, 100.

112. Schäfer, *Piety and Public Funding*, 101. Schäfer offers examples of how the NAE "devoted significant resources to the religious freedom campaign as a way of protecting the missionary activities of evangelical Christians" (101).

113. Anand E. Sokhey, "Church Burnings," in Paul A. Djupe and Laura R. Olson, *Encyclopedia of American Religion and Politics* (New York: Facts on File, 2003), 100; Rose Johnson, Dexter Wimbish, and Mary Ann Mauney, "The Fourth Wave: A Continuing Conspiracy to Burn Black Churches," *Report by the Center for Democratic Renewal for the House Judiciary Hearing on Black Church Burnings* (1997), Box 61, Center for Democratic Renewal records, Auburn Avenue Research Library, Atlanta, GA; and Sarah A. Soule and Nella Van Dyke, "Church Arson in the United States, 1989–1996," *Ethnic and Racial Studies* 22 (1999): 724–42.

114. Christopher Strain, *Burning Faith: Church and Arson in the American South* (Gainesville: University of Florida Press, 2008), 26.

115. This is a conservative figure. Many who have written about the arsons put the number at seventy-five or more. Strain, *Burning Faith*, mentions some of the statistical differences (22–23).

116. Careful reporting was done by Gary Fields and Richard Price, in "Why are Churches Burning? First One Fire, and Then Another and Soon Fear Rises Again," *USA Today*, June 28, 1996, section 01.A; see also Robert Marquand, "Church Fire Phenomenon Goes Beyond Racial Lines," *Christian Science Monitor*, July 10, 1996, https://www.csmonitor.com/1996/0710/071096.us.us.2.html, accessed May 1, 2018.

117. The federal report in 1998 indicated that by late that year, twenty-nine persons had been convicted of hate crimes involving church arson. See "Second Year Report for the President," National Church Arson Task Force, U.S. Department of Justice, October 1998, https://www.justice.gov/crt/image-report-cover, accessed March 12, 2018.

118. Alison Mitchell, "In Town Hit by Church Arson, Clinton Recalls South's Past," *New York Times*, June 13, 1996, https://www.nytimes.com/1996/06/13/us/in-town-hit-by-church-arson-clinton-recalls-south-s-past.html, accessed May 1, 2018.

119. "President William J. Clinton Thank You to Members of Congress for passage of Church Burnings Legislation. July 10, 1996," Clinton Presidential Library, Clinton Digital Library,

NOTES TO PAGES 180–181

https://clinton.presidentiallibraries.us/files/original/5d42b8d96b445ce1cfe7c64373e693d8.pdf. The boilerplate language in the periodic reports of the National Church Arson Task Force is repeated from the first report in 1997 and includes numerous references in every report to the involvement of NCC (1997–2000), and one reference made in passing to the NAE. An example report with drafts of related documents is in the Clinton Presidential Records in Little Rock, AR, Stack S, Row 98, Section 1, Shelf 1, Position 2. Parts of the contents can be read in digital form at National Church Arson Task Force, Third Year Report for the President, January, 2000, https://clinton.presidentiallibraries.us/files/original/82ac02df96fd7124266cefcf1be15add.pdf.

120. "Black Churches Burn in Boligee," *Birmingham News*, January 13, 1996, https://drive.google.com/file/d/0B-BE8fl6oNWaOFhhby1hQkNLcXM/view, accessed March 12, 2018. The Little Zion and Mt. Zoar Baptist churches were destroyed.

121. The document soon was entered into the congressional record. "Statement of Conscience of the National Association of Evangelicals concerning Worldwide Religious Persecution, January 23, 1996," *Consequences of MFN Renewal for China: Hearing before the Committee on Foreign Relations, United States Senate, One Hundred and Fourth Congress, Second Session,* June 6, 1996, vol. 4, pp. 58–59.

122. Pamela Slotte, "Blessed Are the Peacemakers: Christian Internationalism, Ecumenical Voices, and the Quest for Human Rights," in *Revisiting the Origins of Human Rights,* ed. Miia Halme-Tuomisaari and Pamela Slotte (Cambridge: Cambridge University Press, 2015), 293–329.

123. A photocopy of Roosevelt's handwritten notes iterating the Four Freedoms is "FDR and the Four Freedoms Speech," FDR Presidential Library and Museum, https://fdrlibrary.org/four-freedoms, accessed May 12, 2018. The intersection of race and ethnicity with religion and the meanings of Roosevelt's second freedom is discussed by Tisa Wenger, in "Freedom to Worship," in Jeffrey A. Engel, ed., *The Four Freedoms: Franklin D. Roosevelt and the Evolution of an American Idea* (New York: Oxford University Press, 2016), 73–124. Elizabeth Borgwardt emphasizes how FDR emphasized the rights of persons rather than nations and describes the relationship between the Four Freedoms, the founding of the UN, the Atlantic Charter, and the Nuremberg trials (*A New Deal for the World: America's Vision for Human Rights* [Cambridge, MA: Harvard University Press, 2005]).

124. Mark Philip Bradley points out that although the term "human rights" was not present in the text of the Atlantic Charter, Undersecretary of State Sumner Welles promoted the Charter in those terms: "There must be no swerving from the great human rights and liberties established by the Atlantic Charter" (*The World Reimagined: Americans and Human Rights in the Twentieth Century* [New York: Cambridge University Press, 2016], 21).

125. The text is at http://avalon.law.yale.edu/20th_century/decade03.asp, accessed May 1, 2018.

126. John Foster Dulles, "'Six Pillars of Peace' Program of Federal Council of Churches," *New York Times,* May 20, 1943, p. 23.

127. John Foster Dulles, *Six Pillars of Peace,* March 18, 1943. The text is at http://www.ibiblio.org/pha/policy/1943/1943-03-18a.html, accessed May 2, 2018.

128. Bradley, *The World Reimagined,* 73.

129. American Jewish Committee, *Declaration of Human Rights,* https://www.digitalcommonwealth.org/search/commonwealth-oai:ff36jk31r, accessed May 2, 2018. "Declaration of Human Rights issued by American Jewish Committee; Approved by Roosevelt," *Jewish Telegraphic Agency,* December 15, 1944, https://www.jta.org/1944/12/15/archive/declaration-of-human-rights-issued-by-american-jewish-committee-approved-by-roosevelt, accessed May 2, 2018.

130. Rev. Wilfred Parsons, "An International Bill of Rights," in *America's Peace Aims: A Committee Report* (Washington, DC: Catholic Association for International Peace, 1941), 23. On "The Rights of Man," see 13ff.

131. M. Searle Bates, *Religious Liberty: An Inquiry* (New York: International Missionary Council, 1945), 582.

132. Linde Lindkvist, *Religious Freedom and the Universal Declaration of Human Rights* (Cambridge: Cambridge University Press, 2017), 72.

133. The book, nevertheless, drew on the thinking of the French Catholic writer Jacques Maritain, who lectured and taught widely in North America in the 1930s–1940s.

134. United Nations Charter, Chapter 1, Article 3; Universal Declaration of Human Rights, Articles 1 and 2.

135. John Foster Dulles, "The Moral Foundation of the United States," in *Series S. United States Dept. of State. Office of Public Services: 1960* (Washington, DC: U.S. Government Printing Office, 1953–1959), 2. The speech itself is paginated but the collection is unpaginated, and the Dulles speech is located approximately one-third into the collection. The speech was delivered June 19, 1955.

136. Bradley, *The World Reimagined*, 140.

137. Bradley, *The World Reimagined*, 137ff.

138. Benjamin Lazier, "Earthrise; or, the Globalization of the World Picture," *American Historical Review* 116 (2011): 605. I am indebted to Mark Philip Bradley for this observation.

139. Bradley, *The World Reimagined*, 140.

140. Ahmed, "Affective Economies," 17–39; and *The Cultural Politics of Emotion*. Truth as affectual truth and part of the "circulation of affect" is my claim, not Bradley's.

141. Bradley, *The World Reimagined*, 137–48.

142. The author's experiences in a parochial grammar school during the 1950s included many sessions listening to vivid stories about the torture of Christians in China and Russia, some of which he remembers in detail.

143. *Communist Persecution of Churches in Red China and Northern Korea . . . March 26, 1959* (Washington, DC: U.S. Government Printing Office, 1959), 1, 2, 3.

144. *Communist Persecution of Churches in Red China and Northern Korea*, 5, 6.

145. *Communist Persecution of Churches in Red China and Northern Korea*, 28–29.

146. "Asian Christians Bare Red Terror," *New York Times*, June 1, 1959, 9.

147. *American Mercury* 89 (1959): 95, 96, 77.

148. *The Cross and the Flag* 18 (1960): 15, 18.

149. *Issues Presented by Air Reserve Center Training Manual, Hearing Before the Committee on Un-American Activities. Eighty-Sixth Congress, Second Session, February 25, 1960* (Washington, DC: U.S. Government Printing Office, 1960), 1289.

150. Robert D. Dilley, *Message for America: A Handbook for Those Who Will Defend Freedom* (Des Moines, IA: Independence Press Publishers, 1962), 226; Billy James Hargis, *The Facts About Communism and Our Churches* (Tulsa, OK: Christian Crusade, 1962), 99; Forrest Davis and Robert A. Hunter, *The Red China Lobby* (New York: Fleet Pub. Corp., 1963), 222; Herman J. Otten, *Baal or God* (New Haven, MO: Leader Pub. Co., 1965), 283; *Weekly Crusader* 8 (1968): 19.

151. National Association of Evangelicals, *Statement of Faith*, https://www.nae.net/statement -of-faith/, accessed May 1, 2018.

152. *Religious Persecution Behind the Iron Curtain . . . United States Senate, Ninety-Ninth Congress, First Session . . . November 14, 1985* (Washington, DC: U.S. Government Printing Office, 1986), 4.

NOTES TO PAGES 186–190

153. Thomas F. Farr, *World of Faith and Freedom: Why International Religious Liberty Is Vital to American National Security* (New York: Oxford University Press, 2008), 39.

154. Michael Horowitz, "New Intolerance Between Crescent and Cross," *Wall Street Journal*, July 5, 1995, A8. See the related discussion in McAlister, *The Kingdom of God Has No Borders*, 159–75.

155. Nina Shea, "The Origins and Legacy of the Movement to Fight Religious Persecution," *Review of Faith and International Affairs* 6 (2008): 26.

156. *Persecution of Christians Worldwide: Hearing before the Subcommittee on International Operations and Human Rights of the Committee on International Relations, House of Representatives, One Hundred Fourth Congress, Second Session, February 15, 1996* (Washington, DC: U.S. Government Printing Office, 1996), 6.

157. *Hearing before the Committee on International Relations, House of Representatives, One Hundred and Fifth Congress, First Session* (Washington, DC: U.S. Government Printing Office, 1998), 4.

158. *Hearing before the Committee on International Relations, House of Representatives* 28, 44; Paul Marshall, *Their Blood Cries Out* (Nashville: Thomas Nelson, 1997); and Nina Shea, *In the Lion's Den* (Nashville: B and H Publishing, 1997).

159. Farr, *World of Faith and Freedom*, 41.

160. Farr, *World of Faith and Freedom*, 112, 121. In its final form as the International Religious Freedom Act, a core flaw of the bill was the strong residue of "the Horowitz coalition's early emphasis on Christians to the apparent detriment of other religious groups, most notably Muslims" (115).

161. Ira Rivkin, quoted in *Religious Persecution as a U.S. Policy Issue*, ed. Rosalind I. J. Hackett, Mark Silk, and Dennis Hoover (Hartford, CT: Center for the Study of Religion in Public Life, Trinity College, 2000), 57.

162. Ron Kirkemo, *Embraced and Engaged: Grace and Ethics in American Foreign Policy* (Eugene, OR: Wipf and Stock, 2010), 215.

163. The issue was coalescing in 1996, as reflected in "Memorandum, Religious Persecution of Christians in China," Richard Schifter to Stephen R. Neuwirth, April 22, 1996, Clinton Digital Library. It reached a critical point, at which Clinton informed Congress that he would not revoke MFN status for China in June 1997, in letters he wrote to congressional leaders explaining his reasoning. Some of the relevant documents are in the Clinton Digital Library, https://clinton.presidentiallibraries.us/files/original/2102c2d8f0c63398a82fd67e72652e5d.pdf, accessed May 2, 2018.

164. On USA*Engage, see Ken Silverstein, "Persecution Complex," *Mother Jones Magazine* (August 1998): 26–31.

165. Farr, *World of Faith and Freedom*, 114.

166. National Association of Evangelicals, "For the Health of the Nation: An Evangelical Call to Civic Responsibility" (2004), in Ronald J. Sider and Diane Knippers, foreword by Ted Haggard, *Toward an Evangelical Public Policy: Political Strategies for the Health of the Nation* (Grand Rapids, MI: Baker Books, 2005), 363.

167. Winnifred Sullivan, in Hackett et al., *Religious Persecution as a U.S. Policy Issue*, 46; International Religious Freedom Act, Section 2.a.1 (22. U.S.C. 6401).

168. Condit and Bauer, quoted in Jeffrey Goldberg, "Washington Discovers Christian Persecution," *New York Times Magazine*, December 21, 1997, p. 52.

169. Farr is emphatic about this last point throughout *World of Faith and Freedom*.

Chapter Five

1. For a full discussion, see "James Dobson Admits 'We Lost the Culture War,'" interview with James Dobson, YouTube, 2015, https://www.youtube.com/watch?v=_8fOqpMvap4, accessed June 1, 2018; Rod Dreher, "Yes, We Lost the Culture War," *American Conservative*, May 19, 2015, https://www.theamericanconservative.com/dreher/yes-we-lost-the-culture-war-disney-real-oneals/, accessed June 1, 2018; Donald T. Williams, "Discerning the Times: Why We Lost the Culture War and How to Make a Comeback," *Christian Research Journal* 38 (2015): 4–5; Paul Baxter, "Do We Need a Cultural Counter-Revolution?," Marsha West, "70% of Americans are Christians? Seriously?," *Renew America*, August 28, 2015, http://www.renewamerica.com/columns/mwest/150828, accessed June 1, 2018; and *Christian Index*, February 22, 2016, https://christianindex.org/do-we-need-a-cultural-counter-revolution/, accessed June 1, 2018.

2. Robert P. Jones, Daniel Cox, E. J. Dionne Jr., William A. Galston, Betsy Cooper, and Rachel Lienesch, *How Immigration and Concerns About Cultural Changes Are Shaping the 2016 Election* (Washington, DC: Public Religion Research Institute, 2016), 1–2.

3. Robert P. Jones, *The End of White Christian America* (New York: Simon and Schuster, 2016), 49, 133, 50–51.

4. Daniel Cox and Robert P. Jones, *America's Changing Religious Identity*, Public Religion Research Institute, 2016, https://www.prri.org/research/american-religious-landscape-christian-religiously-unaffiliated/, accessed June 1, 2018.

5. Jones et al., *How Immigration and Concerns About Cultural Changes Are Shaping the 2016 Election*, 17.

6. Daniel Cox and Robert P. Jones, *Majority of Americans Oppose Transgender Bathroom Restrictions*, Public Religion Research Institute, March 3, 2017, https://www.prri.org/research/lgbt-transgender-bathroom-discrimination-religious-liberty/, accessed June 1, 2018.

7. Mary Eberstadt, *It's Dangerous to Believe: Religious Freedom and Its Enemies* (New York: HarperCollins Publishers, 2016); Rod Dreher, *The Benedict Option: A Strategy for Christians in a Post-Christian Nation* (New York: Sentinel, 2017); and "God's Not Dead," *Box Office Mojo*, http://www.boxofficemojo.com/movies/?id=godsnotdead.htm, accessed June 1, 2018. *God's Not Dead* appeared in 2014.

8. Melani McAlister, "The Politics of Persecution," *Middle East Report* 249 (2008): 19.

9. Marshall (*Their Blood Cries Out*) offers statistics for various countries and regions throughout the world. While concerned with formerly communist countries (and their atheistic/secularist orientations), he was especially interested in the persecution of Christians in Muslim countries.

10. The methodology, which is continually refined, is described at the Open Doors site, at https://www.opendoorsusa.org/christian-persecution/world-watch-list/about-the-ranking/, accessed June 2, 2018.

11. *World Watch List 2018*, https://www.opendoorsusa.org/wp-content/uploads/2018/01/WWL2018-BookletNew.pdf, accessed June 2, 2018. The United States was not named on that *World Watch List* and never has been.

12. In some reports, persecution of Muslims by other Muslims is deemed an equivalent problem.

13. "Merkel Calls Christianity World's 'Most Persecuted' Religion," *Times of Israel*, November 6, 2012, https://www.timesofisrael.com/merkel-calls-christianity-worlds-most-persecuted-religion/, accessed June 2, 2018.

14. See the related discussion in McAlister, *The Kingdom of God Has No Borders*, 161–63.

NOTES TO PAGES 195–198

15. Dianne Knippers, "They Shoot Christians, Don't They?," *Christianity Today* 36 (July 20, 1992): 35, 34.

16. Knippers, "They Shoot Christians, Don't They?," 33, 35, 34.

17. "Greater Focus on Persecuted Church," *Christianity Today* 40 (August 12, 1996): 62.

18. For example, see Jeffrey Goldberg, "Washington Discovers Christian Persecution," in the *New York Times Magazine* (December 31, 1997), and A. M. Rosenthal in a *New York Times* op-ed column, February 11, 1997, "Persecuting the Christians." Goldberg brought a more critical eye to the topic, but both writers provided strong visibility for the problem.

19. Kevin Boyle and Juliet Sheen, *Freedom and Religious Belief: A World Report* (London: Routledge, 1997), 1. The Trust's Pew-Templeton Global Religious Futures project followed up with a series of reports that progressively raised the level of alarm, such as *Rising Tide of Restrictions on Religion* (Washington, DC: Pew Research Center's Forum on Religion and Public Life, 2012).

20. Elizabeth Castelli, "Praying for the Persecuted Church: U.S. Christian Activism in the Global Arena," *Journal of Human Rights* 4 (2005): 321–51. A useful listing of some of those initiatives by Christians in America to combat persecution of Christians is on pp. 337–44.

21. David Limbaugh, *Persecution: How Liberals Are Waging War Against Christianity* (Washington, DC: Regnery, 2003), ix. The book was ignored by the *New York Times Book Review*.

22. Rick Scarborough, *Enough Is Enough* (Lake Mary, FL: Frontline, 2008), 64.

23. Dana Blanton, "12/01/05 FOX Poll: Courts Driving Religion Out of Public Life; Christianity Under Attack," December 1, 2005, http://www.foxnews.com/story/2005/12/01/120105-fox-poll-courts-driving-religion-out-public-life-christianity-under.html, accessed June 2, 2018.

24. The recurrence of the phrase, and its large overall social media impact in the Twitterverse, on Pinterest, on Facebook, on blogs, in online videos, and elsewhere in social media was evidenced by a Brand 24 search, June 20, 2018, https://app.brand24.com. Brand 24 is a software that searches social media.

25. Janet L. Folger, *The Criminalization of Christianity: Read This Before It Becomes Illegal* (New York: Multnomah, 2005).

26. The organization listed specific occurrences, by year from 2011 to 2014, that it cast as persecution of Christians ("News: Seeds of Persecution," http://www.crossroad.to/News/Persecution/seeds.html, accessed June 2, 2018).

27. Starnes had been fired from the *Baptist Press* in 2003 for falsifying quotes in a story about U.S. secretary of education Rod Paige.

28. Todd Starnes, *God Less America: Real Stories from the Front Lines of the Attack on Traditional Values* (Lake Mary, FL: Frontline, 2014).

29. Fay Voshell, "Persecution of Christians in America: It's Not Just 'Over There,'" *American Thinker* blog, May 10, 2015, https://www.americanthinker.com/articles/2015/05/persecution_of_christians_in_america_its_not_just_over_there.html, accessed June 19, 2019; and Jones et al., "How Immigration and Concerns About Cultural Changes Are Shaping the 2016 Election," 17.

30. Franklin Graham, quoted in "Alan Colmes Says Franklin Graham's Views on Persecution Are Nuts," *Charisma Caucus*, May 5, 2015, https://www.charismanews.com/politics/53043-alan-colmes-says-franklin-graham-s-views-on-persecution-are-nuts, accessed June 2, 2018.

31. Viz. the analogous situation in France detailed in Brown, *Mass Violence and the Self.*

32. Amy Wierman, quoted in Laurie Goodstein, "A Rising Movement Cites Persecution Facing Christians," *New York Times*, November 9, 1998, A1, A14.

33. "Exile Night," *Voices of the Martyrs,* https://www.i-am-n.com/exile-night/, accessed June 2, 2018.

34. Nate Hettinga, "Wear Orange Sunday: The Value of Identifying with Persecuted Christians," May 9, 2016, https://converge.org/news/wear-orange-sunday-the-value-identifying-persecuted-christians, accessed June 2, 2018.

35. Gregory C. Cochran, "Persecution for Every Christian: Why It Is Important to Identify with the Persecuted Church," April 14, 2014, https://gregoryccochran.com/2014/04/14/persecution-for-every-christian-why-it-is-important-to-identify-with-the-persecuted-church/, accessed June 2, 2018.

36. Candida Moss, "The Death of Jesus and the Rise of the Christian Persecution Myth," *Daily Beast,* March 31, 2013, https://www.thedailybeast.com/the-death-of-jesus-and-the-rise-of-the-christian-persecution-myth, accessed June 2, 2018.

37. Candida Moss writes that actual persecutions in the first several centuries of Christianity were rare, but those stories have greatly shaped American Christian self-understanding (*The Myth of Persecution: How Early Christians Invented a Story of Martyrdom* [San Francisco: HarperOne, 2013]).

38. Adrian Chastain Weimer, *Martyrs' Mirror: Persecution and Holiness in Early New England* (New York: Oxford University Press, 2011).

39. See the discussion of White (among others), who is quoted in John Corrigan, *Emptiness: Feeling Christian in America* (Chicago: University of Chicago Press, 2015), 30.

40. It set the box-office record for an R-rated movie.

41. Johnnette Benkovic, "Facing the Challenge," *Women of Grace* blog, http://www.womenofgrace.com/blog/?p=9838, accessed June 2, 2018.

42. Steve Haas, quoted in Goodstein, "A Rising Movement," A14.

43. Bradley, *The World Reimagined.*

44. Laura Jeffery and Mattei Candea, "The Politics of Victimhood," *History and Anthropology* 17 (2006): 289.

45. James A. Kelhoffer, *Persecution, Persuasion, and Power* (Tübingen: Mohr Siebeck, 2010), 28.

46. Ron Dudai, "Entryism, Mimicry and Victimhood Work: The Adoption of Human Rights Discourse by Right-Wing Groups in Israel," *International Journal of Human Rights* 7 (2017): 867.

47. Elizabeth A. Castelli, "Persecution Complexes: Identity Politics and the 'War on Christians,'" *differences: A Journal of Feminist Studies* 18 (2007): 173–74.

48. Sarah Pulliam Bailey, "'Their Dream President': Trump Just Gave White Evangelicals a Big Boost," *Washington Post,* May 4, 2017, https://www.washingtonpost.com/news/acts-of-faith/wp/2017/05/04/their-dream-president-trump-just-gave-white-evangelicals-a-big-boost/?utm_term=.9341bf162bb4, accessed June 3, 2018.

49. Matthew Avery Sutton, *American Apocalypse: A History of Modern Evangelicalism* (Cambridge, MA: Harvard University Press, 2014), 351.

50. Lisa McMinn, "Y2K, The Apocalypse, and Evangelical Christianity: The Role of Eschatological Belief in Church Responses," *Sociology of Religion* 62 (2001): 205–20.

51. Charles Sarno and Helen Shoemaker, "Church, Sect, or Cult? The Curious Case of Harold Camping's Family Radio and the May 21 Movement," *Nova Religio* 19 (2016): 18.

52. Weinland predicted the end in 2012, and Hagee the beginning of the end times in 2014.

53. National Association of Evangelicals: Evangelical Leaders Survey, "Premillennialism

Reigns in Evangelical Theology," January 2011, https://www.nae.net/premillennialism-reigns-in-evangelical-theology/, accessed June 3, 2018.

54. William Martin, "The Christian Right and American Foreign Policy," *Foreign Policy* 114 (1999): 66–80. Military experts have been interested in the influence of millennialism on preparation for national defense for decades, and the topic continues to hold an important place in military planning. See Brian L. Stuckert, *Strategic Implications of American Millennialism* (Fort Leavenworth, KS: School of Advanced Military Studies, U.S. Army Command, 2008).

55. Michael Barkun, "Racist Apocalypse: Millennialism on the Far Right," *American Studies* 31 (1990): 130–34.

56. Carol Mason, *Killing for Life: The Apocalyptic Narrative of Pro-Life Politics* (Ithaca, NY: Cornell University Press, 2002), 105.

57. Paul Boyer, *When Time Shall Be No More: Prophecy Belief in Modern American Culture* (Cambridge, MA: Harvard University Press, 1992).

58. Kenneth L. Waters Sr., "Matthew 27:52–53 as Apocalyptic Apostrophe: Temporal-Spatial Collapse in the Gospel of Matthew," *Journal of Biblical Literature* 122 (2003): 489. On time-space compression, see David Harvey, *The Condition of Postmodernity: An Enquiry into the Origins of Cultural Change* (Cambridge, MA: Blackwell, 1990).

59. Alan Noble, "The Evangelical Persecution Complex," *The Atlantic*, August 4, 2014, https://www.theatlantic.com/national/archive/2014/08/the-evangelical-persecution-complex/375506/, accessed June 3, 2018.

60. Jason Wiedel, *Persecution Complex: Why Americans Need to Stop Playing the Victim* (Edmond, OK: Crowdscribed LLC, 2014), 10–11.

61. Michael Knippa, "No 'Lions of Gory Mane': Persecution of Loss of Predominance in American Christianity," *Concordia Journal* 41 (2015): 299.

62. "The Persecution Complex: The Religious Right's Deceptive Rallying Cry," *Right Wing Watch: In Focus*, June 2014, http://www.rightwingwatch.org/report/the-persecution-complex-the-religious-rights-deceptive-rallying-cry/.

63. Bethany Allen-Ebrahimian, "No, Christians Do Not Face Looming Persecution in America," *Washington Post*, December 12, 2017, https://www.washingtonpost.com/news/democracy-post/wp/2017/12/12/no-christians-do-not-face-looming-persecution-in-america/?utm_term=.57b411ad19f9, accessed June 3, 2018.

64. "Is Christianity Under Attack?," *Hardball with Chris Matthews*, NBC News, March 30, 2006, transcript, http://www.nbcnews.com/id/12079836/ns/msnbc-hardball_with_chris_matthews/t/christianity-under-attack/, accessed June 3, 2018.

65. Kelly Shackelford, quoted in "Faith Under Fire: Persecution of Christians on Rise—In U.S.," *WorldNetDaily* (WND), September 17, 2012, http://www.wnd.com/2012/09/persecution-of-christians-on-rise-in-u-s/ accessed June 3, 2018

66. Conrad Vine, "Discipleship and Suffering: The Christian Response to Persecution," *Journal of Adventist Mission Studies* 12 (2016): 42; and Kevin DeYoung, "Four Thoughts on Persecution in America," *Gospel Coalition*, March 9, 2017, https://www.thegospelcoalition.org/blogs/kevin-deyoung/four-thoughts-on-persecution-in-america/, accessed June 3, 2018.

67. Adam Lee, "Help, Help, I'm Being Repressed! How Conservatives Make a Mockery of the Oppression of Religious Minorities," *The Guardian*, August 17, 2014, https://www.theguardian.com/commentisfree/2014/aug/17/conservative-christian-oppression-religious-minorities, accessed June 3, 2018. The quote is attributed to Cardinal Francis George, archbishop of Chicago.

68. Jesse Lyman Hurlbut, *The Story of the Christian Church* (Philadelphia: Winston, 1918). The book has been repeatedly reissued by Christian publishing houses such as Zondervan.

69. Jeffress, quoted in Gregory Tomlin, "Jeffress Compares Christians to Jews 'Marginalized' by Nazis; Atheist Bill Maher Says Stop Whining," *Christian Examiner*, June 9, 2015, https://www.christianexaminer.com/article/jeffress-compares-christians-to-jews-marginalized-by-nazis-atheist-bill-maher-says-stop-whining/49065.htm, accessed June 3, 2018.

70. Santorum, quoted in David Badash, "Santorum Warns Christians: German Jews Just Before Hitler Weren't Scared Either," *New Civil Rights Movement*, October 31, 2014, https://www.thenewcivilrightsmovement.com/2014/10/rick_santorum_america_s_christians_are_in_same_situation_as_german_jews_before_hitler/, accessed June 3, 2018.

71. Raul Hilberg, *The Destruction of the European Jews*, rev. and definitive ed., 3 vols. (Holmes and Meier: New York and London, 1985; originally published 1961).

72. Vernon J. Sterk, "The Dynamics of Persecution" (PhD diss., Fuller Theological Seminary, 1992), 108–29.

73. Johan Candelin, "Persecution of Christians Today," in *Persecution of Christians Today: Christian Life in African, Asian, Near East and Latin American Countries* (Berlin: Konrad-Adenauer-Stiftung: Berlin, 1999), 16–24; "The Persecution of Christians Today," *St. Mark's Review* 184 (2001): 14–19; and "The Persecution of Christians Today," *Eternal Perspective Ministries*, February 24, 2018. Candelin's ordering of stages was picked up by the Lausanne World Pulse Archives in 2005 (Patrick Sookhdeo, "Persecution of Christians in the Muslim World," *Lausanne World Pulse Archives* 11 [2005], http://www.lausanneworldpulse.com/themedarticles-php/84/11-2005, accessed June 3, 2019).

74. Don McAlvany, *Storm Warning: The Coming Persecution of Christians and Traditionalists in America* (Oklahoma City: Hearthstone Publishing, 1999), 276–86.

75. Gregory H. Stanton originally proposed an eight-stage model and later enlarged it to ten stages ("The 8 Stages of Genocide," Genocide Watch, http://www.genocidewatch.org/genocide/8stagesofgenocide.html, accessed June 3, 2018). The original proposal was a briefing paper for the U.S. State Department ("The Eight Stages of Genocide," http://www.genocidewatch.org/images/8StagesBriefingpaper.pdf, accessed June 3, 2018). The ten stages can be found at http://genocidewatch.org/genocide/tenstagesofgenocide.html (accessed June 3, 2018).

76. Paul Estabrooks and Jim Cunningham, *Standing Strong Through the Storm* (Santa Ana, CA: Open Doors Resources, 2003); and Paul Estabrooks, "Four-Stage Process of Persecution," https://www.biblegateway.com/devotionals/standing-strong-through-the-storm/2092/08/05, accessed June 3, 2018.

77. Thomas Horn, "Persecution of Christians Growing in the United States," *Worthy News*, February 6, 2001, https://www.worthynews.com/1710-persecution-of-christians-growing-in-the-united-states, accessed June 3, 2018.

78. "Hall of Shame Report, 2016," International Christian Concern, https://www.legit.ng/1083032-6-countries-worst-persecutors-christians-number-nigeria-is.html, accessed June 19, 2019.

79. I am indebted to Melani McAlister for pointing out that it may be the case that for some persons the stages-of-persecution model *substitutes* for the excitement of end times theology.

80. Joseph M. Esper, *Spiritual Dangers of the 21st Century* (Goleta, CA: Queenship Publishing, 2012), 84–85.

81. Johnnette Benkovic, "Facing the Challenge," *Women of Grace* blog, October 8, 2011, http://www.womenofgrace.com/blog/?p62194&paged=763, accessed June 3, 2018.

82. Msgr. Charles Pope, "Some Thoughts on the Five Stages of Religious Persecution," *Community in Mission*, November 11, 2012, http://blog.adw.org/2012/11/some-thoughts-on-the-five-stages-of-religious-persecution/, accessed June 3, 2018.

NOTES TO PAGES 207–211

83. Voshell, "Persecution of Christians in America."

84. "Persecution of Christians in America," Berean Publishers, http://www.bereanpublishers.com/persecution-of-christians-in-america/, accessed June 3, 2018.

85. Sharron Angle, quoted in Leon Hadar, "Fear of a Muslim Planet," *American Conservative*, December 13, 2010, http://www.theamericanconservative.com/articles/muslim-planet/, accessed June 3, 2018.

86. Civilus Defendus, "4 Stages of Islamic Conquest," *Civilus Defendus* blog, January 10, 2010, https://civilusdefendus.wordpress.com/2010/01/10/4-stages-of-islamic-conquest/, accessed June 3, 2018.

87. Anita Crane, "Downfall Coming Through a Coalition of Islamists and Marxists?" *WorldNetDaily*, May 8, 2013, http://www.wnd.com/2013/05/downfall-coming-through-coalition-of-islamists-and-marxists/, accessed June 3, 2018.

88. Brannon Howse, "Marxist [*sic*] and Muslims Have United to Bring Down America and Persecute Christians and Conservatives," *Worldview News*, September 13, 2017, https://www.worldviewweekend.com/news/article/marxist-muslims-have-united-bring-down-america-persecute-christians-conservatives-0, accessed June 3, 2018.

89. "Anti-Sharia Law Bills in the U.S," *Southern Poverty Law Center: Hatewatch*, February 5, 2018, https://www.splcenter.org/hatewatch/2018/02/05/anti-sharia-law-bills-united-states, accessed June 3, 2018.

90. Liz Farmer, "Alabama Joins Waves of States Banning Foreign Laws," *Governing*, November 4, 2014, http://www.governing.com/topics/elections/gov-alabama-foreign-law-courts-amendment.html, accessed June 19, 2017; and Tara Culp-Ressler, "Christians Blast Ballot Initiative Banning Sharia Law in Alabama," *Think Progress*, November 2, 2014, https://thinkprogress.org/christians-blast-ballot-initiative-banning-sharia-law-in-alabama-7166c97ae507, accessed June 19, 2017.

91. The initial list of seven was Libya, Somalia, Yemen, Iran, Iraq, Sudan, and Syria. Additions and subtractions were made, so that by summer 2018, that list had been reduced to Iran, Libya, Somalia, Syria, and Yemen, and the ban was expected to apply to a communist nation as well, North Korea.

92. Gregory A. Smith, "Most White Evangelicals Approve of Trump Travel Prohibition and Express Concerns About Extremism," Pew Research Center, February 27, 2017, http://www.pewresearch.org/fact-tank/2017/02/27/most-white-evangelicals-approve-of-trump-travel-prohibition-and-express-concerns-about-extremism/, accessed June 3, 2018.

93. Robert P. Jones, "The Collapse of American Identity," *New York Times*, May 2, 2017, A27, https://www.nytimes.com/2017/05/02/opinion/the-collapse-of-american-identity.html, accessed June 19, 2019.

94. Holger Stark, "How America Lost Its Identity," *Spiegel Online*, January 26, 2017, http://www.spiegel.de/international/world/letter-from-washington-how-america-lost-its-identity-a-1131294.html, accessed June 3, 2018; anonymous quote in Daniel Cox, Rachel Lienesch, and Robert P. Jones, "Beyond Economics: Fears of Cultural Displacement Pushed the White Working Class to Trump," Public Religion Research Institute, May 9, 2017, https://www.prri.org/research/white-working-class-attitudes-economy-trade-immigration-election-donald-trump/, accessed June 3, 2018.

95. Related discussion is in Arlie Hochschild, *Strangers in Their Own Land: Anger and Mourning on the American Right* (New York: New Press, 2016).

Index

Abraham, 32
Acosta, José de, 37
Adair, James, 38
Adams, Brooks, 114, 118, 250n72
Adams, Charles Francis, 114, 116
Adams, Hannah, 28, 29
Adams, James Truslow, 114
Adams, John Quincy, 124
Adams, Samuel, 120
Adams, Samuel Baxter, 114
Adams, William, 59
adoption: of a Constitutional amendment, 12; of foreigners, 256n11
affect, 54, 68, 73, 156, 162, 182, 185, 187, 218n11, 222n24, 224n30, 256n19; circulation of, 158, 182, 264n140
Africa, 4, 25, 75, 76, 77, 108, 131, 154, 175, 176, 194, 262n103; countries, 228n31; slave trade in, 252–53n141
African American churches, 5, 16, 178, 180, 186, 189, 190. *See also* black churches
African Americans, 30, 43, 120, 145, 177, 209; enslavement of, 43; Jim Crow status of, 254n176
Agag, 32, 35. *See also* Amalek; Amalekites
Agassiz, Louis, 127
Ahmed, Sara, 220n14
Alaska Purchase, 121, 122
Albany, NY, 105
Alexander, Jeffrey C., 222n22
Algiers, 97
Amalek, 35, 39, 43, 44, 47, 48, 49, 51, 53, 55, 58, 59; destruction of, 32, 33, 34, 46; hammers of, 40; house of, 52; stories of, 36, 41, 45. *See also* Agag; Amalekites
Amalekites, 15, 34, 58, 61, 226n36; Catholics as, 45, 46, 64; enmity of, 231n79; hammer of, 40;

Mormons as, 48, 49, 52, 53; Muslims as, 210; Native Americans as, 36, 39, 41, 43, 44, 190; in Scripture, 32, 33, 35, 42; story of, 14, 54, 79, 230. *See also* Agag; Amalek
Amazon River, 127
American Annals of Education, 78
American Baptist Woman, 157
American Bible Society, 131
American Board of Commissioners of Foreign Missions (ABCFM), 72, 73, 75, 94, 96, 155; *Proceedings* of, 74
American Cause, The (Kirk), 168
American Christianity, 66, 199, 205
American Christians, 5, 16, 17, 92, 153, 166, 174, 185, 189, 190, 198, 210, 211; conservative, 194, 209; as victims of persecution, 202, 203, 204, 205, 207, 208; white, 171, 193, 195
American Conservative, 192
American exceptionalism, 9, 10, 13, 82, 111, 113, 148, 186, 189, 209, 224–25n35, 259n61
American expansion, 15, 121, 122; westward, 27, 42
American Freedom Law Center, 210
American history, 2, 9, 31, 56, 83, 149
American Home Missionary Society, 52
American Ideals Historically Traced, 1607–1907 (textbook), 113
American Indians, 3, 15, 21, 22, 32, 35, 54, 69, 147, 171, 202, 218n10; as Amalekites, 44, 190; as descendants of the Jews, 37, 38, 39, 44, 45, 231n79; genocide of, 4, 26, 58; relations with, 18, 19, 20, 23, 24, 25, 27, 28, 40, 41, 42, 160; war with, 29, 30, 36, 232n88. *See also* Native American peoples; Native Americans
American internationalism, 14
American Jewish Committee, 165, 181
American Journal of Politics, 29, 142

274 INDEX

American law, 172; history of, 224–25n35
American Mercury, 163, 185
American press, 73
American Protective Association, 47, 62, 138, 143
American Protestant Society, 68
American Quarterly Review, 83
American religious history, 11, 13, 14, 181, 211
American Revolution, 26. *See also* Revolutionary War
American South, 27, 40, 44, 57; and African American churches, 177, 178, 179; antebellum, 124; and the Civil War, 121; representations of, 103; and Wilson, 144, 145, 151
Americans United for Separation of Church and State, 175
American treaties: with Algiers, 97; with Bolivia, 126; with Brazil, 97; with Chile, 97; with China, 97; with Cuba, 122; with Ecuador, 126; with Japan, 97; with Mexico, 97; with Nicaragua, 126; with Paraguay, 126; with Siam, 97; with Switzerland, 98; with Venezuela, 97. *See also* Treaty of Guadalupe Hidalgo
America or Rome, Christ or the Pope (Brandt), 105
Amerindians, 37
Amnesty International, 183, 187, 195
Anderson, Benedict, 33, 217, 218n10, 218n12, 220nn13–14, 220–21n15
Andover Review, 155
Andover Theological Seminary, 72, 93, 152
Angle, Sharron, 208
Anglican Church in America, 69. *See also* Episcopalian Church
Anglo-Saxon, 89, 133, 136; Protestantism, 16, 121, 125, 142, 148, 149, 150, 152, 154; race, 134, 142, 143, 145
Antebellum period, 3, 45, 46, 56, 57, 58, 72, 73, 78, 82, 111; immigration during, 104; periodicals, 75; politics, 99, 100; violence during, 15, 63, 71
Anthony, Susan B., 43
anti-Catholicism, 45, 59, 61, 80, 82, 91, 97, 110, 121, 138, 144, 145, 165; literature, 63, 104, 106, 107, 139, 146; of the NAE, 176, 177; new, 175; politics, 62, 65, 86, 95, 139; rhetoric, 36, 47, 48, 64, 68, 69, 70, 81, 88, 243n118; violence, 3, 15, 47, 60, 66
anti-Mormonism, 49, 50, 59, 61
Antinomian crisis, 23
Anti-Papal Manual, 106
antisemitism, 109, 145–46, 163, 165
Apess, William, 26, 38
apocalypse, 235–36n148
Appleton, Samuel, 40
Appomattox, VA, 122
Aquarian Conspiracy, The (Ferguson), 173
Arabs, 52, 53, 75
Arbella, 34
arbitration, 90

Arena, 138
Arens, Richard, 185
Argentina, 125
Argue, Donald, 187
Arizona, 52
Arkansas, 51
Arlington, VA, 144
Arnold, Gordon, 261n95
arson, 170, 173; of black churches, 17, 178, 179; of Catholic churches, 45, 63; of the Ursuline convent, 67, 81, 82. *See also* Church Arson Prevention Act; National Church Arson Task Force
Asia, 4, 60, 131, 134, 175; missions to, 72, 77, 108, 123, 176; South, 159, 171
Asian Americans, 190
Asian religions, 16, 169, 171, 172, 173, 174, 184, 185, 226n38
Asiatic Exclusion League, 171
Assembly of God General Council, 169
Association of Evangelical Professors of Missions, 156
atheism, 160, 162, 164, 167, 170, 181, 203, 207
Atkinson's Saturday Evening Post, 50
Atlanta, GA, 144
Atlanta Constitution, 172
Atlantic Charter, 180, 263n123
Atlantic world, 25, 26, 59
attachment: dysfunctional, 31, 32, 49, 103, 229n60; emotional, 7, 66, 156, 216; Protestant, 159, 160
auricular confession, 68, 69
Austria, 2, 80, 84, 88, 91, 92
Austria-Hungary, 151
Awful Disclosures of Maria Monk, 63
Axis powers, 180
Azores, 25

Baal or God (Otten), 185
Baha'i, 167, 188
Bailyn, Bernard, 20, 28
Baker, William, 93
Bakhtin, Mikhail, 220n15
Balkans, 151, 167
Bancroft, George, 40, 83, 84, 115, 116, 118
Banks, Nathaniel P., 121
Baptist, 28, 73, 75, 112, 113, 115, 120, 158, 169, 177, 186, 205; American, 180; missions, 132; Southern, 187; United, 111
Baptist Cascade Church, 198
Baptist periodicals: *Baptist Memorial and Monthly Record*, 57; *Baptist Missionary Magazine*, 127; *Baptist Press*, 267; *Baptist Quarterly Review*, 111, 112
Barash, Jeffrey Andrew, 224n33
Barbados, 25
Barry, William, 47
Bartol, C. A., 43

INDEX

Bates, M. Searle, 181
Bauer, Gary, 186
Bavaria, Germany, 75
Baxter, Richard, 63
Beach, Harlan P., 127, 129, 133, 134
Beatles, 172
Bee, Hamilton P., 122
Beecher, Edward, 61
Beecher, Lyman, 60, 61, 64, 81
Beginnings of New England, The (Fiske), 118
Bell, Duncan S. A., 215–16n6, 223n26
Benedict Option, The (Dreher), 193
Benkovic, Johnnette, 199, 207
Bercovitch, Sacvan, 6
Berlin, Germany, 75
Bermuda, 25
Bharati, Agehananda, 173
Bible, 32, 39, 41, 46, 59, 84, 94, 95, 131, 132, 137, 196, 206; belief in, 31; Douai, 65; Jefferson, 66; King James, 42; knowledge of, 34, 38; suppression of, 85, 128
Bible Wars, 54, 65
Birth of a Nation, The (film), 144
black Americans, 218n10, 229n57. *See also* African Americans
black churches, 16, 17, 178, 179, 180. *See also* Congress of National Black Churches
Black Legend of the Americas, 77
Blanshard, Paul, 175
Bloom, William, 218–19n12, 220n15
blot out, 42, 43, 44, 49, 50; the Amalekites, 15, 33; from memory, 33, 46, 47, 53
B'nai B'rith, 112
Boggs, Lilburn, 48
Bolivar, Simon, 77
Bolivia, 125
Bondy, Joseph, 113
Book of Mormon, 52, 167
Boston, MA, 3, 4, 15, 45, 47, 52, 54, 62, 63, 68, 76, 78, 79, 82, 84, 85, 105, 111
Boston Investigator, 46
Bowdoin Street Church, 64
Bradstreet, Anne, 38
brainwashing, 166, 167, 168, 169, 170, 171, 173, 184
Brain-Washing in Red China (Hunter), 168
Branch Davidians, 171
Brandt, John L., 105
Brand 24, 267n24
Brazil, 76, 84, 86, 97, 125, 128, 132, 134
Bridgman, George H., 141
Brief History of the Pequot War (Mason), 19
British, 18, 19, 21, 28, 34. *See also* English
Breckinridge, John C., 122
Bromley, David C., 169
Brookings Institution, 192
Brown, Harold G., 215n3

Brownback, Sam, 197
Brownson, Orestes, 50
Brown v. Board of Education, 178
Brutus, 64
Buchanan, James, 51, 91
Buchman, Frank, 167
Buckingham, William A., 136
Buddhism, 261n96
Budryte, Dovile, 222n24
Buffalo, NY, 106
Burke, Edmund, 29
Burke, Thomas Martin Aloysius, 105
Burleson, Hugh Latimer, 108
Burma, 4, 73, 74
Bushnell, Horace, 147

Cahoon, B. B., 29
California, 51
California Baptist University, 198
Caligula, 29
Calvin, John, 84, 114
Calvinism, 115, 116, 148
Campbell, Alexander, 35
Campbell, David, 223n28
Campbell, James, 85
Campbell, Joan, 179
Campbell, Joseph, 172
Camping, Harold, 201. *See also* May 21 Movement
Campus Crusade for Christ, 196
Canaan, 18, 38, 40, 44
Canaanites, 40, 41, 43
Canada, 46
Candelin, Johan, 206
capital punishment, 35
Cardenas, Cuba, 123
Carey, Mathew, 82
Caribbean, 25, 121, 122, 123, 125
Cass, Elizabeth, 91
Cass, Lewis, 90, 91, 92, 93, 95, 96, 97, 123, 138, 142, 151, 244n129, 244n134
Cass, Lewis, Jr., 91
Catholic Association for International Peace, 181
Catholic church, 4, 29, 58, 63, 64, 67, 69, 70, 75, 85, 86, 87, 92, 103, 135, 139, 141, 142, 164, 176; persecution of, 84, 100, 131
Catholic Eucharistic Congress, 106
Catholic Guild, 258n40
Catholicism, 46, 47, 49, 50, 65, 78, 88, 104, 107, 115, 142, 175, 177; American, 109; Austrian, 80; influence on Protestantism, 147; liberal, 167; Portuguese, 126; Spanish, 126
Catholics: American, 36, 58, 105, 109, 143, 164, 176; Irish, 63, 65, 70, 104, 242n104; Spanish, 79, 123, 135
Caul, David, 173
Central America, 125

276 INDEX

Channing, William Ellery, 67
Chaos of Cults, The (van Baalen), 166, 167
Chapin, Edwin, 67
Charles I, 19
Charles River, 64
Charleston, SC, 63
Charlestown, MA, 3, 64, 67, 78, 81, 82, 84, 88, 91, 92. *See also* Ursuline convent riots
Chauncy, Charles, 229n46
Chautauquian, 127
Cheeseman, Lewis, 60
Cheng, Samuel W. S., 184
Chicago, IL, 106, 113, 138, 139, 156, 172, 174
Chicago Daily Tribune, 117
Chicago Methodist Ministers Meeting, 139, 140, 141, 142, 143
Chico Courant, 42
Child, Lydia Marie, 26, 73
Chile, 92, 97, 132
China, 4, 5, 16, 61, 76, 88, 97, 190, 209; Christians in, 157, 194, 264n142; communist, 160, 161, 162, 166, 176, 184, 186, 202; loss of Most Favored Nation status, 188, 265n163; missionaries to, 128, 134, 152, 153
Chinese Exclusion Act, 171
Christian periodicals: *Christian Advocate*, 118, 157; *Christian Advocate and Journal*, 80, 86; *Christian Crusade Weekly*, 185; *Christian Examiner*, 81; *Christian Index*, 192; *Christianity and Crisis*, 157; *Christianity Today*, 195; *Christian Monitor*, 46; *Christian Nationalist Crusade*, 185; *Christian Observer*, 75, 85, 132; *Christian Register*, 85; *Christian Research Journal*, 192; *Christian Secretary*, 79; *Christian Statesman*, 76; *Christian Union*, 68; *Christian Watchman*, 81; *Christian World*, 93
Christian Anticult Movement (CAM), 169, 170
Christian Coalition, 173, 187; of Alabama, 210
Christian Crusade, 162
Christian Identity, 201, 202
Christianity, 3, 16, 29, 34, 37, 49, 52, 59, 61, 62, 90, 93, 95, 152, 162, 163, 164, 166, 172, 180, 184, 192, 195, 203; American, 66, 197, 199, 205, 209; early, 157; persecution of, 5, 153; progress of, 74, 86; Protestant, 4, 13, 73, 121, 145, 167; World, 154, 155, 156, 159, 160, 161, 183, 198, 211. *See also* Catholicism; evangelicalism; Protestantism
Christian Research Institute, 170
Christian Right, 186, 188, 192
Christmas, 26; Eve, 158; tree, 158
Church Arson Prevention Act, 179, 262–63n119
Church of England, 229n46
Church of Jesus Christ of Latter-Day Saints, 48, 143, 234n118. *See also* Book of Mormon; Mormonism
Cincinnati, OH, 47, 50, 111

city on a hill, 13, 24, 111, 189
civil liberty, 89, 123, 137, 138, 141
Civil Marriage Bill, 141
Civil Rights Act, 178
Civil Rights movement, 178
Civil War: American, 15, 40, 43, 50, 61, 102, 111, 121, 122, 123, 144, 151, 218n10; Spanish, 164
Clark, Francis E., 127
Clark, John B., 48
Clark, R. F., 69
Cleaveland, J. P., 44
Cleveland, Grover, 141
Clinton, Hillary Rodham, 90
Clinton, IA, 47
Clinton, Bill, 179, 188, 262–63n119, 265n163
Cloven Foot, The (Rector of Oldenwold), 62
Cochran, Gregory C., 198
Cold War, 5, 16, 17, 153, 154, 163, 182, 183, 186, 191, 201, 202, 258n43; anti-Catholicism during, 175, 177; early period, 157, 160, 165, 166, 190; late period, 168, 194; NRMs and, 170, 171, 172, 174
Colombia, 125
colonialism, 159, 221–22n20, 222n21
Colson, Chuck, 186, 262n105
Columbia College, 87
commerce, 85, 86, 87, 90, 91, 97, 98, 136, 137
Commission to Study the Bases of a Just and Durable Peace, 181
communism, 157, 160, 190, 208; and Catholicism, 175, 177; in China, 185; as a cult, 166, 167, 168, 169; as a religion, 5, 161, 162, 163, 164, 165, 258n43
Communism, Democracy, and Catholic Power (Blanshard), 175
Conant, Eben, 44
Concordia Journal, 203
Condit, Philip, 190
Confederacy, 40, 121, 122, 233n107
Confusion of Tongues (Ferguson), 166
Congregationalism, 28, 152, 229n46
Congregationalist, 131
Congress of National Black Churches, 179
Connecticut, 63, 112, 117; General Assembly of, 20
Connecticut River Valley, 19
conspiracy: Amalekite, 48, 59; Catholic, 16, 62, 63, 77, 79, 80, 176; communist, 161, 165, 167, 169, 170, 185; Jewish, 110; Muslim, 207, 209; NRM, 171, 172, 173; and secrecy, 62, 64, 68, 70, 107, 115; and sectarianism, 60; threat from, 17, 49, 58, 60, 71, 235–36n148
Cook, Harold, 156
Cook County, IL, 138
Cooper, Thomas, 65
Copts, 75
Costa Rica, 125
Cotton, John, 18

INDEX

covenant, 34, 38, 51
Covenant of the League of Nations, 150
Cradlebaugh, John, 51
Crawford, Charles, 38
Criminalization of Christianity, The (Folger), 197
Crocker, Joseph Henry, 113, 248n38
Cross and the Flag, The, 185
Crowe, W. S., 113, 117
Cuba, 121, 122, 123, 124, 125, 133
Cuban Americans, 105
Cults in Our Midst (Singer), 169
culture, 1, 7, 11, 12, 39, 53, 80, 171, 216n7, 222n21; American, 32, 54, 59, 152, 208; colonial New England, 25; European, 72; evangelical, 197, 203; Jewish, 38; local, 183; material, 37, 135; Native American, 24, 37, 147; political, 164; popular, 161, 172; print, 154; Protestant, 59, 73, 103, 147; South American, 131, 137; war, 192, 194
Cunningham, Jim, 206
Curtis, George Ticknor, 109

Dabney, Robert Lewis, 40
Daily Sun, 86
Daniel, Marjorie L., 150
David, King, 35
Davidson, James West, 46
Davis, Andrew Jackson, 67
Davis, Ashabel, 233n109
Davis, David Brion, 59
Davis, Forrest, 185
Davis, Thomas J., 114
Day, William Rufus, 141
Dayton, TN, 146
Dearborn Independent, 109
Decalogue, 52
Declaration of Human Rights, 181
Declaration of Independence, 132, 135
Deism, 72, 80
democracy, 9, 59, 65, 71, 77, 82, 112, 114, 148, 164, 166; American, 15, 61, 62, 76, 80, 104, 149, 171, 177; Protestantism and, 69, 150
Dennis, James S., 131
Denver, CO, 199
Deseret, 107
Detroit, MI, 91, 164
Deuteronomy, 33
Devil, 21, 38, 162, 168
Dickens, Charles, 233n109
Diderot, 81
Dieffenbach, Albert C., 120, 248n36
Dilley, Robert D., 185
diplomacy, 7, 90, 124, 136, 142, 188, 189
Disciples of Christ, 35
discrimination, 12, 128; against American Muslims, 193; against Asians, 171, 174; against

Christians, 193, 196; against immigrants, 104; against Jews, 98, 205
Dobson, James, 192
Dolma, Tsultrim, 187
domestic policy, 7, 10, 99, 108, 122, 124, 129, 179, 218–19n12
Domino Theory, 171
Dreher, Rod, 192, 193
Druses, 61
Dudley, Irving B., 141
Dulles, John Foster, 163, 180, 181, 182, 183, 255n4, 264n135
Dulles Commission, 155
Dwight, Timothy, 27, 80

Early, Jubal, 122
East, 61, 172, 173, 221n20. *See also* Orient; *Orientalism* (Said); Said, Edward
Easter, 161
Eberstadt, Mary, 193
economics, 121, 123, 171, 243n118
Ecuador, 125
ecumenism, 154, 164
Edinburgh Missionary Conference, 155
Edwards, Jonathan, 34, 38, 80
Eggleston, Edward, 41
Egypt, 32, 33, 52, 186, 198
Eisenhower, Dwight D., 161
Elements of General History (Woodhouselee), 114
Eliot, John, 37, 231n81
Ellis, George Edward, 117
Elson, Ruth Miller, 113, 248n45
Emancipation of Massachusetts, The (Adams), 114, 118
emotion, 7, 71, 183, 188, 191, 202, 217n8, 218n11; connection, 152, 159, 211, 222n24; feeling, 7, 10, 23, 31, 67, 68, 70, 81, 83, 103, 138, 147, 157, 160, 182, 198, 208, 211, 217n8, 218–20n12, 220n14, 257n25; language, 58, 80, 93, 167, 185; responsivity, 67, 160, 190, 197; scripts, 156
empathy, 159, 215n3
empire, 74, 76, 77, 78, 117, 121, 122, 154
Encyclopedia of the Social Sciences, 6
Encyclopédie, 81
End of White Christian America, The (Jones), 193
England, 18, 20, 38, 57, 75, 145, 226n37
English, 19, 33, 35, 46; colonists, 20, 21, 22, 23, 24, 27, 36, 37, 40, 44; settlements, 1; writers, 24, 29, 39, 45, 58. *See also* British
Enlightenment, 14
Episcopalian Church, 28. *See also* Anglican Church in America
Erikson, Erik, 218n12, 220n15
Esau, 32. *See also* Amalekites
eschatology, 46, 194, 201, 235–36n148
Esper, Joseph M., 207

278   INDEX

Estabrooks, Paul, 206
Ethiopia, 186
ethnicity, 6, 171, 224–26n35, 243n110, 263n123
Europe, 4, 25, 56, 71, 72, 75, 95, 125, 130, 134, 140, 151; Catholics in, 84, 85, 86; early modern, 2, 59; Eastern, 5, 167, 168, 194; Protestantism in, 154; religious intolerance in, 92, 93
Evangelical Alliance, 97, 121, 140
evangelicalism, 27, 70, 76, 161, 175, 176, 186, 191, 195; and American politics, 2, 5, 17, 201; and anti-communism, 163, 165; conservative, 146, 162, 185; and missions, 52, 132, 133, 134, 152, 156, 194; organizations, 96, 131, 177, 188, 196; persecution complex, 203, 205, 210; white, 192
Evarts, William M., 151
Eyerman, Ron, 229n57

Facebook, 267n24
Facts About Communism and Our Churches, The (Hargis), 185
Falwell, Jerry, Jr., 201
Family Research Council, 189
Faneuil Hall, 81
Farr, Thomas F., 186, 188, 189
Father Coughlin, 164, 165
Father Divine, 169
Fawkes, Guy, 61
Federal Bureau of Investigation, 161, 260n80
Federal Council of Churches, 155
federalism, 81
Female Seminary, 65
Ferguson, Charles Wright, 166, 167
Feuerbach, Ludwig, 222n21
Fiery Cross, 146
Fight with Rome, The (Fulton), 139
Finney, Charles Grandison, 34, 60
Finney, Patrick, 216n7
First Amendment, 12, 54, 71, 100, 224–25n35
First Inaugural Address, 149
First Liberty Institute, 204
First Settlers of New England, The (Child), 26
Fish, Hamilton, 121, 124, 127
Fisher, George Parker, 114
Fisher, Sydney George, 67
Fiske, John, 118, 250n71
Florence, Italy, 94
Folger, Janet L., 197
Ford, Henry, 109
Ford, Samuel Howard, 111
Foreign Conspiracy Against the Liberties of the United States, The (Morse), 62, 64, 79
Foreign Missions Conference of North America, 155, 181
foreign policy, 4, 10, 91, 96, 98, 99, 110, 125, 216–17n7, 218n12, 223n27, 224–26n35; American, 11, 88, 90, 94, 122, 141, 142, 148, 162, 165, 189, 208,

211; Protestant efforts to influence, 5, 15, 108, 177, 201
forgetting, 2, 7, 29, 30, 31; extermination and, 44, 45; national, 8, 33, 54, 114, 218n10, 218–19n12, 221–22n20; practice of, 9, 12, 13, 34, 113, 223n26, 224–26n35. See also remembering
Forrest, Edwin, 26
Fort Wayne, IN, 59
Four Freedoms, 180, 263n123
"4 Stages of Islamic Conquest," 208
Fourth of July, 48, 57, 59, 65
Fox News, 197
France, 98, 113, 215n3, 218n10, 224n35
Franco, Francisco, 164, 181
Franklin, Benjamin, 27, 28
Freedom and Religious Belief: A World Report, 196
freedom of worship, 97, 140, 180
freemasonry, 59, 61
French, 30, 37, 44, 46, 61, 94, 121, 122
French and Indian War, 45
French Canada, 104
Freud, Sigmund, 220n14, 222n21
Friends' Review, 115
frontier, 27, 41, 42
Frost, Stanley B., 106, 107
Fry, Birkett T., 122
Fuller Theological Seminary, 156, 201, 206, 260n84
Fulton, Justin D., 139
fundamentalism, 120, 155

Galveston, TX, 63
gender, 63, 170, 216–17n7, 224–26n35, 228n43
genocide, 13, 42, 53, 237n29; of Native Americans, 3, 4, 19, 33, 54, 58; of the Pequot, 41, 226n3
Genocide Watch, 206
geology, 127
Georgia, 28, 144, 149; state senate, 144
Germantown, IL, 106
Germany, 61, 92, 104, 113, 148, 151
Gladden, Washington, 62
Gleason, Philip, 6, 215n4
Glover, Robert Hall, 156
Goa, 76
God, 18, 20, 22, 23, 37, 39, 42, 51, 57, 134, 136, 158, 161, 162, 184, 189, 207, 232n88; commands violence, 3, 15, 20, 32, 33, 34, 35, 41, 46; obedience to, 133; providence of, 135, 156; worship of, 38, 43, 81, 90, 180; wrath of, 52
God Less America (Starnes), 197
God's Not Dead (film), 193
Goldberg, Jeffrey, 196
Gonzaga, Mary, 67
Gould, Philip, 228n43
Graham, Billy, 155, 160, 163, 201, 258n50
Graham, Franklin, 197
Grant, Ulysses S., 121

INDEX

Gratz, Benjamin, 84
Gratz, Rebecca, 84
Great Depression, 35, 107, 229n57
Greece, 93, 245n138
Greek Orthodox, 94
Greeleyville, SC, 178
Green, William Henry, 43
Greenwood, A. B., 42
Gregg, Josiah, 243n110
Griffith, D. W., 144
Gunpowder Plot, 61
Guy Fawkes Day, 47

Hagee, John, 201
Haight, Isaac C., 51
Halbwachs, Maurice, 223n26
Hale, John, 43
Hale, John P., 90
Hale, Salma, 27
Hallgren, Mauritz A., 144, 145
Hamburg, Germany, 75
Hanover, Germany, 75
Hardball, 204
Hare Krishna, 170
Hargis, Billy James, 162, 163, 185
Hart, Albert Bushnell, 115
Hartford, CT, 79
Harvard, 118, 127, 152, 169
Haun's Mill, MO, 48
Havana, Cuba, 105
Hay, John, 141, 142
Heathen Woman's Friend, 140
Hegel, Georg Wilhelm Friedrich, 220n15
Helms, Jesse, 168
Henry, Carl, 161
Henry Luce Professorship of World Christianity, 154
Heresies Exposed (Irvine), 166
heresy, 48, 58, 59, 70
Hessia, Germany, 75
Heyrman, Christine, 72
Hickok, Laurens P., 67
Higham, John, 104
Hilberg, Raul, 205
Hinduism, 74, 174, 261n96
History of All Nations, A (Goodrich), 43
History of American Baptist Missions in Asia, Africa, Europe, and North America (Merriam), 75
History of the American Indians (Adair), 38
History of the American People, A (Wilson), 149, 254n174
History of the Indian Tribes of North America (McKenny), 29
History of the Thirty Years' War (Schiller), 2
History of the United States (Hale), 27
History of the United States, from the Discovery of the American Continent to the Present Time, A (Bancroft), 40, 83, 115
History of the Work of Redemption, A (Edwards), 34, 38
History of Virginia, A (Howison), 57
Hixson, Walter L., 223n27
Hocking, William Ernest, 152
Hocking Report, 152. See also *Re-Thinking Missions* (Hocking)
Hodel, Donald, 187
Hofstadter, Richard, 235n148
Holocaust, 183, 202, 205, 222n23
Holy Land, 44, 61, 78, 79
Hong Kong, 76, 184
Hoover, J. Edgar, 161, 164, 165
Hope Leslie, or, Early Times in the Massachusetts (Sedgwick), 27
Hope of Israel (Israel), 37
Horn, Thomas, 205, 206
House Human Rights Committee, 186
House Un-American Activities Committee (HUAC), 162, 165, 176, 184, 185
Howison, Robert Reid, 57
How Religious Liberty Was Written into the American Constitution (Bondy), 113
Hubbard, William, 22
Hudson Institute, 186
Hughes, John, 95, 96, 98, 244n134
Huguenots, 30
human rights, 90, 155, 186, 263n124; movement in the U.S., 180, 181, 182, 185, 191, 200; organizations, 188, 224–25n35; violations, 190
Human Rights Watch, 195
Humboldt Times, 42
Hungarian Revolution, 91
Hunter, Edward, 168
Hunter, Robert M. T., 91
Huntington, Frederick D., 41
Hurlbut, Jesse Lyman, 205
Hyde, Orson, 50

Iberia, 61, 79
identity, 2, 96, 215n4, 215–16n6, 216n7, 217n8; American, 1, 6, 11, 13, 24, 30, 31, 54, 55, 99, 129, 143, 147, 163, 202, 203, 209; Anglo-Protestant, 102, 147, 175; black, 178, 229n57; collective, 220n14; construction of, 25, 27, 103; English, 24; male, 236n11; national, 6, 7, 8, 9, 10, 11, 14, 31, 54, 99, 103, 130, 160, 209, 217n8, 218nn11–12, 221–22n20, 222n21, 223nn27–28; New England, 25; racial, 25, 149; religio-national, 111; religious, 146, 147, 211; spatial, 110; white, 26
Iews in America (Thorowgood), 38
Illinois, 54, 138
Imagined Communities (Anderson), 217n8, 218n10, 220n13

280 INDEX

imagined community, 33, 217n8, 220–21n15
immigration, 15, 63, 210; Asian, 171; Catholic, 69, 103, 104, 142; Muslim, 1
Immigration Act: of 1917, 171; of 1924, 171
imperialism, 138, 159. *See also* empire
Independent, 76, 77
India, 73, 74, 167, 172, 261n96
Indians, The (Apess), 38
Indian Wars, 22, 23, 24, 26, 30
indigenes, 135
Ingersoll, Robert, 30
Inquisition, 77, 79, 85, 106, 113, 117, 130, 131, 132
internal orientalism, 102, 246n1
International Christian Concern, 208
International Day of Prayer for the Persecuted Church, 196
International Foreign Missions Association, 156
International Jew, The, 109
International Missionary Council, 181
International Peace Mission, 170
international relations, 2, 6, 7, 8, 9, 10, 13, 14, 90, 116, 124, 148, 176, 182, 191, 218–19n12, 224–25n35; American, 15, 31, 67; cultural turn in, 216n7; religion in, 181, 210; researchers, 11, 218n11
International Religious Freedom Act of 1998 (IRFA), 5, 180, 188, 265n160
In the Lion's Den (Shea), 187
Introduction to the Science of Government (Young), 57
Iowa, 50
Iowa Conservative Party, 185
Iran, 186, 209, 271n91
Iraq, 203, 204, 209
Ireland, 86, 87
Ireland, John, 140
Iron Curtain, 16, 185, 194, 202
Irvine, William C., 167, 259n64
Irving, Washington, 67
Islam, 52, 53, 67, 180, 195. *See also* Muslim
Islamophobia, 210
Israel, 37, 38, 39, 40, 41, 200; American relations with, 201; children of, 52
Israel, Menasseh ben, 37
Italy, 4, 60, 76, 85, 86, 87, 93, 105, 113
It's Dangerous to Believe (Eberstadt), 193

Jackson, Andrew, 31, 91
Jackson, Thomas "Stonewall," 40
Jacobs, George, 112
Jamaica, 25
Japan, 97, 148, 224n35, 261n96
Jefferson, Thomas, 65, 66, 71, 122, 149, 244n129, 254n181
Jeffress, Robert, 205

Jehovah's Witnesses, 36, 102, 110, 167, 170
Jesuit Juggling (Baxter), 63
Jesuits, 62, 65, 76, 139
Jesus Christ, 37, 169, 186, 199
Jewish: Americans, 98, 165, 172; culture, 37, 38; discrimination, 98, 102, 109, 110, 111, 151, 205; identification, 201, 202; people, 5, 84, 86, 109, 110, 112, 144, 162, 186, 205, 243n118; relationship to Amalekites, 14, 15, 31, 32, 35, 58; self-understanding, 109
John, Atilio Okot, 187
Johnson, Andrew, 136
Johnson, Lyndon B., 161
Johnston, Albert, 51
Joint Committee on Religious Liberty, 181
Jones, Robert P., 192–93
Jonesboro, TN, 46
Joshua, 40, 52
Judah, 37, 41
Judaism, 109, 165
Judson, Adoniram, 73, 74
Judson, Ann Hasseltine, 73
Jung, Carl, 172
justice, 14, 22, 34, 35, 54, 191; racial, 149

Kasson, John A., 151
Kendall, George Wilkins, 77
Kennedy, John F., 176
Kentucky, 89
Kenya, 209
Kidd, Thomas S., 232n88
Kim, Kyung Rai, 184
King, Charles, 87
King, Jeff, 205
King, Jonas, 93
King, Martin Luther, Jr., 178
Kingdom of the Cults, The (Martin), 169
King Philip's War, 21, 22, 24, 25
Kinney, Bruce, 53
Kirk, Russell, 168
Kirtland, OH, 50
Klansmen (White), 120
Knights of Columbus, 145, 164
Knowles, James D., 73
Knowles riot, 47
Know-Nothingism, 62, 66, 86, 145
Know-Nothing Party, 62, 95
Korean War, 164, 169
Kosovo, 222n25
Kremlin, 175
Kristeva, Julia, 220n15, 222n24
Ku Klux Klan (KKK), 5, 107, 117, 120, 144, 146, 167, 170, 174, 178
Kung Fu (television show), 172
Kupperman, Karen, 228n26

INDEX

LaHaye, Tim, 201
Lamanites, 52
Land, Richard, 186
Landscape of Freedom (Hallgren), 145
Las Casas, Bartolomé de, 37
LaRouche, Lyndon, 173
Late, Great Planet Earth (Lindsey), 201
Latin: language, 68, 69; race, 129
Latin America, 4, 121, 124, 125, 135, 136, 137, 157, 194, 252–53n141
Lausanne, 156
Lazier, Benjamin, 182
League for the Protection of American Institutions, 47
League of Nations, 148, 150, 155
Lebanon, 241n64
Lebow, Richard Ned, 223n28
Lee, John, 138, 139, 143, 150, 151
Lee, John D., 51
Legal Society, 188
legislation, 13, 17, 179, 186, 210
Leo XII (pope), 139
León, Pedro Cieza de, 37
Lepore, Jill, 24, 229n58
Levin, Lewis C., 86, 243n118
Levinas, Emmanuel, 220n15, 221n16
Liberator, The, 70
Liberia, 89
Liberty University, 201
Libya, 271n91
Life, 118
Life of Mrs. Ann Judson, Late Missionary to Burmah (Knowles), 73
Lifton, Robert Jay, 169
Limbaugh, David, 196
Limbaugh, Rush, 196
Lincoln, Abraham, 44, 139, 145
Lindsell, Harold, 156
Lindsey, Hal, 201
literature: Anglophone, 34; anti-Catholic, 63, 146; anti-NRM, 168; colonial, 23, 25; English, 44; missionary, 72, 74; religious, 36, 62, 82, 162, 166, 169, 197
Littel's Living Age, 52
Little Rock, AR, 262–63n119
Liu, Tsin-tsai, 184
Lollards, 85
Lorimer, George, 115
Lost Cause, 148, 254n174
Louisiana, 66, 100
Lovewell, John, 40
Lowery, Charles, 162
Lowrie, John M., 59
Luce, Henry, 163
Lutherans, Missouri Synod of, 203

Macao, 76
Madiai, Francesco, 94
Madiai, Rosa, 94
Madiai Affair, 93, 94, 95
Madison, James, 1, 71
Madriz, José María Castro, 136
Magnalia (Mather), 38
Magruder, John B., 122
Maine, 22, 63
Malony, Newton, 171
Manifest Destiny, 27, 89
Manypenny, George W., 42
Maritain, Jacques, 264n133
market revolution, 85, 243n115
Markham, Reuben, 163, 167
Marlborough, Duke of, 39
Marshall, Paul, 187
Martin, Harry V., 173
Martin, Walter Ralston, 169, 170
martyrdom, 40, 131, 195, 198, 199, 200, 204
Marvel Comics, 161
Marxism, 17, 208
Maryland, 45, 47
Mason, Carol, 202
Mason, John, 19, 20
Massachusetts, 18, 29, 30, 83, 112, 114, 118, 119, 174
Massachusetts Bay colony, 19, 23, 34, 84, 158
Massachusetts Historical Society, 117
Massasoit, 21
Masters of Deceit (Hoover), 165
Mather, Cotton, 22, 36, 38, 115
Matthews, Chris, 204
Maximilian I (emperor), 121
Mayflower Hotel, 186
Mayhew, Jonathan, 57, 229n46
May 21 Movement, 201. *See also* Camping, Harold
McAlvany, Don, 206
McCarthy, Joseph, 164, 165, 176
McDuffie, James Y., 42
McGilvary, Daniel, 74
McGuffey's New Fifth Eclectic Reader, 57
McKenney, Thomas Loraine, 29
McKim, Randolph H., 131
McKinley, William, 136, 141
McLoughlin, William G., 163
McNeilly, James H., 135
Memorial and Remonstrance Against Religious Assessments (Madison), 71
memory, 69, 100, 221–22n20; American, 44, 96, 147, 224n33; collective, 7, 12, 22, 23, 33, 44, 218–20n12, 223n26, 224n33, 237–38n29; of enemies, 42, 44, 45, 47; process of, 8, 29, 31, 43, 233n109; repressed, 2, 3, 58, 126, 237n29; of trauma, 4, 10, 30, 53, 130, 216–17n7. *See also* forgetting; remembering

282 INDEX

Mennonite, 159
Merchants' Magazine and Commercial Review, 87
Meriden, CT, 112
Merkel, Angela, 195
Merriam, Edmund, 132
Message for America (Dilley), 185
Messenger and Advocate, 50
Metacom, 21, 22, 26. *See also* Massasoit; Philip, King
Metamora (Stone), 26
Methodism, 50, 75, 108, 120, 131, 134, 137, 138, 139, 145, 167, 205
Methodist League Against Communism, Fascism, and Unpatriotic Pacifism, 165
Methodist Review, 47, 133
Methodist Rock River Association, 142
Mexican War, 77, 89, 99
Mexico, 47, 77, 78, 79, 84, 89, 97, 99, 121, 122, 125, 133
Miami, FL, 105
Michelet, Jules, 68
Michigan, 90, 91, 207, 208
Michigan Christian Advocate, 157
Middle Ages, 132
Middle East, 241n64
Midway, 121
militia, 48, 50, 51
millennialism, 202, 269n54
millennium, 38, 39, 46
Miller, Perry, 32
Milwaukee, WI, 47
missionaries, 37, 73, 74, 79, 90, 123, 128, 130, 139, 146, 158, 167, 206, 241n64, 243n108, 243n110
Missionary Herald, 140
mission field, 75, 108, 123, 129, 134, 135, 152, 162, 176
missions, 108, 133, 150, 151, 156, 183, 206; in Africa, 176; American, 152, 159, 177, 224–25n35; Catholic, 76, 86, 175; evangelical, 132, 133, 134, 156, 194; overseas, 72, 73; Protestant, 16, 78, 93, 108, 123, 128, 129, 135, 137, 181; in South America, 134, 135, 136
Mississippi, 90
Mississippi River, 48, 127
Missouri, 48, 50, 52, 54
Mitchell, Samuel Augustus, 86, 243n108
modernism, 120
Mohammed, 53
Monroe, James, 122
Monroe, WA, 198
Monroe Doctrine, 121, 124, 125
Moody Bible Institute, 156
Moon, Sun Myung, 170, 172, 182
Moorti, Sujata, 220n14
Moral Re-Armament, 167
Moran, Patrick, 95
Mormon, 112, 234n113, 234n118; communities, 48,

108, 109; leaders, 50, 51, 52, 53, 59; scripture, 52, 59; violence, 70
Mormonism, 33, 49, 50, 59, 60, 70, 109, 235n133; as the Amalekites, 52, 53; as a foreign country, 108
Mormonism: The Islam of America (Kinney), 53
Mormon Usurpation, The (Nimmo), 108
Mormon Wars, 54, 88, 150
Morris, Samuel W., 90
Morse, Jedidiah, 80
Morse, Samuel, 62, 64, 79, 80, 81, 82
Moses, 33, 35, 40, 52
mosque, 225–26n35
Moss, Candida, 268
Most Favored Nation (MFN) status, 188, 265n163. *See also* China
Mott, John, 146
Mountain Meadows massacre, 51, 70
multiculturalism, 152
Murch, James DeForest, 176
Muslim, 17, 74, 79, 152, 171, 180, 190, 207, 245n137; American, 193; immigration, 1, 210; nations, 5, 75, 181, 208, 209, 210, 266n9; persecution, 186, 209, 266n9. *See also* Islam
Mystery of Israel's Salvation Opened, The (Mather), 38
Mystic, CT, 19, 20, 21, 27, 41
mysticism, 61, 173
myth, 10, 23, 165, 203, 223n26, 223n27, 223–24n28
myth of Ham, 43
Myths and Memories of the Nation (Smith), 215–16n5

Name of War, The (Lepore), 24
Napa Sentinel, 173
Napoleon III, 121
Narrative of the Late Massacres, A (Franklin), 27
Narrative of the Texan Santa Fé Expedition (Kendall), 77
Narrative of the Wars in New England (Hubbard), 22
Nash, Gary B., 239n41
nation, 1, 9, 10, 17, 26, 28, 31, 50, 61, 62, 80, 82, 93, 110, 112, 121, 122, 129, 136, 137, 149, 191, 217n8, 218nn10–11, 222n21, 222n24; Catholic, 77, 84; Christian, 6, 90, 145, 166, 167, 192, 196, 209, 210, 212; danger to, 103, 107; essence of, 7, 8, 13, 94, 99, 100, 185, 189; and race, 134; and religion, 11, 51, 55, 128, 162, 169, 179, 224–26n35. *See also* state
Nation, The, 144
National Association of Evangelicals (NAE), 179, 186, 196, 262–63n119
National Church Arson Task Force, 179, 262–63n119
National Council of Churches (NCC), 177, 179, 188, 262–63n119

INDEX

National Council of Congregational Churches, 136
National Era, 96
nationalism, 209, 211, 215–16n6, 217n8
Native American, 86
Native American Party, 65, 66
Native American peoples: Algonquians, 19; Cherokee, 26; Mohawks, 22; Mohegans, 19; Mosquito, 125; Narragansett, 19, 39; Niantic, 19; Pequot, 19, 20, 21, 27, 41, 53, 226n3, 228n43; Sioux, 37; Wampanoag, 19, 21, 22
Native Americans, 3, 12, 18, 21, 28, 37, 42, 54, 67, 70, 108, 218n10, 221n16; as Amalekites, 32, 34, 35, 36, 40, 41, 43, 45. *See also* American Indians; Native American peoples
nativism, 102, 243n118
Nativist Party, 62
Nauvoo, IL, 48, 50
Nauvoo Times and Seasons, 50
Neal, Lynn S., 120
Neely, Thomas B., 137
Nephites, 52
Nero, 29
Neumann, Iver B., 220n15, 221n16
Nevins, William, 63
New Age, 169
new anti-Catholicism, 175
Newark, NJ, 44
Newark Daily Advertiser, 95
New England, 3, 19, 20, 23, 38, 113, 117; anti-Catholicism in, 47; colonial, 13, 14, 24, 25, 26, 34, 36, 39, 54, 82, 111, 114, 115, 121; Native Americans in, 41; as the Promised Land, 18; Puritans in, 116, 158; self-understanding, 21; seventeenth-century, 6
New Englander, 60
New Englander and Yale Review, 69
New Englanders, 18, 20, 22, 23, 24, 25, 26, 34, 36, 37, 39, 46, 115; colonial, 3, 32, 40; early, 28, 45, 53, 57, 69, 82, 117, 145
New-England Magazine, 79
New England's Crisis (Tompson), 22
New France, 25
New Hampshire, 27, 90
New Haven, CT, 79
New Jersey, 63, 113
New London, 20
New Mexico, 52
New Order, 201
New Orleans, LA, 62, 63
New Religious Movements (NRMs), 16, 166, 190, 261n100
New Spain, 25, 221n16
New Testament, 37, 46, 49, 158, 198
New World, 34, 116, 117, 127, 145
New York, 28, 48, 52, 63, 95, 105, 154, 181

New York City, 62, 68
New York Evangelist, 75, 84
New York Freeman's Journal, 95
New York Herald, 131
New York Observer, 59, 74
New York Times, 50, 112, 117, 172, 181, 185, 190, 196
New Zealand, 167
Nickles, Don, 188
Niebuhr, H. Richard, 158
Niebuhr, Reinhold, 157
Niles, Hezekiah, 56
Niles' Weekly Register, 56
9/11, 208, 209
Noah, Mordecai Manuel, 71
Noble, Alan, 203
non-governmental organizations (NGOs), 180
Noonan, John T., Jr., 224n35
Norfolk, England, 37
North America, 11, 15, 23, 28, 34, 60, 68, 72, 100, 102, 111, 127, 218n10, 229n47, 234n116; British, 30, 36; colonial, 37, 40; pre-Columbian, 52
North American Review, 30, 40, 47, 61
North British Review, 29
North Carolina, 57
North Korea, 5, 168, 184, 187, 195, 271n91
Norton, Anne, 221n16
Norway, 92
Norwich, CT, 117
Notre Dame College, anti-KKK riot, 146
Nun, The (Sherwood), 63
Nuremberg trials, 263n123
Nusaris, 61

Obama, Barack, 17, 209, 210
Obergefell v. Hodges, 192, 193
Odeon theater, 26
Office of International Religious Freedom, 186
Ohio, 90, 155
Oklahoma Baptist University, 203
Oklahoma Wesleyan University, 196
Oldenburg, Germany, 75
Old South Church, 64
Old Testament, 3, 14, 15, 30, 37, 39, 41, 42, 45, 50, 53, 61; Amalekites in the, 31, 32, 33, 34, 43, 46, 52, 58
Old World, 72, 116, 117, 121
O'Leary, Catherine, 139
O'Leary, Patrick, 139
Olive Branch, The, 60
Open Doors USA, 195, 208
Operation Rescue, 202
oppression, 15, 17, 18, 75, 83, 161; Catholic, 131, 143; political, 87; Puritan, 84; religious, 5, 181, 203
Orient, 9, 72, 222n21
Orientalism (Said), 9, 221n18, 221–22n20, 222n21
Orr, Charles, 19

Ostend Manifesto, 122
othering: spatial, 102, 103, 107, 109, 110, 111, 129; temporal, 116, 120
Otis, Harrison Gray, 81
Otten, Herman J., 185
Our South American Cousins (Taylor), 127

Pacific Northwest, 42
paganism, 60, 87, 161
Pakistan, 186, 198
Palestine, 78, 93
Papacy and the Civil Power, The (Thompson), 69
Papal Conspiracy Exposed and Protestantism Defended, The (Beecher), 61
Paraguay, 125
paranoid style, 68, 115, 146–47, 235n148, 244–45n134
Paranoid Style in American Politics and Other Essays, The (Hofstadter), 235–36n148
Park Street Church, 64
Passion of the Christ, The (film), 199
Penn, William, 38
Pennsylvania, 27, 28, 65, 90, 198
Pentecostalism, 177, 186
Penzotti, Francisco G., 131, 140
People's Church in Chicago, 113
Peoples Temple, 170
Peoria, IL, 139
Pequot River, 20
Pequot War, 19, 20, 21, 25, 87
Perkins, Tony, 204
Pernambuco, Brazil, 128
Persecution (Limbaugh), 196
persecution complex, 200, 203
Peru, 125
Pew Research Center, 195, 196
Phases of Religion in America (Crowe), 113
Philadelphia, PA, 3, 4, 15, 45, 54, 63, 64, 66, 76, 105, 117
Philadelphia Riots of 1844, 60, 65, 67, 68, 70, 78, 80, 84, 85, 86, 87, 88, 89, 91, 92, 100
Philip, King, 22, 26. *See also* Massasoit; Metacom
Philippines, 129, 130, 133, 136
Philistines, 39
Piazza Santa Maria Novella, 94
Piedmont, 28
piety, 23, 118
Pilgrims, 21, 41, 117
Pillar of Fire Church, 120
Pinterest, 267
Pius IX (pope), 94, 104
Plea for the West, A (Beecher), 61, 64
Plymouth Colony, 21, 22, 41
political liberty, 112, 116, 119, 120, 137
politics, 2, 9, 23, 147, 157, 200, 215–16n6, 229n46, 235n148, 243n118; affectual, 182, 183, 218n11; do-

mestic, 122; and economics, 121; and missions, 89, 155; partisan, 196, 197; and religion, 96, 103
Polk, James K., 122, 124, 135
polygamy, 51, 53, 70, 143
Pong, Peter Chu, 184, 185
pope, 62, 85, 105, 128, 140, 175
Pope, Charles, 207
Pope Day, 47
Popery (Brownlee), 106
populism, 120
Porter, W. C., 128
Portugal, 4, 76, 77, 80, 126, 130
Portuguese Sephardim, 71
post-Christian America, 210, 212
postcolonialism, 9
power, 2, 12, 14, 30, 41, 53, 84, 85, 109; American, 97, 102, 125, 134, 235–36n148, 243n118; Catholic, 76, 77, 80, 132, 139, 244n134; economic, 11; European, 122, 124, 125, 127; and international relations, 7, 91, 122, 164, 183, 189, 223n27; political, 17, 194; Protestant, 121, 146; religious, 65, 69, 70, 155, 188, 200, 203, 211, 224–25n35
praeparatio evangelica, 37
Presbyterianism, 50, 65, 66, 120, 157
Presbyterian Ministerial Association, 50
Preston, Andrew, 142, 143
Prince, Thomas, 19
Princeton, 131
Princeton Review, 65, 66
Prison Fellowship, 196
projection, 9, 17, 125, 176, 209, 221n20, 222n21, 224n35; of intolerance, 56, 134, 178; spatial, 15, 224–26n35
Promised Land, 18, 23, 28, 111
Protestant Episcopal Church, 41, 69
Protestant International, 154, 155, 175, 255n1. *See also* world Christianity
Protestantism: American, 4, 12, 15, 17, 22, 34, 46, 54, 77, 95, 126, 134, 145, 156, 157, 223n27; and Catholicism, 48, 49, 61, 63, 64, 68, 69, 75, 76, 85, 96, 98, 107, 143, 147, 175, 237n29, 240n51, 260n81; and communism, 164, 165, 166, 176; evangelical, 152, 176, 192; and intolerance, 3, 5, 47, 67, 78, 82, 83, 84, 88; and Jews, 110; mainline, 155, 165; and the Middle East, 78, 79; and missions, 16, 73, 74, 113, 123, 135, 177; and Mormonism, 108; and South America, 130, 131, 132, 139, 140, 141; and space, 103, 104, 105; white, 12, 150, 193; world, 154, 155, 183, 198. *See also* evangelicalism
Protestant Missions in South America (Beach et al.), 127
Protestant Reformation, 46, 59
Protocols of the Elders of Zion, 109
Provins, Capuchin Pacifique de, 37
Prozorov, Sergei, 116
Prussia, 75

INDEX

psychoanalysis, 218n10, 218n12, 224n33, 237n29
psychohistory, 169
Public Religion Research Institute (PRRI), 192
Puebla Institute, 195
Puritan Origins of the American Self, The (Bercovitch), 6
Puritans, 3, 15, 24, 29, 47, 147, 228n34, 229n47; conflict with Native Americans, 27, 40, 41, 158, 159, 160; and intolerance, 113, 114, 115, 116, 117, 118, 119; memory of, 82, 83, 84, 116, 117, 118, 119, 120, 145; in New England, 28, 34, 36, 44, 88, 115, 119; theology, 38
Putnam's Monthly Magazine, 40

Quakers, 28, 30, 54, 66, 123, 150, 242n104, 255n182
Quarterly Review, 29
Quebec, 62

race, 7, 127, 225–26n35, 228n31, 228n34, 243n110, 261n96, 263n123; definitions of, 11; and gender, 63, 170, 216n7; and religion, 16, 23, 31, 148, 149, 151, 171, 177; and space, 25, 26, 27
Racial Equality Clause, 148, 149
Rajneeshpuram ashram, 173
Rauschenbusch, Walter, 180
Reagan, Ronald, 161, 162, 163
realpolitik, 157
Reconstruction, 151
Red China Lobby, The (Davis), 185
Reed, Rebecca, 64
religion, definition of, 224–26n35
Religion and State Project, 195
religious community, 12, 70, 192
religious conflict, 12, 14, 28, 34, 48, 54, 96, 149, 218n10. *See also* religious intolerance; religious persecution; religious violence
religious cult, 166, 168, 169, 172
religious difference, 29, 63, 71, 171, 229n45
religious diversity, 65
religious doctrine, 11, 13, 14, 178
religious freedom, 1, 12, 14, 28, 56, 57, 75, 120, 177, 224–26n35; and commerce, 87, 89, 90, 137; enemies of, 208; and foreign policy, 90, 93, 99, 142, 143, 180, 181; promotion of, 31, 71, 111, 112, 113, 117, 129, 130, 143, 150, 155, 178, 182, 188, 189; protection of, 13, 16, 197; and the state, 81, 102, 136, 190, 224n35. *See also* religious liberty
religious hierarchy, 80
Religious Intelligencer, 73, 74, 79
religious intolerance, 14, 45, 80, 111, 112, 138, 216n7; in America, 53, 54, 120, 126, 130, 134, 135, 140, 142, 143, 149, 154, 165, 166, 178, 189, 211; and foreign policy, 96, 97; history of, 1, 2, 5, 6, 11, 13, 17, 29, 30, 113, 114, 115, 224–26n35; international, 71, 73, 76, 77, 78, 92, 93, 132, 133, 151; justifications for, 14; of NRMs, 170, 177; overseas, 16, 17,

58, 88, 89, 91, 98, 179, 183, 244; problem of, 4, 10, 72, 74, 87, 100; and Protestantism, 81, 83, 85, 94; and violence, 15, 28, 102. *See also* religious conflict; religious persecution; religious violence
"Religious Intolerance in England," 75
religious liberty, 5, 87, 89, 93, 95, 140, 141, 177, 203; as ideal, 12, 56, 76, 116, 129, 130, 143, 170; overseas, 98, 99, 150, 151; and political liberty, 119, 128, 132, 135, 136, 137, 138, 142; the triumph of, 57, 58, 111, 112, 113, 114, 115, 117, 120. *See also* religious freedom
Religious Liberty: An Inquiry (Bates), 181
Religious Liberty in America (Snow), 248n33
Religious Liberty in South America (Lee), 140
Religious Liberty Task Force, 1, 11
Religious Liberty: The Great American Illusion (Dieffenbach), 120
religious militia, 30
religious opponents, 5, 28, 33, 42, 53, 61, 63, 82, 103, 108, 143, 146
religious persecution, 11, 74, 82, 149, 150, 180, 186, 187, 188, 189, 190, 195. *See also* religious conflict; religious intolerance; religious violence
Religious Persecution Behind the Iron Curtain, 186
religious policy, 67, 94
religious practice, 13, 68, 134, 143, 166, 178
religious press, 57, 72, 87, 95, 97, 110, 133, 140, 155
religious rhetoric, 43
Religious Right, 17, 188, 189, 190, 197, 200, 204, 211
religious rights, 57, 91, 94, 95, 98
religious ritual, 38
religious studies, 105, 224–25n35
religious tolerance, 85, 91, 100, 113, 116, 233n109
religious violence, 2, 14, 31, 55, 59, 79, 84, 114, 130, 224–26n35; colonial, 3, 28, 29; condemnation of, 4; memory of, 12, 13; and trauma, 30, 113, 143. *See also* religious conflict; religious intolerance; religious persecution
religious wars, 28, 29, 215n3
religious worldview, 23, 235–36n148
remembering, 2, 8, 10, 31, 33, 34, 44, 45, 119, 218n10, 218–19n12; process of, 7, 9, 29; and trauma, 13, 30, 54, 96, 114. *See also* forgetting
Renan, Ernest, 7, 217n9, 218n10
Renew America, 192
Republic, 56, 71
republicanism, 50, 228n43
Republican Party, 173, 193, 200, 208
Resende, Erica, 222n24
Reshetar, John Stephen, 168
Re-Thinking Missions (Hocking), 152
Revere, Paul, 120
Revolutionary War, 27, 64
Rhode Island, 19, 22, 28

286   INDEX

Rigdon, Sidney, 48
Rivkin, Ira, 188, 265n161
Rock River Annual Conference, 142
Rock River Association, 142
Rocky Mountains, 107
Rodino, Peter, 164
Roe v. Wade, 193
Romania, 75
Romanism, 59, 131, 132, 140. *See also* anti-Catholicism
Romanism and the Pope, 70
Rome, 46, 60, 62, 76, 86, 91, 95, 104, 105, 106, 109, 139, 140, 160
Rome's Policy Toward the Bible (Campbell), 85
Roosevelt, Franklin D., 180, 181, 263n123
Roosevelt, Theodore, 125
Rosenthal, A. M., 196
Rosicrucianism, 61
Rough Riders, 133
Rowlandson, Mary, 22, 35, 227n21
Russia, 88, 92, 109, 157, 160, 162, 165, 176, 181, 186, 209, 224n35
Russo-Turkish War, 151
Ruth, 32

Sabbath, 43
Said, Edward, 9, 72, 102, 221n18, 221n20, 222n21
Salem, MA, 30, 43
Salmanasar, 37
Salt Lake City, UT, 51, 52
same-sex marriage, 1, 17, 192, 200
Samuel, 32, 33, 35, 41
Sandwich Islands, 87
San Francisco, CA, 50
San Salvador, 125
Santiago, Chile, 132
Santo Domingo, 122, 124
Santorum, Rick, 205
Sassacus, 27
Satan, 39, 43, 46, 162, 163, 174, 235–36n148
Satanic panic, 171
Satanism, 160, 161
Saul, 32, 33, 34, 233n107
Scarborough, Rick, 197
Schäfer, Axel, 176
Schiller, Friedrich, 2
Schlafly, Phyllis, 197
School of World Mission, 156, 206
school prayer, 17, 200, 211
Scientific American, 70
Scopes, John, 146
Scopes trial, 185
Seaman, Ezra C., 69
Sears, E. H., 61
Second Vatican Council, 175, 176
secrecy, 33, 45, 48, 49, 54, 58, 59, 60, 62, 64, 68,

70, 71, 80, 107, 115. *See also* conspiracy; sect; sectarianism
sect, 59, 60, 61, 65, 67, 68, 74, 84, 115. *See also* sectarianism
sectarianism, 68, 70, 71, 116; accusations of, 58, 59; feeling of, 67; Protestant, 72; spirit of, 60, 65, 66, 115. *See also* sect
Sectarianism Is Heresy (Wylie), 65
secular, 113, 168, 203
secularism, 6, 17, 181, 193, 196, 207, 209
secularity, 164, 224–26n35
Sedgwick, Catharine Maria, 27, 228n43
Seeds of Persecution, 197
Sehat, David, 12
Seoul, South Korea, 184
Servetus, 114
Sessions, Jeff, 1, 11
Seventh-day Adventism, 35, 112, 119, 199
Sewall, Samuel, 38, 231n81
Seward, William, 121
sexuality, 21, 200, 211
Shackelford, Kelly, 204
Shakers, 60
Sharia law, 17
Shea, Nina, 186
Sheela, Ma Anand, 173
Sheen, Fulton J., 164
Shepard, Thomas, 20
Sherwood, Mary Martha, 63
Shupe, Anson D., 169
Siam, 74, 97, 119
Siberia, 92
Sims, Walter, 139
sin, 42, 43, 68, 69, 78, 83, 114, 134, 143, 199
Singer, Margaret, 169, 170, 172, 260n77
Sisters of Charity, 65
Sister St. John, 64
Six Nations Indians, 27
Six Pillars of Peace, 181
16th Street Baptist Church, 178
Sketches of China (Wood), 76
slaveowners, 63
slavery, 25, 40, 43, 122, 124, 238n30
slaves, 25, 28, 30, 43, 63, 89, 122, 148
Slotkin, Richard, 23, 24, 228n33
Smelser, Neil J., 222n23
Smith, Anthony D., 215–16n6
Smith, Chris, 188
Smith, George, 76
Smith, Gerald L. K., 185
Smith, Joseph, 48, 49, 50, 51, 53, 234n120
Smith, Michael E., 223n28
Smoot, Reed, 235n133
Snow, Charles M., 248n33
Social Gospel, 62, 180. *See also* Gladden, Washington; Rauschenbusch, Walter

INDEX

socialism, 60

social media, 267n24

Social Sources of Denominationalism (Niebuhr), 158

society, 59, 62, 80, 83, 137, 205, 215n2, 229n46; American, 49, 145, 173, 196; foundations of, 87; secret, 61

Somalia, 271n91

South Africa, 157

South America, 14, 101, 125; Catholicism in, 4, 77, 130, 135, 139, 160, 176; Protestants and, 15, 131, 132, 133, 134, 135, 136, 137, 138, 140, 141, 143, 150; and "twin" North America, 17, 89, 126, 127, 128, 129. *See also* missions

South Bend, IN, 146

South Carolina, 44

South Dakota, 108

Southern Baptists, 187

Southwark, PA, 65

space, 14, 15, 111; construction of, 25, 26, 27; cultural, 170; foreign, 103, 105, 106, 116, 134; and time, 157, 202

Spain, 25, 80, 88, 92, 160, 181; Catholic, 4, 77, 79, 83, 84, 87, 92, 164; conflict over Cuba, 122, 124, 126

Spanish American War, 123, 125, 132, 133

Specter, Arlen, 187

Speer, William, 128

Spiritual Dangers of the 21st Century (Esper), 207

Spiritual Direction, and Auricular Confession (Michelet), 68

Stalin, Joseph, 162

Stamp Out the Aquarian Conspiracy (LaRouche), 173

Standing Strong Through the Storm (Cunningham and Estabrooks), 206

Stanton, Gregory H., 206

Starnes, Todd, 197, 267n27

state, 8, 9, 69, 99, 221n16, 223n27; church and, 30, 88, 104, 120, 128, 130, 158, 162, 175, 176, 200, 210, 211; identification with the, 8, 103, 218–19n12, 223–24n28; individuals and the, 7, 218n10; slave, 122, 124. *See also* nation

Statement of Conscience, 180

St. Augustine Church, 65

St. Bartholomew massacre, 30

Stephens, Alexander H., 90

Sterk, Vernon J., 206

St. Louis, MO, 158

St. Michael's Church, 65

Stoler, Ann Laura, 257n25

Stone, John Augustus, 26

Stone, Nathan, 46

Stone Mountain, GA, 144

Storm Warning (McAlvany), 206

St. Paul, MN, 140

St. Philip Neri Church, 65

Straus, Oscar S., 115

Strong, Josiah, 121, 143

Stuart, Charles E., 90

Stuart, Elizabeth Emma, 93

Stuarts, 29

Stuttgart, Germany, 75

Sudan, 186, 187, 204, 271n91

Sunday schools, 41, 42

Suzuki, D. T., 172

Sweden, 92

Swedenborgians, 60

Switzerland, 98

Syllabus of Errors (Pius IX), 104

Symmes, Thomas, 232n88

Syracuse University, 172

Syria, 61, 156, 271n91

Systematic Theology (Finney), 34

Taft, William Howard, 117

Taiwan, 184

Taoism, 60

Taylor, Bayard, 151

Taylor, Clyde, 176, 177

Taylor, Fitch W., 77

Taylor, John L., 90

Taylor, William, 127

Temple, Oliver Perry, 119

Temple, William, 157

Ten Lost Tribes of Israel, 37, 38, 39, 44

Texas, 77, 78, 169, 197, 205

textbooks, 1, 57, 113, 114, 248n45

Their Blood Cries Out (Marshall), 187

Theosophists, 167

Thomas, H. W., 113

Thompson, John F., 139, 141

Thompson, Richard W., 69

Thorowgood, Thomas, 38

Thoughts on Popery (Nevins), 63

Tibetans, 188

Times and Seasons, 50

Todorov, Tzvetan, 221n16

Toledo, OH, 62

Tompson, Benjamin, 22, 25

Toombs, Robert A., 122

translocation, 105

trauma, 2, 3, 7, 9, 10, 12, 13, 23, 118; American, 15, 69, 209, 224; collective, 215n3, 216n7; cultural, 222; forgetting, 31, 54, 211, 238n30; memory of, 30, 36, 54, 55, 96, 129, 130, 216–17n7, 223n26, 224n33, 237–38n29; repressed, 58; violence and, 71, 72, 143, 190

Treasure Chest, 161

treaty-making, 96, 98

Treaty of Guadalupe Hidalgo, 89, 100

Truman, Harry, 158, 161, 164

288 INDEX

Trump, Donald, 1, 2, 193, 194, 201, 203, 205, 209, 210, 228n31

Truth Unveiled, The, 66, 67

Turner, Frederick Jackson, 67, 254n174

Tuttle, Daniel, 158

Twain, Mark, 51, 233n109

Tweed, Thomas A., 105

Twitter, 267n24

Tyndale, William, 85

ultramontanism, 16, 95

UN Charter, 182

Underhill, John, 20, 21, 87

Underwood, Joseph R., 89, 90, 92, 95, 244n123

UN Economic and Social Council, 182

UN General Assembly, 182

Unification Church, 170, 172, 173, 260n80

Union, 40, 44, 53, 78, 122

Union of Soviet Socialist Republics (U.S.S.R.), 5, 16, 152, 160, 161, 162, 164, 166, 168, 181, 190, 194

Union Theological Seminary, 154

United Baptist Congregations, 111

United Nations (UN), 160, 180

United States Catholic Miscellany, 82

United States Magazine and Democratic Review, 29

Universalists, 60, 67

Universal Statement of Human Rights, 182

University of Pennsylvania, 168

UN Security Council, 182

Upon the Propagation of the Gospel (Crawford), 38

Ursuline convent riots, 3, 64, 67, 78, 81, 82, 83, 88, 92

Ursuline sisters, 64, 81

Uruguay, 125

USA*Engage, 188

U.S. Bill of Rights, 56

U.S. Catholic Conference, 187

U.S. Commission of Indian Affairs, 39

U.S. Commission on Civil Rights, 174

U.S. Congress, 15, 17, 50, 86, 98, 121, 136, 148, 160, 190, 203; members of, 90, 179; testimony before, 157, 168

U.S. Constitution, 51, 56, 84, 128, 135

U.S. Department of State, 4, 11, 16, 17, 96, 140, 141, 142, 187, 189

U.S. Labor Party, 173

USS Maine, 124

U.S. Supreme Court, 17, 192, 210, 236n3

Utah, 50, 51, 53, 70, 107, 108

Vaiden, Thomas J., 60, 68

van Baalen, Jan Karel, 166, 167

van Dusen, Henry, 154, 157

van Dyke, Joseph, 106

Vatican, 106, 162, 164, 175

Vaughan, Alden T., 231n79

Vega, Garcilaso de la, 37

Venezuela, 97, 121, 125

vengeance, 14, 15, 36

Vico, Giambattista, 222n21

victimhood, 2; Christians claiming, 17, 199, 200, 202, 203, 208, 210; white, 145, 146

Vietnam, 5, 171, 187, 202

Vincent, Philip, 20

Virginia, 91, 203

Virginia Company, 36

Voice of the Martyrs (VOM), 195, 198

Voshell, Fay, 197, 207

Waco, TX, 17, 124

Waite, Morrison, 236n3

Waldenses, 85

Wall Street Journal, 186

Walsh, Robert, Jr., 242n104

Wang, Shih-Ping, 184

Warner, John, 128

Warner, Sam Bass, 239n41

War of 1812, 90

"War on Christians" conference, 197

Warsaw, IL, 49

Washington, DC, 89, 144, 186, 197, 207, 210

Washington, George, 26, 94, 120

Washington Times, 173

Watch Tower Bible and Tract Society, 110. *See also* Jehovah's Witnesses

waterboarding, 185

Watson, Thomas E., 144

Weber, Max, 115

Weinland, Ronald, 201, 268n52

Wendt, Alexander, 221n16

West, 9, 37, 41, 42, 61, 144, 157, 159, 162, 170, 172, 222n21

West Church, 43

Western Christian Advocate, 81

Western Monthly Magazine, 42

Westminster Confession, 43

Wheaton, 156

Whig, 46

White, Alma, 120

White, Ellen Gould, 35, 199

white Christian America (WCA), 192

White House, 17, 98, 141, 150, 158, 187, 188

Whitney, Caspar, 133

Whiton, James M., 41

Wiedel, Jason, 203

Wierman, Amy, 198

Wilcox, John Allen, 90

Willard, Emma, 114

Willard, Frances E., 140

Williams, Roger, 18, 19, 21, 38, 57, 111, 112, 113, 114, 115, 227n16

INDEX

289

Wilson, Woodrow, 16, 148, 149, 150, 151, 254n174, 254n176, 254n178
Winthrop, John, 23, 25, 28, 34, 115
Wirz, Henry, 44
witchcraft, 28, 75
Wolf, Frank, 187
Wolf–Specter bill, 187, 188, 189, 190
women, 6, 11, 68, 70, 162; and missions, 123, 144, 152, 156, 183; and sexual violence, 187; social role of, 200, 211
Women of Grace, 207
Women's Christian Temperance Movement, 140
Woodhouselee, Lord (Alexander Fraser Tytler), 114
world Christianity, 154, 155, 156, 159, 160, 183, 198, 255n5. *See also* Protestant International
World Council of Churches, 155, 255n5
World Evangelical Alliance Religious Liberties Commission, 206
WorldNetDaily, 208

World Parliament of Religion, 139
World War II, 153, 157, 164, 165, 255n5
World Watch List, 195
Wycliffe, John, 85
Wylie, Andrew, 65

Y2K, 201
Yale University, 27, 80, 115, 117
Yemen, 271
Yesidees, 61
yoga, 260n77
Young, Andrew W., 57
Young, Brigham, 51, 235n132
"Young Americans," 94
Young Men's Christian Association (YMCA), 128
Young People's Missionary Movement, 137

Zionism, 109
Zion's Herald, 67, 134
zoology, 127